COUNSELING: SELECTED READINGS

COUNSELING

SELECTED READINGS

Edited by **HERMAN J. PETERS**
The Ohio State University

BRUCE SHERTZER
Purdue University

JAMES B. HECK
The Ohio State University

RICHARD R. STEVIC
The Ohio State University

RALPH E. VAN ATTA
The Ohio State University

CHARLES E. MERRILL BOOKS, INC.
Columbus, Ohio

Library of Congress Catalog Card Number: 62-13623

PRINTED IN THE UNITED STATES OF AMERICA

PREFACE

Here, for the first time, is a compilation of the major published contributions to school counseling. In this volume, the reader will find ideas that touch on all aspects of counseling—basic psychological principles, empirical studies, ethical considerations, special problems in high school counseling, the counselor-counselee interview. This broad focus will encourage school psychologists, school counselors, counselor educators, counselor trainees, and interested laymen to do more conceptualizing, experimenting, and researching in the area of school counseling.

The main criterion in selecting the articles has been the extent to which new ideas and methods were presented. The variety of the articles will be a stimulus to creative understanding and study of the complexity of this intimate human relationship—counseling.

The book is divided into seven sections. Section One proposes to set the stage of the counseling function in high school. Section Two emphasizes the need for the counselor to consider the kind of counselees with whom he works. Section Three deals with general principles of counseling. Section Four contains articles of a more definitive nature about the counseling process. Section Five discusses group methods in counseling. Section Six presents discussions of ethics and values in the counseling process. Section Seven presents articles on evaluation and research in counseling.

In addition to the primary criterion mentioned above, the editors made an effort to select articles which gave scope and depth to factors which are known to be of paramount importance in counseling objectives. The variety of journals represented also makes available articles which would not otherwise be easily accessible.

Grateful acknowledgment is given the publishers and the authors for their kind permissions to use their materials. Identification of journal and author is made at the beginning of each reading.

April, 1962

Herman J. Peters
Bruce Shertzer
James B. Heck
Richard R. Stevic
Ralph E. Van Atta

CONTENTS

Section One

THE COUNSELING FUNCTION

Section Two

THE COUNSELEES

Section Three

GENERAL PRINCIPLES OF COUNSELING

Section Six

VALUES IN THE COUNSELING PROCESS

Section Seven

EVALUATION AND RESEARCH

xi

COUNSELING: SELECTED READINGS

Section One

THE COUNSELING FUNCTION

The central activity of the guidance process is the counseling function. Counseling is basic to all guidance and pupil personnel work. Of all the guidance activities, the counseling function is the unique differential between guidance and teaching. Counseling is the integrating process in the more encompassing guidance function. Counseling is concerned with the total functioning of the individual. In contrast to the instructional process, counseling focuses on the individual rather than on the subject matter to be used and learned.

Counseling in the secondary school emphasizes the normal developmental aspects of a boy or girl growing to maturity. This emphasis has arisen out of and in contrast to the clinical or pathological emphasis of counseling in other settings of the helping relationship. The main purpose of the high school counseling process is to assist the student to gain a sense of identity as a basis for real fulfillment in living. In a world barraged by "togetherness," "groupiness," and "mediocrity," there is need for this guidance function which assists the individual to understand himself and his potential.

In relating counseling to the total process of education, Brown discusses the purposes of general education and the purposes of counseling. Emphasizing the developmental concept in counseling, he gives seven ways by which a sound counseling program supports the total school effort.

In Masoner's article, the reader will find the setting for

counseling in the larger framework of the world today. Twelve key functions of counseling are given. "Counseling stands on the threshold of true, professional status" indicates the contemporary maturation of the guidance field. Balancing this broad treatment is Stiller's article, which attempts to analyze the counseling process in the more delimited sphere of its purposes and functions.

Yates and Schmidt emphasize the importance of the counselor's self-concept. This is one of the crucial factors in the counseling function. The reader will want to keep this in mind as he proceeds to the following six sections of this book.

The article by Riccio and Wehmeyer is included here because it emphasizes the context of pupil concerns within which the counseling function takes place. Although focused on elementary pupils, the article points out that guidance and counseling continue to be viewed from a problem orientation by teachers. As the reader will note, there was difficulty in finding articles which emphasize developmental counseling. Most articles emphasize the remedial or therapeutic functions of counseling.

1. COUNSELING VITAL TO EDUCATION

Stuart C. Brown

Counseling has become a major responsibility in modern schools.
This article describes current theories of guidance and indicates
the objectives of an effective counseling program.

For some years now guidance has been a prominent word in educational terminology. An increased awareness of the complex causes
which determine the success or failure of our young people in school
has made educators seek new means for helping students out of their
confusion. Many types of objective testing devices have been developed to measure personality traits, vocational and mental aptitude,
vocational interest and emotional adjustment. Innumerable organizational plans for school guidance programs have found their way
into current publications, and much has been done in schools to
put these theories into practice.

An important phase of guidance programs is the relationship
which develops between counselor and student, particularly when
the situation demands special attention to personal problems of one
kind or another. Some schools make use of specially trained personnel while others depend primarily upon members of the regular
teaching staff. Schools usually try to work out a combination of these
two procedures, using the specialist only for the more difficult situations.

This article will attempt to show that by accepting a proper rationale, counseling programs are effective in their influence upon
the lives of our young people. The counseling programs with which
the writer has been associated have been instituted too recently to
warrant objective conclusions and statements of success or failure.
It would be a mistake, therefore, merely to list as evidence a few
isolated cases in which these counseling programs have affected the

Reprinted by permission of the author and *Educational Leadership,* XI,
No. 7 (April, 1954), 404-8.

students' lives. It is possible, however, through a process of deductive reasoning to focus our attention on the results expected of a counseling program which has as its philosophy and basic structure certain clearly defined principles. Naturally it is dangerous, even under the best of circumstances, to make predictions in the area of human behavior. It is possible, nevertheless, to gain confidence in a program if it has been developed according to a plan that can be supported on the basis of the philosophy and of the psychology which it represents.

The counselor's work is but one phase of the school guidance program. More accurately, any counseling situation, scheduled or otherwise, is an integral part of the total process we call education. I firmly believe, as do many other educators, that no phase of the school program can be justified unless it provides experiences which can be expected to contribute toward realization of the school's objectives. If a phase of the program is not instituted for the purpose of effecting changes in students in keeping with philosophies and objectives of the total program, it stands on indefensible grounds. Insofar as a counseling program does not meet this test, it can be classified as part of a patchwork curriculum which is aimless, time-consuming and expensive. The fruits of such a program would be unpredictable in terms of quality and frequency. It is discouraging enough when a course of study fails to bring about for students the behavioral changes which were expected and for which the course was carefully designed. It is even more inexcusable for a school, year after year, to continue practices or phases of a program which are aimless or are in actual conflict with the school's philosophy. The first question that must be answered, therefore, is whether or not harmony exists between the purpose of general education and the purpose of a counseling program.

Assistance in Adjustment

The true purpose of general education is to provide for the child significant experiences which will promote the growth and development of his potentialities including those which make him an effective participant in a democratic society. Such growth and development will be assisted by courses of study that challenge and interest the student. To enable him to become an effective participant in a democratic society, the school must offer the student experiences which produce a deep appreciation for democracy.

The counseling program has as its purpose helping the student to adjust more quickly to all phases of school life so that he may better achieve his educational aims. It is concerned with the student's emotional life and also serves to help him see more clearly his role in an educational and occupational world. The results hoped for are that students will arrive at a synthesis of their aspirations, potentialities and opportunities. Very definitely, a counseling program can be in agreement with the purposes of general education.

An effective counseling program must be related to the laws of human behavior. There have been times in our historical development when it would have been questionable to conduct a program of counseling for the purpose of helping the student make proper adjustment to life situations.

From the time of primitive man to the Middle Ages, it was assumed that behavior was controlled by forces outside the individual. Evil spirits had to be cast out to free the individual of his evil behavior and this was done by mysterious methods. The Puritan was of the opinion that all behavior was controllable, the will being the determining factor.

The exponent of the theory of heredity claimed that the individual had no responsibility since his behavioral pattern was predetermined through factors beyond his control. The environmentalist was concerned with controlling the environment rather than helping the individual gain insight into his problems. None of these theories of human behavior would serve to justify a modern counseling program.

Modern counseling programs generally accept the present theory which assumes that all people share common basic needs and drives. These urges pattern the individual's behavior as he attempts to satisfy them. He learns to meet these basic needs by developing certain mechanisms of adjustment. Some of these mechanisms are not socially acceptable and others lead the individual away from reality. Under these circumstances, it would be difficult for the student to achieve the basic objective of general education until such time as

he begins to appreciate reality and to adopt socially acceptable
habits. It is the role of the counseling program to try and help him
face up to reality and make a socially acceptable adjustment.

CURRENT THEORIES OF ~~GUIDANCE~~ Cnslg,

It seems reasonable to claim that any school accepting the tenets
of present theories of human behavior can successfully use counseling programs, provided these are in harmony with the basic philosophy of general education in a democratic society.

What assurance is there that counseling is a desirable and effective
device in a school concerned with helping the student develop to the
utmost his potentialities for effective living in a democracy? To answer this question, it is necessary to learn from the expert counselor
what he has discovered and which techniques of counseling have
produced most effective results.

It should be made very clear at this point that one paragraph or
two cannot do more than mention the various techniques which are
widely accepted by counselors today. The reader is urged to use the
references listed at the end of this article for a fair and complete explanation of each technique.

Non-Directive Counseling

Non-directive counseling, which Carl R. Rogers has promulgated,
can be and has been brought successfully into the school program.
Five sequential steps are outlined by Rogers:[1]

1. The counselee seeks the help of the counselor.
2. The counselee gives free expression to his emotionalized attitudes.
3. The counselee gains insight.
4. The counselee formulates plans.
5. The counselee terminates the counseling contact.

The counselor uses reflection and acceptance of expressed attitudes
to help the counselee gain insight and enable him to formulate plans
for the solution of his problem. At no time does the counselor be-

---

[1] Carl R. Rogers and John L. Wallen, *Counseling with Returned Servicemen*,
New York: McGraw-Hill Book Co., Inc., 1946, p. 47.

come critical or suggestive in his relationship with the counselee. It is important to note that one element of this technique is the original contact by the counselee, indicating that routine counseling situations predetermined by the counselor in a school situation would not fit this type of program.

Clinical Method

Another major counseling method applicable to public school situations involves the clinical approach of which E. G. Williamson[2] is a leading exponent. The first step in this approach requires gathering of pertinent information which will shed light on the problem as well as lead to its solution. These facts are synthesized into meaningful and related unity which, in application, help the counselor diagnose the problem much as the physician, skilled in his work, diagnoses after he seeks out symptoms of the illness. Logically, then, and with the help of his own experience, training and skill, the counselor helps the counselee to better appreciate his problem, discover the causes, and plan for the future. ,

The trained counselor is a necessary element of this program for only he will be able properly to find significant data and interpret it. The school is in a position to make such a technique possible since testing programs and knowledge of the home and environment from which the student comes are accessible to the counselor.

An Eclectic Approach

A third major concept deserves attention. There are those who believe, as do Shirley A. Hamrin and Blanche B. Paulson,[3] that a purposeful selection of techniques from other types of counseling and proper application of techniques according to the problem of the individual constitute a sound approach. This eclectic point of view assumes that each individual possesses varying degrees of ability to carry full responsibility and that many students with problems are unable to solve these by increased insight or action. The eclectic

---

[2] E. G. Williamson, *How to Counsel Students,* New York: McGraw-Hill Book Co., Inc., 1939, p. 57.

[3] Shirley A. Hamrin and Blanche B. Paulson, *Counseling Adolescents,* Chicago: Science Research Associates, 1950, p. 82-99.

believes that there are cases in which the problem is created by the school program or some other extraneous factor not under control of the student. The non-directive assumption that each individual has the capacity to solve most of his problems through increased insight is also one of the bases of the eclectic rationale. A non-directive counseling situation is employed, therefore, for those cases in which the counselor feels it to be most applicable.

Each one of the previously mentioned concepts has abundant evidence to show that success has consistently been attained. These points of view have received wide recognition not because they fulfill the requirements of sound psychology, but because the individual through their use has experienced improved adjustment. Each has enabled the counselee to overcome maladjustment whether this be primarily emotional, educational or vocational in nature. Each has helped the counselee make a more effective contribution to our democratic society.

An Effective Instrument

Counseling, therefore, can be an effective instrument of the public school in its attempt to develop a program suitable for the attainment of the basic goals of general education. There is sufficient evidence to indicate that if the counselor has been trained in one of the three philosophies of counseling presented here, the results of his effort will be in keeping with the basic philosophy of the school. There exist unanimity of purpose, a defensible theory and suitable methodology.

Briefly, a sound counseling program will support the total school effort by helping the student attain the objectives of general education. This support will come in several ways:

1. The youngster facing disturbing problems will find release for his emotional tensions.

2. A clearer appraisal of his purpose in school will help the student maintain a more successful scholastic record.

3. Wiser curricular choices will result from a counseling relationship.

4. Vocational information and appraisal will give a student confidence and direction.

5. Basic human needs of security and adequacy can be satisfied.

6. Misunderstandings occurring between students and teachers can be resolved.

7. The student will become a more effective participant in a democratic society.

These conclusions are not mere platitudes. No technique will produce all of the desired results and counseling is no exception. We can be confident, nevertheless, that if we apply a reasonable rationale to such a program, boys and girls in school will respond.

Suggested Readings

Blos, Peter. *The Adolescent Personality*. New York: D. Appleton-Century Co., 1941.

Clark, Willis W. *Vocational Guidance for Junior and Senior High School Pupils*. Educational Bulletin No. 15, Los Angeles: California Test Bureau, 1945.

Hamrin, Shirley A. and Paulson, Blanche B. *Counseling Adolescents*. Chicago: Science Research Associates, 1950.

Prescott, Daniel A. *Emotion and the Educative Process*. Washington, D. C.: American Council on Education, 1938.

Reed, Anna Y. *Guidance and Personnel Services in Education*. New York: Cornell University Press, 1944.

Rogers, Carl R. *Counseling and Psychotherapy*. Boston: Houghton Mifflin Co., 1942.

Rogers, Carl R. and Wallen, John L. *Counseling with Returned Servicemen*. New York: McGraw-Hill Book Co., 1946.

Sherman, Mandel. *Basic Problems of Behaviour*. New York: Longmans, Green and Co., 1946.

Thorpe, Louis P. *Appraising Personality and Social Adjustment*. Educational Bulletin No. 11, Los Angeles: California Test Bureau, 1945.

Thorpe, Louis P. *Guiding Child and Adolescent Development in the Modern School*. Educational Bulletin No. 16, Los Angeles: California Test Bureau, 1946.

2. THE ROLE OF THE COUNSELOR IN A NEW WORLD

Paul H. Masoner

A NEW WORLD

Few will deny that we are on the threshold of a new world. It was little more than a decade ago that the explosion of a bomb over Hiroshima opened a new era of the atom. The V-2 missile over England presaged a new and exciting conquest of time and space which culminated in the 18,000-mile-per-hour satellite encircling the globe. The constantly-shrinking world has indeed suddenly become a small planet. Developments in industry—in electronics, in automation, in chemistry, in physics—have suddenly created a new life that overshadows the industrial revolution in its potential consequences. Perhaps, almost without our knowing it, the new world that we have always spoken of in the future tense is already a reality.

In this new physical world which he has created, man seeks self-realization. Faced with problems which grow out of the environment which is largely a product of his own inventiveness and intelligence, he looks for assistance in achieving his needs. Although counseling has been variously defined since its emergence as a profession, perhaps the most effective indication of the role of the counselor arises from a description of certain needs of man.

Man desires to develop the best that is in him. In order to achieve this kind of self-realization, it is necessary that he gain a full understanding of himself—of his interests, his abilities, his needs. Both his own happiness and the welfare of society become important personal goals. To achieve these goals man frequently must have the assistance of others who will help him to gain the understandings, the knowl-

A paper presented at the Thirty-Seventh Annual Meeting of the Pennsylvania Association of Deans of Women, November 2, 1957, Pittsburgh, Pennsylvania. Reprinted by permission of the author and the *Journal of the National Association of Women Deans and Counselors,* XXI, No. 3 (March, 1958), 115-25.

edges, and the skills that are necessary to make the decisions that are necessary to self-realization.

Here then is the raw material from which the role of the counselor must be formulated. This role involves the kind of activity that will make it possible for man to gain self-understanding, to develop goals in the light of this understanding, and to achieve these goals. All of this happens through a counselor-client relationship which results, not in decisions on the part of the counselor, but rather in thoughtful decisions by the client himself, in the development of changes in the individual which will enable him to make wise decisions in future situations, and in the growth of intellectual, social, and emotional attitudes in respect to his basic problems.

If this role were to be performed in a static society, then it might be possible to describe it in minute detail so that the role could be performed like that of an actor in a dramatic presentation. However, this role is one which is constantly affected by the environment in which both the counselor and the client live. Decisions concerning educational plans, vocational goals, social problems, moral and spiritual issues, and the responsibilities of citizenship are vitally affected by the changing world in which all of us live.

Hence, what may appear to some to be a somewhat stable role must be carried out in a dynamic society and becomes a dynamic role. If this world of today is truly a new world, then the basic responsibilities of the counselor must be considered in terms of the impacts of the environment, the personal needs of individuals, and the needs of the social structure.

In few occupations have responsibilities and duties escaped change. Change has been welcomed as the opportunity to improve the task to be accomplished, as the opportunity to adjust to a new environment with its problems and its opportunities. If we are to look at the role of the counselor in this new world, we must indeed look to the world itself. We must look to the challenges that the new world presents to man. We must identify the major responsibilities of the counselor to those whom he counsels. We must look at the counselor himself to see the kind of individual the profession demands.

In investigating the role of the counselor in a new world, we might ask three important questions:

1. What are the characteristics of this new world that create for man situations demanding careful self-evaluation, accurate information, and wise decisions in the interests of his own happiness and the welfare of society?

2. What are the major responsibilities of the counselor in his attempt to help man and society meet the problems of the world today?

3. What kind of individual, what type of preparation, what sort of job organization is important if the counselor is to fulfill his professional responsibilities?

Perhaps these questions might be considered under three topics—the setting, the job, and the counselor.

THE SETTING

It is obvious that the total setting in which man lives will affect the nature of the problems he faces and the decisions that he must make. To attempt to describe all the characteristics of the present world is a task far beyond our opportunities here today. Yet, it is clear that today there are certain major and critical aspects of the national and world setting which have a vital and important relationship to man's need for counseling. Some of these characteristics are briefly discussed in the paragraphs which follow.

A Conflict of Ideologies

One of the major problems of society lies in the ideological conflict between the East and the West. The democracy for which Americans have died, its promise of opportunity to all men, the goal of a free world—all these are threatened by a totalitarian group of nations which seek to enslave the rest of the world. The cold war is a reality in the lives of all individuals. Men are faced with new and serious problems almost completely foreign to the American scene. Youth is faced with an uncertain future. A standing military organization must be manned by almost 3 million youth who must postpone entrance into a chosen career. The emotional stability of individuals is threatened as society moves uneasily under the constant threat of total war, perhaps even of total annihilation. Occupations have become subject to the dictation of an economy which has many of its roots in war rather than peace.

All of this has produced a new and different setting in which man must resolve his problems—a setting in which new occupations develop almost overnight, educational needs and opportunities undergo constant change, increasing tensions cause social and emotional problems, and, above all, a setting in which as never before the best education and development of the individual is important to the survival of the free world. Counseling, with its concern for the individual, must indeed assume a role of significance and importance in a world which threatens the inalienable rights of mankind.

An Occupational Revolution

Almost overnight new industries have appeared in this new world. Electronics, guided missiles, atomic power, automation, high-speed transportation—all these are manifestations of new developments which have brought comforts to man and, at the same time, sudden and difficult occupational adjustments. Many industries are devoting their major energies to the production of manufactured items that were not even in existence a decade ago. Automation has invaded not only the factory but also the office, and many of the tasks that were commonplace only a short time ago have been taken over by mechanical hands and electronic brains.

A defense economy has greatly affected the nature of occupational opportunities for youth. In addition to the 3 million in the armed services, another million persons are employed as civilians in military activities, and additional millions work in industries wholly devoted to the production of defense materials.

Along with new and different occupational developments, major realignments have occurred in respect to the nature of jobs themselves. Job trends show amazing changes. Semi-professional and technical jobs are on the increase. The number of persons required for professional tasks threatens to double in a relatively short time. The requirements for jobs also have taken on a new complexion. There are increasing demands for individuals of high intellectual ability to design and create the automation equipment that continues to affect the nature of jobs. Skills grow in their importance with the development of complicated mechanical and electronic equipment. At the same time there is a growing need for individuals who can think in abstract terms. Muscle-power is giving way to brainpower.

Educational requirements of jobs have become increasingly important in a situation in which educational and intellectual job standards are in a constant process of moving upward. Courses in science and mathematics have taken on a new significance. The new manpower quota must include individuals whose talents have been developed to their maximum potential if the needs of the new revolution in occupations is to be met.

There is little need here to indicate the relevance and importance of occupational changes like these to the counselor. His traditional responsibility of assisting individuals to make wise occupational choices has become of major importance in the new world of jobs.

A Changing Population

One of the significant signs of the new world in which Americans live is the great change in the composition of population—a real phenomenon of our times. Although the population of the United States had increased steadily over a long period of time, suddenly, in the depression years of the 1930's, a decreasing birthrate and a declining immigration resulted in the lowest net increase in three-quarters of a century. However, beginning with 1940, Americans witnessed a sudden and unprecedented increase in the birthrate that has continued to the present. Already the population of the nation has reached approximately 170 million, a figure that experts a few years ago were predicting would not be reached until the end of the century. The Educational Policies Commission, in *Manpower and Education,* discusses this changing population.

The Commission, in an excellent analysis, states that with this growth, other major changes create conditions that are of concern to those who study social, economic, and educational problems. Of special importance is the distribution of the population in the various age groups. If the productive years of men are those between the ages of 20 and 64, we can see an interesting and important change that has occurred. In 1900 this productive group accounted for 51 per cent of the population and as much as 60 per cent in 1950. However, since 1950, this group has continued to decrease in its proportion to the total population. Increasing birthrates have increased the numbers of children and youth. Advances in medical science, improvements in health services, and developments in improved living standards have greatly increased man's life span and consequently have added to the number of those beyond age 64. This means that for a period of time, at least the next dozen years, the labor force from which all workers must be drawn will be small. On the other hand this trend may reverse itself by 1970 with a consequent surplus of manpower until a new equilibrium is reached.

Other population changes are equally significant. The population continues to be an extremely mobile one. Large numbers of people move to those areas in which new industries are being developed. More and more leave the farm and rural areas and become part of large cities and metropolitan areas. As a result there is a continual change occurring—social, political, and economic—that affects the lives of people in many ways.

Here, too, the counselor sees real problems that become a part of his responsibility in helping individuals make the best possible adjustments in a changing environment.

Education for All

The new world of education is as startling as any aspect of our changing environment. Always a nation in which education has been important, we have suddenly witnessed a number of events which have made education of even greater importance. American education has literally opened its doors wide to all youth. A national realization of the importance of education for all citizens, an increased desire of youth for learning, the demands of a changing occupational picture for higher educational attainments—all these have brought into or retained in our schools millions of young people who a few years ago would have completed only a minimal educational program.

Coupled with the almost astronomical increase in population of the last two decades, these causes have brought about the oft-mentioned "Tidal Wave" of students that threatens to engulf all our educational institutions. Statistics concerning enrollments in elementary schools and secondary schools are relatively common knowledge. The elementary school population of 16 million at the beginning of the century will have doubled by 1960. The high school enrollment of less than 1 million in 1900 will have increased twenty-fold by 1970. But, perhaps less well-known are the facts concerning college enrollments, though within the past year we have become painfully aware that a remarkable change is occurring. At the beginning of the century there were only a few more than 200 thousand youth in colleges and universities. Today the figure has passed the 3 million mark. By 1970 it will probably be in excess of 6 million.

These changes in school and college populations have been accompanied by considerable changes in educational structure and educational programs. Obviously, a high school program geared to a selected enrollment of 10 per cent of the youth of high school age has had to undergo a considerable change to become adaptable to the needs of almost 90 per cent of the youth of that same age group. And, undoubtedly it will continue to change.

It is equally obvious that colleges and universities and other post-high school institutions are witnessing considerable changes in the curriculum, in their structure, and in the nature of the total educational experience in view of an enrollment that has increased from 4 per cent of the college age to 35 per cent of that same group between 1900 and 1957. And, in all probability, by 1970 those attending post-high school institutions will have increased to 50 per cent of the college age group. In this new picture of higher education, students are faced with the necessity of choosing from an increasing number of institutions and from an increasing variety of curriculums. New and different institutions are developing in the face of this unprecedented demand for higher education. The community junior college, common now in only certain parts of the nation, appears to be on the way to becoming an institution of nation-wide importance.

In this new world of education, the traditional role of the counselor for educational guidance has become even more important in the face of the growing number of youth in our schools and the increasing opportunities for education.

THE JOB

The role of the counselor has always been important. The development of organized programs of guidance around the beginning of the twentieth century and their development during the subsequent years was only a formal recognition of the importance of counseling in the lives of individuals. But, important as counseling has been, the changes that have brought about the new world of today have tended to make it even more important to individuals and to society. Most commentaries on current problems have made specific mention of counseling and its critical importance.

Manpower and Education, a report of the Educational Policies Commission, has this to say:

> . . . the situation emphasizes for education today the importance of guidance as a function of democratic education. Guidance programs have developed as a unique characteristic of American education, and their importance was never more apparent than now.

The Commission, in a later publication, *Higher Education in a Decade of Decision,* added:

> To secure the highly gifted students for the colleges, counseling services will have to be expanded and improved at both the elementary and secondary school levels. It is a task of the counseling services to encourage talented students to pursue higher education, and to give them educational guidance toward the particular programs which seem most advantageous for the individuals concerned.

A very recent report, that of the President's Committee for Education Beyond the High School, stated:

> The committee urges all school systems to strengthen their guidance and counseling services, and urges colleges and universities to expand and improve their programs for training well-qualified guidance counselors.

Later this report added:

> The need for guidance and counseling does not stop at the secondary school level. The early years of college are, for many students, critical ones in the selection of life goals.

With this growing importance of the counselor in society, it is important that we look at his responsibilities and tasks. It is not necessary here to define the traditional role of the counselor. This definition can be found in any basic text in the field of guidance. What is more important is that we look especially at certain of the responsibilities that grow out of the new world of today.

1. In today's world it is especially imperative that counseling services be expanded so that all individuals will have the opportunity to receive suitable assistance in achieving self-realization. In a world in which our nation stands at the head of the free peoples in a struggle for democratic ideals, in a world in which we constantly affirm our belief in the supremacy of the dignity and worth of the individual, increased concern must be shown for the development of counseling services for all youth and adults. With almost all youth attending high school and large numbers going beyond high school, the counselor must be prepared to provide professional services from the elementary school through the college and university. This enlarged concept of counseling services arises from the firm belief that in a democracy the individual must have the opportunity to develop to the maximum of his potential, that he must be given the freedom to make his own choices, and that he must have the chance to grow in the kind of wisdom that will enable him to make decisions in the best interests of his own welfare and that of society.

2. Counseling must be especially concerned with the identification of the talents of each individual and the best development of those talents through educational and vocational opportunities. With a constant demand for the development of individual abilities to the highest potential, the counselor faces the task of helping each individual in the identification of his abilities and aptitudes and interests so that educational and vocational choices can be made in the light of his best potential. Particularly, with the current need for an increasing educational level for occupational tasks, gifted youth must be identified and given the opportunity to complete educational programs that will equip them for the important tasks of today. When we realize that currently about one-half of the most able youth in our high schools do not even enter college, then the importance of this task becomes even more apparent. Certainly the complexities of modern life, the increasing occupational require-

ments in business and industry, the demands of government and the military services for well-educated individuals, the scientific advances that are a part of everyday living—all combine to make it imperative that each individual have the opportunity to develop the best that he has to offer for his own happiness and the welfare of his fellow men.

3. Counseling services must give special attention to those groups which in the past have been denied an opportunity to achieve in terms of their abilities and interests. Of particular importance are those minority groups who by reason of race, color, religion, ethnic background, or physical disability have found many opportunities either difficult to reach or completely closed. In a world which professes to provide equal opportunity to all in terms of their abilities, counseling must be the initial means by which these minorities achieve their search for equality of opportunity. This means that special attention must be given to measurement of abilities, to the provision of opportunities for education and training, and to the identification of vocational opportunities for all individuals who have been denied these opportunities in the past.

4. Counseling services should develop particularly strong programs of career guidance. The manpower needs of today are possibly more critical than ever before in our history. Shortages of workers for important occupations, a need for the maximum development of the talents of each individual, and rapidly changing trends in jobs and job needs make the task of wise career choosing a source of increasing difficulty for youth and adults. It is important that counselors provide the best possible methods of individual analysis and evaluation, accurate information concerning present and future occupational needs, and assistance in developing in individuals the capacity to make wise decisions about education and careers.

5. Counseling services must provide and develop high level programs of educational guidance with special attention to the post-high school educational needs and opportunities of youth. The diversity of educational opportunity, the increased educational requirements of almost all occupations, and the constantly increasing group of youth who seek education beyond the high school make improved educational counseling an imperative. Youth must have guidance that will provide information concerning the wide variety

of educational offerings, the relationship of education to career, the opportunities for continued education beyond the high school, and their own qualifications for entrance into educational programs.

6. Counseling must show strong concern for helping individuals in personal problems, in the solution of emotional problems, in the exploration of social problems that are a common phenomenon in this world of tension and unrest. The increasing strains that grow out of a disordered international scene, the dislocations that arise from compulsory military service, the personal frustrations in respect to educational and vocational goals, the feelings of insecurity that develop in a complex world—all place upon the counselor a responsibility that is constantly growing in its seriousness.

7. With large numbers of youth facing military service and with many others finding their career opportunities determined largely by defense needs, counseling services must be prepared to provide information concerning military careers, opportunities for educational experiences in the armed forces, and occupations in the defense industries. Youth need to know, in a world in which this entire new group of occupations has suddenly become important, how they can make the best use of their talents, give service to society, and achieve their own personal goals.

8. Counseling services must provide increasing assistance to the parents of the youth whom they serve. Much of the unrealistic educational and vocational planning of youth can be attributed to the unrealistic goals of parents themselves and to the pressures of family and friends upon youth. In a world that has changed so rapidly and in which a great premium has been placed upon education, it is not at all difficult to realize how parents adopt for their children goals that are entirely out of accord with either abilities or interests of their children. This means that counseling services must provide parents with information that will enable them to understand the problems of educational and vocational planning and the importance of permitting each individual to make his own decisions.

9. Counseling services must work cooperatively with other agencies that are serving youth. Today a growing number of organizations provide for youth various kinds of services. Counselors in educational institutions must not only be aware of these youth-serving agencies but must actually coordinate their programs in a coopera-

tive enterprise. Unless this cooperation is achieved, there may be not only a duplication of effort but actual confusion to hinder the adjustment of the individuals concerned.

10. Counseling services must accept the responsibility for providing in-service education for all those in the institution who serve the counseling needs of youth. With the probable growth of counseling services and with the continued importance of all teachers providing at least informal advisory services to youth, it will be particularly important that a good program of in-service education be developed to aid all counseling personnel in the development of skills and acquisition of information that will enable them to serve youth well.

11. Counseling services must engage in research designed to result in improved programs of guidance. The techniques of counseling must undergo the scrutiny of constant evaluation. Follow-up of youth who have been counseled will provide important data which may be used in the development of improved procedures, improved organizational methods, improved methods of counselor selection, and improved methods of counselor preparation.

12. Although counseling services have a basic responsibility to the individual, there is a corresponding responsibility to society as well. That counseling should accept an obligation to society is not at all inconsistent with its acceptance of a responsibility to the individual. It is true that each individual must have the right and opportunity to make his decisions in the light of information about himself and the environment. Yet, counseling that failed to give assistance to individuals in developing a knowledge of social needs and personal obligations to society would indeed be failing to meet its responsibilities.

THE COUNSELOR

It is clear that both the setting in which the counselor operates and the special tasks which he must perform should affect the nature of the job, the organization of the counseling services, the qualifications of the counselor, and the program of counselor preparation. It would appear then that the new world which we have tried to describe dictates a number of important characteristics of counseling.

1. The increasing demand for counseling services and the expanding number of potential clients requires a great expansion of the ranks of professionally-trained counselors.

2. In view of the wide variety of tasks and responsibilities of counseling, it is important that counseling be regarded as a team endeavor rather than the responsibility of a single individual.

3. Counseling staffs must be developed in terms of this team concept with a staff consisting of a director, of staff counselors, as well as special consultants in related fields such as medicine, psychiatry, and social work.

4. The staff counselors must be selected in terms of their special competencies for the various responsibilities of counseling since it is highly unlikely that all the competencies and backgrounds will often be found in a single individual.

5. The counseling program must make complete use of the teaching staff of the institution as an important resource in the total counseling program.

6. To meet the increasing complexity of the counseling task, a careful organizational plan must be developed which will include provision for adequate administration, for counseling, for consultative services, for in-service education, and for research.

7. Procedures for recruitment and selection of candidates for the growing profession must be based upon steadily increasing requirements in terms of both personal and educational qualifications.

8. The educational program for the preparation of counselors must be one of both breadth and depth. Obviously the counselor must be a well-educated person with a broad background of general education. Special educational fields of importance include human growth and development, clinical and counseling psychology, educational and vocational counseling, occupational information, and related backgrounds in the areas of education, social work, human relations, and administration.

9. Special attention in the educational program must be given to the development of a concept of research and its importance to counseling, and a knowledge of the techniques that are essential to good research.

10. Academic requirements for the counselor must, in view of the increasing professional obligations placed upon him, approximate those of other professions with the doctorate or a similar professional degree as the eventual goal.

11. The program for the preparation of counselors must include opportunities for adequate experience in counseling services and educational institutions through an internship program. This internship should provide extensive and meaningful experiences in teaching, in counseling, in research, and in administrative responsibilities.

Conclusion

Counseling stands on the threshold of true professional status. The new world in which we live looks to this new profession to provide both to individual and to society those professional services which will result in happiness and well-being for man. How well we achieve professional status—and more importantly, how well we meet our new and important responsibilities—will depend upon those who are members of the profession. This is our challenge in a new world.

One over-riding responsibility that, in a sense, encompasses all these specific responsibilities that have been mentioned is one of leadership. Perhaps no professional group in education today, more than counselors, has the background and knowledge that is so vital in a time when critical problems face the nation. I believe that it is clear, if you will agree with the analysis that I have made today, that the major problems relate, somehow or other, to the counseling function. Hence, with professional counseling background that you have, you have a major responsibility to give this leadership—in the bringing about of changes in the curriculum, in the development of new structures and organization to meet educational needs, in helping business and industry to look clearly at manpower needs and their relationship to education and training, in assisting men and women everywhere to look anew at education and its importance and to give it their confidence and support. This, indeed, is a responsibility that you can fulfill through a role of leadership.

3. THE HIGH SCHOOL GUIDANCE COUNSELOR— GUIDANCE OR COUNSELOR?

Alfred Stiller

There are today several potent factors which can be expected to influence the trends of tomorrow's education and of the specialized services of the school. Of these, the best-known probably is the impact of "Sputnikism," the evaluation of our educational system in terms of the progress which Russia has effected in a short time. Another factor, less known but no less important, is the sociological development of our past history and its implications for the near future. Because of the relatively low birth rate of the 1930's and the relatively high birth rate of the post-World-War II era, coupled with rapidly increasing technological improvement, we can foresee an expanding economy with greater demands for talent and leaders than ever before, but with a smaller pool of talent from which to draw. A third factor is increasing concern with mental health and mental illness; Fein has estimated the direct and indirect costs of mental illness to be more than $2.4 billion a year (7:57). Even more sobering were his quotes of remarks made in 1953 at a hearing of the Committee on Interstate and Foreign Commerce of the House of Representatives. Among other things, these quotes indicated that:

1. Mental illness is the nation's number one health problem.
2. More than half of all hospital beds in this country are occupied by the mentally ill.
3. About 50 per cent of patients who are treated in general practice have psychiatric complications.
4. At least 6 per cent of our total population—about 9 million people—suffer from a serious mental disorder. (7:3-4)

A fourth factor is our recognition of the increasing complexity of modern life and the inability of the home and other institutions to

---

This article was originally published under the title, "The High School Guidance Counselor." Reprinted by permission of the author and *The Bulletin of the National Association of Secondary School Principals*, XLV, No. 265 (May, 1961), 150-59.

provide all the guidance needed by youth. Because of the factors cited above, the number of guidance counselors has increased rapidly and is expected to increase still more in the near future. The Honorable Lawrence G. Derthick, former Commissioner of Education of the United States and now with the National Education Association, has pointed to guidance as a basic answer to the problem of making the best possible use of tomorrow's talent (4). Congress, by means of the National Defense Education Act, has asked guidance to assist in the identification and motivation of academically talented youth. Conant (3) and others are asking the same function of guidance counselors. It can be expected that great emphasis will be placed on the diagnostic and appraisal functions of the counselor, which along with orientation, information-giving, and placement, have traditionally comprised the major duties of the secondary-school counselor.

To date little attention has been paid by school counselors to the mental health problem, partly because of pressure of other duties, partly because of lack of training, and partly because of the belief that this function should be left to the clinical psychologist. However, the nature and adequacy of the functions and the basic philosophy of the school counselor are today being challenged by the leaders of the counseling movement in colleges and industry, a group known as counseling psychologists.

Counseling psychology as a separate discipline began only in 1953, but it has its roots in the vocational guidance and individual testing movements, just as does public school guidance. Counseling psychologists have used—and to a great extent have discarded—the notion that successful vocational counseling consists of determining an individual's aptitudes, abilities, or traits and then of finding an occupation which requires that particular constellation of factors. They have observed the frequency with which personal factors affect an individual's behavior and, consequently, now look beyond the problem as stated by the client to the personal difficulties which prevent him from solving his own problem. Super has traced this development—". . . the movement which started as vocational guidance in the United States, first with an emphasis on vocational orientation activities and then with a parallel and eventually merging emphasis on aptitude testing, both leading to placement, recently also assimilated a psycho-therapeutic approach and has emerged as the 'new' field of counseling psychology. While it includes vocational guidance, it goes beyond it to deal with the person as a person, attempting to help him with all types of life adjustments. *Its underlying principle is that it is the adjusting individual who needs help, rather than merely an occupational, marital, or personal problem which needs solution.*" (26:4) (Italics mine)

The questions that are being raised concerning the functions of the counselor are not merely academic in nature. In the words of one group which has studied the problem of counselor training, "States are not in a position to guarantee that certification of a counselor means good counseling. The universities that educate counselors in their specialty have to assume a major responsibility for the quality of background training that is provided." (10) Counselor-trainers—those who train school counselors—belong by and large to this group of counseling psychologists. The books, pamphlets, and other publications used in training school counselors reflect to a great extent the counseling psychology view. It is extremely likely that recently trained counselors have assimilated this point of view to a greater or lesser degree. For example, a survey of "Theses in Counseling and Student Personnel Work" (28) for the years 1953-1956 reported on 144 Doctoral dissertations and 60 Master's theses. Only 37 of the Doctoral dissertations dealt with topics related to guidance or personnel work *per se.* The others considered topics of personality and adjustment, topics of greater interest to psychologically oriented workers. At the Master's level, 27 theses dealt with other guidance topics, and 33 with personality or adjustment questions. Yet, by and large, these new counselors work in a school setting in which the administrator has little or no concept of counseling psychology and, possibly, even less faith in its practicability. The administrator is likely to consider the counselor as an educator who worked in the subject field of guidance, whereas the counseling psychologist looks upon him as a brother psychologist who works in an educational setting. It is the purpose of this article to demonstrate that there is a difference between the concept of the guidance function held by school administrators and that held by counseling psychologists and to present the author's views toward the reconciling of these differences.

THE PARTS OF THE PROBLEM

The problem of the function and role of the high-school guidance counselor is manifold and complex. This article will discuss the problem in terms of the following questions:
1. What is counseling? How does it differ from guidance?
2. What are the counselor's functions?
3. Who should become a counselor?

WHAT IS COUNSELING? HOW DOES IT DIFFER FROM GUIDANCE?

To the layman, including the educator, any time a guidance worker engages in an individual interview he is "counseling." To others, counseling means the giving of advice (5). For the counseling psychologist, however, this word has a special meaning. To him, "Counseling has distinctive functions involving an emphasis upon personality development and upon an environmental understanding of the client." (33:2) Pepinsky has indicated that the current tendency is to group all psychotherapies under the term "counseling" as a psychological function. (13:3) A recent textbook on guidance techniques (which mentions counseling little, if at all) states that, "The point will bear repeating that guidance as defined by those who approach the problem rationally implies, first of all, recognition and understanding of the individual and creation of conditions that will enable each individual to develop his fullest capacities and ultimately to achieve the maximum possible self-guidance and security both economically and socially." (29:9) Traxler

Judging from these citations, the counseling psychologist views counseling as a process designed to promote an individual's understanding of himself and of his environment. It differs from guidance in the personal nature of the process and in the depth of penetration into the individual's perceptions. It differs also in the emphasis placed upon the influence of the perceptions. To the educator, counseling is one of the guidance services; to the counseling psychologist, it is *the* guidance function.

WHAT ARE THE COUNSELOR'S FUNCTIONS?

It would follow from the above that education and counseling psychology would differ in their concept of the function and role of the school counselor. There have been many attempts made to define this role, but generally these attempts have been made by members of a relatively homogeneous group who might be expected to agree. Thus, educators may easily agree upon the functions of the counselor, counselor-trainers will also agree, but there will be little agreement between the two disciplines. That a difference of opinion does exist, and that this difference is reflected in actual counselor work practices, may be easily demonstrated. Derthick (4) has indicated that some counselors spend as much as half their time in duties which are considered to be more administrative than counseling. He further states that, although guidance and counseling are essential to the realization of our educational objective, we are falling far short of realizing adequate guidance programs in many schools. A study by Tennyson of 152 certificated guidance workers in Missouri (27) has shown that these workers spend almost as much time in administrative duties as they do in counseling. In some cases, as much as 80 per cent of a counselor's time has been spent on clerical and/or administrative duties (24). However, the argument goes far beyond the question of the percentage of time spent on various duties. Even if the school counselor were to spend all of his time upon such guidance functions as orientation, the occupational and educational library, individual analysis, and placement—even then the psychologically oriented counselor would argue that this is not counseling.

What does education feel should be the guidance function? Generally, its concept is that the guidance worker should acquaint the student with the pertinent and necessary facts about himself and about the world; the student will be able to accomplish the rest. Thus, those papers on guidance given at the 42nd Annual Convention of the National Association of Secondary-School Principals dealt primarily with those guidance services which provide information (16). Thus, Ginzberg (8) says that it is more important to ensure that information is made available to people who need it than it is to work on psycho-dynamics. He indicates that the counselor can do little to change the basic attitudes of young people to school and to work, and, therefore, the counselor should work in the direction of making the youngster aware of the resources available in the community and in himself. The Educational Policies Commission (6:95) has said, "There is at least one clear need which is stressed by the manpower situation and which calls for imaginative and creative development. This is the need to develop adequate methods of identifying the best abilities of every individual to the end that his further education may result in their optimum development." The National Defense Education Act, by its emphasis on the function of guidance to identify talent (8), supports this view that the most important part of guidance is to supply knowledge to students. The principals of two New York state high schools, in a workshop on "The Wise Use of a Counselor's Time—Whose Responsibility?" (32), have said that the counselor's function is to know as much as possible about the pupil to help him function as effectively as possible. They go on to say that all specialized services in the schools—including guidance—exist only to facilitate learning; the classroom is the focal point of instruction and the counselor should put his primary emphasis on those conditions which affect learning. And they further state that the counselor tends to spend too much of his time in the personal interview; instead, he should extend his activities to include such functions as discipline and attendance. The certification requirements for counselors in New York state (17), by their emphasis on the non-counseling aspects of counselor training, support this information giving view. Perhaps the most extreme position is that taken by Conant, who assigns to the counselor the function of giving advice and of "steering" pupils in the right direction. "The function of the counselor is not to supplant the parents but supplement parental advice to a youngster" (3:44-5). In several other cases, Conant uses the words "counsel" and "guide" as synonymous with "advise" or "urge."

To the counseling psychologist, the primary function of the counselor is counseling with students, and he should retain only those functions connected with this. (32) In the preface of his book *Counseling in the Secondary School,* Smith states flatly that "throughout this book counseling is considered to be central service of the guidance program with all other services occupying a supporting role."

(22:v) Or Rothney and Roens say "the guidance program must become essentially a counseling program" (19:8) and claim that all common (group) guidance functions are merely contributory to the counseling process. Stewart, in his *Bill of Rights for Counselors* (24), includes "the right to enough time to do his real job—to engage in counseling *per se.*" These counselor-trainers take the point of view that experience has shown that psychological problems will prevent, or lessen the capacity for, learning and that the giving of information is of little value unless accompanied by the ability of the student to use this information in a purposeful manner. They further say, that if the factors preventing individual learning are removed, then the individual can, and will, seek out the necessary information by himself, thus allowing the counselor more time to work on counseling with others. There are plenty of resources available to furnish information, but few to remove psychological blocks. Therefore, this should become the specialized function of the counselor.

Perhaps the best manner of pointing out the differing emphases on counselor functions is to compare those functions as stated by the Educational Policies Commission and by the Committee on Professional Training, Licensing, and Certification of the American Personnel and Guidance Association.

Educational Policies Commission (10)	*American Personal and Guidance Association* (18)
1. To gather information about occupational requirements, opportunities, and prospects; and to maintain a system for making such information readily accessible to teachers and students.	1. To increase the accuracy of the individual's self-percepts.
2. To set up and maintain cumulative records about each student.	2. To increase the accuracy of the individual's environmental perceptions.
3. To help all teacher colleagues to increase skill and understanding in guidance.	3. To integrate the individual's self-percepts with environmental realities and perceptions.
4. To give personal counseling to individual students with special problems.	4. To present relevant information.
5. To plan and coordinate school-wide activities such as "career	5. To improve the individual's ability to make and execute plans.

days," special assemblies, and
testing programs.

6. To maintain liaison with out-of-
school agencies, including other
guidance services, labor unions
and prospective employers, and
with alumni and other former
students.

Who Should Become a Counselor?

In a survey of counselor employment policies and practices in the
48 states (31), Weitz discovered that most states will not hire, as a
guidance counselor, a person highly trained as a guidance worker
but not certifiable as a teacher. This seems to represent a view of
education that the guidance counselor should be a competent
teacher who seems to have the right "temperament" for guidance
and who meets certification requirements. Pierson (15) seems to express this view best when he says that the counselor should think of
himself as an experienced teacher with special training whose job
is to help teachers, administrators, and parents to carry on the
process of educating the student.

Counselor-trainers will argue that it is personal, motivational, or
emotional problems which interfere with the learning process.
Therefore the counselor must be highly trained in the techniques
and skills of dealing with adjustment problems; this professional
skill constitutes a unique discipline in itself which may be applied
to any field of work. Thus the guidance counselor in the high school
should be a psychologist or psychologically trained worker who can
function anyplace but who happens in this case to be operating in
an educational setting. As Bordin puts it (2), "counselors speak with
many tongues and identify with varied disciplines and professional
groups." A book review by Arbuckle (1) seems best to sum up the
attitude of counselor-trainers toward the view of counseling as educational in nature:

> The statement that "because counseling takes place in an edu-
> cational setting, it follows logically that its purpose also should
> be educational" . . . might seem to some to be a rather illogical

statement. The author's statement that we should "try to get counseling back into its rightful role as an educational instrument" . . . is also highly debatable. It may be that one of the reasons that so few school counselors do any real counseling is that they think of themselves as educators, and they think of counseling as an "educational instrument."

A Suggestion for Counseling in the High School

At one time secondary schools operated on an attrition basis—survival of the fittest. Those whose ability, motivation, and study skills were adequate for the task succeeded. Many of these then went on to provide educational, vocational, social, and political leadership. This system worked in pre-World War II America in which there existed a large unskilled class of workers, a smaller semi-skilled class, and still smaller skilled and professional classes, although even then there was growing recognition of the need for a more personalized service. The guidance service was inaugurated to help youngsters make educational and vocational choices in a world rapidly becoming more complex. It was added to an educational system which could still operate by the process of attrition.

Today the problem of educational and vocational planning is even more complex, made so by a growing demand for highly trained personnel and narrowing opportunities for unskilled workers. Added to this is the rapid growth in the sum total of human knowledge over the past fifty years. In order to solve these problems alone, it would be necessary for the secondary school to abandon its policy of attrition in favor of one which assists each student in employing his abilities to their maximum. However, superimposed upon these problems is the additional sociological emergency which exists in the United States, that of the dearth of leaders in the foreseeable future. This makes it even more imperative that the potentially superior student not only be identified, but also be motivated to develop his talents to their full capacity. The superior student who has ceased to perform must be retrieved. All others must be encouraged to perform their best.

In line with the history of the development of the guidance service in the secondary school, there exists today a wealth of information upon career and educational opportunities, offered to the student free of charge. A plenitude of free advice is also available—from family, friends, college or societal representatives, religious leaders, social agencies, and teachers. For some students, this information and advice provides all the direction needed. In a very large percentage of the cases, however, the student fails to take advantage of the information and/or advice. In most of these cases in this writer's experience, failure of a student to plan adequately for the future or to achieve to his full capacity has been caused at least in part by emotional, social, or motivational problems. It is for these students who for some reason cannot take advantage of the normal guidance functions of school and society that the counselor should exercise his special training.

At the present time this service is either lacking or present only in a very limited sense. The school psychologist, if one is present, works mainly with abnormal cases. The guidance staff is busy with orientation, program planning, scheduling, and educational and vocational information-giving. In many cases, no counselor has been trained to work with students who fall within the normal range of personality characteristics, but whose full development is impeded by some psychological factor. Yet these problems must be cleared before the student can take advantage of the guidance services being offered. This indicates that professional counseling service—as distinct from guidance service—must be available in the secondary school for all whose school progress seems to be blocked by psychological factors.

At the present time, a great deal of money is being spent by secondary schools to provide guidance services. Much of this money is being wasted because the service does not help those who need it the most. The need for greater efficiency and less waste alone would indicate that secondary-school administrators must modify their concept that the function of guidance is to provide the student with information about himself and about educational and vocational opportunities to include the concept that guidance must eliminate any blocks to increased self-understanding and self-direction by the pupil.

The system for providing this professional counseling service may vary from school to school. In large city districts, a central counseling office may be established to which school guidance staff may make referrals. Smaller schools may prefer to have one or more of their current staff trained to assume this function. Very small or rural units may prefer a cooperative plan, similar to the Board of Co-operative Services system existing in New York state. Regardless of the system employed, there should be available at least one counselor, fully trained, whose sole duty is to work with students referred by other guidance staff. Should this counselor be able to solve student problems which would otherwise harry teachers, guidance staff, and administrators for years to come, he would pay for himself many times over. It has been demonstrated in many instances in the past that prevention is far cheaper than cure.

A Synthesis of the Problem

From the above discussion, it seems clear that the basic difference between education and counselor-trainers lies in their philosophies. Education feels that guidance is the providing of information and instruction, whereas counselor-trainers would hold that guidance is the prevention of mental imbalance or illness. From this basic difference stems the afore-mentioned differences in counselor selection, training, and functions. There is even an inherent difference in the meaning assigned to the word "counseling."

Guidance is being asked to furnish an ever-increasing role in our attempts at solution of the pressing economic, political, and social problems of today. Because of this, it is necessary for educators and counselor-trainers to agree on their concepts of what constitutes counseling. As a start, they might attempt to find a common meeting ground for the answers to the following questions:

1. Should the school accept the responsibility of a positive attempt at fostering mental health through counseling? If not, what agency, if any, should accept this responsibility?
2. What should be the training of the school counselor?
3. What should be the functions of the school counselor?
4. Will the counselor's function encroach upon that of the school psychologist?
5. Should a different title be given to the school counselor?

BIBLIOGRAPHY

1. Arbuckle, Dugald S. Review of "New Dimensions in Counseling Students" by Carolyn A. Sechrest, *The Personnel and Guidance Journal,* Vol. 37, March 1959, p. 519.
2. Bordin, Edward S. *Psychological Counseling.* New York: Appleton-Century-Crofts, Inc. 1955.
3. Conant, James B. *The American High School Today.* New York: McGraw-Hill Book Company. Inc. 1959.
4. Derthick, Lawrence G. "Guidance and the Nation's Needs," *The Personnel and Guidance Journal.* Vol. 37, Oct. 1958, pp. 107-113.
5. Drasgow, James. "Are You Counseling or Advising?" *The Vocational Guidance Quarterly.* Spring 1959, pp. 193-195.
6. Educational Policies Commission. *Manpower and Education.* Washington, D. C.: National Education Association. 1956.
7. Fein, Rashi. *Economics of Mental Illness.* New York: Basic Books, Inc. 1958.
8. Ginzberg, Eli. "Guidance in a World of Skill." Keynote address to convention of New York State Counselors Assoc., April 19, 1959.
9. Hitchcock, Arthur A. Executive Director, American Personnel and Guidance Association, "Guidance and the National Defense Education Act." Speech before New York State Counselors Association, April 21, 1959.
10. "Identification and Guidance of Able Students," *Report of Conferences on Testing and Counseling,* University of Michigan, May 28-31, 1958.
11. Mathewson, Robert Hendry. *Guidance Policy and Practice.* New York: Harper and Brothers. 1949, p. 167.
12. Mathewson, R. H. "The General Guidance Counselor," *The Personnel and Guidance Journal,* Vol. 32, pp. 544-547.
13. Pepinsky, Harold B., and Pauline N. Pepinsky. *Counseling: Theory and Practice.* New York: Ronald Press Co. 1954.
14. Peters, Herman J., and Gail F. Farwell. "What Is Different About High-School Counseling," *The School Counselor.* Vol. 5, May 1958, pp. 67-70.
15. Pierson, G. A. "Aesop and the School Counselor," *The Personnel and Guidance Journal.* Vol. 32, pp. 326-329.
16. "Proceedings of the 42nd Annual Convention," *The Bulletin of the National Association of Secondary School Principals.* Vol. 42, April 1958.
17. "Regulations of the Commissioner of Education," New York State Education Dept., Certificates Valid for Guidance Service.

18. "Report of the Committee on Professional Training, Licensing, and Certification," *The Personnel and Guidance Journal*. Vol. 37, Oct. 1958, p. 163.

19. Rothney, J. W. M., and B. A. Roens. *Counseling the Individual Student*. New York: The Dryden Press, Inc. 1949.

20. Shear, Bruce E., Chief, Bureau of Guidance, New York State Education Department, "Guidance and the National Defense Education Act." Speech before New York State Counselors Association, April 21, 1959.

21. Shoben, Edward J. "Student Personnel Work: A Worry and a Vision," *The Personnel and Guidance Journal*. Vol. 33, 1954, pp. 152-156.

22. Smith, Glenn E. *Counseling in the Secondary School*. New York: The Macmillan Co. 1955.

23. "Statement by the Executive Director," *The Personnel and Guidance Journal*. Vol. 37, March 1959, p. 528.

24. Stewart, C. C. "A Bill of Rights for School Counselors," *The Personnel and Guidance Journal*. Vol. 37, March 1959, pp. 500-503.

25. Stoops, Emery, and Gunnar L. Wahlquist. *Principles and Practices in Guidance*. New York: McGraw-Hill Book Co., Inc. 1958.

26. Super, Donald E. "Transition from Vocational Guidance to Counseling Psychology," *The Journal of Counseling Psychology*. Vol. 2, No. 1, 1955.

27. Tennyson, Willard W. "Time: The Counselor's Dilemma," *The Personnel and Guidance Journal*. Vol. 37, Oct. 1958, pp. 129-135.

28. "Theses in Counseling and Student Personnel Work," *The Journal of Counseling Psychology*. Vol. 3, No. 4, 1956, pp. 272-277.

29. Traxler, Arthur E. *Techniques of Guidance*. New York: Harper and Brothers. 1957.

30. Warters, Jane. *High School Personnel Work Today*. New York: McGraw-Hill Book Company, Inc. 1956.

31. Weitz, Henry. "The Role of the Guidance Worker in the Schools," *The Personnel and Guidance Journal*. Vol. 37, Dec. 1958, pp. 266-272.

32. "The Wise Use of a Counselor's Time—Whose Responsibility?" Workshop Conference, New York State Counselors Association, April 19-21, 1959.

33. Wrenn, C. G., editorial comment. *The Journal of Counseling Psychology*. Vol. 4, No. 1, 1957, p. 2.

4. THE COUNSELOR'S SELF CONCEPT

J. W. Yates and Lyle D. Schmidt

The counselor's self concept may be rather simply identified as what he perceives himself to be in the counseling relationship. This may not be what is perceived by the client and in some ways the counselor himself may recognize the difference. But when the counselor's concept of self can allow him to be himself and this is acceptable to the client, counseling comes to be a real and effective experience.

It is not likely that the counselor becomes a totally different person during the counseling hour than he is in his other interpersonal relationships. It should be noted, however, that the energy devoted toward being understanding and accepting may be exhausting to the counselor and he may feel he cannot try as hard to do this in all relationships as he does in the counseling one. Nevertheless it is probable that to a considerable degree the type of personal relationships developed during the counseling hour might represent the kinds of relationships the counselor otherwise maintains.

What the counselor sees himself to be as a person will be reflected in his relationship with the client. A person's psychological development, including his response to training, may cause him to be dominant, controlling, or rigid in structure on the one hand; accepting, understanding, and flexible on the other, or, more likely, something between these two extremes. But whatever his structure may be it is quite sure to have an important place in the relationship and be revealed to the client.

It sometimes happens that the counselor intellectually recognizes a need to be accepting and understanding and in his self concept must be such a person. If in the perception of the client he is not, the relationship will become confusing to both the client and the counselor. But if the counselor is willing and able to accept what the client says as it pertains to the counseling relationship, he may begin to see himself as the client sees him. In this way the counseling

Reprinted by permission of the authors and *Vocational Guidance Quarterly,* VII, No. 3 (Spring, 1959), 151-54.

hour may offer to the counselor as well as the client the opportunity to examine and modify his self concept.

It seems that a training program for counselors built around the strengths of the trainee may allow him to develop more of this awareness of self in relation to how others see him. As the counselor can come to accept himself in the manner in which he actually enters into the counseling relationship he may develop strength to deal with the relationship which is not available if he is forced to protect himself from what the client sees him to be.

An unhelpful defensiveness can become a part of the counselor's counseling when in training the demands of what he should do differ in his experience from what he is able to do at that time. It is very difficult to deal effectively with a situation in which one is expected to be something he is not. We recognize that the demands placed on counselors in training are usually sound in terms of ultimately desirable competencies, but wonder about the best way of reaching them.

COUNSELING, A LIFE EXPERIENCE

Counseling is a special situation in life in which two people come together with a common goal of helping one of them. Each person brings into the counseling hour what he is as a person and the counseling process becomes an experience in life for both participants. The quality of the interpersonal relationship may differ from any the client previously has experienced.

In this relationship the counselor directs his energy toward understanding the client's difficulties and his effort helps the client to again gain interest in those aspects of himself which he may have hidden, distorted, overevaluated, or inhibited. Here the client can experience and examine himself as a living human being and become aware of the counselor's interest and desire to understand. This may give the client the support that allows him to feel more secure in the shared understanding of previously hidden or distorted aspects of himself.

The counselor also provides warmth and acceptance which makes possible the development of a deep but controllable emotional relationship. He frankly recognizes that he is emotionally involved, is not detached, and yet is not overly involved. He must remain very sensitive to both his own and to the client's needs in order to control his own identification and maintain a constructive relationship.

The counselor's acceptance provides strength for the client to accept himself as he is, to attempt to understand how he became what he is, and to move toward taking constructive steps for himself as he is. He can discover that his defenses are not always necessary to justify his feelings and behavior and perhaps for the first time he can drop defense mechanisms and overcompensations, enabling him to examine more effective ways of dealing with the world. He then can evaluate his feelings, actions, choices, and conflicts as he lives them in the interpersonal interaction with the counselor. He can do this since he is free from the necessity of defending himself from attack on one hand and is protected from overdependence on the other.

The client has this protection, provided the counselor directs his efforts at maintaining the constructive relationship previously described. Therefore, through a wholehearted understanding of the relationship and its meaning to both the client and the counselor, the counseling hour becomes a living experience.

Some Training Influences

The potential counselor on entering training, like everyone else, has some sort of self concept which may in part be consciously definable and understood by the individual. In the process of training, this concept of self is modified, reinforced, accepted, or rejected. Many of the pressures, tensions, and anxieties felt by clients may also be experienced to a degree by the counselor in training.

In brief, the trainee is expected to intellectually master various theories, methods, and techniques of counseling, skill with counseling tools, and to integrate these into his own system of counseling. This might remain academic in the trainee's experience since it is sometimes necessary in training to verbalize acceptance and integration of philosophy and academic knowledge, at least to an appreciable degree. When this occurs and is not really felt in the way it is verbalized, the trainee may become at least partially aware of it and feelings of insecurity or inadequacy can result. A desire to maintain status with his supervisors and fellow trainees by doing the "right" things can be more important than trying to understand his own self concept as it influences his relationships with others. Unless a careful structure is provided during the practicum phase of training, the academic preparation may be difficult to assimilate into the trainee's self concept.

Since a person needs understanding and acceptance in order to be able to understand himself, some of the dangers of academic pressures brought to bear on trainees become obvious. This leads to the problems of screening, selection, and retention of trainees within the counseling profession but it is not the purpose of this paper to deal with these questions. It only attempts to indicate that training programs deeply affect the counselor's self concept and seeks to ask those who deal with trainees to examine their relationships with students in terms of self concepts.

These comments are not at all intended to be critical. Many, if not most, counselors have experienced the atmosphere conducive to self evaluation, made possible by effective relationships with graduate advisors and counselor-trainers. They are only to suggest that this area is important enough to the process of the development of the counselor's self concept to be evaluated carefully. One must consider that to deal differently with people than we expect them to deal with others, can be defended, but perhaps not understood.

If the purposes of training resemble the goals of counseling, in that growth is an anticipated result, then it seems that psychologically the same principles are operative. If the trainee feels that he is compelled to accept something which he does not seem able to accept, a very frustrating situation may exist. Of course this may eventuate in growth provided the frustration is within the individual's capacity to accept it, but we must be aware of the trainee's perceptions and deal accordingly if we are to afford him maximum opportunities for development.

It is possible that a lack of understanding of the trainee's self concept on the part of the counselor-trainer, in a limited program of training experiences, may be reflected by the feelings of some counselors of the inability to do counseling. They may be further adversely affected by attitudes of competency conveyed to them by others who have experienced a more complete program of training, although if this is so, maybe a few of the latter do not feel as competent as they would like.

In the formulation of each counselor's self concept he seeks to define for himself his competencies as a counselor in relation to his colleagues. It is important that he be accepted and understood as an individual so that he may feel comfortable in doing his work consistently with himself rather than feel inadequate and insecure in relationship to others.

A Conclusion or Two

A counselor cannot effectively accept others or be of help to them, through maintaining a permissive structure, until he can accept and understand himself within this structure. If he feels the need to maintain himself through controlling others, he is left in a poor position to be able to accept and understand them.

The counselor needs to be understanding of himself and his relationships with others. He needs to be able to be himself in such a manner that relationships with others become "real." Suc¹ implies the acceptance and understanding of himself and th for what they are and for what they must be at any given mo Then the counselor and client have less need to defend themsc and confuse the existing relationship through being somethi..g which they are not, or in other words, sharing an "unreal" relationship.

In the process of counseling insofar as the conditions on the part of the counselor can be as described, it seems that positive client movement occurs. If we can accept that "life is," and that our only control over it is in controlling ourselves in relationship to others, we may be able to come nearer to one of the meanings of counseling —that of being accepting and understanding of others in the process of becoming themselves.

In the final analysis it seems ultimately more rewarding to try to see an individual as he sees himself and provide the understanding and acceptance necessary for him to become himself than it is to feel we have caused him to change and become what we think he should be. If people are basically positive and really need meaningful relationships with others, it is reasonable that they should be allowed and encouraged. It could be that relationships of these types offer man his only real hope for the future.

5. GUIDANCE SERVICES RECOMMENDED BY PUBLIC- AND PAROCHIAL-SCHOOL TEACHERS

Anthony C. Riccio and Donald J. Wehmeyer

In a recent report, Leona E. Tyler indicates that there is a definite need to improve guidance services in private schools. Further, she notes the effort "to get private school counselors into the [National Defense Education Act] program has been almost completely unsuccessful." [1] Many persons believe that private-school personnel do not enroll in guidance and counseling training institutes because they do not receive the handsome stipends afforded public-school participants. Others think that the problem is more basic. They hold that guidance services are not as well received in private as in public schools, primarily because of the emphasis on traditional approaches to education in private schools. They see the issue as directly related to conflicting philosophies of education.

This paper reports a study designed to ascertain whether there are noticeable or significant differences in the guidance services recommended by public and private (parochial) elementary-school teachers for particular problem situations. By law neither public nor private elementary-school teachers are allowed to enroll in NDEA counseling and guidance training institutes and thus are ineligible to profit professionally or financially from external pressures to improve the quality of counseling and guidance services; it seemed desirable, therefore, to use elementary-school teachers to measure genuine attitudinal differences toward guidance services. The study incidentally yielded data pertinent to the future of guidance services at the elementary-school level.

Several attempts have been made to study the reactions of educa-

Reprinted by permission of the authors and *Educational Research Bulletin,* XL (January 11, 1961), 12-18.

[1] *The National Defense Counseling and Guidance Training Institutes Program: a Report of the First 50 Institutes,* Washington, D. C.: Office of Education, U. S. Department of Health, Education and Welfare, 1960, p. 73. (Bulletin No. 31).

tional groups to the kind of guidance services that should be employed in particular problem situations. Lawrence H. Stewart administered Robinson's "What Should Be Done?" questionnaire to 94 counselors and 169 classroom teachers in the San Francisco Bay area to learn whether these groups had different conceptions of the guidance services most appropriate for particular problem situations. He found few outstanding differences in the recommendations of the two groups and noted that large numbers in both groups recommended actions which were "inadequate and often inappropriate." He suggested that his findings conceivably were related to the current practice of assigning teachers to counseling positions rather than persons qualified in the field.[2]

Mangan conducted a similar study using a sample of elementary- and secondary-school teachers in Ohio. He administered the same questionnaire to 111 secondary-school teachers and an adaptation of it to an equal number of elementary-school teachers. Observing few differences between the guidance services recommended by the groups under study, he discerned a tendency for secondary-school teachers to suggest intensive guidance procedures for students with various kinds of academic difficulties.[3] The writers used this adaptation in the present study. The questionnaire follows:

WHAT SHOULD BE DONE?

Following are brief descriptions of pupils in the sixth grade of an elementary school. The members of the staff are discussing the relationship which their guidance program should have to each pupil. As a preliminary step they are placing each pupil in one of the following five categories. If you were there, what rating would you give each pupil? (Place a category number before each pupil.)

0 Probably no need for guidance program to work with this pupil.

1 Routine use made of conferences and activities with pupil and/or parents; nothing especially planned for pupil at this time.

---

[2] "Teachers and Counselors Look at Students: Some Implications for Guidance Practice," *Personnel and Guidance Journal*, XXXV (May, 1957), pp. 565-68.

[3] Mangan, John C. "Teachers' Recommendations for Guidance Services." 1959. A Master's thesis on file in the library of Ohio State University. The writers make grateful acknowledgment for permission to use the questionnaire and other data appearing in the thesis.

2 Special plans made to fit this pupil's needs with particular emphasis placed on non-conference personnel methods, e.g., activities, change of grade, enrichment, etc.

3 Special plans made to fit this pupil's needs with particular emphasis placed on the school providing intensive counseling help or play therapy.

4 Refer the pupil to some agency outside of school for help.

........Athlete	A natural athlete. Is the star in all physical education held in class. Has average intellectual ability and achievement to match; has a pleasing personality.
........Bright	Very bright pupil; I.Q. 170. Particularly likes arithmetic but gets outstanding grades in all class work with little or no effort (his success with poor study methods makes it difficult to convince other pupils that they might benefit from learning better study methods). Accepted by others; often a leader.
........Cqueer	He's so odd we spell it "Cqueer." Tense, withdrawn, and often smiles or talks to himself. Erratic in behavior. Doing very poor school work; rejected by other pupils.
........Dumb and Deficient	Doubly troubled, I.Q. 75. Three grades below level in school; has difficulty in doing class work. He is older and bigger than other pupils and is accepted by them in such activities as physical education.
........Engineer	Has his heart set on becoming an engineer. He has high ability and grades. Has many mechanical and electrical hobbies. Not too socially inclined, but is well liked by pupils.
........Failing	Pupil has average ability and is doing satisfactory work in everything but arithmetic which he is failing. Much upset by failing grade. Has always had trouble with arithmetic, just as his mother did. Liked by fellow pupils.
........Gauche	Not particularly liked by other pupils. Dresses in poor taste. Not always clean, poor manners, seems awkward for age, does good work in school however.
........Homely	She just isn't good looking at all. She has a pleasant personality, good social skills, and is ac-

cepted by other pupils in class work. Outside of school, however, she is not in a group and other girls tend less often now to be seen with her. Has been pubescent for one year. Does good work in school.

........Ill
Constantly has colds or other respiratory ailments. Lately has had a bad cough and has lost weight. Says she doesn't feel well. When she does attend school, she does good work and is liked by the pupils.

........Jerk
A "teacher's pet." Does well in school; goes out of his way to please his teacher. Rushes home after school "to be with Mother." Immature, even "babyish" in his relations with other pupils, disliked by other pupils.

........Kiddish
Girl's behavior is immature; baby talk, over-dependency on mother, fails to make own decisions, etc. Her "cute" manner makes her popular with many of the boys. To get average grades in school her parents force her to study and help her with school work.

........Loafer
Very high ability; average grades. Liked by pupils; active in school affairs. Plans to go to a private high school which has very high standards.

........Medicine
Wants to become a doctor; but has low ability and low grades. Will probably have difficulty in high school; parents want him to be a doctor.

........Not Known
Not mentioned by anyone on a Guess Who test. Does average work in school but doesn't discuss in class; teacher says nothing about her stands out. Comes from a farm nearby; not active in group work. Not rejected; just sort of "mousy."

This questionnaire was administered to 103 parochial elementary-school teachers in attendance at the 1960 Summer Session of the University of Notre Dame. Their responses were compared to Mangan's data (1959) on 111 public elementary-school teachers in Ohio in two ways. First, a comparison was made of the percentage distribution of choice of guidance services by both groups for each of the fourteen problem situations. Second, in accordance with Mangan's treatment of his data, the five categories listed in the directions accompanying the questionnaire were reduced to two. Categories 0, 1, and 2 were termed "routine"; categories 3 and 4 "intensive." The chi-square test was used to determine whether there were significant differences in the extent to which the study groups recommended routine or intensive guidance services. The .05 level of confidence was selected as the criterion of significance.

Table I presents a percentage breakdown by category of the responses of the study groups. The table should be read as follows: for the case called Athlete, 58 per cent of the parochial and 52 per cent of the public elementary-school teachers thought that no guidance was needed; 37 per cent of the parochial and 43 per cent of the public-school teachers suggested a routine conference; and so on. An analysis of Table I indicates a remarkable similarity in the categories selected for each problem situation. In only four of the fourteen categories (Cqueer, Engineer, Homely, and Kiddish) were there different modal responses, and in only one case (Cqueer) was there a difference larger than 20 per cent. In addition, there was a decided tendency for both groups to suggest intensive counseling or referral for students characterized by social or academic deficiencies. This observation was also reported by Robinson and by Stewart.[4]

On the other hand, less than 10 per cent of the members of either group suggested intensive guidance services for the superior or well-adjusted students (Athlete, Bright, and Engineer). This finding runs counter to one of the purposes of the National Defense Education Act: to use guidance services as a means of helping talented students to make optimal contributions in the interests of national defense. It also suggests that Mr. Conant's recent interest in using guidance services to identify, encourage, and develop talented students[5] has yet to be accepted or practiced at the grass-roots level, for guidance services were viewed by study-group members as remedial and preventive rather than developmental.

The data contained in Table I does not augur well for the future. Since there are relatively few elementary-school counselors at present, elementary-school teachers will have to bear the brunt of guidance activities. If the study-group members are representative of

---

[4] Robinson, Francis P. "Guidance for All: in Principle and in Practice," *Personnel and Guidance Journal*, XXXI (May, 1953), pp. 500-504; Stewart, *op. cit.*

[5] Conant, James B. *The American High School Today: a First Report to Interested Citizens.* New York: McGraw-Hill Book Company, 1959, pp. 44-46.

TABLE I

PERCENTAGE OF PAROCHIAL AND PUBLIC ELEMENTARY-SCHOOL TEACHERS'
RESPONSES FOR GUIDANCE ACTION, BY CATEGORY

STUDENT	No GUIDANCE NEEDED 0		ROUTINE CONFERENCE 1		SPECIAL NON-CONFERENCE 2		INTENSIVE COUNSELING 3		REFERRAL TO OUTSIDE AGENCY 4	
	Par.	Pub.	Par.	Pub.	Par.	Pub.	Par.	Pub.	Par.	Pub.
(1)	(2)	(3)	(4)	(5)	(6)	(7)	(8)	(9)	(10)	(11)
Athlete..........	58	52	37	43	4	5	1	0	0	0
Bright...........	7	7	15	15	69	70	6	8	3	0
Cqueer..........	0	0	0	4	3	3	25	53	72	40
Dumb and Deficient......	1	0	2	10	20	25	43	40	34	25
Engineer........	15	26	43	33	33	35	8	4	1	2
Failing..........	0	2	30	28	38	49	29	20	3	1
Gauche.........	2	2	32	29	6	21	52	43	8	5
Homely.........	7	3	28	25	16	36	42	32	7	4
Ill..............	4	3	10	24	3	5	8	10	75	58
Jerk............	0	1	17	18	14	14	63	61	6	6
Kiddish.........	0	2	38	29	20	22	37	41	5	6
Loafer..........	2	3	20	24	62	52	15	21	1	0
Medicine........	0	0	46	47	18	18	32	33	4	2
Not Known......	3	6	29	27	26	32	40	35	2	0

their co-workers, they will devote much time to working with the deficient and maladjusted at the expense of the superior and the well-adjusted student. Since the elementary-school counselors of the future in all probability will come from the present crop of elementary-school teachers, there is reason to believe that to a large extent they will continue to view guidance services as remedial and preventive. The talented and potentially superior students in our society will suffer—as will the entire nation—if this negative view of guidance services is not radically altered. Undoubtedly one of the major tasks of both teacher- and counselor-education programs in this decade will be to communicate to future teachers and counselors the belief that guidance services have just as much, if not more, to offer to the development of the superior student as to the rehabilitation of the deficient or unmotivated student.

TABLE II

ANALYSIS OF OBSERVED DIFFERENCES BETWEEN PUBLIC AND
PAROCHIAL ELEMENTARY-SCHOOL TEACHERS' RECOMMENDA-
TIONS OF ROUTINE AND INTENSIVE GUIDANCE SERIVCES*

Student	Chi Square	Level of Significance
(1)	(2)	(3)
Athlete.................	.0071	.95
Bright..................	.0275	.90
Cqueer.................	2.0208	.20
Dumb and Deficient......	3.6019	.10
Engineer................	1.7099	.20
Failing.................	3.5422	.10
Gauche.................	3.3291	.10
Homely.................	3.4297	.10
Ill.....................	6.3347	.02
Jerk....................	.1254	.80
Kiddish.................	.5625	.50
Loafer..................	.9644	.50
Medicine...............	.0144	.95
Not Known.............	.9883	.50

* Degree of freedom = 1

Table II presents the results of a chi-square analysis of the significance of the differences between public and parochial elementary-school teachers' recommendations of routine and intensive guidance services. The table shows that in one case only (Ill) was there a significant difference in the recommendations of the study groups. In view of the data contained in Table I, this finding is not surprising. It should be noted, however, that there were greater differences in the guidance recommendations of the Ohio elementary- and secondary-school groups studied by Mangan[6] than in the responses of the parochial and public elementary-school teachers. It is conceivable that the elementary-secondary dimension may be more important than the public-private school one. This possibility bears further investigation.

To the extent that the study groups are representative of public- and private- (parochial) school teachers, it is possible to conclude

---

[6] *Op. cit.*, p. 34.

that there are no distinguishing general attitudes toward guidance services between these two groups. It seems, therefore, that if administrators in parochial schools were to place guidance services at the disposal of teachers, they would be used at least as often by parochial-school teachers as by public-school teachers. What is most noticeable, however, is that both private and public elementary-school teachers perceive guidance services as means of rehabilitating the deficient rather than as avenues of developing the talented. Here, perhaps, is a major challenge to elementary-school administrators. Through in-service education or other means, they must make their teachers aware of the advantages of the developmental approach to guidance services. A successful developmental guidance program may obviate much of the work required by remedial or preventive guidance programs.

Unfortunately, students also have a tendency to view guidance services from other than a developmental point of view.[7] They share with their teachers the notion that guidance is for those who are performing at a less than satisfactory level on some behavioral dimension. They do not view it as a means of assisting the mediocre to perform at a superior level or as a vehicle for helping the superior student to perform at an exceptional level. They must come to realize that the counseling interview is basically a learning situation and that the well-motivated, intelligent student stands to profit far more from counseling than does the unmotivated, less intelligent student.[8] Perhaps it is in this area that Mr. Conant's report will make its greatest contribution to the modern school; for as students who are known to be excellent are seen in fairly frequent contact with guidance personnel, the stigma currently attached to taking part in a counseling interview will gradually disappear. In sum, until there is a radical departure from a negative, problem-oriented conception of guidance services on the part of teachers and students, the concept of guidance for all youth will be but a counselor-educator's dream.

---

[7] Heilfron, Marilyn. "The Function of Counseling as Perceived by High School Students," *Personnel and Guidance Journal,* XXXIX (October, 1960), pp. 133-36.

[8] Peters, Herman J. "Counseling Services for Talented Students" in *Working with Superior Students: Theories and Practices,* edited by Bruce Shertzer. Chicago: Science Research Associates 1960, p. 203.

Section Two

THE COUNSELEES

Both theoretical formulations and factual knowledge concerning adolescence may facilitate the school counselor's building of adequate conceptual models of his counselees. Even though many of the constructs developed by the counselor should arise inductively from the data provided by the counselee, it seems true that the counselee cannot be fully understood apart from the adolescent stage of life, his peer group culture, and the context of the times in which we live. In this section, several articles are presented which depict adolescence in the contemporary American scene.

The high school student of today, as seen through O. E. Thompson's research perspectives, does not appear to be beset with value conflicts insofar as occupational values are concerned. Rather clearly, the adolescent is portrayed as aspiring to move upward in the occupational hierarchy but not so far, in terms of his own abilities, as to appear unrealistic. However, there are threads of evidence in Thompson's research which imply that new values related to self-expression, security, and social service are replacing those values which emphasize individual freedom.

As if to amplify Thompson's portrayal, Peters depicts the growing adolescent as "reflecting the image of many of his peers and, in particular, the significant adults of his daily living." Peters describes eight growth processes from the zero moment of conception to the maturity of becoming. In concluding his paper, this author lists eight specific goals for the teachers, parents, and school counselors of high school boys and girls.

Even though it may be agreed that counseling can serve all boys and girls, it is also clear that there are many pupils who could benefit from counseling but are reluctant to voluntarily initiate counseling. Nelson's topic, "Reaching High School Pupils Who Need Counseling," gives many practical suggestions concerning techniques and procedures. In his conclusions, the writer cites evidence to the effect that the personal qualities of the counselor may overshadow techniques in importance in the relationship-building process.

A section concerning counselees would hardly be complete without evidence concerning pupil reactions to counseling. Jenson's article provides a normative picture of counselee feelings about counseling. Contrary to some views are Jenson's findings that the pupils in his sample seemed generally to prefer being counseled by counselors rather than by the teachers, parents, or peers. The reader should be cautioned, as Jenson indicates, that pupils recognize that there are many potential avenues for counseling help other than counselors.

6. WHAT IS THE HIGH SCHOOL STUDENT OF TODAY LIKE?

O. E. Thompson

What is the high school student of today like? What is his home situation? Does his mother work? With whom does he live? Does he attend church regularly? Has he made an occupational choice? What is important to him in selecting a vocation?

Answers to these and similar questions about the high school student should be of interest not only to the general public but particulary to those in curriculum planning, pupil personnel work, and educational and vocational guidance, and those responsible for the over-all administration of the school.

It is often stated that the high school student of today is different from one of a decade ago. Undoubtedly this is partially true, for as our society progresses, the occupational values, personal values, and attitudes of students will reflect the culture of the particular era.

Today the family situation is in transition. The general economic level of the American family is near an all-time high. Education in general is undergoing critical evaluation. Atomic energy and space research are forging ahead at an unbelievable pace. The conflict in ideologies among world powers is at fever pitch. These and many other developments and problems cannot help but influence and direct the thinking, action, and general characteristics of the modern teen-ager.

THE PROBLEM

The problem under study was—what are some of the sociological and psychological characteristics of the modern high school student

Reprinted by permission of the author and *Journal of Secondary Education*, XXXVI, No. 4 (April, 1961), 210-19.

and how do these characteristics relate to his vocational choice and his reaction to selected vocational values and desires?

PROCEDURE

The questions already listed, plus others, were posed to freshmen and seniors in five central-California high schools—two small ones in rural areas, one medium-sized school in an industrial area, and two moderately large schools, one in a semi-rural community and the other in a strictly urban center. Thus, this is a cross section of the various kinds of high schools, and might well be considered a sample of typical California high schools.

Each freshman and senior completed a survey form asking for personal information and reactions to certain occupational values plus a personal differential values inventory. A random sample of 100 boys and 100 girls from each of the classes was drawn for analysis from the total population of about 1400 students. This report deals with only the personal information and occupational values of the students.

DISCUSSION

Home Situation

The home situation is often a factor with mentally disturbed children as well as with those who exhibit tendencies toward delinquency. Here, the idea was not to try to correlate family situation with any other characteristics but merely to find the proportion of high school students that came from atypical home situations.

It was found that about one in eight students came from an abnormal home. About two-thirds of those not living with both parents were living with the mother. Home situation differed little between boys and girls, and between freshmen and seniors.

In some areas the place of residence is known to influence the opportunities students have in high school, their attitudes and values, and the curriculum they follow. This study, however, found little difference between rural students and their city cousins. In this study at least, rural students did not necessarily live on farms. Thus, only one-third of the parents of rural students were farmers. About one-fifth were in each vocational class, skilled and unskilled, whereas over one-tenth were in the professional-managerial category, only slightly less than the proportion for the parents of city students. This perhaps accounts for the lack of major differences between rural and city students.

The only stratification showing significant differences between rural and city students was whether the mother worked outside the home for pay. Significantly fewer (at one per cent level) of the rural mothers worked outside the home. That is logical when one considers items such as employment opportunity and child care facilities.

No differences were apparent between rural and urban students in high school curriculum, vocational choice, academic achievement, church attendance, or occupational values and desires.

High School Curriculum

Although the curriculums followed by rural and urban students were very similar, the same is not true for other stratifications of the sample. It will be noted in Table 1 that slightly over two-fifths (43.5 per cent) of the entire group were taking a program designed for entrance into college. Almost one-fourth were in each curriculum, business and general. About one-tenth didn't know what curriculum they were enrolled in. Probably it was a general curriculum, for they likely would have been aware of any special choice they might have made.

Differences between boys and girls in curricular choice were large enough to be significant at the one per cent level. Significantly more boys than girls were in the college preparatory curriculum, whereas the reverse was true in the business field. Likewise, more boys than girls were in the general major.

Differences in curricular choice were also large enough to be significant between freshmen and seniors, but not as great as between boys and girls. More seniors were in the business and general curriculum, whereas more freshmen than seniors did not know what curriculum they were in.

The decrease in the number of seniors unsure about their major

TABLE 1

CURRICULUM FOLLOWED IN HIGH SCHOOL (ALL FIGURES ARE IN PER CENT)

Curriculum	All Boys N = 200	All Girls N = 200	Freshmen N = 200	Seniors N = 200	Total N = 400
College Preparatory	48.5	38.5	43.5	43.5	43.5
Business-Commercial	6.5	38.5	19.0	26.0	22.5
General	32.0	16.0	23.0	25.0	24.0
Don't Know	13.0	7.0	14.5	5.5	10.0

chi square = 62.074   chi square = 10.442
(significant 1% level)   (significant 5% level)

could mean one of two things—either a proportion had settled upon a specific major or had withdrawn from school.

Academic Achievement

Academic achievement was measured by the grades students stated they received. Although the grade distribution for all the students does not follow a normal curve, it is probably quite typical for the average high school. Failures because of deficient grades are generally quite rare.

Grades earned by students during the 1959-60 school year were compared with the grades students indicated they received. There was no demonstrable difference between grades earned and grades indicated. Girls proved to get better grades than boys, enough so to be significantly superior at the one per cent level. Likewise, grades for seniors were enough higher than those of freshmen to be significant at the one per cent level. Undoubtedly the dropping out of some of the low-ability students had up-graded the average for the seniors. See Table 2.

It was also found that, in general, students with high ability were in the college preparatory majors, and the less capable students were in the less demanding majors. Of the 32 students in the A grade category, 87 per cent were in college preparatory work. Likewise, B students tended to be oriented toward the college preparation majors. Actually, about two-thirds of this group were preparing for college and one-fifth were in the business major.

Students earning mostly C grades were about equally distributed

TABLE 2

ACADEMIC LEVEL OF ACHIEVEMENT (ALL FIGURES ARE IN PER CENT)

Grades	All Boys N = 200	All Girls N = 200	Freshmen N = 200	Seniors N = 200	Total N = 400
Mostly A's	4.00	12.06	8.54	7.50	8.02
Mostly B's	27.50	35.17	23.11	39.50	31.33
Mostly C's	54.50	44.72	52.26	47.00	49.62
Mostly D's	13.50	8.04	15.57	6.00	10.78
Below D	0.50	—	0.50	—	0.25

chi square = 14.675 (significant 1% level)   chi square = 17.796 (significant 1% level)

among the majors, whereas the D students were primarily in the general curriculum group. It is evident that students in general, either on their own or with the assistance of counselors, are seeking the kinds of educational preparation that are in line with their abilities. Naturally, there are minor departures from this.

When students whose mothers worked outside the home were compared with those whose mothers did not, the differences in grades were significant at the 5 per cent level. Students whose mothers worked received significantly higher grades than those whose mothers did not.

Church Attendance

Studies of student characteristics ordinarily omit consideration of the spiritual side of students' lives. Since this one aspect may be a factor influencing others, it is included in this study. The frequency with which a student attended church was used as an indicator of his religious interest.

It is obvious from Table 3 that there is a difference in the frequency with which the different groups attended church. Girls were by far the most regular in attendance, with the differences between boys and girls significant at the one per cent level. Freshmen attend church more frequently than seniors, though the difference was not as great as between boys and girls (5 per cent significance). It can be concluded that boys, and senior boys in particular, have poor church attendance records.

TABLE 3

FREQUENCY OF CHURCH ATTENDANCE (ALL FIGURES ARE IN PER CENT)

Frequency	All Boys N = 200	All Girls N = 200	Freshmen N = 200	Seniors N = 200	Total N = 400
More Than Once Weekly	7.00	12.50	11.00	8.50	9.75
Once a Week	36.00	52.50	49.00	39.50	44.25
About Once Monthly	15.00	15.50	16.50	14.00	15.25
Seldom	42.00	19.50	23.50	38.00	30.75

chi square = 25.741   chi square = 9.933
(significant 1% level)   (significant 5% level)

A comparison of the church attendance of A, B, C, and D students showed a distinct relationship. Over 71 per cent of A students attended church at least once a week, compared with 54 per cent of B students, and 51 per cent of C and D students. Only 6 per cent of the A students seldom attended church, whereas this percentage was respectively 32, 30, and 41 for the B, C, and D groups.

Occupation of Father and Vocational Choice of Students

Each student was asked to state what his father did to support his family. These jobs were then classified into seven major categories by the Dictionary of Occupational Titles.[1] Student vocational choices were classified similarly. Table 4 compares the occupations of the fathers and vocational choices for boys, girls, and both.

Students in general aspire to occupations that are higher on the socio-economic ladder than those of their fathers. For example, over three times as many boys chose professional-managerial kinds of vocations as there were fathers in these occupations. Many girls were interested in clerical-sales vocations. The vocation with the closest relation between fathers and students was agriculture-forestry. Here, almost as many boys (14.5 per cent) planned to enter the vocation as there were fathers presently in the vocation.

It is readily apparent that most high school students have made at least tentative vocational choices. When freshmen were considered separately, only 22 per cent were undecided, some 8.5 per cent more

[1] U. S. Department of Labor, Bureau of Employment Security, *Dictionary of Occupational Titles: 1949,* Vol. II, Occupational Classification and Industry Index.

TABLE 4

COMPARISON OF THE VOCATIONAL CHOICES OF STUDENTS
WITH THE OCCUPATION OF THE FATHERS
(All Figures Are in Per Cent)

Kind of Occupation	Father's Occupation All Boys N = 200	Choice of Boys	Father's Occupation All Girls N = 200	Choice of Girls	Father's Occupation Totals N = 400	Choice of Students
1 Professional-Managerial	11.50	38.00	17.00	36.00	14.25	37.00
2 Clerical-Sales	11.50	3.00	8.00	32.50	9.75	17.75
3 Services	5.00	9.00	7.50	11.50	6.25	10.25
4 Agriculture-Forestry	16.00	14.50	19.00	0.50	17.50	7.50
5 Skilled	27.50	13.50	17.50	—	22.50	6.75
6 Semi-Skilled	6.00	1.00	5.50	1.00	5.75	1.00
7 Unskilled	13.00	4.00	17.00	—	15.00	2.00
8 Unemployed, Retired, Undecided	9.50	17.00	8.50	18.50	9.00	17.75

than for seniors. This refutes the contention of some educators that students of this age are too immature even to consider this important decision.

Also, it is interesting to note that girls were as vocation conscious as were boys. On the data sheets many girls indicated that being homemakers was their ultimate goal. Nevertheless, most were planning for another vocation first.

Some interesting inferences can be drawn when the vocational choices of students are compared with academic achievement. Three-fourths of the students in the A group were interested in professional-managerial vocations, with none choosing semi-skilled or unskilled work. The C students, which included about one-half the entire group, were interested in a wider range of vocations. Slightly over one-fourth chose the professional types of vocations, and about 15 per cent were interested in clerical work. About 10 per cent were interested in service, agricultural, and skilled kinds of vocations. The D students likewise chose a wide range of vocations, with some one-fourth (the largest group) interested in service kinds of vocations.

It is interesting to note that the undecided students were primarily in the C and D groups: over 20 per cent in these groups, compared with 10 per cent in the A and B groups. In one sense it can be said that students are reasonably realistic in choosing vocations that are in line with their academic achievement.

One might observe, however, that far too many of the C and D students are considering vocations that require a four-year college degree. Also, too many are avoiding the semi-skilled, skilled, and unskilled occupations.

Over 43 per cent of the fathers were employed in these categories, yet only 9 per cent of the students showed an interest in these areas. Granted, there has been a decrease in the need for unskilled laborers; but the same is not true for semi-skilled and skilled workers. The missile industry has created a terrific demand for such technicians.

It is highly desirable to have students raise their levels of aspiration, but care must be taken to ensure that these are in line with the students' mental and physical abilities. One might conclude that a number of these students, particularly those with average academic accomplishments and below, are being over-sold on the "prestige vocations."

Occupational Values and Desires of Students

Interesting information resulted from findings on student values regarding a job or vocation. Student values were assessed by having each student record whether each of the items below was important or not important to him in deciding on the vocation of his choice:

1. A job where you could be a leader.
2. A very interesting job.
3. A job where you will be looked upon very highly by your fellow men.
4. A job where you could be boss.
5. A job you are absolutely sure of keeping.
6. A job where you could express your feelings, ideas, talents, or skills.
7. A very highly paid job.
8. A job where you could make a name for yourself or become famous.

9. A job where you could help other people.
10. A job where you could work more or less on your own.

The above statements were adopted from items developed by Centers.[2] The sincerity with which students responded to the ten items is exemplified by the fact there were only six omissions out of a possible 4000 responses.

It is apparent in Table 5 that the high school student of today places high emphasis on a vocation that provides interesting experiences, a means of self-expression, security, and an opportunity to give social service. Also important to him, though less so, is independence, esteem of fellow workers, and a high salary.

The values and desires given very little importance, and in a way almost rejected, were drive to be the leader, desire to be the boss, and desire to become famous. It is disturbing to see so many young people reject the values and desires that many would attribute to the successful man of today. The three low-rated values are an integral part of our emphasis on freedom of the individual.

One might wonder if students are reflecting the emphasis that schools may be placing on the fact that the things we do should benefit society as a whole and not be for personal gain or recognition. In any event, these interesting findings deserve study with more refined instruments. These results compare favorably with the findings of Centers[3] and Wilson,[4] who used similar measuring instruments.

There was general agreement among stratifications in the responses of students to individual values and desires, but significant differences did appear. Boys rated leadership important to them significantly more times than did girls, even though both rated this item rather low. Likewise, boys were significantly more interested than girls in positions giving power and a high salary. Girls were significantly more interested in providing social service. Freshmen were significantly more interested than seniors in having security, high salary, and recognition in their vocations.

---

[2] Richard Centers, *The Psychology of Social Classes,* Princeton: Princeton University Press, 1949. P. 152.

[3] *Ibid.* P. 152.

[4] W. Cody Wilson, "Value Differences Between Public and Private School Graduates," *The Journal of Educational Psychology,* Vol. 50, No. 5, Oct. 1959, p. 213.

TABLE 5

STUDENT REACTIONS TO VARIOUS OCCUPATIONAL VALUES AND DESIRES
(Per Cents stating that this value or desire was important to him personally.)

Values—Desires	All Boys N = 200	All Girls N = 200	Freshmen N = 200	Seniors N = 200	Total N = 400
1 Leadership	38.5*	21.5	33.0	27.0	30.0
2 Interesting Experiences	95.5	98.0	96.5	97.0	96.7
3 Esteem	64.0	58.5	64.0	58.5	61.2
4 Power	33.5*	9.0	23.0	19.5	21.2
5 Security	92.0	83.0	91.0*	84.0	87.5
6 Self Expression	88.0	91.5	87.5	92.0	89.7
7 Profit	69.5*	52.0	68.5*	53.0	60.7
8 Fame	25.0	18.0	27.0*	16.0	21.5
9 Social Service	72.5	91.5*	84.5	79.5	82.0
10 Independence	65.0	60.5	61.0	64.5	62.7

* Significantly different from its counterpart at the 5% level.

A comparison of the occupational values and desires of students, stratified by academic achievement, showed some definite trends. As grades went from A to D, interest in being boss, high salary, and job security increased substantially. The opposite was true of interest in self-expression. Others showed practically no variation among grade categories.

Stratification by frequency of church attendance showed that student interest in being boss, getting a high salary, or becoming famous increased as regularity of church attendance decreased. No other categories were correlated with church attendance.

CONCLUSIONS

There are certain recognized dangers in attempting to arrive at a composite picture of the high school student of today by a study of any kind. This study was intended to give some insight into this problem and not necessarily to arrive at any conclusions. Even so, from these data we might venture to describe the modern high school student as follows:

1. Chances are seven to one that he is living with both parents.

2. Whether he lives in the country or in the town or city will not noticeably influence his high school program.

3. If he is a high-achieving student, the chances are that he is taking a college preparatory major, plans to enter a professional field, and attends church at least once a week.

4. If he is a low-achieving student he is probably enrolled in the general major, may be undecided about vocational plans or is interested in a service kind of vocation, and is quite irregular in church attendance.

5. If the student is a boy his grades are probably lower than the average for the girls.

6. If his mother works outside the home, chances are he gets higher grades than if she did not work.

7. He has made at least a tentative vocational choice, and this decision will conform in general to his academic ability as measured by achievement. The vocation of his choice will probably be on a higher socio-economic level than that of his father.

8. When considering a vocation he will place high emphasis on a job that offers interesting experiences, a means of self-expression, job security, and an opportunity for social service.

9. He will place moderate emphasis on a vocation that provides for independence, esteem of fellow workers, and a high salary.

10. He will attach only minor importance to a vocation that will enable him to be a leader, to be a boss, or to become famous.

The reader is reminded that these are group characteristics and may not be representative of a single individual. Perhaps the most important outcome of the study is that patterns do appear to exist among certain of the sociological and psychological characteristics of freshmen and seniors in high school.

7. WHAT IT MEANS TO GROW UP

Herman J. Peters

At no time in the history of mankind, with the possible exception of the Golden Age in Greece and the Renaissance, has the
concept of the individual as an entity been nearer to general acceptance than today. According to this concept, the individual as
a whole is something more than the sum of his parts: he is a
totality of 'body-mind,' an end result of the dynamic inter-rela-
tionship of many parts.[1]

Despite the concern for the individual, much of the effort of the
educator and the psychologist has been focused on the exceptional
child with the normal child or adolescent becoming the hidden
agendum of every class and guidance program. "While normal can
seldom be defined in precise quantitive terms, there are ranges in
motor and sensory abilities, in intelligence, in educational achievement, in emotional control, in social behavior, and in other aspects
of behavior within which the majority of children fall." [2] In child
and adolescent psychology books, usually the characteristics of nor-
malcy in each of these above named categories are given as resultants
of growth and development. There is a minimum of discussion on
the processes of becoming an adult. Therefore, it might prove interesting if we gave some attention to the psychological processes—
on-going behaviors—building toward a oneness called "adulthood."

It is on this basis that I wish to think *with* you, the reader, "What
It Means to Grow Up"—growing up from childhood to maturity,
from the school days to adult days, from infancy to the twenties,
from the agony of the kindergarten to the joy of college freedom
or to the joy of a full-time job. We shall cover some of the high-
points in this long journey of growth. First, let us keep in mind some

---

Reprinted by permission of the author and *High School Journal*, XLI,
No. 8 (May, 1958), 340-47.

---

[1] Liss, Edward. "The Individual Medical Guidance" Harms, Ernest (ed.) *Handbook of Child Guidance*, New York: Child Care Publications, 1947.

[2] Louttit, C. M., *Clinical Psychology of Exceptional Children*, New York:
Harper and Brothers. 1957.

of the important "givens" which a baby has when he enters this world, then let us briefly consider some of the psychological processes of growing up, processes which permeate the entire period of developing—in fact, all of life. Lastly, let us consider what you may do to guide the direction of these processes so that they do not like torrents of water rush on without control and positive use.

GIVENS

When the child enters this world, he has a certain potential for characteristics, traits, and physical features which are in a real sense given to him at the critical point of life—conception—truly a zero moment in the person's life span. The child is given his *physical system* within which nature has set susceptibilities, good and poor, and limits—limits which combine to defy man's intellectual ingenuity to change them.

The child is also given a family—his mother, his father and others. He is given the family's background, their hopes and failures, their joys and sorrows, their reputation—good or bad. Through his family he is given his first outlook on life ranging from an optimistic one to a pessimistic one. He is given an immediate setting in which he may grow to his fullest or be thwarted, not because of his inherent limitations, but because of those who manage his first years, his family.

Surrounding the immediate setting, the infant is given *a community*—a town, a city or a rural area. Encompassing this, he is given *a wider community* whose limits are bounded only by the provincialism of the next smaller community. The many forces in the community exert a powerful force on the shaping, the molding of the child and later the adolescent.

With inexorable impact, the child is given an *"age in history,"* a *time* in the history of man, during which he must develop. No matter how it might have been, he is living at a certain time with all of its advantages and disadvantages.

Most important of all, the normal infant comes into this world with great potentiality, flexibility, and readiness for the journey into maturity—a journey so long in prospect, so very short in retrospect.

LOOKING

One of the key processes is *looking*. The young infant learns that looking is important—looking at mom and dad. If he looks with a smile, he knows that this brings added dividends in more food, a kiss or a hug. He is experiencing "looking" as a process for developing. He thrills to the joy of seeing, animals at the zoo, the clown in the circus, or the creatures of a Disneyland. He sees toys as a part of his life. This young child begins—just a beginning—to see people—his sisters, brothers, and adults coming into the family.

In middle childhood, the boy or girl sees toys as a means of doing *something,* as a means of playing with *someone.* In adolescence, the boy or girl sees uses of gadgets and games. He or she sees relationships with persons, not people as separate individuals. In adolescence, the youth interprets his self-concept in terms of his relationships with others and his abilities to compete successfully in adolescent revered activities.

However, it is not enough to see objects. A child or adolescent is also experiencing how to interpret what he sees. It is the *meaning* in what he sees, the inference of what he is watching, the potential for making this boy that gives frightening importance to that at which he is looking. If a child is looking at a "dirty old animal" in a zoo—"dirty old animal" as mama says—then looking at animals may be discarded from his desire to see more animals—if he is told "nice boys and girls sit still all the time" then he may retreat from activity and not look at physical activities as a way of growing up. His looking involves more than just seeing—it involves what this means to him as a personality, which he and others are making. What a boy or girl sees that makes a difference in growing up is seen in terms of his needs based on what he has learned.

What one sees in looking at one age may need to be re-interpreted at another age. The kindergarten boy looks around only to feel lost in a sea of legs—table legs, chair legs, and human legs. In adolescence, he tables the difficulty with the legs of the inorganic but oh how enticing become the feminine legs. Looking is a part of growing up.

LISTENING

If looking is one of the basic experiences of a normal child's growing up, then listening must also be considered. It is in the privacy of listening that the inner core of personality is translating into meaning what he hears. What a child hears, so that child develops.

> Listening is a magnetic and strange thing, a creative force. . . . The friends that listen to us are the ones we move toward, and we want to sit in their radius as though it did us good, like ultraviolet rays. . . . When we are listened to, it creates us, makes us unfold and expand. Ideas actually begin to grow within us and come to life. . . . It makes people happy and free when they are listened to. . . . When we listen to people there is an alternating current, and this recharges us so that we never get tired of each other. We are constantly being re-created.
>
> Now there are brilliant people who cannot listen much. They have no ingoing wires on their apparatus. They are entertaining but exhausting too. I think it is because these lecturers, these brilliant performers, by not giving us a chance to talk, do not let us express our thoughts and expand; and it is this expressing and expanding that makes the little creative fountain inside us begin to spring and case up new thoughts and unexpected laughter and wisdom.[3]

Directly and indirectly the child is listening. Through this listening he is growing up—growing up in the direction of his listening or growing in doubt of what he hears. It is through looking in combination with listening that the boy or girl senses the importance or lack of importance of practicing what is being preached. When he listens to the adult saying one thing and then looking at him do the other, the child learns "talk is cheap."

Listening is the adolescent's check-point on his own behavior. He may or may not follow what he hears but it acts as a screen against which he checks his decisions for action.

---

[3] Moustakas, Clark E., *The Teacher and the Child,* New York: McGraw-Hill Book Company. 1956, pp. 42-3.

THINKING

Today's boy or girl lives in a world where "to do" means to be "physically active." To sit in silent thought is frowned upon. Much is said of the well rounded person. The well rounded person, in particular a pupil, is thought of as one who studies a minimal amount, but who engages, in band, glee club, the yearbook, the senior play, the junior prom and who holds minor offices in five school clubs, the titles of which defy categorization. Stop, let us be startled by the fact that thinking *is* an activity—an important activity. Learning how to think is a part of growing up. Yet is it really encouraged?

And remembering? To memorize is often looked upon by teacher and parent as a waste of time. You know the defensive attack is "You can always look it up." Yet time and again, have you not told your children "If you don't remember where you put it, you'll have to do without it." Just recently a high school girl told me, "I don't let anyone know of my thinking ability as measured on the IQ test." She went on to say, "If I'm average, they'll think I'm really in the know."

One bright little boy said, "I keep thinking that I am doing well in school and then instead of a report card, I get a letter home saying, 'Jimmy is making progress.' I often wonder, 'progress to what places?'"

A senior high boy says, "I keep thinking about boy-girl relations. Sure would like to ask some questions. Don't dare at home. Dad said, 'You'll learn soon enough.' Must be some of the girls are learning soon enough—guess you get to leave town if you learn soon enough—I just don't understand it."

The development of sound thinking is a continuing process in the boy or girl's growth toward maturity.

FEELINGS

Feelings are facts. One develops a process of feeling as one develops other personality facets. To understand our own emotional tendencies is a vital concern to most persons. When used in a positive way, emotions are forceful ingredients for growth. Lawrence Frank states that "until recently we have not realized the need for a consciously planned education of the emotions, although each culture favors and cultivates some kinds of emotions, and denies and suppresses others." Each individual is forced to become sensitized to his emotions. How he or she handles these emotions is resolved, *in part,* in terms of how the individual perceives himself as a person.

The feelings which one high school girl has are illustrated in the problems which bother her. Here are some of them as taken from her Science Research Associates Youth Inventory:

> I'm easily excited.
> I have trouble keeping my temper.
> I'm nervous.
> I can't help daydreaming.
> I'm not popular with boys.
> I don't see much future for myself.
> I'm not ready for any job when I graduate.
> I prefer to be alone.
> I wonder if I am normal in the way my mind works.
> I worry about tests.
> I'm trying to get rid of an undesirable habit.
> I'm afraid of failure or humiliation.
> I'm afraid of making mistakes.
> I'm afraid to speak up in class.

This girl is growing in the direction of these feelings. One of the contributions of an effective guidance program is to assist boys and girls in developing proper attitudes toward life and their concomitant feelings.

SEARCHING FOR MEANING

A fifth process in growing up involves the difficult area of *searching for meaning*—a searching for meaning into many aspects of life, in fact, into life itself.

In early childhood, meaning is centered on simple concepts such as the description of familiar objects—a round ball or a familiar adult—a nice aunt. In middle childhood, there is a searching for understanding of one's self as in one's masculine or feminine role. In adolescence there is a searching for the meaning of independence from parents, a career choice and a philosophy of life. It is in late adolescence that many boys and girls experience a searching for the meaning of God. This is on a conceptual abstract plane in contrast with the five or six year old's trying to understand a Supreme Being in terms of a human person.

VALUING

A sixth process of growing up is the process of valuing. Valuing is an attaching of significance to a part or parts of one's life. Valuing is the establishment of what is precious to me—what is important for me. Valuing may involve a consideration of ranking "one good" act or thing or concept ahead of another "good" act, thing or concept. Valuing involves looking, listening, thinking and feeling. Valuing is a summing up of what to keep in one's life pattern.

To a great degree, the child values what his parents value. As the child grows into adolescence, conflict may result because the parents become satisfied with their son or daughter's childhood values and do not wish to change or do not grow with changing conditions. Parents can be active interpreters for the often confused adolescent in his valuing process.

FOCUSING

Within each age level there seems to be a focusing on what life's experience means for the boy or girl. We might call this process of focusing, a seventh kind of action in growing up. Excessive amounts of this turn into prolonged daydreaming. However, this taking stock of where one has been and where one is going is a real growth experience for the person. Often the boy or girl needs the help of someone to assist in this appraising process. The competently trained school counselor is in an excellent position to help boys and girls make this focusing process a most beneficial one for gaining new insights into one's self.

It is as a result of the focusing process that a boy or girl may better know what his next step should be in school, at home or in a peer relationship. The adult must keep in mind that the boy or girl may center on a situation in terms of routine procedure even though current conditions have indicated the necessity for a change in behavior.

Choosing

The eighth process is one of choosing. From infancy through adulthood, choosing results from the other processes. Because each person is in motion, in orbit, he must make choices. Choice is based on knowledge, feeling, and environmental pressures. One makes choices in terms of something. Here too the adolescent, more so than the child, often needs the experience of counseling wherein he can be helped to see the possible effects of the choices he plans to make. As you choose, so you become.

Becoming

All of the previously discussed processes interact in the individual's total development as he is becoming the best possible person one can become. The concept of becoming does not ignore the past nor deny the present. Rather it states that man may use the past to live better in the present for his best becoming in the future. We must emphasize that becoming is the key to successful living. Fixation on the past denies the resiliency of the human personality.

A Look Forward

What can you do? What teaching processes are in order? What guidance functions are necessary? You can work toward the following goals which are applicable at all ages.

1. Help your boys and girls to learn the contradictions of what is acceptable at different ages of development.
2. Teach them respect for property and the other person's rights.
3. Teach them to do more than they have to do.

4. Teach them to be responsible.
5. Teach them to "risk failure lest they surrender success."
6. Teach them the enchantment of learning.
7. Teach them respect for teachers, subject matter, and homework.
8. Teach them limits. Help them to understand that freedom follows discipline and that one is not the alternative of the other. Do this with compassion and love; yet, be firm.

It must be kept in mind that all of these processes are inter-related in the complex of a dynamic growing boy or girl changing imperceptibly in the short-time space but so very much in a longitudinal way. In some way or ways, each parent, teacher and school counselor helps to shape the developing boy or girl. The image of the adolescent growing toward maturity reflects the image of many of his peers and, in particular, the significant adults in his daily living.

8. REACHING HIGH SCHOOL PUPILS WHO NEED COUNSELING

A. Gordon Nelson

But little space in the literature of pupil personnel work has been devoted to one of the first problems that faces a beginning high-school counselor; namely, that of identifying and establishing a relationship with students who can benefit from counseling. The purpose of this article is to consider a number of principles and procedures which a counselor may follow in his attempt to reach these individuals.

PUPIL-INITIATED COUNSELING

Pupils either seek interviews voluntarily or are summoned by a counselor or are referred to him by another person. The consensus

Reprinted by permission of the author and *Bulletin of the National Association of Secondary School Principals*, XXXVIII, No. 200 (February, 1954), 9-15.

among educational personnel workers is that pupil-initiated counseling is ordinarily more effective than the other two types. It is believed that an individual who takes the step of asking for assistance thereby demonstrates not only a desire to solve his personal problems but also a certain amount of confidence in the ability of the counselor to help him. He is, therefore, more ready for, and more receptive to, counseling than is the individual who presents himself for an interview only because he has been "called" or "sent." The self-referred counselee is in a frame of mind or state of motivation which increases the probability that he will benefit from whatever assistance a counselor can provide.

Because it is desirable to have as much pupil-initiated counseling as possible, a counselor should do everything he can to encourage self-referral on the part of pupils. If he merely sits in his office and waits for clients to come to him, some, no doubt, *will* come. But he can do more than wait—he can stimulate pupil desire for counseling.

One technique is to publicize counseling services widely and recurrently by means of talks before groups of pupils or through announcements in pupil handbooks, newspapers, bulletins, and posters. Both oral and written announcements should be carefully phrased in order that pupils may not be given the impression that the counselor is either a fortune teller or a person who thinks he has "all the answers" or be led to believe that to seek counseling is a sign of weakness.

A counselor should take pains to make his services known not only to pupils themselves but also to adults who have daily contacts with adolescents. If fellow staff members, parents, and workers in community agencies understand the objectives of counseling and believe it to be worth while, they will tend to encourage young people to ask for interviews. Conversely, if they are not well informed concerning the aims of counseling and are not satisfied that it is of value, they will tend to be overtly or covertly indifferent or antagonistic, and their attitudes may well discourge pupils from going to a counselor voluntarily.

Another factor that has a bearing on the amount of pupil-initiated counseling is the counselor's reputation. Pupils who think of him as a person who is friendly, trustworthy, and helpful will be inclined to seek his assistance; and, if he helps them, they will tend to "advertise" his services and thus encourage others to go to him; satisfied clients often talk about their satisfaction. It behooves a counselor, therefore, to establish good relations *early* in his career in a given school—by *being* friendly, trustworthy, and helpful, not only in interviews but also in his other contacts with pupils.

A desire for counseling can be stimulated through group guidance activities. If, for example, a counselor administers a battery of interest and aptitude tests to a group, he may find that many members of the group will be so interested in their own performances on the battery that they will request interviews in order that they may discuss their educational and vocational plans in the light of the test results. Or, to give another illustration, a counselor may conduct a group discussion on boy-girl relationships in such a way that at least some of the members of the group will seek his help concerning their own problems relative to such relationships. To stimulate pupil interest in counseling is, of course, not the only objective of group guidance, but it is an important one.

COUNSELOR-INITIATED INTERVIEWS

In spite of whatever a counselor and others may do to encourage pupil-initiated interviews, not all who can benefit from counseling will seek it voluntarily. For this reason, most high-school counselors feel that it is desirable to have "call-in" interviews. Two procedures are followed: one is to confer with every pupil at least once each year, and the other is to summon individuals who have been identified by various means as persons who need help.

Interviews with All Pupils

When a counselor calls in one individual after another in accordance with a systematic schedule for reaching all pupils, he ordinarily utilizes at least part of the interview time to help each one plan an academic program for the following term or year. Several things may be said in favor of this procedure. First, to help an individual decide upon the subjects he will take is in itself a worthy enterprise. In the course of a school year, a pupil invests a considerable portion of his time and energy in studying various subjects; if counseling increases the probability that he will plan his program of study wisely, it is worth while. Undoubtedly, some pupils can and do make excellent educational plans without assistance, but even if a counselor does no more than examine and agree with an individual's choices, he is not wasting time, for the investment planned is of sufficient consequence to warrant review.

Another advantage of calling in all pupils to discuss with them their curricular plans is that this practice tends to lessen whatever resistance to counseling there may be. When every pupil has a conference with a counselor, no one needs to feel that he is singled out for special attention or that any special stigma of weakness is attached to participation in a counseling interview.

A third advantage of having conferences with all pupils concerning their academic schedules is that interviews of this type sometimes serve as ice-breakers—that is to say, they give a counselor an opportunity to "sell" himself to individuals who would not voluntarily seek an initial interview. If such pupils, in reviewing their educational plans with a counselor, discover that he is "easy to talk to," they may be willing to discuss with him, later in the same interview, other problems that have been troubling them. Furthermore, if in a compulsory conference a counselor can establish friendly and helpful relationships with these pupils, they may conclude that counseling is not such an unpleasant or worthless experience as they had thought, and at a later time they may go to the counselor without being summoned. Thus, counselor-initiated interviews on one occasion may lead to pupil-initiated counseling on subsequent occasions.

Counseling with Selected Pupils

In addition to, or instead of, interviewing all pupils periodically, some counselors call in those who seem to need special help. A major problem associated with this plan is that of identifying the pupils who are to be summoned. In connection with this problem, several procedures have been found to be useful.

Examination of report cards—One of the most simple and common practices is that of examining, at the end of each marking period, the grades which teachers have recorded on report cards in order to note pupils who have failed one or more subjects. These individuals are then called in for counseling. Some school administrators ask teachers to submit mid-marking reports so that counselors may "spot" pupils who are in danger of failing and attempt to help them improve their work before they receive final grades for the period in question. This is a type of preventive counseling and is highly commendable.

Inspection of attendance records—Research has shown that poor or irregular attendance is frequently associated not only with illness but also with such factors as poverty, maladjustment in school, and adverse parental attitudes. It is not surprising, therefore, that counselors have found that by examining attendance records they can often discover individuals who need some type of help. Instead of being a symptom of a full-blown, immediate problem, frequent absence from school may be an early indication of an incipient problem. It may, for example, be a portent that a pupil is thinking of quitting the halls of learning as soon as he reaches the age when he can legally do so. If a counselor can ferret out the factors underlying such a pupil's dissatisfaction, he may be able to prevent him from leaving school before graduation.

Scrutiny of cumulative record cards—When he carefully looks over a set of comprehensive cumulative record cards, a counselor often finds information about individuals which leads him to believe that they should be called in for counseling. Pupil A's record, for example, shows that he has consistently evidenced superior scholastic aptitude on standardized tests, but that he has just as consistently achieved mediocre or poor grades in the subjects he has taken. He is apparently an under-achiever, a proper candidate for counseling. Pupil B has an excellent academic record, but he has participated in no extracurricular activities during his first two years in high school. Pupil C is taking an industrial arts course, but he has on several occasions claimed, according to the cumulative record card, that professional mechanical engineering is his vocational objective.

Review of pupil questionnaires—In some schools, pupils are asked to fill out self-report forms. These are then reviewed by the counselor. If a pupil's responses suggest, intentionally or unintentionally, that he needs help, the counselor summons him for an interview. The *SRA Youth Inventory* and the *Mooney Problem Checklist,* as well as most of the so-called personality "tests" of the paper-and-pencil variety, are examples of questionnaires which may be used to identify those who need counseling. Home-made forms are also used. For example, a counselor may devise and utilize a form which asks questions such as the following: What do you plan to do when you finish high school? Do you need information concerning schools, colleges, or occupations? Is there any other way in which a counselor can be of service to you?

Observation—Counselors who cultivate the habit of noticing the behavior of pupils find that by this means they can sometimes discover individuals who are in need of help. Pupils may be observed in interviews; during group discussions and testing periods; on the corridors, streets, and athletic field; and in other places.

Scattergram analysis—A scattergram, sometimes called a scatter-diagram, is a device which helps a counselor to identify quickly pupils who have achieved much more or much less, academically, than one would expect them to achieve in view of their performances on scholastic aptitude tests. A counselor is interested in discovering under-achievers because he may be able to help them to do better work. He is interested in "spotting" over-achievers because they may be doing above-capacity work at the expense of their mental, physical, or social health. Several detailed descriptions of the scattergram-analysis technique are available in the literature.[1] A counselor who wishes to use this means of identifying under-achievers and over-achievers should read such descriptions carefully in order to learn about the various ways of making a scattergram and to become aware of the values and limitations of this device.

COUNSELING INITIATED BY REFERRAL

An interview may take place not because a pupil has requested it, or because he has been "called in," but because he has been sent by a teacher, parent, community agency worker, or someone else who believes that counseling will be or may be helpful. Individuals who

---

[1] Froehlich, C. P., and Benson, A. L. *Guidance Testing*. Chicago: Science Research Associates. 1948. Pp. 53-68; Froehlich, C. P., and Darley, J. G. *Studying Students*. Chicago: Science Research Associates. 1952. Pp. 260-276; Germane, C. E., and Germane, E. G. *Personnel Work in High School*. New York: Silver Burdett Company. 1941. Pp. 97-115.

have frequent contacts with pupils are in a favorable position to observe and identify those who may properly be referred.

The number of pupils sent to a given counselor depends to a considerable extent upon his reputation. If he is able to help the first few who are sent to him, the persons who made these referrals will tend to send others from time to time. If he continues to do effective counseling, he will gradually acquire a reputation which will tend to influence more people to refer individuals to him. Counseling that is initiated by referral gives a counselor an opportunity to make his services known and to enhance their prestige in the school and in the community.

It is difficult to have a worth while interview with a person who has been referred in an abrupt or awkward manner. A counselor should, therefore, try to induce individuals and agencies to make referrals in a way that will facilitate the establishment of an effective counseling relationship. A desirable procedure is one which prepares both the pupil and the counselor for their first interview together. The pupil should be given a clear explanation of the type of service which the counselor can provide and should be assured that he will be welcomed when he presents himself. The counselor should be told that the pupil will come to see him and should be given information about the circumstances that suggested the need for referral. The person who plans to make a referral should, if he can, *first* talk to the counselor, because, otherwise, there is a possibility that the pupil may go to the counselor before the latter has had an opportunity to learn anything about him. Moreover, discussion before referral sometimes results in the conclusion that a given pupil should not be referred because there appears to be a better way to help him.

Establishing Rapport

Whether a pupil has come voluntarily or has been summoned or has been referred, his mere presence in a counselor's office does not automatically lead to an effective counseling relationship. Reaching an individual who needs help involves not only the bringing about of a meeting between counselor and counselee but also the establishment of rapport in the interview.

Simply stated, "to establish rapport" means to create a relationship in which the counselee feels "at ease" in the counselor's presence. When a pupil talks freely and indicates by his general bearing that he is "comfortable," there is reason to believe that the interview has started well. Signs of lack of rapport include: a tense manner, fidgeting, blushing, and perspiring; hesitancy in speech; long periods of silence; and statements indicative of embarrassment, annoyance, or evasiveness. It is obvious that, if a pupil does not feel free from constraint, an interview with him will not be very fruitful. If he is ill at ease, he will not be inclined to discuss readily the various aspects of the personal problems he faces. A counselor should, therefore, be familiar with conditions and techniques that tend to facilitate the process of establishing rapport.

The importance of a counselor's reputation has been discussed previously in another connection, but it should be mentioned again here for it has a bearing on rapport. In respect to the creation of a good interview relationship, a counselor who has a favorable reputation enjoys an advantage over a counselor who is not favorably regarded; a counselee is more likely to be at ease in the presence of a person whom other pupils have pictured as "a good guy' than in the presence of an individual whom they have described in disapproving terms.

Although no objective evidence is available concerning the effect of physical surroundings on the establishment of a good counseling relationship, it is reasonable to assume that the *milieu* in which an interview takes place is, to some extent, related to the ease with which rapport is brought about. It is generally agreed that a desirable setting for interviews is one in which there is: a pleasant and informal atmosphere, quiet, privacy, adequate lighting, optimum temperature and humidity, and a comfortable chair for the counselee.

The literature of interviewing is replete with techniques believed to be conducive to the establishment of rapport. Several of these are listed here; none, of course, should be used in a stereotyped or self-conscious way:

1. Greet the individual cordially by name when he enters the office; shake hands with him.

2. Start the conversation informally by introducing a subject in which the counselee is likely to be interested.

3. Avoid giving the impression that you are in a hurry; do whatever you can, before the interview, to forestall distractions and interruptions.

4. Be collected, friendly, accepting, sympathetic.

5. Be a good listener; give full attention to what the counselee says.

6. Do enough talking yourself to put the interviewee at ease.

7. Adjust your vocabulary to the intellectual level of the person to whom you are talking to the extent that you can do so without appearing unnatural.

Many counselors achieve rapport without making conscious use of any special techniques. Such individuals seem to behave spontaneously in ways which lead clients to feel comfortable in their presence. The personality of the counselor is apparently far more important than the techniques he uses. Strang, after commenting that . . . "The personal qualities of an ideal interviewer have been the occasion of much speculation but of little or no research . . ." goes on to say:

> Three qualities seem to be of special importance: (1) a constructive attitude toward people; (2) an understanding of their motives, of the world as they variously perceive it, of actual environmental influences, and of common patterns and sequences of behavior; and (3) a sensitivity to the individual to whom he is talking, an alertness to indications of mood and attitude, and an ability to adapt himself to the other person's changes in feeling as any clever conversationalist does. It is only through thinking and feeling with the other person—empathy and sympathy—that the interviewer knows when to be silent, when to reflect his feeling, when to interpret.[2]

---

[2] Strang, Ruth, *Counseling Techniques in College and Secondary School.* New York: Harper and Brothers. 1949. P. 126.

9. STUDENT FEELING ABOUT COUNSELING HELP

Ralph E. Jenson

How do high school youth feel about the counseling help they have received? To what extent do high school students feel their counselors have been of real assistance to them in finding improved solutions to some of their problems? To whom do students prefer taking their different categories of problems—teachers, counselors, parents, deans, or friends their own age? Answers to these questions can provide the kind and quality of information which are needed to plan and promote better counseling service.

In 1952 the writer undertook the responsibility of making an appraisal of the guidance program, with special attention to the counseling service, in the Phoenix Union High Schools. Rather than make the study a one man show, it was decided to make it an in-service research project involving a representative district-wide planning and steering committee made up of school administrators and school counselors.[1]

Part of the design for the study called for finding answers to the questions above. It was speculated that if the project was cooperatively planned and conducted by individuals who were directly represented, affected by, and who were daily participants in the counseling program, that our findings would stimulate more interest and enthusiasm for improving student counseling services.

Unfortunately, no systematic attempt was made to check the validity of this hypothesis. From the amount of unsolicited favorable opinion, however, and the number of changes in our counseling services (conjectured as representing improvements) coming soon after the findings were released to the schools and public, we feel rather confident that the cooperative planning paid off. For our

Reprinted by permission of the author and *Personnel and Guidance Journal*, XXXIII, No. 9 (May, 1955), 498-503.

[1] Dr. Raymond Emery, Curriculum Coordinator; Dr. Harold L. Gear, Superintendent; Mrs. Muriel Gurr, Counselor; Mr. Avery Olney, Reading Consultant; Mrs. Jewell Rasbury and Mrs. Myrtle Rodgers, Deans of Girls; Mr. John Schoolland and Miss Eleanor Wallingford, Counselors.

purpose, home-spun research seemed to have a distinct advantage over facts and figures collected by somebody else in some ego-remote school district. There is likely very little which is novel or unique about this approach, but there is perhaps much to be learned about its dynamics and limitations. More systematic research planned to explore its possibilities may prove fruitful.

PROCEDURE

The criteria tried and suggested for measuring the effectiveness of counseling are legion. Researchers in counseling are loath to place much faith in any of them. Yet, those who "want to know" argue, and it would seem sensibly so, that one must be content with using his rough tools until more refined and dependable ones are available.

In planning the phase of the study reported here, we were aware of the weaknesses of using student reactions as evidence for or against counseling. Nevertheless, it struck us that consumer reaction determines the destiny of most, if not all, professional service. This notion should not be interpreted to mean that we think counseling service should be molded entirely by subjective feelings of students. The dangers of evaluating counseling on a continuum of personal feelings are well known. We know that it is possible to "play up" to students in such a way that they are temporarily elated without the elation being significantly related to real personality change. In fact, this transitory feeling of self-satisfaction or personal worth may last long enough for a naive investigator to be fooled into thinking that counseling has produced permanent personality changes of a miraculous character. Also, "good" counseling may be labeled bad by students. High ethical standards of service must be observed in counseling.

Despite these known weaknesses of the criterion of student feeling, the writer is inclined to agree with Grant (1) that it at least provides us with an index to what students think about counseling and counselors—how they think their self-understanding and adjustment have been affected. Grant (1, 2), among others, was interested in this same problem. Regrettably, we cannot make valid comparisons with Grant's findings since our research designs, methods, and sample differ so greatly.

The data reported in Table 1 and 2 represent a 20 per cent random sampling of approximately 8,000 boys and girls distributed among seven high schools, grades nine through twelve. The average counselee load for counselors was about 650. All counselors had master's degrees with an average of 12-15 semester hours of college or university credit in guidance-type course work. The student reaction sheets were administered under the supervision of classroom teachers according to carefully prepared, written instructions.

RESULTS

Students' feelings about help received from counselors—In this part of the study we were interested in finding out how those students who had "talked" with their counselors about problems which were presumably bothering them actually felt about the counseling help they had received.

The list of district-wide counseling objectives were stated so that students could express their feelings anonymously toward each. The order of feeling alternatives were randomized for each question to control for halo effect. The alternatives from which students chose were worded so that a student could mark one of five degrees of feeling toward each counseling-objective-problem-area. We were more interested in student reactions to broad expected outcomes of counseling rather than to specific problem areas like vocational, educational, social, emotional, and so on. It may be seen from the areas of help described in Table 1 that our objectives emphasized increased student self-understanding, independent and realistic decision making, and personal-social responsibility for decisions and actions.

Table 1 presents students' feeling reactions for all high schools combined. There were some differences among schools but they did not appear significant. It would appear from the distribution of per cents along the arbitrarily determined continuum of feeling that, in general, our boys and girls were pleased with the help they had received from their respective counselors. Less than one-fifth made negative reactions. Two per cent or less felt hypernegatively toward counseling help. Over sixty per cent felt counselors had helped them very much or helped some. As might be expected, a minority (less than one in five) were "on the fence."

A comparison of student reactions to the various areas of help reveals at least two interesting tendencies. First, students seemed to feel they had received the most help in understanding themselves better in terms of their abilities, interests, ambitions, and personality —area A. Eighty-one per cent had positive feelings toward help received in this area. We might speculate that our counselors are doing a "good" job of helping students appraise themselves in terms of their personal assets and liabilities.

TABLE 1

STUDENT FEELING ABOUT COUNSELOR HELP

	Per Cent				
Areas of Help	Helped Very Much	Helped Some	Not Sure	No Help	Worse Than Nothing
A. Better understanding of abilities, interests, ambitions, and personality.	31	50	11	6	2
B. Discovery of things best suited to do or be happiest doing both while in school and after finishing school.	25	43	15	16	1
C. Making progress toward realistically chosen while-in-school and after-school goals.	23	38	19	19	1
D. Learning to get along better with friends and others at school, at home, or in the community.	27	40	15	17	1
E. Increasing capacity and self-confidence in making decisions and solving adjustment problems both now and in the future.	27	40	15	16	2

The second seemingly significant tendency appears in students' feelings about help they had received in making progress toward realistically chosen goals—area C. Only sixty per cent felt they had received much or some help in this regard. This response may be as much or more a reflection of inadequate school-community life adjustment opportunities as ineffective counseling. It may also represent the level of help adolescents are least capable of using. However, the response requires guarded interpretation. Reaction tendencies in areas B, D, and E are very nearly the same—about two-thirds positive, fifteen per cent uncertain, and approximately seventeen or eighteen per cent felt counseling was of no help or worse than none at all.

In summary, our sample of students seemed to feel counselors had helped them considerably in evaluating their potentialities. In this area of help, counselor effectiveness does not depend so much upon supporting environmental adjustment opportunities within the school, home, and community as might be the case in some of the other areas of help, especially area C. Psychometric appraisal may also be easier for an adolescent to accept than the personal appraisal necessary to choose and make progress toward remote adult goals.

To whom do students wish to take their problems?—In almost any school system one is likely to hear comments something like the following:

> Students will go to teachers for help just as much as they will go to counselors.
>
> The counseling process is not threatened if counselors are required to discipline their counselees.
>
> Parents can do a better job of counseling their children than counselors.
>
> Students get more help from talking with their friends than from talking with counselors or teachers.

Many criticisms of counseling like those above are difficult to investigate scientifically. Each of them would require redefinition and a carefully designed research project if we were to hope to arrive at a valid answer. Our approach was not highly experimental. Our planning committee agreed to ascertain what the "student-problem" popularity of different individuals might be who were readily available to students for help. Consequently six counseling-objective-problem-areas were prepared. Students were instructed to rank in order of first, second, and third choice, those key individuals (parents, counselors, teachers, deans, friends their own age, and other individuals in the community like doctors, lawyers, ministers, and Scout leaders) to whom they would go for help. The order of individuals was randomized for each problem area to minimize halo effect.

The student preference score for each of these individuals was computed by assigning a weight of three to a first choice, a two to a second choice, and a one to a third choice. The sum of these weighted values divided by the total weight of each choice-individual represents the preference score for each category of choice-individual. These percentages of preference may also be interpreted as "popularity" scores of the individuals to whom students would go for help with problems which they felt were represented by the six counseling-objective-problem-areas.

Table 2 shows the student preference scores in the six problem areas. To the first problem, "desire to know more about their real abilities, interests, ambitions, and personality," it seems that students gave the nod to counselors and parents over all other sources of help. Teachers and friends were more popular than deans or the miscellaneous category of individuals. It seems significant to point out that deans were responsible for school discipline. They were definitely unpopular as "relief" agents.

It would seem that students had high respect for help associated with counselors. On the other hand, there is considerable evidence to suggest that many students solicit the opinions of parents, teachers, and friends in whom they may have confidence. One tentative conclusion which may be drawn from these data is that counselors and others must recognize the influences different resource individuals may have upon students. Although counselors rate high, they are not invariably revered by students.

In the second problem area (desire to discover the most promising kinds of school activities and work), counselors seemed to cinch first place. Parents and teachers ranked second. Deans and friends ranked much lower. Counselors were pictured by students as being the most helpful in exploring and identifying school-work goals which would promise to provide adequate expression of their capabilities and interests. Again, however, we cannot ignore the inclinations of numerous students to go to parents and teachers. Some few preferred deans or their own friends.

Following the identification of suitable activities to develop one's abilities and interests, a student is faced with the problem of making real progress toward his goals. Student reaction to problem area C (finding out how to make progress toward selected goals in school and work) reveals counselors to be considerably more popular than anyone else. Teachers are favored over parents. Deans again rank considerably lower than counselors, teachers, and parents, but somewhat more popular than friends own age or miscellaneous persons.

Adolescents as a group are very much concerned about making and holding friends and getting along amicably with others in the school, home, and community. In problem area D we see parents and counselors rated about the same. It is interesting to note that the importance of friends their own age as a source for help com-

TABLE 2

STUDENT PREFERENCE FOR DIFFERENT INDIVIDUALS TO HELP THEM
WITH CERTAIN KINDS OF PROBLEMS

Problem Areas	Parents	Counselors	Teachers	Deans	Friends	Misc.
A. Desire to know more about real abilities, interests, ambitions, personality, etc.	27	28	19	7	15	4
B. Desire to discover most promising kinds of school activities and work.	20	38	22	9	8	3
C. Finding out how to make progress toward selected goals in school and work.	18	36	28	13	4	1
D. Desire to learn how to get along better with friends and others at school, at home, or in the community.	28	27	13	7	22	3
E. Help in developing more confidence in ability to make "good" decisions about problems which bother now and those which may pop up in the future.	34	30	14	9	9	4
F. Help in learning to do the things known to be "best" for me and society but which are not easy to do.	29	30	17	9	9	6

Per Cent Preference for

pares very favorably with that expected from parents or counselors. Adolescents apparently think of their peer group as a real adjustment resource with problems falling in this category. This fact should not be ignored but rather recognized and used constructively in counseling work. Deans consistently ranked low.

Another objective of counseling is to help the student improve his ability to make "good" decisions about how to handle problems that arise from time to time. From Table 2 it appears that students placed a little more but perhaps not significantly more confidence in their parents than counselors or any of the other individuals. Teachers fall decisively lower than parents and counselors and deans and friends still lower as prospective sources of assistance with problems associated with this area of help.

Making proper decisions about problems constitutes real accomplishment but if decisions are not acted upon appropriately, the decision-making may simply become energy wasted in wheel-spinning. In problem area F students were given an opportunity to rank those individuals to whom they would go to learn how to do the things known to be "best" for them and society yet which were not easy to do. From Table 2 we may see that parents and counselors were accorded equal ratings. Teachers seemed to run a weak third. Deans and friends their own age ran a poor fourth.

SUMMARY AND CONCLUSIONS

The feeling reactions of a 20 per cent random sample of 8,000 high school boys and girls (grades nine through twelve) who said they had "talked" with the school counselors about problems which had bothered them were solicited and evaluated to learn: (1) how students felt about the counseling help they had received from counselors; and (2) how students rated counselors compared with other individuals (teachers, deans, parents, friends own age) as sources of help with adjustment problems.

The objectives of counseling service in the Phoenix Union High Schools were used as problem areas of adjustment. It was thought this approach would put the emphasis upon an evaluation of the expected outcomes of counseling and provide the counseling planning committee with the kind of information it should have to improve the quality of service. The major counseling-objective-problem-areas to which students reacted were:

A. increased understanding of personal abilities, interests, ambitions, personality, etc.;
B. the discovery of the things for which one is best suited to do and be happiest doing while in school and after finishing school;
C. finding out how to make real progress toward selected goals in school and work;
D. learning how to get along better with friends and others at school, at home, or in the community;
E. developing more confidence in ability to make "good" decisions about problems which bother now or those which may arise in the future; and
F. learning to do the things known to be "best" for self and society but which are not easy to do.

The findings of the survey suggested the following conclusions:

1. In general, the feeling of students was positive toward the help they had received from counselors in all counseling-objective-problem areas. Counseling seems to meet some real felt need among students.

2. Table 1 also tends to show that students felt counselors were most helpful in assisting them to appraise their abilities, interests, and personalities and, compared with other areas of help, of least assistance in helping them make progress toward their realistically chosen while-in-school and after-school goals. Judging from students' expressed confidence in anticipated help from counselors in this latter problem area compared with that expected in other areas shown in Table 2, one is tempted to strongly speculate that students expect more help from counselors in making progress toward their school-work goals than they feel they are getting. This being the case, counselors might concentrate more effort on providing more life adjustment opportunities in which students can find appropriate expression of their personal potentialities.

3. As individuals to whom students might go for help, students preferred counselors over parents, teachers, deans, and friends their own age when the problems were concerned with discovering and making progress toward realistically chosen while-in-school and after-school goals. Students looked most to counselors for help in these areas of adjustment.

4. With the exception of the areas mentioned in (3) above, parents and counselors were about equally favored by students. Both were preferred to teachers, deans, or friends own age. Counselors appeared to compete strongly with parents as a source of help.

5. Teachers received their strongest vote from students for help with problems related to making progress in school. However, they were ranked lower than counselors. Parents were thought to be of less help than teachers. Counselors seem more strongly identified as help agents in matters related to discovering and progressing toward realistically chosen school and work goals than teachers.

6. Deans of boys and deans of girls who are known by the students to be responsible for school discipline received few student choices. It would seem that students would definitely avoid seeking help from individuals who assume authoritative roles.

7. Students seemed to prefer going to friends their own age for help in learning how to get along better with their friends and others at school, at home, and in the community about as much as going to parents or counselors. Counselors should recognize and make constructive use of peer group activities as a potent resource in helping students learn to relate effectively with one another.

8. Although students tended to prefer rather decisively the help of counselors over that of teachers, deans, and friends own age, it was also observed that some students still preferred some of the latter mentioned individuals. Counselors are obliged to recognize and accept the fact that teachers, deans, friends own age, or other individuals in the community are perceived by students as potential sources of "counseling help." In individual work with students, these potential influences should be kept firmly in mind and if possible utilized to facilitate adjustment. Counselors do not have a monopoly on the counseling market. The results of this survey suggest especially convincingly that parents should somehow be made a vital part of student counseling help. Teachers and others must also be

incorporated, but perhaps to a lesser extent, depending upon the individual student and his problems.

REFERENCES

1. Grant, C. W. How students perceive the counselor's role. *Personnel & Guid. J.*, 1954, 32, 386-388.
2. Grant, C. W. The counselor's role. *Personnel & Guid. J.*, 1954, 33, 74-77.

Section Three

GENERAL PRINCIPLES OF COUNSELING

Many people, professional and otherwise, conduct interviews and advise others. The truly competent counselor will be an individual with an understanding of himself, his counselee, and the interaction that takes place between them; he will be one who can prepare for, conduct, and carry through a counseling interview that results in behavioral changes for the counselee. Such an individual must know the principles upon which he bases counseling activity. The principles of counseling are derived from the philosophies of our democratic society. Democratic principles permeate our economic, social, political, and educational institutions. A study of the principles of counseling reveals that they are rooted in our democratic ideals, values, and faith. Such basic principles include the belief in the worth and dignity of the individual, belief in the right and responsibility of individual freedom and choice, and the belief that life, happiness, and well-being are to be respected and valued above all else.

The school counselor must be knowledgeable about the theoretical structures and general principles undergirding counseling and must understand their implications for his work. Only through such an understanding can he evaluate what he is doing, why he is doing it, and what he can expect. Otherwise his work will be a hit-or-miss, trial and error operation which is inadequate to meet the needs of his students. With a knowledge of procedures, methods, and philosophical assumptions, the counselor can adapt his work to the school situation. The school setting has some inherent characteristics that are inconsistent with some of the basic principles of counseling; for example, most counseling orientations have as one of their assumptions that the counselee will come of his own volition to the counselor because he is aware of a problem and seeks help in alleviating or resolving it. In the school setting it is common practice to "call in" students for interviews on the assumption that the need for counseling is evident and it is too important to wait for the student to volunteer. The school counselor's grounding in theory and principles of counseling will make it possible for him to determine what is applicable to his situation and the changes that he will need to make.

The counselor can find considerable literature on instructions and suggestions but few attempts at describing what really goes on in counseling. The lists of "dos and don'ts" are plentiful but not too satisfying in understanding the interaction between the counselor and the counselee. Over the years more and more attention has been directed to the task of developing a more adequate theoretical model for the "why" of the counseling relationship. The professional school counselor should view counseling principles as a means for translating his ideas into actions. The seven articles in this section serve as a means of presenting how others working in the counseling relationship view the basic principles of their work. It is hoped that the articles will illuminate and clarify some of the directions which you as a counselor have taken.

In the first article Calia views counseling methodology as a function of social theory. His point is that the social implications of behavior have been grossly neglected in both counseling theory and practice. He illustrates the relationship of directive and nondirective counseling concepts to three social theories and examines some of the incongruities inherent in counseling principles having a socially isolated conceptual scheme.

In the next article, Thorne questions the cultism which

seems to have developed with the popularity of the Rogerian, nondirective counseling method. Through his eclectic approach Thorne seeks to integrate the principal contributions of the main schools of psychology into a basic set of principles that underlie the eclectic approach to counseling.

In his article, Callis recommends a theoretical model of counseling organized around the causes or motivation of human behavior, the ways and forms of behaving, and the counseling methods to be utilized in correcting inadequate counselee behavior. His analysis is that the counselor will have to be competent in more than one method of counseling and skilled in diagnosing counselee behavior. Diagnosis is the key to determining the basis for the counselor's behavior and counselee treatment. He illustrates his recommendations by proposing two hypotheses as to the kind of counselor behavior necessary for the correction of counselee inadequacies.

Carl Rogers, focusing on the process of counseling, identifies some of "The Characteristics of a Helping Relationship" in one-to-one and group settings that facilitate growth, maturity, and better functioning of the individual. Drawing upon knowledges gained from studies in the area of attitudes involved in the helping relationship, studies of operant conditioning, and studies of group and individual psychotherapy, Rogers then proposes some of the behaviors of the counselor that go into the making of a helping relationship.

Can the school counselor rightfully expect his work to be the same regardless of the age and grade level of the counselee? Peters examines a number of factors such as the pupil's maturity, psychological development, concept of time, and school organization and curriculum and suggests they constitute meaningful differences in counseling pupils at the elementary and secondary school levels. Peters believes these differential factors affect the nature of the counseling process and content and calls for further research of counseling at the elementary level. Research in the area of counseling has been largely concentrated at the college level or in a clinical setting. In the next article Peters and Farwell raise the question as to whether such research findings in the counseling in these settings have equal validity and relevance for counseling conducted at the secondary level. By citing ten major distinguishing characteristics between the two levels, they question the almost universal acceptance of the applicability of such research to counseling pupils at the secondary school level.

The counselor's basic responsibility is to understand the counselee with whom he works. To understand the multi-faceted personality of the counselee, Tyler believes each counselor needs to personally organize many varieties of theoretical concepts originating from the physiological and psychological laboratories, the psychiatric consulting room, the social disciplines, and from philosophy and religion. For her, the basic principle of such a synthesis is that of understanding the developmental patterns of the counselee.

10. COUNSELING, CONFUSION, AND SOCIAL THEORY

Vincent F. Calia

This writer has been continuously plagued by the many inconsistencies and contradictions prevalent in counseling theory, practice, and research. The theoreticians either get so involved in creating and then trying to define intervening variables or become so entrenched in their own operational quagmire that they can't see "the end for the means." Hopefully, the practitioner examines the multitude of available research and is rewarded with the importance of the criterion variable in research, the inherent pitfalls of computing and interpreting reliability and validity co-efficients, the promise of the new Q-Technique, "The Trouble with Q-Technique," "Q Technique: Its Rise and Fall," "P-Technique, a Promising Research Tool," "The Trouble with P-Technique," and so on it goes. Somewhat confused at this point, but nevertheless determined, the practitioner turns to the seemingly fruitful meandering of the clinician. The case study approach, the resulting one case generalizations, the emphasis on the intuitive and affective aspects, the multitude of intangibles and, in army parlance, the seemingly haphazard "Kentucky windage and Tennessee" elevation approach to clinical work in general and counseling in particular, leaves the foundering practitioner conceptually breathless. Finally, in despair, the practitioner locates the antithetical contributions of the pure-research clinician, the professional schizophrenic. The practitioner reads of their ethical aches and pains in shifting from one role to another. He reads further of the need for closer communication between the two areas, but finds channels for such communication lacking.

It is not the sole intent of the writer to wantonly criticize the

Reprinted by permission of the author and *Journal of Educational Sociology*, XXXI, No. 7 (March, 1958), 271-77.

confusing state of affairs in counseling, but rather attempt to locate some of the difficulties and attempt a piece-meal, highly unoriginal and perhaps far from satisfying compromise solution. The solution represents a direction in counseling that has heretofore been ignored in practice, discussed informally if idealistically at conventions and rarely mentioned and considered in the journals of research, and other formalized avenues of communication.

The Sine Qua Non of Counseling

Eminent psychological theorists of today bewail the need for relating the individual to the "greater whole." Counselors are warned not to lose sight of the "broad perspective." In spite of these occasional reminders, a kind of "social vacuum" approach to counseling ideology and methodology persists to this day. The need for a broader perspective would suggest the need for a kind of theory that is more all-inclusive, that deals not only with the isolated individual, but with the area that surrounds, engulfs, immanently affects and interacts with the behavior and structure of the individual, viz., *relations;* relations with things, with people, with institutions, with oneself. In essence, the social implications of behavior have become increasingly neglected in both counseling theory and practice. Perhaps what is needed is a recapitulation in counseling theory to the Sullivan-Horney era of inter-personal relations.

The need for a social re-orientation in counseling theory and practice suggests the lack of a consistent socio-psychological frame of reference in which the counselor can effectively operate.

Counseling Methodology as a Function of Social Theory

By way of illustrating the kinship of counseling to social theory it may be well to relate some central counseling concepts to a small number of familiar but radically different social schemes.

Atomism

The phenomenological approach, currently in vogue, appears to be an outgrowth of the atomistic school of rugged individualism with its emphasis on the "private world" of the individual. What the individual perceives is real, and it becomes the task of the skillful counselor to "see things" from the counselee's frame of reference. The counselor-counselee relationship is one of equality, character- ized by lack of authority. Emphasis is placed on creating an atmos- phere of permissiveness, acceptance, and understanding. The counselee is allowed freedom of expression, so long as the private rights of the counselor are respected (e.g., physical violence is pro- hibited).

The self-concept or "private world" of the individual receives most of the attention in atomistic counseling. The individual is en- couraged to "talk about himself," his needs, his frustrations, his aspirations, his strengths, his weaknesses, his past, his future. The *self* is all-consuming, all-important. The ends of counseling stress individual gains only: decrease in tension, increased growth and maturity, independence, increased skill in interpersonal relations, and a concomitant rise in occupational status and class mobility.

In essence, the individual *is* the end in counseling, to which every- thing else (methods, theory and counselor) is the means.

There are, of course, some variations of atomistic counseling. Warner (6) suggests that since a class system in a democracy is in- evitable, it becomes the task of the counselor in an educational setting to be as realistic and candid as possible, since there is not room enough for everyone at the top. Thus, while the counselor assumes a more aggressive role, the individual is still granted the prerogative of freedom of choice. Again, the emphasis is placed on class mobility, rugged individualism and inalienable rights.

Organicism

Central counseling concepts in, say, a fascistic society would prob- ably stress such terms as the "public world" of the citizen, "direc- tive" counseling, ego-ideal and superego. These latter two terms refer to the state concept of the ideal citizen and the will and conscience of the state. It becomes the task of the counselor to inculcate the values of the state. The individual is encouraged to grow in the direction of a universally-defined citizen-ideal. There can be no "private world" or concept-of-self, since the very being of the individual is given to him by the state. The counselee-citizen must see himself only as an instrument to the ends of the state. It is interesting to note that an important criterion of recovery, in regard to the psychiatrically-disturbed, in the Soviet State, is not freedom from tension, or increased skill in interpersonal relations, but the ability to function effectively on the job or on the farm. Likewise, considerable emphasis for cure is placed on methods of physical insult and occupational therapy. Since increased production is essential to the preservation, improvement, and expansion of the state, all methods and techniques are directed towards the attainments of these fundamental ends.

Corporatism

Dewey, Jordan, Tawney and our present-day Walter Lippmann subscribe to the corporate theory of social structure. Corporatism represents an attempt to meet the criticisms associated with the two points of view discussed above. It is a blending of the particular (in philosophical terms) with the universal (i.e., diversity within uniformity). Society serves as a means to the ends of the individual, and in turn the actions and ends of the individual promote and develop the ends of society. Corporatism stresses a mutuality and identity of ends and means, an interdependence of individuals, institutions, and society. The corporate society is a classless society that would relegate status not to the acquisition of wealth and class mobility, but to the performance of functions. A function is thought of as the performance of a service having a social purpose. Occupations are not associated with a class system having differential status and prestige and promoting isolated individual ends, but rather as a function, vital to the individual, to the institution for which he works, and to the society in which he lives.

The corporate counselor would probably think in terms of the "corporate world" rather than the "private world" of the individual. While the atomist would imply that the self-concept is to a large extent an isolated, given, and unique entity, the corporatist would theorize about a "corporate-self," a related interdependent, bio-social concept. The corporatist cries, *"we are what we are, in and through relations."*

The corporate approach to counseling would utilize both the internal and external frame of preference to relate the individual to reality and to clarify his position and purpose in the general scheme of things. Both the actions and ends of the individual and society must be clarified and evaluated, for it is not the self-concept that needs clarification, reorganization, and assimilation, but the corporate-self—a connected, intrinsically related bio-social concept.

The counselor as a member of the corporate society is aware that he is functioning in a culture that has a core of relatively stable social norms, and a common system of values that are definable at the level of social conduct. It is apparent then, that direction in counseling is culturally defined, and if on occasion the client seeks the solution to a problem involving values, or resulting in the adoption of an anti-cultural alternative, it is the task of the counselor (not in the role of God, but as a representative of what is real and ideal) to commit himself accordingly.

This would imply that the counseling process is not characterized by freedom from restraints. Lippmann (2) would not define freedom of speech as the total disregard for restraints. Crying "fire" in a theatre in which there is no fire cannot mean freedom of speech.

The counselor's use of the cultural core as a frame of reference does not mean conformity in the sense of a rigid and static concept of adjustment. It means, instead, creativity within uniformity, uniqueness and stability, autonomy and social purpose.

The corporatists' emphasis on relations, interpersonal behavior and the interdependence of individuals and institutions suggests the increasing need for group methods of counseling. Individual counseling should be supplemented by techniques, stressing group deliberation and processes.

The resulting increased skill in interpersonal relations is not to be thought of in the atomistic sense of manipulating people for selfish ends, but rather the cooperative "working through" of problems relevant to the growth and development of the individuals composing the group and having repercussions beyond that.

SUMMARY AND CRITIQUE

It is not the purpose of this article to examine exhaustively the detailed relationships of the three social theories considered. Rather, an attempt was made to illustrate the resulting confusion and inconsistencies prevalent in counseling ideology having a socially isolated conceptual scheme. The significance of three social theories in regard to a number of counseling concepts was further considered, with particular regard for the contributions of the corporate scheme.

Atomism is said to result in unrestrained egoism, the oppression of the weak, class antagonism, war and the negation of life. Similarly, organicism becomes identified with the ends of the ruling element, resulting in mass subordination, expansion, war, and again, the negation of life. By identifying the means and ends of society with those of the individuals that compose it, stressing interpersonal relations and interdependence of people and functions, corporatism attempts to meet the criticisms of the previous two social systems.

IMPLICATIONS FOR COUNSELING

1. A major contribution of the corporate scheme suggests that the counselee is affected by and, in turn, affects his socio-cultural milieu. Individual growth in counseling must be evaluated in terms of broader social objectives.

2. Passive exploration and clarification represent what Neff (3) refers to as a "retreat to neutrality." There are times in a counseling relationship when a counselor *must* commit himself.

3. A recent study by Pearl (4) suggests that the group process is superior to individual therapy as a method of effecting attitude change in regard to ethnocentrism. It would appear that individuals need the experience of participating in groups if relationships are to be fostered and improved. Both individual and group methods are deemed essential to the total counseling process, if the ends of counseling are to be attained.

4. The heretofore forbidden areas of values, philosophy of life

and purpose should be considered the vital but hardly exclusive province of the effective counselor. The fine points of dogma, doctrine or theology need not concern nor deter the general counselor as long as he operates within the dictates of the cultural core. When problems of a theological nature arise, pastoral referral may be warranted.

5. Group methods may well be the solution to the dilemma of the theoretician, research worker and the clinician. John Dewey's (5) proposal of the "application of cooperative intelligence as displayed in science" to areas other than technological, may well be the answer. The scientific method does not appear to be the exclusive domain of the "white rat" experimentalist. Putting our "collective heads" together and sharing information, pooling and exchanging ideas, discussing implications and possible interpretations, and modifying our theories and practices in light of all this may well resolve a long standing dilemma. National and local professional organizations such as the *American Psychological Association* and its many sub-branches may well provide the machinery for inter-disciplinary organization. Sheer speculation, unfounded and untested counseling practices, inconsistent outcomes, unwarranted assumptions: such are the data that the research worker may "take away" with him for controlled experimentation, following cross-sectional group deliberations. The practitioner, on the other hand, may note discrepancies between his practice and the newer research findings, clarify implications of recent findings, adopt more promising conceptual schemes and develop methods and techniques that are in keeping with the new research. The correlation of private and public ends and its significance for progress and growth is seen to apply to the whole counseling process, affecting the theoretician, clinician, and client alike.

6. A further aspect regarding the consolidation of resources, is the trend toward group research. In fact, cooperative ventures are not unusual at the pre-doctorate level. While individual initiative and pioneering are not to be discouraged, group projects do offer the advantages commonly associated with the "two heads are better than one" concept. The development of individual initiative and the ability to work with others are the necessary pre-requisites of all research specialists.

DANGERS

Katz (1) warns of the conceptual confusion prevalent in systems relating social concepts to concepts of behavior. "If anthropology is on a different level of interpretation than psychology of the same phenomenon, then we can not talk about the interdependence of the phenomenon."

Assuming, "we are what we are, in and through relations," the implication is, without relations we are nothing! Hence it is not a question of different conceptual levels, but one and the same level of interpretation.

While the corporative scheme would appear to offer advantages not afforded by other systems, the author cannot accept its theoretical postulates in toto. Followed to its logical conclusion, the precepts of corporatism and their implicit extensions possess a strong socialistic-Marxist bent. To the extent that such a system stresses the importance of social-relatedness, the interdependence of individuals, functions and institutions, and encourages change and diversity within the frame-work of a stabilized structure; to this extent then is corporatism positive in its contributions. The author cannot, however, accept its agnostic, materialistic implications. The counselor, functioning solely within a cultural context need not inculcate his spiritual values, but neither must he convey the notion that culture is finite, for such a conception would transcend the notion of unrestrained egoism prevalent in the atomistic society.

BIBLIOGRAPHY

1. Katz, Daniel, "Special Review: Handbook of Social Psychology," *Psychological Bulletin,* July, 1955, **52,** pp. 346-353.
2. Lippmann, Walter, "Our Need for a Public Philosophy," *The Atlantic Monthly,* April, 1955.
3. Neff, Frederick, "The Retreat from Heresy," *Scientific Monthly,* April, 1954, pp. 43-49.
4. Pearl, David, "Psychotherapy and Ethnocentrism," *Journal of Abnormal and Social Psychology,* March, 1955, **50,** pp. 227-229.

5. Ratner, J., *Intelligence in the Modern World:* John Dewey's Philosophy, 1939.
6. Warner, William L., *Who Shall Be Educated,* Harper, 1944.

11. PRINCIPLES OF DIRECTIVE COUNSELING AND PSYCHOTHERAPY

Frederick C. Thorne

INTRODUCTION

Clinical psychology has emerged from the prescientific into the scientific era of development. There is urgent need for a comprehensive integration of all scientific data into a "system" of practice which would be genuinely eclectic and provide a basis for the standardization of practice throughout the world. Such a system would be based upon the most modern scientific principles and methods, and would attempt to relate the most recent discoveries with the great mass of information accumulated during the history of the profession. An example of this phase of development in the medical field was the work of Sir William Osler who wrote the first systematic text on the practice of medicine and laid the foundations of the great medical center at Johns Hopkins University. Characteristic of the newer theory of professional education has been the insistence that the orientation must be genuinely eclectic with every student being required to familiarize himself with the latest developments in every clinical specialty.

Prior to World War II, uniform training was non-existent in clinical psychology and every student operated more or less on his own with whatever tools and qualifications he had been able to acquire informally. This situation is being rapidly remedied during the post-war period through the efforts of the APA committees on graduate training in cooperation with the universities, but in spite

Condensed from a paper presented at a symposium under the auspices of the Division of Consulting Psychology at the Detroit meeting of the American Psychological Association, September 10, 1947. Reprinted by permission of the author and *American Psychologist,* III, No. 5 (May, 1948), 160-65.

of this desirable trend clinical psychology in America is still characterized by a primitive state of organization in which the leaders in the field operate more or less independently. Until the recent popularity of nondirective methods, there was no general agreement on any theoretical viewpoint with the result that there were almost as many brands of clinical psychology as there were clinical psychologists. Lacking any formally systematized viewpoint, the theoretical biases of clinical psychologists literally represented all the permutations and combinations of behaviorism, experimentalism, Gestalt psychology, Freudianism, Adlerian individual psychology, Jungian analytic psychology, purposivism and many other minor schools. Most of the leaders in clinical psychology were represented by groups of adherents who were well-trained only in the methods of their teachers. So divergent were the different ideologies and terminologies that proponents of the various schools were frequently unable to communicate with each other. In view of these theoretical differences, it is easy to understand why clinical psychologists have been viewed with suspicion by their experimental colleagues to say nothing of psychiatrists and psychoanalysts who have theoretical biases all their own.

ORIGINS OF DIRECTIVE PSYCHOTHERAPY

The purpose of this paper is to review the basic principles of the comprehensive system of directive psychotherapy described in the series of papers appearing in the *Journal of Clinical Psychology* beginning in 1945, and to make a definitive statement concerning the eclectic orientation which is the basis for the proposed system of practice. The primary motivation was to formulate a comprehensive system of counseling and psychotherapy which would integrate and relate the positive values of newer viewpoints with traditional methods. This system would be more than a compilation of isolated facts, and would be based primarily on the objective foundations of experimental psychology. Its basic orientation would be determined by a detailed system of psychopathology derived from a more comprehensive method of personality analysis than had ever been attempted before. Modifying the classical psychiatric methods involving (a) Kraepelinian descriptive classifications, (b) psychobiological longitudinal studies, and (c) psychoanalytic depth analysis, the new method would seek to systematically evaluate and, if indicated, to modify *all known important personality traits* by the eclectic utilization of all available methods according to their indications and contraindications.

Although recognizing the undesirability of designating a system of psychotherapy by the term "directive," the choice was partially determined by our apprehension that the sudden popularity of Rogerian nondirective methods to the exclusion of traditional methods was a dangerous development both for the profession and for the student. This critical attitude was directed not so much toward nondirective methods which are admitted to have great value in their place, but toward the attitude of uncritical enthusiasm and cultism associated with the new development. It appeared that there was definite need for a comprehensive system which would relate directive and nondirective methods in their proper perspective and emphasize the values of eclecticism in clinical science.

TERMINOLOGICAL CONSIDERATIONS

The term *directive* seemed particularly appropriate to designate a system of therapy which is based upon a formal plan for the identification and modification of etiologic factors in maladjustment. Based upon the historical study of the evolution of clinical methods in science which have been outlined elsewhere (9), it was our opinion that any valid therapeutic system must be oriented about a comprehensive knowledge of psychopathology and the uses and limitations of *all* known clinical methods. It is presupposed that persons representing themselves as clinical psychologists should have training and experience to enable them to adequately utilize all known methods according to the standards of time and place. Possession of such training and experience beyond that which might be expected of the most intelligent and best-informed layman implies that the basic responsibility for the *direction* of all stages of case handling lies with the therapist even though he may choose to delegate some portion of this responsibility to other persons including the client himself. In our opinion the possibility of a completely nondirective method is nonexistent since by the very nature of the therapist-client relationship (a) the client comes to a therapist considered to be of superior experience and training which thereby establishes a relationship of dominance through prestige, (b) the therapist determines the method to be used, and (c) what happens in the therapeutic relationship must be evaluated not only in terms of what the therapist thinks he is doing but also in terms of what the therapy means to the patient. Rather than involving a dichotomy of either-or directive or nondirective, we are dealing with a continuum involving various degrees of directiveness of which nondirective methods may be regarded as being at one extreme along with other "passive" techniques. We are in disagreement with Rogers' contention that any lapse from complete nondirectiveness is a grave therapeutic error, since our experience indicates that all degrees of directiveness may be used with a single case according to the indications of each individual situation.

The concepts of *directive* and *direction* also imply straightforwardness, i.e. straight, leading by the shortest way to a point or end. *Directed* movements of an organism are those which are observed to be related to a specific stimulus or goal. *Direction* is an attribute of behavior indicative of specific function and variously expressed in terms of needs, drives, goals, purposes and other concepts descriptive of integrated behavior. One of the principal characteristics of the maladjusted or disordered person is the inability to resolve problems unaided. Although self-direction is the highest democratic goal and evidence of integration, the maladjusted person either asks for help spontaneously or is induced to do so for his own good. Until such time as the person demonstrates his ability to regulate his behavior within the limits of what is socially acceptable, he is subjected to varying degrees of direction or regulation from the environment. The general rule may be stated that *the need for direction is inversely correlated with the person's potentialities for effective self-regulation,* i.e., the healthier the personality, the less the need for direction; the sicker the personality, the more the need for direction. It is to be assumed that the well-trained psychological scientist is the person best equipped to provide whatever degree of direction may be necessary to catalyze therapeutic processes by the shortest route. Judiciously utilized, psychological knowledge may have specific action in facilitating curative processes in much shorter time than might be accomplished by the client working by trial and error even assuming that homeostatic resources would be sufficient. While recognizing the dangers of over-regulation and over-interpretation in cases of mild personality disorder, it is our opinion that failure to institute the indicated degrees of direction in more serious cases may constitute malpractice since the therapist has the obligation to protect the interests of the client when the client is unable to do so himself.

The significance of these facts is that the therapist is supposed to *direct* the overall details of case handling according to tested scientific procedures whether he is utilizing nondirective methods or authoritarian methods in an institution. It is assumed that training and experience will provide the therapist with the knowledge concerning when to be directive or relatively nondirective. The validity of the results will be determined by the skill with which any method is used with reference to etiological diagnosis and the indications of each individual case. *The critical factor is not what method is used but rather the skill with which it is used.* We are not in agreement with the ideological bias of many nondirective therapists to the effect that all which is directive is bad, while all that is nondirective is good. In his basic text, Rogers (6) attacks directive methods by setting up the straw man of criticizing the most crude and unacceptable forms of directive methods and implying that all directive techniques are subject to the same handicaps. Directive methods can only be fairly judged when they are employed with maximum skill; it is unrepresentative to base criticisms on atypical examples which would be condemned by all experienced directive therapists. Long before the development of nondirective methods, psychoanalysis had demonstrated the errors of over-interpretation, too much leading, crude interference and other pitfalls of the beginning counselor. The nondirective viewpoint appears to have gone to the extreme of rejecting direction in any form simply because it has frequently been misused. Hahn and Kendall (5) and others have recently pointed out the logical inconsistencies involved in many of the theoretical criticisms made by Rogers and his pupils against directive methods. Perhaps most important is it to emphasize that all valid therapy is client-centered and that nondirective therapy has no monopoly on methods which are to the best interests of the client. As pointed out by Blain (2), effective therapy frequently involves a compromise between what a patient sincerely believes he wants and what he needs according to the most objective judgment of the experienced therapist. Although it is theoretically desirable to place major dependence upon the growth principle and homeostatic processes as emphasized by Rogers and many others before him, there are many cases in which the client's resources and growth potentialities are so deficient or damaged that adjustment without outside help and direction is impossible.

A further application of the concept of *directness* is illustrated in our attempt toward a systematic application of the Law of Parsimony (Lloyd Morgan's canon). In contrast with the current popularity of psychoanalytically oriented approaches which seek to discover latent meanings, symbolism, unconscious complexes and other depth processes in personality, our viewpoint is that primary weight should be assigned to direct interpretations of manifest behavior according to the principles of scientific psychology and particularly the laws of learning. Much is lost by failing to make the simplest possible interpretations and also by proceeding in the most direct manner consistent with the needs of the client. In our own practice, we systematically avoid complex psychoanalytic interpretations, preferring to communicate whatever minimum amount seems indicated in the simplest of terms. It is an axiom of directive therapy, as well as nondirective, that the less said by the therapist the better.

Finally, we would specifically refute the implication made by Snyder (8) and apparently accepted by others, that the term *directive psychotherapy* was coined by us simply to refer to traditional methods of therapy and involving little which is new. While it is true that many of the methods included under directive therapy have long been utilized, there has not been any systematic attempt known to us in the English literature to reevaluate them in terms of modern psychopathology with the objectives of determining their nature, indications and contraindications. Traditionally, these methods have been described and utilized as isolated units with no attempt being made to construct an integrated system about a central theory of personality.

The Basic Method

The theoretical foundations for directive psychotherapy are derived from a survey of the historical development of clinical science carrying over the principles and methods which appear to be valid for clinical psychology. As pointed out elsewhere (9), clinical psychology has a medico-psychological heritage dating back to ancient Egypt and one must be familiar with the evolution of medical psychology in order to evaluate any development in proper perspective. Utilizing standard techniques of description, classification, statistical evaluation and integrative interpretation, directive psychotherapy attempts to discover the causal conditions resulting in maladaptation and then to utilize treatments specific for each pathological condition. Unless comprehensive etiologic studies are carried out with every case, it is difficult to understand how any objective evaluation in case handling may be made. However, this unending search for the causation of morbidity must never be allowed to conceal the basic objective of satisfying the needs of the client.

The basic pattern of directive therapy in which the therapist, though client-centered, assumes responsibility for the conduct of all details of case handling according to the highest ethical and professional standards of time and place is given in another paper (10).

Gregg (4) states a cardinal axiom that the human organism involves such a complex relationship of constituent parts that one cannot be modified without effecting all others; that, therefore, a given result comes usually not from one cause but from a combination of causes, sometimes a sequence, sometimes a constellation or pattern; and similarly, that a given cause has not one but many results, sometimes in sequence, sometimes in pattern. With such a complex situation, it is inevitable that a wide armamentarium of therapeutic tools will be needed, each used as skillfully as possible based on a valid knowledge of what each tool can be expected to accomplish.

PSYCHOPATHOLOGICAL RATIONALE

One of the most important contributions of Adolf Meyer's psychobiological approach to personality was his recognition that pathological processes of different types may involve personality functions as a whole or in parts. By careful appraisal of all the known functions of personality, it becomes possible to identify areas of dysfunction, to postulate etiologic factors, and to outline specific plans of treatment. The psychobiologic approach is genuinely eclectic in the sense that it seeks to assess all known functions with proper weight being assigned to dysfunctions of each in the longitudinal study of personality. In this respect, the psychobiologic viewpoint may be contrasted with that of psychoanalysis in its various forms. In our opinion, psychoanalytic theory is one-sided in that it overemphasizes latent, unconscious, affective-impulsive components of personality while almost disregarding the direct, manifest, rational intellectual components characteristic of the higher mental functions and which are best understood by the psychology of learning and thinking. When the psychoanalytic viewpoint is carried to its logical conclusions as in nondirective therapy, the main emphasis is placed on affective-impulsive components which are regarded as involving the principal etiologic factors in maladjustment. Snyder (8) even defines the objective of psychotherapeutic counseling as to "modify emotional attitudes that are socially maladjusted" and omits any reference to intellectual factors which may also be productive of maladjustment.

The system of directive psychotherapy which has been outlined in our published series of papers is theoretically oriented upon psychobiological approaches to the whole organism with perhaps more emphasis on rational intellectual components than on affective-impulsive since we believe that the highest potentialities for adaptation are related to the maturation and effective utilization of the higher cortical functions. The developmental phenomena associated with the maturation of the cerebral cortex are now well known and may be summarized in the statement that although the biologically more primitive affective-impulsive components of personality are constantly operative throughout life, the maturation of the cortex with the development of the higher mental functions results in the achievement of rational intellectual control through cerebral inhibition of lower functions and the acquisition of tremendously enhanced powers of learning. The dominance of the cerebrum over mid and hind-brain functions is achieved very slowly and only incompletely in the average person so that learning self-regulation, making the most of one's resources, and achieving insight into the meanings of behavior and life in general is a very gradual process.

In outlining the theoretical foundations of directive psychotherapy, we have attempted to integrate the principal contributions of the main schools of psychology. From behaviorism comes a major emphasis on the role of learning and of environmental stimulation in the development of acquired patterns of behavior. Experimental psychology of the traditional type contributes important information concerning sensation, memory, association, physiological reactions, and other relatively elemental phenomena. Gestalt psychology is important because of its emphasis on wholes, and its detailed studies of the perceptual process. Psychoanalysis gives most important emphasis to depth psychology, with its developmental studies of the affective-impulsive life. Finally, hormic psychology contributes the stimulating viewpoint that organic phenomena are largely determined by purposive factors as yet not clearly understood. Following the psychobiological approach which assumes that the psychologist will have detailed and extensive training and experience in the basic sciences of anatomy, biochemistry, physiology, pathology, as well as in normal psychology, directive psychotherapy depends for its validity upon the psychological sophistication and broadness of the person who attempts to utilize it. The better oriented is the clinician to the psychological sciences and to life in general, the more able is he to avoid the pitfalls which are recognized as inherent in any active (directive) method. Any method is no better than the skill of the person who makes it. We have come to regard psychotherapy as involving the hardest kind of work for both therapist and client, since deviant personality patterns become chronic over the years and can hardly be expected to be unlearned and relearned with startling rapidity.

Directive psychotherapy accepts the concept of *distributive analysis and treatment* developed by Meyer and described by Diethelm (3). The distributive principle assumes that it is most effective to budget time and energy during the treatment process giving major emphasis to trends which appear to be most etiologically important. Instead of spending hundreds of hours more or less passively exploring the channels taken by the client, considerable saving may be accomplished without violence to the client-centered principle by directing the course of treatment along what may seem to be the most profitable lines. In addition to etiologic studies exploring the developmental history of the person, it seems important also to assess learning ability and accomplishment in all areas of activity. Directive psychotherapy is particularly concerned with maximizing the self-regulatory functions of personality with particular emphasis on self-control and conative life. It seems important to deal with certain phenomena usually denied or ignored in traditional psychology including the study of the nature of consciousness, nonconscious mental functions, volition, suggestion, hypnosis, deviant personalities of all types, and other phenomena which have important significance for psychopathology.

The directive principle that intellectual resources constitute the highest potentialities for adaptation in the organism and that therapy must be realistically distributed to deal with both affective-impulsive and rational-intellectual factors as they are encountered in the individual case, is based on the important distinction concerning primary and secondary etiologic factors in maladaptation. Etiologic factors may be identified as precipitating, predisposing or perpetuating. To explain our conception of the relative psychopathological importance of affective vs. intellectual factors in personality would require much more time than is here available. In summary, it seems important to reevaluate the entire etiologic role of affective factors in maladjustment with particular reference to the distinction between (a) *reactive* affective disorders, and (b) deeper habitual affective reactions based on constitutional or acquired personality complexes. In our opinion, affective disorders of reactive type have a much higher incidence and have most hopeful prognosis with or without treatment (although perhaps more quickly with treatment) when the stimulating factors are modified. In these cases, affective disorders are recognized to be symptomatic and therapy is primarily directed toward the intellectual failure to react adaptively. It may be necessary to treat affective-impulsive disorders first in order to prepare the stage for rational problem-solving activity but it should clearly be recognized that treatment of such reactive affective disorders results in only transient alleviation of symptoms which are prone to recur unless effective intellectual solutions are achieved. A basic diagnostic question therefore becomes: "Is the client maladjusted because he is emotionally disturbed, or is he emotionally disturbed because he is maladjusted?" The solution to this hen-egg problem is not always easily achieved, since reactive affective states may be of long duration. The degree of directiveness indicated in the individual case will be determined by the client's demonstrated ability to solve the problem alone.

Recognition of the need for maximally potentiating intellectual resources of personality in problem solving behavior has important implications in both theoretical orientation and practical application. If human behavior is determined by unconscious, instinctual, affective-impulsive components in personality, it follows that maladjustment is caused by mechanistic, physiological factors over which a person can exert little conscious, voluntary control unless his growth resources or homeostatic tendencies are sufficiently strong to fortunately effect a cure. On the other hand, if it is accepted that rational-intellectual factors may supersede and control impulsive behavior, then the normal person may be expected to achieve some success in solving problems by conscious use of intellectual resources. This viewpoint does not necessarily involve the postulation of such mental functions as will or volition. On the contrary, the acquisition of self-regulatory abilities is regarded as a function of past training, usually by directive methods since few individuals are gifted enough to work out optimal methods by themselves, nor would such a trial and error process be economically desirable even if possible. Important areas of maladjustment are regarded as being caused by failure to *learn* to solve such problems using intellectual resources. This learning would normally take place in early life, thus normally preventing maladaptation. Since the basic factor in most psychotherapy is commonly recognized to be reeducation, it follows that the treatment process is essentially a training situation. It is occasionally necessary to resolve emotional attitudes before training can be begun, but this is not inevitable, since training may proceed even in unfavorable conditions. If latent, subconscious, unverbalized affective-impulsive reactions are important determiners of behavior, so are acquired intellectual traits and attitudes operating on manifest conscious levels. The goal of therapy is to replace emotional-compulsive behavior with deliberate rational-adaptive behavior based on the highest utilization of intellectual resources. To accomplish this may require the use of many directive techniques over and above the simple nondirective handling of emotional reactions which may be understood as simply the first step in therapy.

Status of Directive Methods

Unfortunately, the traditional discussions of directive methods have dealt primarily with theoretical considerations with very little detail concerning the actual mechanics of case handling. Since each clinician has largely been forced to develop techniques by himself, it is understandable that the actual execution of these techniques ranged from literal perfection in the hands of the masters to the crudest bungling in the hands of amateurs. The situation is further complicated by the fact that the practical details have been taught by the apprenticeship method and only rarely described objectively. One of the purposes of the medical internship is to teach many small details of case handling which have never appeared in print, and which can only be learned by actually doing. No matter how rigidly and experimentally the treatment process may be controlled, the actual success is largely a function of the skill and intuitiveness of the individual practitioner in making the patient comfortable while attempting to treat the basic condition.

Before any extensive research program could be planned or undertaken, it has been necessary to achieve a theoretical formulation of the principles and methods of directive therapy and this has been attempted in the series of papers appearing in the *Journal of Clinical Psychology*. The failure to produce more quantitative evidence in support of the validity of directive psychotherapy is a function of its youth. Experimental work with any of the traditional methods has been almost completely lacking. Directive methods are only now being formally described and related to a system of therapy, and it will take many years to accumulate objective validation as evidenced by the fact that the basic outlines of psychoanalysis have still not been confirmed after almost fifty years of research. Although slightly more objective research has been accomplished with nondirective methods, it is insufficient either to establish the rather optimistic claims of its proponents or, conversely, to offer objective evidence that directive methods are invalid.

The status of all methods of psychotherapy is in such an elementary stage of evolution that clinical psychologists find themselves in the position of the chemists who having discovered some of the rarer elements did not know what to do with them. Some of the neglected methods such as suggestion, hypnosis, reconditioning or reassurance may well turn out to have such startling possibilities when properly used as did uranium in relation to the atom bomb. When psychologists devote as much time and energy to training themselves in the use of any of these methods as do professional athletes or craftsmen, much of the crudeness which is now so much in evidence will inevitably disappear. In our experience, nondirective methods constitute just a beginning with respect to what the clinical psychologist may be expected to do. Some cases will show some improvement with the use of any superficial method, but others become progressively more maladjusted and constitute a challenge which will require the most effective use of all resources if the problem is to be solved. Directive psychotherapy requires that the therapist will be trained and able to make use of every known method in his field as indication may arise.

References

1. Alexander, F., French, T. M., et al. *Psychoanalytic therapy*. New York: Ronald, 1946.

2. Blain, D. The psychiatrist and the psychologist. *J. clin. Psychol.*, 1947, **3**, 4-9.

3. Diethelm, O. *Treatment in psychiatry*. New York: Macmillan, 1936. Pp. 111-133.

4. Gregg, A. Transition in medical education. *J. Assoc. Med. Coll.* 1947, **22**, 226-232.

5. Hahn, M. E., and Kendall, W. E. Some comments in defense of non-nondirective counseling. *J. consult. Psychol.*, 1947, **11**, 74-81.

6. Rogers, C. R. *Counseling and psychotherapy*. Boston: Houghton-Mifflin, 1942.

7. Rogers, C. R. Significant aspects of client-centered therapy. *Amer. Psychologist*, 1946, **1**, 415-422.

8. Snyder, W. U. The present status of psychotherapeutic counseling. *Psychol. Bull.*, 1947, **44**, 297-386.

9. Thorne, F. C. The clinical method in science. *Amer. Psychologist*, 1947, **2**, 159-166.

10. Thorne, F. C. Theoretical foundations of directive psychotherapy. *Annals N. Y. Acad. Sci.*, 1947, in press.

12. TOWARD AN INTEGRATED THEORY
OF COUNSELING

Robert Callis

INTRODUCTION

First, let me apologize for being so presumptuous as to choose to talk about an integrated theory of counseling. I feel very inadequate to the task. However, I have chosen this topic more because of its need to be considered than because of what I will be able to do with it. There is entirely too much talk abroad in the land of counseling of the "either-or" and "what school do you belong to?" variety. Such talk is unhealthy for the profession in that it substitutes belief and convictions for creative thought and research. We need to organize our knowledge (theories and facts) in such a manner that the result is a consistent and unified guide to counseling thought, research and practice. We need a theory that is useful in our day by day practice; one that is not just a rag-bag collection of unrelated constructs, but a unified theory with high internal consistency. This paper is an attempt to take a step in that direction.

Before we get into the age-old hassle of theory vs. practice, let me commit myself at least to the notion that the most practical thing I know of is a good theory. The definition of a theory is an organized set of ideas which will explain a maximum amount of the phenomena with which we are concerned. The test of a theory is—will it work? A good theory will work more often and in a greater variety of situations than a poor theory. Actually, there is no dichotomy between theory and practice. If a theory is adequate it is practical.

This paper is organized around three questions:

1. *What energizes behavior?* What causes the human organism to move, to act, to respond, to behave?
2. *How does the human organism develop a behavior repertoire?* When is one's behavior repertoire adequate or inadequate? What is the nature of the inadequacies?

Reprinted by permission of the author and *The Journal of College Student Personnel*, I, No. 4 (June, 1960), 2-9.

3. *How can the several kinds of inadequacies in behavior repertoire be corrected?* Which counseling method is most effective in correcting which inadequacy in behavior repertoire?

WHAT ENERGIZES BEHAVIOR?

Perhaps first we should state what appears to be a basic law of behavior: *The primary goal of an organism is to behave in such a fashion that he is able to extract from his environment the satisfaction of his needs not only at the moment but in a sustained manner in the future.* Most behavioral scientists agree that the stuff that energizes behavior is the need of the organism. Thus, if we are to understand behavior, we must understand the needs that the organism is trying to satisfy. So that we won't get bogged down by terminology, let us assume that needs and drives have to energize behavior.

Various authors have developed lists of needs. Maslow (1954) has ordered these needs into a hierarchy according to their power or priority relative to each other. This order is typical but individual variation from it can be observed. The following list is a modification of Maslow's list. It contains seven needs: two biological and five psycho-social. These are presented in order of their power or priority with the most powerful one first

1. Self-Preservation

This drive to survive physically has been rather well established in all forms of life. Immediately, we can think of instances in which some other need supercedes this supposedly most basic and powerful one. Suicide, for example, violates this basic drive. It seems to me that in the human organism we must introduce an additional construct here in order to understand self-preservation. Biologists describe self-preservation as a drive for physical survival. However, as we grow and develop, we develop a psychological self as well as a physical self. Somehow these two selves get intertwined. If we consider this drive for self-preservation to encompass both the physical and the psychological self, we can leave it stand as the highest priority and most powerful drive. Take, for example, the soldier who throws himself on a live grenade to protect his buddies from certain death; knowing full well that in doing so he will be killed. Some need more powerful than that to survive physically has motivated him. We can explain this act of heroism by invoking the notion of preservation of the psychological self and postulating that the soldier was acting in accordance with a concept of himself as a good soldier, one loyal to his buddies and one willing to risk his life to protect his buddies.

2. Reproduction of the Species

This is the second most powerful drive which biologists have identified. It also seems to be biologically inherited. The absence or malfunction of either the drive to physical survival or the drive to reproduce the species will cause that particular genetic strain to die out. We are here today only because our ancestors possessed these two drives in sufficient quantity. The genetic argument is perhaps the most powerful argument for these two biological drives being considered first in priority in relation to all the other drives. This puts preservation of the psychological self in second place. Dead heroes do not reproduce themselves.

3. Security

Security is a widely used term and perhaps loosely so at times. Security here has to do with a feeling of confidence within the individual that he will be able to satisfy his needs now and continuously in the future. When this security need is not satisfied, the person is fearful and apprehensive that he will not be able to interact with his environment in such a way that his needs will be satisfied. The magnitude of this fear may reach catastrophic proportions producing extreme anxiety and panic.

4. Respect for Self

Each person needs to feel that he is worthy of dignity and respect. This is an attitude toward self; an approval of oneself. It is not necessarily associated with social or economic status. It is a need of everyone regardless of his status in life.

5. Acceptance by Others

This includes heterosexual love, family and other close friendships, and general gregariousness. In adolescence acceptance by peers is highlighted.

6. Self Expression and Accomplishment

We have a need to use our abilities in manners suggested by our interests to create or accomplish something. Ability in itself has drive properties. This expression may take occupational forms or it may take recreational and hobby forms. Ability here is not restricted to intellectual ability.

7. Esthetic Experiences

The need for esthetic experience accounts for the existence of art, music, drama, etc.

Maslow's hierarchy principle states that in general until the most basic need has been satisfied in our perception or expectation, but not necessarily in reality, we cannot attend to the higher order but less powerful needs. The implications for the counselor are two-fold: (1) at what need level is the client functioning or having difficulty functioning? and (2) at what level is the counselor functioning and is the counselor able to distinguish between his own need level and that of his client? When the counselor understands at what need level the client is having difficulty, he is able to see more clearly the goal of counseling and is able to choose an appropriate counseling method for this instance.

Once we have satisfied our more basic needs, we are then able to "upshift" and attend to higher order needs. When the satisfaction of these lower order needs is threatened, we "downshift" to attend to them.

If we can accept the notion that needs motivate our behavior, we are ready to consider the behavior repertoire that we have at our command which we can use to interact with our environment for the purpose of satisfying our needs.

How Does One Develop His Behavior Repertoire?

Needs provide the motivating force which energizes behavior and sets the goal to be attained as well. But what sort of behavior does one employ in attempting to satisfy his needs? What patterns of behavior response does he have at his command; i.e., what repertoire of behavior responses does he have available for use? How does he choose a single course of action from among the several that may be in his repertoire? What happens if the choice is wrong? What happens if the behavior repertoire cupboard is bare? Where does counseling fit into such a scheme? These are a few of the questions which must be answered. Pepinsky and Pepinsky (1954) have dealt with several of these questions at length. You will see that my treatment of the questions has been influenced by the Pepinsky's.

We can define behavior repertoire as the total of all behavior response that the individual is capable of making. We start with our inherited capacities and through maturation and experience build a behavior repertoire. Our behavior repertoire changes or is subject

Figure 1—Behavior Repertoire

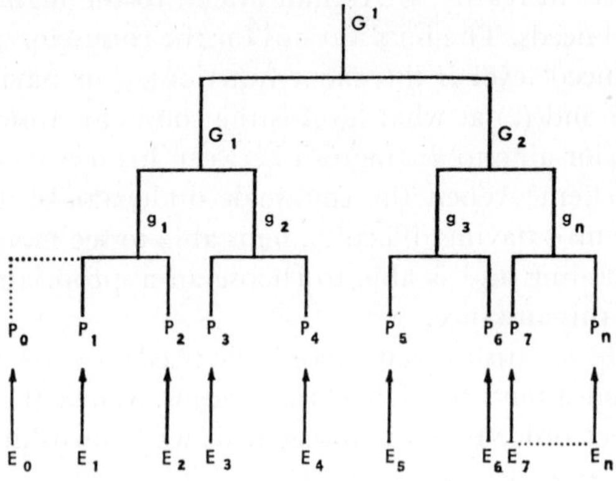

CODE

E—*experience;* P—*Perception;* g—*first order generalization;* G—*second order generalization;* G'—*third order generalization*

Figure 1: Schematic Diagram of Behavior Repertoire Showing the Relationship of Experience, Perception and Generalization

to change with each new experience. Thus, experience becomes the first level in a schematic diagram (Figure 1) which we can construct to represent behavior repertoire.

For our purposes here, the unit of experience can be conceived of as being of any size. Experience is an objective occurrence external to the "psyche."

The second element is *perception*. Perception is the individual's interpretation of the experience or that which is interiorized by the individual.

The third element is *generalization*. We seem to have a natural tendency to group perceptions which appear to us to be of a similar kind and draw one rule or generalization from the whole class of events. We use this generalization to guide our behavior at any time in the future when we encounter an event perceived to be of the same class of events as those about which the generalization was drawn. For example, if we go into a strange room which is dark and wish to turn on the light, where would we look for the light switch? Most of us have had experiences with light switches and from these experiences and our perceptions of them, we have concluded or generalized that usually the light switch is located on the wall adjacent to the door frame a little above waist high. We have also learned, that is, concluded or generalized that light switches are not to be found on the ceiling or in the floor. Consequently, we look for the light switch near the door and not on the floor or ceiling. Thus, the generalization based on past experience guides our behavior in this present situation.

Before we apply a generalization to a new situation we must determine that the new situation is identical for our purpose to the class of situations from which our generalization came. Thus, if the dark room mentioned above were in a rustic log cabin in an isolated wooded area we should suspect that there would be neither lights nor light switches in the room. The ability to differentiate between apparently identical situations and actually identical situations must be admitted into the scheme of thinking which we are developing here. Dollard, Auld and White (1953) have indicated that improvement in accuracy of differentiation and discrimination is a major goal in psychotherapy. They describe instances in which psychiatric patients try to apply generalizations developed out of childhood experiences to situations which they encounter as adults.

Although the generalizations were valid for the childhood situations, the apparently identical adult situations were in reality not identical, and, consequently, the behavior repertoire employed was ineffective in satisfying the patient's needs.

The constellation of all generalizations developed out of past experience gives direction and selectivity to our behavior tendencies in our attempts to interact with present environment to satisfy present needs. If this constellation of generalization which we have labelled behavior repertoire directs our behavior in such a way that our needs are satisfied we can consider it adequate.

When a client comes to a counselor saying, "I have a problem. I would like for you to help me with it," he is, in effect, saying, "My behavior repertoire is inadequate. Will you help me correct the inadequacies?" No matter what language he uses, in the model we are developing here, that is the translation.

What kinds of inadequacies in behavior repertoire can there be? There are three general classes of inadequacies: (1) lack of experience, (2) distortions in perception, and (3) errors in generalization.

Lack of experience simply means that we have not had the kind of experience necessary to develop generalizations appropriate for the situation with which we are confronted. This includes lack of information about ourselves as well as our environment. Most counseling effort devoted to increasing understanding of self and of the world of work is attacking this first kind of inadequacy. (See E_o in Figure 1.)

Distortion in perception can occur even though our experience or exposure is adequate. For example, our need to regard ourselves highly may be so pressing that we distort or deny all evidence or experience which suggests that we may not be as intelligent or popular as our current self-concept suggests. Generalizations based on distorted perceptions are apt to be invalid and will direct us into behavior which will not satisfy our needs.

Errors in generalization are more difficult to describe in concrete terms. We could say that they are faulty logic but this is not very helpful. Errors in grouping perceptions from which we draw a generalization would produce a faulty generalization, but, also, there can be errors in actual generalization itself. The process of creating an idea resists definition and description. We can test the validity of an idea, hypothesis or generalization once it has been invented, but we know very little about how these inventions were produced. In our model, we must include errors in generalization even if we cannot describe exactly how they occur.

In addition to the three types of inadequacies, there is a fourth notion that needs mentioning. That is the *spread of effect of errors.* Lack of experience or distortion in perception does not stop there. They cause, in turn, erroneous generalization based this time on the original error. One is reminded here of the children's ditty: "For the lack of a nail, the shoe was lost. For the lack of a shoe, the horse was lost. For the lack of a horse, the rider was lost. For the lack of the rider, the battle was lost."

Let us return to our client who has said to us (translated), "My behavior repertoire is inadequate. Will you help me correct the inadequacies?" It seems to me that the problem calls for two discoveries: (1) discovery of the error, and (2) discovery of a way to correct the error. Who is to make the discoveries? We have two choices— the counselor or the client. Or, to say it another way, there are two general methods of counseling—(1) client self discovery and (2) counselor discovery followed by interpretation.

WHICH COUNSELING METHOD IS MOST EFFECTIVE IN CORRECTING WHICH INADEQUACY IN BEHAVIOR REPERTOIRE?

This question suggests that the counselor's behavior repertoire should include more than one counseling method. Is there any justification for a counselor being competent in and using more than one counseling method? Or, is some one counseling method sufficient to solve all client problems as many counselors contend? Reasoning by analogy does not always lead to valid conclusions but let's take that risk for a moment.

Suppose that you move to a new town and shortly thereafter you develop a severe head cold. You consult a physician and he gives you a shot of penicillin. You get well. You conclude that he is a good physician. Later on you break your arm. You go back to your physician. He gives you a shot of penicillin and starts to dismiss you. You say, "But Doc, how about this broken bone? Aren't you going to set it?" He replies, "I don't believe in bone setting. I'm a penicillin man." Do you still consider him a good physician? If not, why not?

Because he is a one-tool physician. He refuses to vary his treatment according to the problem. Should we not also condemn counselors for this "one-tool" attitude?

Suppose your car has blown a head gasket. You take it to a garage for repair. The mechanic starts banging on the head bolts with a screwdriver. You say, "Why don't you use a wrench on these head bolts?" and he replies, "Oh, I couldn't do that, you see, I'm a screwdriver man." Would you judge him to be a competent mechanic? If not, why not? Would you really condemn him for being a one-tool mechanic? He has such strong *faith* in his screwdriver and such strong *conviction* that it is proper to limit himself to only one tool. Isn't faith and conviction a sufficient basis for determining one's professional behavior? Since it seems to be a sufficient basis for many counselors, it would seem only fair that we also permit physicians and mechanics the privilege of restricting their tools on the basis of faith and conviction.

Many counselors restrict themselves to the client self-discovery method solely. Since all of us must agree that counseling is a learning process, at least in some broad sense of the word, let's try another reduction to absurdity. Suppose we instruct every third grade teacher that he is to employ the self-discovery method solely, and, in addition, we set the standard that every third grader must know the multiplication tables before he can go on to the fourth grade. How many grey-bearded third graders would we have hobbling around in our schools because they hadn't yet discovered the multiplication tables? Of course, someone did discover the multiplication tables years ago, but, it was not a third grader. However, millions of third graders have learned the multiplication tables by having them interpreted to them. Many a client has learned what occupational groups his interests are similar to through interpretation within a few hours time. Most of these would expend hundreds of hours to acquire the same understanding of themselves by self-discovery method.

I have tried to show that a single counseling method cannot solve all types of problems, and that client self-discovery method of counseling cannot solve certain client problems and will be grossly inefficient with others. But, how about the converse? Can counselor discovery and interpretation be effective in all instances? Let's return to our discussion of distortion in perception. It was shown that distortion in perception can occur even though the client has had adequate and appropriate experience or exposure. Certainly, interpretation by the counselor is an experience or exposure for the client. Therefore, it is quite possible and conceivable that the client may distort or reject a counselor's interpretation which would in turn produce an erroneous generalization. An erroneous generalization is an inadequacy in behavior repertoire so the client is still unable to satisfy his needs. Counseling has failed.

We now come to the major point in this paper. Clients consult counselors because they have found that their behavior repertoire is inadequate. Inadequacies in behavior repertoire can be of three different kinds and counseling methods are basically of two kinds, neither of which can be effective with all kinds of inadequacies. Therefore, it is absolutely necessary that counseling include differential diagnosis which will form the basis for differential choice of treatment, i.e., counseling method. The one-tool counselor must go. He is just as unscientific, unprofessional, unethical and immoral as the penicillin physician or the screwdriver mechanic. The only instance in which a counselor would be justified in restricting himself to one method, would be for him to limit his practice to one type of inadequacy. Even then, he would have to engage in diagnosis to determine if this particular client is the type of case he would accept. Diagnosis in counseling is not a new topic, nor is it a completely forgotten one. (See Apostal and Miller, 1959; Berezin, 1957; Bordin, 1946; Pepinsky, 1948; Weiner, 1959; Williamson and Darley, 1937.)

In spite of all of the important contributions Rogers (1931, 1939, 1942, 1951) has made, he has damaged the field quite significantly by making most of us feel guilty about diagnosis, and yet if you read his works carefully this should not have happened. Rogers limits his method to certain kinds of cases and makes the determination (diagnosis) at the outset that the case is appropriate to his method (client-self-discovery) before accepting the case. I have a bone to pick with the pseudo-Rogerians, not Rogers himself.

If the word diagnosis makes you feel squeamish, if it rankles you, I believe we can avoid that very nicely by substituting "working hypothesis" for "diagnosis." Of course, we are still talking about the same thing, but "working hypothesis" may be more palatable to many counselors. Each counselor, whether he admits it or not, draws generalizations (working hypotheses) about his client on a moment-to-moment basis throughout the entire counseling process. On the

basis of these hypotheses the counselor determines what his behavior
will be, what method he will employ at the next moment. In reality,
every counselor employs differential diagnosis and differentially
chooses his treatment method accordingly. My plea, simply, is to
make these operations explicit so that we can begin to think about
and conduct some research on the effectiveness of various counseling
methods in correcting the several kinds of inadequacies in behavior
repertoire.

As a starting point for this line of investigation, let me propose
two hypotheses. Earlier three kinds of inadequacies in behavior repertoire were described: (1) lack of experience, (2) distortion in perception and (3) erroneous generalization. I will deal here with the
first two only. Also, I will not attempt to distinguish between the
two kinds of discoveries to be made. However, I suspect that the
following hypotheses are more appropriate to discovery of a way to
correct an inadequacy than to discovering the inadequacy in the
first place.

> *Hypothesis A.* Lack of experience is most effectively dealt with by
> the method of counselor discovery and interpretation.
>
> *Hypothesis B.* Distortion in perception is most effectively dealt
> with by the method of client self-discovery.

There are several arguments to support these two hypotheses as a
starting point. Lack of experience includes lack of information about
self the environment. Experience can be direct or vicarious. The
client is motivated by his needs to obtain the result of the experience which he is lacking. Typically the counselor is able to obtain
the necessary information, understandings and insights by virtue of
his superior knowledge of human behavior, his superior knowledge
of environment, and his superior methods of assessing psychological
characteristics. The counselor can supply the client with the proper
information (experiences) and the client can correct his inadequacies
in a straightforward learning situation. However, if the client is
unable to utilize these counselor discoveries, the problem is not one
of lack of experience but one of distorted perceptions. The client
does not need more information or experience to distort. He needs
to correct his distortions. Since his distortions are in part a defense
against encroachment from the outside, he cannot accurately utilize
information from the counselor. Therefore, he must discover for

himself. The counselor can aid by creating a situation in which the client need not spend all of his attention and energy defending himself against his environment but can attend to the things in his own make-up which are causing him trouble. The counselor can provide a safe situation in which the client can work on material he already has on hand.

To summarize very briefly, I have suggested a theoretical model for counseling which includes the following points:

1. Biological and psycho-social needs are the energizers of behavior.
2. Behavior repertoire is made up of three elements—experience, perceptions and generalizations.
3. Behavior repertoire may be inadequate for any of three reasons —lack of experience, distortion in perception or erroneous generalizations.
4. The goal of counseling is to discover and correct inadequacies in behavior repertoire.
5. These discoveries can be made by either client or counselor. Therefore, counseling methods can be grouped under general methods: client self-discovery, and counselor discovery accompanied by interpretation.
6. Any one counseling method will not be equally effective in discovering and correcting all types of inadequacies in behavior repertoire.
7. There is an urgent need for attention to the problem of differential diagnosis leading to differential choice of treatment. Two attractive research hypotheses as a start on the problem are: (a) Lack of experience can be most effectively dealt with by counselor discovery and interpretation. (b) Distortions in perceptions can be most effectively dealt with by client self-discovery.

REFERENCES

Apostal, R. A and Miller, J. G. A manual for the use of a set of diagnostic categories. Columbia: University of Missouri Testing and Counseling Service Report No. 21, 1959.

Berdie, R. F. Counseling principles and presumptions. *J. Counsel. Psychol.*, 1959, **6**, 175-182.

Berezin, Annabel G. The development and use of a system of diagnostic categories in counseling. Unpublished doctoral dissertation, University of Missouri, 1957.

Bordin, E. S. Diagnosis in counseling and psychotherapy. *Educ. Psychol. Measmt.*, 1946, **6**, 169-184.

Dollard, J., Auld, F. W., and White, Alice M. *Steps in psychotherapy.* New York: Macmillan, 1953.

Maslow, A. H. *Motivation and personality.* New York: Harpers, 1954.

Pepinsky, H. B. The selection and use of diagnostic categories in clinical counseling. *Psychol. Monogs.*, 1948, No. 15.

Pepinsky, H. B. and Pepinsky, Pauline N. *Counseling: Theory and practice.* New York: Ronald, 1954.

Rogers, C. R. *Test of personality adjustment.* New York: Association Press, 1931.

Rogers, C. R. *The clinical treatment of the problem child.* Boston: Houghton-Mifflin, 1939.

Rogers, C. R. *Counseling and psychotherapy.* Boston: Houghton-Mifflin, 1942.

Rogers, C. R. *Client-Centered therapy.* Boston: Houghton-Mifflin, 1951.

Weiner, I. B. The role of diagnosis in a university counseling center. *J. Counsel. Psychol.*, 1959, **6**, 110-115.

Williamson, E. G., and Darley, J. G. *Student personnel work.* New York: McGraw-Hill, 1937.

13. THE CHARACTERISTICS OF A HELPING RELATIONSHIP

Carl R. Rogers

My interest in psychotherapy has brought about in me an interest in every kind of helping relationship. By this term I mean a

This address was delivered during the APGA Convention, held at the Sheraton-Jefferson Hotel, St. Louis, Missouri, March 31-April 3, 1958. Reprinted by permission of the author and *Personnel and Guidance Journal,* XXXVII, No. 1 (September, 1958), 6-16. This article also appears in Dr. Rogers' book, *On Becoming a Person* (Boston: Houghton Mifflin Company, 1961), pp. 39-58.

relationship in which at least one of the parties has the intent of promoting the growth, development, maturity, improved functioning, improved coping with life of the other. The other, in this sense, may be one individual or a group. To put it in another way, a helping relationship might be defined as one in which one of the participants intends that there should come about, in one or both parties, more appreciation of, more expression of, more functional use of the latent inner resources of the individual.

Now it is obvious that such a definition covers a wide range of relationships which usually are intended to facilitate growth. It would certainly include the relationship between mother and child, father and child. It would include the relationship between the physician and his patient. The relationship between teacher and pupil would often come under this definition, though some teachers would not have the promotion of growth as their intent. It includes almost all counselor-client relationships, whether we are speaking of educational counseling, vocational counseling, or personal counseling. In this last-mentioned area it would include the wide range of relationships between the psychotherapist and the hospitalized psychotic, the therapist and the troubled or neurotic individual, and the relationship between the therapist and the increasing number of so-called "normal" individuals who enter therapy to improve their own functioning or accelerate their personal growth.

These are largely one-to-one relationships. But we should also think of the large number of individual-group interactions which are intended as helping relationships. Some administrators intend that their relationship to their staff groups shall be of the sort which promotes growth, though other administrators would not have this purpose. The interaction between the group therapy leader and his group belongs here. So does the relationship of the community consultant to a community group. Increasingly the interaction between the industrial consultant and a management group is intended as a helping relationship. Perhaps this listing will point up the fact that a great many of the relationships in which we and others are involved fall within this category of interactions in which there is the purpose of promoting development and more mature and adequate functioning.

THE QUESTION

But what are the characteristics of those relationships which *do*
help, which do facilitate growth? And at the other end of the scale
is it possible to discern those characteristics which make a relationship unhelpful, even though it was the sincere intent to promote
growth and development? It is to these questions, particularly the
first, that I would like to take you with me over some of the paths
I have explored, and to tell you where I am, as of now, in my thinking on these issues.

THE ANSWERS GIVEN BY RESEARCH

It is natural to ask first of all whether there is any empirical research which would give us an objective answer to these questions.
There has not been a large amount of research in this area as yet,
but what there is is stimulating and suggestive. I cannot report all
of it but I would like to make a somewhat extensive sampling of the
studies which have been done and state very briefly some of the findings. In so doing, over-simplification is necessary, and I am quite
aware that I am not doing full justice to the researches I am mentioning, but it may give you the feeling that factual advances are being
made and pique your curiosity enough to examine the studies themselves, if you have not already done so.

STUDIES OF ATTITUDES

Most of the studies throw light on the attitudes on the part of the
helping person which make a relationship growth-promoting or
growth-inhibiting. Let us look at some of these.

A careful study of parent-child relationships made some years ago
by Baldwin and others (1) at the Fels Institute contains interesting
evidence. Of the various clusters of parental attitudes toward children, the "acceptant-democratic" seemed most growth-facilitating.
Children of these parents with their warm and equalitarian attitudes
showed an accelerated intellectual development (an increasing IQ),
more originality, more emotional security and control, less excita-

bility than children from other types of homes. Though somewhat slow initially in social development, they were, by the time they reached school age, popular, friendly, non-aggressive leaders.

Where parents' attitudes are classed as "actively rejectant" the children show a slightly decelerated intellectual development, relatively poor use of the abilities they do possess, and some lack of originality. They are emotionally unstable, rebellious, aggressive, and quarrelsome. The children of parents with other attitude syndromes tend in various respects to fall in between these extremes.

I am sure that these findings do not surprise us as related to child development. I would like to suggest that they probably apply to other relationships as well, and that the counselor or physician or administrator who is warmly emotional and expressive, respectful of the individuality of himself and of the other, and who exhibits a non-possessive caring, probably facilitates self-realization much as does a parent with these attitudes.

Let me turn to another careful study in a very different area. Whitehorn and Betz (2, 18) investigated the degree of success achieved by young resident physicians in working with schizophrenic patients on a psychiatric ward. They chose for special study the seven who had been outstandingly helpful, and seven whose patients had shown the least degree of improvement. Each group had treated about 50 patients. The investigators examined all the available evidence to discover in what ways the A group (the successful group) differed from the B group. Several significant differences were found. The physicians in the A group tended to see the schizophrenic in terms of the personal meaning which various behaviors had to the patient, rather than seeing him as a case history or a descriptive diagnosis. They also tended to work toward goals which were oriented to the personality of the patient, rather than such goals as reducing the symptoms or curing the disease. It was found that the helpful physicians, in their day by day interaction, primarily made use of active personal participation—a person-to-person relationship. They made less use of procedures which could be classed as "passive permissive." They were even less likely to use such procedures as interpretation, instruction or advice, or emphasis upon the practical care of the patient. Finally, they were much more likely than the B group to develop a relationship in which the patient felt trust and confidence in the physician.

Although the authors cautiously emphasize that these findings relate only to the treatment of schizophrenics, I am inclined to disagree. I suspect that similar facts would be found in a research study of almost any class of helping relationship.

Another interesting study focuses upon the way in which the person being helped perceives the relationship. Heine (11) studied individuals who had gone for psychotherapeutic help to psychoanalytic, client-centered, and Adlerian therapists. Regardless of the type of therapy, these clients report similar changes in themselves. But it is their perception of the relationship which is of particular interest to us here. When asked what accounted for the changes which had occurred, they expressed some differing explanations, depending on the orientation of the therapist. But their agreement on the major elements they had found helpful was even more significant. They indicated that these attitudinal elements in the relationship accounted for the changes which had taken place in themselves: the trust they had felt in the therapist; being understood by the therapist; the feeling of independence they had had in making choices and decisions. The therapist procedure which they had found most helpful was that the therapist clarified and openly stated feelings which the client had been approaching hazily and hesitantly.

There was also a high degree of agreement among these clients, regardless of the orientation of their therapists, as to what elements had been unhelpful in the relationship. Such therapist attitudes as lack of interest, remoteness or distance, and an over-degree of sympathy, were perceived as unhelpful. As to procedures, they had found it unhelpful when therapists had given direct specific advice regarding decisions or had emphasized past history rather than present problems. Guiding suggestions mildly given were perceived in an intermediate range—neither clearly helpful nor unhelpful.

Fiedler, in a much quoted study (7), found that expert therapists of differing orientations formed similar relationships with their clients. Less well known are the elements which characterized these relationships, differentiating them from the relationships formed by less expert therapists. These elements are: an ability to understand the client's meanings and feelings; a sensitivity to the client's attitudes; a warm interest without any emotional over-involvement.

A study by Quinn (15) throws light on what is involved in understanding the client's meanings and feelings. His study is surprising in that it shows that "understanding" of the client's meanings is essentially an attitude of *desiring* to understand. Quinn presented his judges only with recorded therapist statements taken from interviews. The raters had no knowledge of what the therapist was responding to or how the client reacted to his response. Yet it was found that the degree of understanding could be judged about as well from this material as from listening to the response in context. This seems rather conclusive evidence that it is an attitude of wanting to understand which is communicated.

As to the emotional quality of the relationship, Seeman (16) found that success in psychotherapy is closely associated with a strong and growing mutual liking and respect between client and therapist.

An interesting study by Dittes (4) indicates how delicate this relationship is. Using a physiological measure, the psychogalvanic reflex, to measure the anxious or threatened or alerted reactions of the client, Dittes correlated the deviations on this measure with judge's ratings of the degree of warm acceptance and permissiveness on the part of the therapist. It was found that whenever the therapist's attitudes changed even slightly in the direction of a lesser degree of acceptance, the number of abrupt GSR deviations significantly increased. Evidently when the relationship is experienced as less acceptant the organism organizes against threat, even at the physiological level.

Without trying fully to integrate the findings from these various studies, it can at least be noted that a few things stand out. One is the fact that it is the attitudes and feelings of the therapist, rather than his theoretical orientation, which is important. His procedures and techniques are less important than his attitudes. It is also worth noting that it is the way in which his attitudes and procedures are *perceived* which makes a difference to the client, and that it is this perception which is crucial.

"Manufactured" Relationships

Let me turn to research of a very different sort, some of which you may find rather abhorrent, but which nevertheless has a bearing upon the nature of a facilitating relationship. These studies have to do with what we might think of as manufactured relationships.

Verplanck (17), Greenspoon (8) and others have shown that operant conditioning of verbal behavior is possible in a relationship. Very briefly, if the experimenter says "Mhm," or "Good," or nods his head after certain types of words or statements, those classes of words tend to increase because of being reinforced. It has been shown that using such procedures one can bring about increases in such diverse verbal categories as plural nouns, hostile words, statements of opinion. The person is completely unaware that he is being influenced in any way by these reinforcers. The implication is that by such selective reinforcement we could bring it about that the other person in the relationship would be using whatever kinds of words and making whatever kinds of statements we had decided to reinforce.

Following still further the principles of operant conditioning as developed by Skinner and his group, Lindsley (12) has shown that a chronic schizophrenic can be placed in a "helping relationship" with a machine. The machine, somewhat like a vending machine, can be set to reward a variety of types of behaviors. Initially it simply rewards—with candy, a cigarette, or the display of a picture—the lever-pressing behavior of the patient. But it is possible to set it so that many pulls on the lever may supply a hungry kitten—visible in a separate enclosure—with a drop of milk. In this case the satisfaction is an altruistic one. Plans are being developed to reward similar social or altruistic behavior directed toward another patient, placed in the next room. The only limit to the kinds of behavior which might be rewarded lies in the degree of mechanical ingenuity of the experimenter.

Lindsley reports that in some patients there has been marked clinical improvement. Personally I cannot help but be impressed by the description of one patient who had gone from a deteriorated chronic state to being given free ground privileges, this change being quite clearly associated with his interaction with the machine. Then the experimenter decided to study experimental extinction, which, put in more personal terms, means that no matter how many thousands of times the lever was pressed, no reward of any kind was forthcoming. The patient gradually regressed, grew untidy, uncommunicative, and his ground privileges had to be revoked. This (to me) pathetic incident would seem to indicate that even in a relationship to a machine, trustworthiness is important if the relationship is to be helpful.

Still another interesting study of a manufactured relationship is being carried on by Harlow and his associates (10), this time with monkeys. Infant monkeys, removed from their mothers almost immediately after birth, are, in one phase of the experiment, presented with two objects. One might be termed the "hard mother," a sloping cylinder of wire netting with a nipple from which the baby may feed. The other is a "soft mother," a similar cylinder made of foam rubber and terry cloth. Even when an infant gets all his food from the "hard mother" he clearly and increasingly prefers the "soft mother." Motion pictures show that he definitely "relates" to this object, playing with it, enjoying it, finding security in clinging to it when strange objects are near, and using that security as a home base for venturing into the frightening world. Of the many interesting and challenging implications of this study, one seems reasonably clear. It is that no amount of direct food reward can take the place of certain perceived qualities which the infant appears to need and desire.

Two Recent Studies

Let me close this wide-ranging—and perhaps perplexing—sampling of research studies with an account of two very recent investigations. The first is an experiment conducted by Ends and Page (5). Working with hardened chronic hospitalized alcoholics who had been committed to a state hospital for 60 days, they tried three different methods of group psychotherapy. The method which they believed would be most effective was therapy based on a two-factor theory of learning; a client-centered approach was expected to be second; a psychoanalytically oriented approach was expected to be least efficient. Their results showed that the therapy based upon a learning theory approach was not only not helpful, but was somewhat deleterious. The outcomes were worse than those in the control group which had no therapy. The analytically oriented therapy produced some positive gain, and the client-centered group therapy was associated with the greatest amount of positive change. Follow-up data, extending over one and one-half years, confirmed the in-hospital findings, with the lasting improvement being greatest in the client-centered approach, next in the analytic, next the control group, and least in those handled by a learning theory approach.

As I have puzzled over this study, unusual in that the approach to which the authors were committed proved *least* effective, I find a clue, I believe, in the description of the therapy based on learning theory (13). Essentially it consisted (1) of pointing out and labeling the behaviors which had proved unsatisfying, (2) of exploring objectively with the client the reasons behind these behaviors, and (3) of establishing through re-education more effective problem-solving habits. But in all of this interaction the aim, as they formulated it, was to be impersonal. The therapist "permits as little of his own personality to intrude as is humanly possible." The "therapist stresses personal anonymity in his activities, i.e., he must studiously avoid impressing the patient with his own (therapist's) individual personality characteristics." To me this seems the most likely clue to the failure of this approach, as I try to interpret the facts in the light of the other research studies. To withhold one's self as a person and to deal with the other person as an object does not have a high probability of being helpful.

The final study I wish to report is one just being completed by Halkides (9). She started from a theoretical formulation of mine regarding the necessary and sufficient conditions for therapeutic change (14). She hypothesized that there would be a significant relationship between the extent of constructive personality change in the client and four counselor variables: (1) the degree of empathic understanding of the client manifested by the counselor; (2) the degree of positive affective attitude (unconditional positive regard) manifested by the counselor toward the client; (3) the extent to which the counselor is genuine, his words matching his own internal feeling; and (4) the extent to which the counselor's response matches the client's expression in the intensity of affective expression.

To investigate these hypotheses she first selected, by multiple objective criteria, a group of 10 cases which could be classed as "most successful" and a group of 10 "least successful" cases. She then took an early and late recorded interview from each of these cases. On a random basis she picked nine client-counselor interaction units—a client statement and a counselor response—from each of these interviews. She thus had nine early interactions and nine late interactions from each case. This gave her several hundred units which were now placed in random order. The units from an early interview of an unsuccessful case might be followed by the units from a late interview of a successful case, etc.

Three judges, who did not know the cases or their degree of success, or the source of any given unit, now listened to this material four different times. They rated each unit on a seven point scale, first as to the degree of empathy, second as to the counselor's positive attitude toward the client, third as to the counselor's congruence or genuineness, and fourth as to the degree to which the counselor's response matched the emotional intensity of the client's expression.

I think all of us who knew of the study regarded it as a very bold venture. Could judges listening to single units of interaction possibly make any reliable rating of such subtle qualities as I have mentioned? And even if suitable reliability could be obtained, could 18 counselor-client interchanges from each case—a minute sampling of the hundreds or thousands of such interchanges which occurred in each case—possibly bear any relationship to the therapeutic outcome? The chance seemed slim.

The findings are surprising. It proved possible to achieve high reliability between the judges, most of the inter-judge correlations being in the 0.80's or 0.90's, except on the last variable. It was found that a high degree of empathic understanding was significantly associated, at a 0.001 level, with the more successful cases. A high degree of unconditional positive regard was likewise associated with the more successful cases, at the 0.001 level. Even the rating of the counselor's genuineness or congruence—the extent to which his words matched his feelings—was associated with the successful outcome of the case, and again at the 0.001 level of significance. Only in the investigation of the matching intensity of affective expression were the results equivocal.

It is of interest too that high ratings of these variables were not associated more significantly with units from later interviews than with units from early interviews. This means that the counselor's attitudes were quite constant throughout the interviews. If he was highly empathic, he tended to be so from first to last. If he was lacking in genuineness, this tended to be true of both early and late interviews.

As with any study, this investigation has its limitations. It is concerned with a certain type of helping relationship, psychotherapy. It investigated only four variables thought to be significant. Perhaps there are many others. Nevertheless it represents a significant advance in the study of helping relationships. Let me try to state the findings in the simplest possible fashion. It seems to indicate that the quality of the counselor's interaction with a client can be satisfactorily judged on the basis of a very small sampling of his behavior. It also means that if the counselor is congruent or transparent, so that his words are in line with his feelings rather than the two being discrepant—if the counselor likes the client, unconditionally, and if the counselor understands the essential feelings of the client as they seem to the client—then there is a strong probability that this will be an effective helping relationship.

Some Comments

These then are some of the studies which throw at least a measure of light on the nature of the helping relationship. They have investigated different facets of the problem. They have approached it from very different theoretical contexts. They have used different methods. They are not directly comparable. Yet they seem to me to point to several statements which may be made with some assurance. It seems clear that relationships which are helpful have different characteristics from relationships which are unhelpful. These differential characteristics have to do primarily with the attitudes of the helping person on the one hand and with the perception of the relationship by the "helpee" on the other. It is equally clear that the studies thus far made do not give us any final answers as to what is a helping relationship, nor how it is to be formed.

Some ques. Carl Rogers says the counselor
Questions you should ask himself

How Can I Create a Helping Relationship?
in creating a " " in C.C.-thera

I believe each of us working in the field of human relationships has a similar problem in knowing how to use such research knowledge. We cannot slavishly follow such findings in a mechanical way or we destroy the personal qualities which these very studies show to be valuable. It seems to me that we have to use these studies, testing them against our own experience and forming new and further personal hypotheses to use and test in our own further personal relationships.

So rather than try to tell you how you should use the findings I have presented I should like to tell you the kind of questions which these studies and my own clinical experience raise for me, and some of the tentative and changing hypotheses which guide my behavior as I enter into what I hope may be helping relationships, whether with students, staff, family, or clients. Let me list a number of these questions and considerations.

1. Can I *be* in some way which will be perceived by the other person as trustworthy, as dependable or consistent in some deep sense? Both research and experience indicate that this is very important, and over the years I have found what I believe are deeper and better ways of answering this question. I used to feel that if I fulfilled all the outer conditions of trustworthiness—keeping appointments, respecting the confidential nature of the interviews, etc.— and if I acted consistently the same during the interviews, then this condition would be fulfilled. But experience drove home the fact that to act consistently acceptant, for example, if in fact I was feeling annoyed or skeptical or some other non-acceptant feeling, was certain in the long run to be perceived as inconsistent or untrustworthy. I have come to recognize that being trustworthy does not demand that I be rigidly consistent but that I be dependably real. The term congruent is one I have used to describe the way I would like to be. By this I mean that whatever feeling or attitude I am experiencing would be matched by my awareness of that attitude. When this is true, then I am a unified or integrated person in that moment, and hence I can *be* whatever I deeply *am*. This is a reality which I find others experience as dependable.

2. A very closely related question is this: Can I be expressive enough as a person that what I am will be communicated unambiguously? I believe that most of my failures to achieve a helping relationship can be traced to unsatisfactory answers to these two questions. When I am experiencing an attitude of annoyance toward another person but am unaware of it, then my communication contains contradictory messages. My words are giving one message, but I am also in subtle ways communicating the annoyance I feel and this confuses the other person and makes him distrustful, though he too may be unaware of what is causing the difficulty. When as a parent or a therapist or a teacher or an administrator I fail to listen to what is going on in me, fail because of my own defensiveness to sense my own feelings, then this kind of failure seems to result. It has made it seem to me that the most basic learning for anyone who hopes to establish any kind of helping relationship is that it is safe to be transparently real. If in a given relationship I am reasonably congruent, if no feelings relevant to the relationship are hidden either to me or the other person, then I can be almost sure that the relationship will be a helpful one.

One way of putting this which may seem strange to you is that if I can form a helping relationship to myself—if I can be sensitively aware of and acceptant toward my own feelings—then the likelihood is great that I can form a helping relationship toward another.

Now, acceptantly to be what I am, in this sense, and to permit this to show through to the other person, is the most difficult task I know and one I never fully achieve. But to realize that this *is* my task has been most rewarding because it has helped me to find what has gone wrong with interpersonal relationships which have become snarled and to put them on a constructive track again. It has meant that if I am to facilitate the personal growth of others in relation to me, then I must grow, and while this is often painful it is also enriching.

3. A third question is: Can I let myself experience positive attitudes toward this other person—attitudes of warmth, caring, liking, interest, respect? It is not easy. I find in myself, and feel that I often see in others, a certain amount of fear of these feelings. We are afraid that if we let ourselves freely experience these positive feelings toward another we may be trapped by them. They may lead to demands on us or we may be disappointed in our trust, and these outcomes we fear. So as a reaction we tend to build up distance between ourselves and others—aloofness, a "professional" attitude, an impersonal relationship.

I feel quite strongly that one of the important reasons for the professionalization of every field is that it helps to keep this distance. In the clinical areas we develop elaborate diagnostic formulations, seeing the person as an object. In teaching and in administration we develop all kinds of evaluative procedures, so that again the person is perceived as an object. In these ways, I believe, we can keep ourselves from experiencing the caring which would exist if we recognized the relationship as one between two persons. It is a real achievement when we can learn, even in certain relationships or at certain times in those relationships, that it is safe to care, that it is safe to relate to the other as a person for whom we have positive feelings.

4. Another question the importance of which I have learned in my own experience is: Can I be strong enough as a person to be separate from the other? Can I be a sturdy respecter of my own feelings, my own needs, as well as his? Can I own and, if need be, express my own feelings as something belonging to me and separate from his feelings? Am I strong enough in my own separateness that I will not be downcast by his depression, frightened by his fear, nor engulfed by his dependency? Is my inner self hardy enough to realize that I am not destroyed by his anger, taken over by his need for dependence, nor enslaved by his love, but that I exist separate from him with feelings and rights of my own? When I can freely feel this strength of being a separate person, then I find that I can let myself go much more deeply in understanding and accepting him because I am not fearful of losing myself.

5. The next question is closely related. Am I secure enough within myself to permit him his separateness? Can I permit him to be what he is—honest or deceitful, infantile or adult, despairing or over-confident? Can I give him the freedom to be? Or do I feel that he should follow my advice, or remain somewhat dependent on me, or mold himself after me? In this connection I think of the interesting small study by Farson (6) which found that the less well adjusted and less competent counselor tends to induce conformity to himself, to have clients who model themselves after him. On the other hand, the better adjusted and more competent counselor can interact with a client through many interviews without interfering with the freedom of the client to develop a personality quite separate from that of his therapist. I should prefer to be in this latter class, whether as parent or supervisor or counselor.

6. Another question I ask myself is: Can I let myself enter fully into the world of his feelings and personal meanings and see these as he does? Can I step into his private world so completely that I lose all desire to evaluate or judge it? Can I enter it so sensitively that I can move about in it freely, without tramping on meanings

which are precious to him? Can I sense it so accurately that I can catch not only the meanings of his experience which are obvious to him, but those meanings which are only implicit, which he sees only dimly or as confusion? Can I extend this understanding without limit? I think of the client who said, "Whenever I find someone who understands a *part* of me at the time, then it never fails that a point is reached where I know they're *not* understanding me again. . . . What I've looked for so hard is for someone to understand."

For myself I find it easier to feel this kind of understanding, and to communicate it, to individual clients than to students in a class or staff members in a group in which I am involved. There is a strong temptation to set students "straight," or to point out to a staff member the errors in his thinking. Yet when I can permit myself to understand in these situations, it is mutually rewarding. And with clients in therapy, I am often impressed with the fact that even a minimal amount of empathic understanding—a bumbling and faulty attempt to catch the confused complexity of the client's meaning—is helpful, though there is no doubt that it is most helpful when I can see and formulate clearly the meanings in his experiencing which for him have been unclear and tangled.

7. Still another issue is whether I can be acceptant of each facet of this other person which he presents to me. Can I receive the client as he is? Can I communicate this attitude? Or can I only receive him conditionally, acceptant of some aspects of his feelings and silently or openly disapproving of other aspects? It has been my experience that when my attitude is conditional, then he cannot change or grow in those respects in which I cannot fully receive him. And when—afterward and sometimes too late—I try to discover why I have been unable to accept him in every respect, I usually discover that it is because I have been frightened or threatened in myself by some aspect of his feelings. If I am to be more helpful, then I must myself grow and accept myself in these respects.

8. A very practical issue is raised by the question: Can I act with sufficient sensitivity in the relationship that my behavior will not be perceived as a threat? The work we are beginning to do in studying the physiological concomitants of psychotherapy confirms the research by Dittes in indicating how easily individuals are threatened at a physiological level. The psychogalvanic reflex—the measure of skin conductance—takes a sharp dip when the therapist responds

with some word which is just a little stronger than the client's feelings. And to a phrase such as, "My, you *do* look upset," the needle swings almost off the paper. My desire to avoid even such minor threats is not due to a hypersensitivity about my client. It is simply due to the conviction based on experience that if I can free him as completely as possible from external threat, then he can begin to experience and to deal with the internal feelings and conflicts which he finds threatening within himself.

9) A specific aspect of the preceding question but an important one is: Can I free him from the threat of external evaluation? In almost every phase of our lives—at home, at school, at work—we find ourselves under the rewards and punishments of external judgments. "That's good"; "that's naughty." "That's worth an A"; "that's a failure." "That's good counseling"; "that's poor counseling." Such judgments are a part of our lives from infancy to old age. I believe they have a certain social usefulness to institutions and organizations such as schools and professions. Like everyone else I find myself all too often making such evaluations. But, in my experience, they do not make for personal growth and hence I do not believe that they are a part of a helping relationship. Curiously enough a positive evaluation is as threatening in the long run as a negative one, since to inform someone that he is good implies that you also have the right to tell him he is bad. So I have come to feel that the more I can keep a relationship free of judgment and evaluation, the more this will permit the other person to reach the point where he recognizes that the locus of evaluation, the center of responsibility, lies within himself. The meaning and value of his experience is in the last analysis something which is up to him, and no amount of external judgment can alter this. So I should like to work toward a relationship in which I am not, even in my own feelings, evaluating him. This I believe can set him free to be a self-responsible person.

10) One last question: Can I meet this other individual as a person who is in process of *becoming,* or will I be bound by his past and by my past? If, in my encounter with him, I am dealing with him as an immature child, an ignorant student, a neurotic personality, or a psychopath, each of these concepts of mine limits what he can be in the relationship. Martin Buber, the existentialist philosopher of the University of Jerusalem, has a phrase, "confirming the other," which has had meaning for me. He says "Confirming means . . .

accepting the whole potentiality of the other . . . I can recognize in him, know in him, the person he has been . . . *created* to become . . . I confirm him in myself, and then in him, in relation to this potentiality that . . . can now be developed, can evolve" (3). If I accept the other person as something fixed, already diagnosed and classified, already shaped by his past, then I am doing my part to confirm this limited hypothesis. If I accept him as a process of becoming, then I am doing what I can to confirm or make real his potentialities.

It is at this point that I see Verplanck, Lindsley, and Skinner, working in operant conditioning, coming together with Buber, the philosopher or mystic. At least they come together in principle, in an odd way. If I see a relationship as only an opportunity to reinforce certain types of words or opinions in the other, then I tend to confirm him as an object—a basically mechanical, manipulable object. And if I see this as his potentiality, he tends to act in ways which support this hypothesis. If, on the other hand, I see a relationship as an opportunity to "reinforce" *all* that he is, the person that he is with all his existent potentialities, then he tends to act in ways which support *this* hypothesis. I have then—to use Buber's term— confirmed him as a living person, capable of creative inner development. Personally I prefer this second type of hypothesis.

CONCLUSION

In the early portion of this paper I reviewed some of the contributions which research is making to our knowledge *about* relationships. Endeavoring to keep that knowledge in mind I then took up the kind of questions which arise from an inner and subjective point of view as I enter, as a person, into relationships. If I could, in myself, answer all the questions I have raised in the affirmative, then I believe that any relationships in which I was involved would be helping relationships, would involve growth. But I cannot give a positive answer to most of these questions. I can only work in the direction of a positive answer.

This has raised in my mind the strong suspicion that the optimal helping relationship is the kind of relationship created by a person

Rogers says

who is psychologically mature. Or to put it in another way, the degree to which I can create relationships which facilitate the growth of others as separate persons is a measure of the growth I have achieved in myself. In some respects this is a disturbing thought, but it is also a promising or challenging one. It would indicate that if I am interested in creating helping relationships I have a fascinating life-time job ahead of me, stretching and developing my potentialities in the direction of growth.

I am left with the uncomfortable thought that what I have been working out for myself in this paper may have little relationship to your interests and your work. If so, I regret it. But I am at least partially comforted by the fact that all of us who are working in the field of human relationships and trying to understand the basic orderliness of that field are engaged in the most crucial enterprise in today's world. If we are thoughtfully trying to understand our tasks as administrators, teachers, educational counselors, vocational counselors, therapists, then we are working on the problem which will determine the future of this planet. For it is not upon the physical sciences that the future will depend. It is upon us who are trying to understand and deal with the interactions between human beings— who are trying to create helping relationships. So I hope that the questions I ask of myself will be of some use to you in gaining understanding and perspective as you endeavor, in your way, to facilitate growth in your relationships.

REFERENCES

1. Baldwin, A. L., Kalhorn, J., & Breese, F. H. Patterns of parent behavior. *Psychol. Monogr.,* 1945, **58,** No. 268, 1-75.

2. Betz, B. J., & Whitehorn, J. C. The relationship of the therapist to the outcome of therapy in schizophrenia. *Psychiat. Research Reports #5. Research techniques in schizophrenia.* Washington, D. C.: American Psychiatric Association, 1956, 89-117.

3. Buber, M., & Rogers, C. Transcription of dialogue held April 18, 1957, Ann Arbor, Mich. Unpublished manuscript.

4. Dittes, J. E. Galvanic skin response as a measure of patient's reaction to therapist's permissiveness. *J. abnorm. soc. Psychol.,* 1957, **55,** 295-303.

5. Ends, E. J., & Page, C. W. A study of three types of group psychotherapy with hospitalized male inebriates. *Quar. J. Stud. Alcohol,* 1957, **18,** 263-277.

6. Farson, R. E. Introjection in the psychotherapeutic relationship. Unpublished doctoral dissertation, University of Chicago, 1955.

7. Fiedler, F. E. Quantitative studies on the role of therapists' feelings toward their patients. In Mowrer, O. H. (Ed.), *Psychotherapy: theory and research.* New York: Ronald Press, 1953, Chap. 12.

8. Greenspoon, J. The reinforcing effect of two spoken sounds on the frequency of two responses. *Amer. J. Psychol.,* 1955, **68,** 409-416.

9. Halkides, G. An experimental study of four conditions necessary for therapeutic change. Unpublished doctoral dissertation, University of Chicago, 1958.

10. Harlow, H., & Associates. Experiment in progress, as reported by Robert Zimmerman.

11. Heine, R. W. A comparison of patients' reports on psychotherapeutic experience with psychoanalytic, nondirective, and Adlerian therapists. Unpublished doctoral dissertation, University of Chicago, 1950.

12. Lindsley, O. R. Operant conditioning methods applied to research in chronic schizophrenia. *Psychiat. Research Reports #5. Research techniques in schizophrenia.* Washington, D. C.: American Psychiatric Association, 1956, 118-153.

13. Page, C. W., & Ends, E. J. A review and synthesis of the literature suggesting a psychotherapeutic technique based on two-factor learning theory. Unpublished manuscript, loaned to the writer.

14. Rogers, C. R. The necessary and sufficient conditions of psychotherapeutic personality change. *J. consult. Psychol.,* 1957, **21,** 95-103.

15. Quinn, R. D. Psychotherapists' expressions as an index to the quality of early therapeutic relationships. Unpublished doctoral dissertation, University of Chicago, 1950.

16. Seeman, J. Counselor judgments of therapeutic process and outcome. In Rogers, C. R., & Dymond, R. F. (Eds.), *Psychotherapy and personality change.* Chicago: University of Chicago Press, 1954, Chap. 7.

17. Verplanck, W. S. The control of the content of conversation: reinforcement of statements of opinion. *J. abnorm. soc. Psychol.,* 1955, **51,** 668-676.

18. Whitehorn, J. C., & Betz, B. J. A study of psychotherapeutic relationships between physicians and schizophrenic patients. *Amer. J. Psychiat.,* 1954, **111,** 321-331.

14. DIFFERENTIAL FACTORS BETWEEN ELEMENTARY AND SECONDARY SCHOOL COUNSELING

Herman J. Peters

"Paradoxical though it may seem, society as a whole must come to the aid of the individual—finding ways to identify him as a unique person, and to place him alongside his fellow men in ways which will not inhibit or destroy his individuality. By its educational system, its public and private institutional practices, and perhaps most importantly, by its attitude toward the creative person, a free society can actively insure its own constant invigoration."—"The Rockefeller Report" on Education. (Quoted in the U. S. Office of Education Circular No. 553—Guide to the National Defense Education Act of 1958.)

Interest in guidance, and in particular counseling, at the elementary and secondary school has prompted me to raise questions as to either one's singularity of distinguishing hallmarks. It is in the pupil's school career that many of the pristine encounters with one's individuality form patterns of the self. The foundation and direction of a vigorous adulthood of productivity has so very often its nurturing in the school years.

For too long, many of us have been so busy in the doing that we have had little time to challenge our guidance activities. Perhaps more fundamental to our activities is a concern for thinking through the rationale for our guidance procedures. The importance of an intellectual look at our work is well emphasized by the Pepinskys: "Theoretical Approaches, which have the function for gaining and accounting for the behavior of clients, can serve as useful guides to counselor activities with clients, as in the broad field of scientific endeavor, or behavior science in particular, a theoretical approach to the behavior of clients calls for conceptual rigor." (9:19) With this set, let us proceed to look at some of the differential factors between elementary and secondary school counseling.

Reprinted by permission of the author and *The School Counselor,* VII, No. 1 (October, 1959), 3-11. Copyright 1959 by The American School Counselor Association.

The Question

Should we accept the current thinking and research findings in counseling as being fully or partly applicable to the elementary and/or secondary school? Should we be encapsulated in the college and clinic approaches, as excellent as some of them are? Too, are there differences between counseling in the elementary school and counseling in the secondary school? Might we do a better job in counseling in the elementary and secondary schools, if we better understood the distinguishing characteristics that define the counseling relationship?

At this point, it is well to give my definition of counseling. Counseling is a one to one psychological relationship where in privacy a competently trained counselor assists a pupil to think through his concerns. The focus of this paper is on differential factors in counseling rather than the larger area of guidance. Of course, any consideration of differences will overlap with other phases of guidance work. It is hoped that this discussion might serve as a stimulus for research in the area of counseling in the elementary or secondary school.

Some Major Differences

One of the major differences between counseling in the elementary and secondary schools lies within the general framework of the central purpose of guidance in each school level. "Guidance in the elementary school should assist the pupil to develop a harmonious and integrated personality core through carefully planned school experiences which reflect the integration of the forces impinging on the individual. This is in contrast to guidance services in the secondary school which assist adolescents to extend themselves to the optimum in all the various aspects of adolescent and adult living, such as educational planning, career choice, personal relationships, and living with one's self." (6:445) The integration of the various aspects of living begins to change to differentiation during the junior high school years. Thus, this becomes a crucial period for effective counseling of the pupils. The pupil has become accustomed to correlating his behavior with the group during the elementary school years. Then with a seemingly disconcerting suddenness the high school student must differentiate his life plans in terms of his unique abilities and interests.

The impact of the organizations of the elementary and secondary schools defines very often the possibilities in counseling. The extended and intensive relationship with one teacher or at most two or three in the elementary school is in contrast to the brief and often superficial relationship with school staff in the secondary school. Unless the elementary school is large, the opportunities for environmental manipulation as an outcome of counseling are non-existent. The flexible structure within the day long elementary classroom permits possibilities for counseling through activity interviews and conferences. The comparatively unstructured time sequence may permit a teacher to engage in his secondary role of counselor with a child in helping him look at his behavior as he progresses through a class activity which allows for differential performances by the many pupils. Other aspects of the organization have their impact on counseling, e.g. the limited or non-existent course choices in the elementary grades versus the increasing number of courses for possible selection in senior high school. Thus, *course* choice is not a problem of counseling in the elementary school. However, should not there be concern for *subject* matter choice in the elementary school? Is it not here that interest must begin for the almost irreversible choice of high school? How may this difference be reconciled in counseling the pupil?

A third major difference is the significantly greater dependency relationship involving parents of elementary school children. Not only the approbation of behavior but also the support of the counseling relationship by the adult is almost a universal when counseling with elementary school children. Although the parental rights continue throughout high school, the very nature of the growing adolescent in our culture reduces the adolescent's concern about what parents think. The paradox of this situation is that in many ways the elementary child has more freedom to act and thus fewer problems for counseling. The adolescent is on the search for maturity and to the dismay of his elders breaks through the limits of behavior as set by the adults. Thus, counseling on the search for meaning is unique to the adolescent and adult as contrasted to the elementary child. Jersild states that, "As they grow older, children tend to become somewhat subdued in their quest for meaning. By the time they have reached adolescence, there are many who have learned that it is not good to inquire too much into the meaning of things. It is this attitude that makes it possible for many adolescents to learn what is assigned at school even when it has little or no personal significance. There are many who do not have as much freedom as they had when they were small to ask questions of what, where, whether, and why? Yet in all adolescents, as in all human beings, this search for meaning is an essential quality and it goes on in various ways." (7:25) Do we through counseling activity help the adolescent in his search for meaning?

Fourth, the nature of the elementary curriculum usually focuses on subject matter which is non-personal in the sense that it does not require a close look at one's abilities and past performances. The secondary curriculum is similar, but because of the parcelled organization of the secondary schools, there are a number, often many, of discrete school events where the pupil is encouraged to look at himself in relation to a program of studies to be selected. This in itself assists some pupils to be in a state of readiness for counseling. Blair and Burton state that in pre-adolescence "if school subjects were so organized as to include the personal and social problems of these children rather than chronological organization of history or the logical organization of geography, opportunity could be provided for these boys and girls to use their abilities to be realistic and begin to see the causal relations in human behavior." (3:73) Does the curriculum make a difference for counseling purposes?

A fifth difference overlaps with the nature of the school and may be tersely stated in terms of the core of psychological development. The focus of childhood psychological functioning is on security, especially in his family relationships. In the junior high school pupil, self-expression seems to be the core from which spring phases of behavior. The senior high school student centers his behavior in terms of peer relationships. Should not many counseling concerns be considered in terms of these key factors determining behavior? More specifically, we will look at the junior high school pupil. Piaget, Isaacs, and Gruenberg (3) report in their individual studies that it is in pre-adolescence that the individual begins to seek reality, objectively, and a concept of self distinguishable from the outer world. Thus, the reports indicate, this gives us some basis for the counseling of junior high school pupils involving dissemination of facts and materials, e.g. vocational information. Insight is also approaching a high level of development, thus affording a more verbalized counseling relationship.

Before discussing more of the differences relating specifically to the counseling process, it is in order to reflect for a moment on who does the counseling in the elementary and secondary schools.

The responsibility for counseling varies greatly between the elementary and secondary schools. Currently, the organizational pattern of the elementary schools gives the teacher the counseling role, secondary only to the instructional assignment. The benefits of this secondary type of counseling must be limited. The high school counselor has counseling as a primary function. Also, the worker usually is strongest in his major role. Therefore, too often the counseling function in the elementary school becomes a burden rather than an important secondary function. Too many teachers today may do effective counseling by chance rather than on a basis of sound training. Thus, a sixth difference lies in the primary responsibility for counseling in the elementary and secondary schools.

Specific to the counseling process is motivation to seek or to refer one's self for counseling. The adult who seeks counseling comes with a concern. The adolescent may voluntarily seek an appointment with his school counselor. The elementary school child does not come to the counseling setting ready to work on a concern. Probably the child comes sensing that it is he upon whom the counselor (teacher to him) will work. The referral of self would subsume a state of readiness to begin counseling on the individual's concern. Thus, the extrinsic motivation most always required for starting counseling with the elementary school child distinguishes it from the many voluntary self-referrals by adolescents.

As we look more closely at the counseling process, we shall see some areas of profound differences as relates to elementary and secondary school counseling. Although guidance is primarily concerned with normal pupils, we may gain from considering the thinking of those who deal with severely disturbed boys and girls.

Bijou states that "Historically, Anna Freud initially attempted to apply the techniques developed for the neurotic adult to the child.

It soon became apparent to her that the child treatment situation differed from that of the adult in many significant details and that techniques applicable to adults would have to be modified. Many other therapists recently concurred with her impressions." (2:611) Perhaps nowhere else is this statement substantiated as in the variance between the child and the adolescent in the capacity to relate feelings and concerns. The child cannot verbalize as extensively as the adolescent nor is he inclined to do so if he does have an unusual verbal capacity. Also, the child is beginning to think through the nature of problem solving but maturationally and experimentally, he has far to go. Too, the capacity to relate feelings is clouded by the child's inability to discern with clarity the differences in his fantasy concerns and those which are fantasy but have the additional ingredient of trouble. Thus, the counseling function in the elementary school runs into a barrier, a rather typical one, of the child's minimal ability to relate his feelings. Too, the emotional tones of adolescence may give pressure to an adolescent to relate his feelings.

A ninth difference is the child or adolescent's concept of time. The younger child views time as NOW. The adolescent can view actions not only in the present but also in the future. He also begins to think back to "When I was a little boy." Thus, the adolescent has a number of reference points other than the immediate present. It is difficult to counsel when one has few conscious time reference points. Behavior as viewed primarily in the present may not seem to the pupil to need revision or change. Behavior viewed as a basis for future action does imply the need for at least a consideration of change to meet the continuing demands of daily living—now and in the future. For the younger pupil, contiguity of behavior with time makes both almost congruent. With the adolescent years there comes a pulling apart of the circle of behavior and its contiguous time dimensions. Thus, there may be an adolescent need to think through next steps in daily living.

The therapeutic relationship in the counseling interview is considered by many to be the vital force for change in the counselee. Certainly it is this phase of counseling, above all others, that the elementary teacher can and often does employ in individual work with boys and girls. The firm yet permissive, the free yet limited, the just never punitive, the authoritative never authoritarian climate can foster changes, often imperceptible, in the sensitive, albeit not fully developed, rational young child. The same might apply to the adolescent in the counseling interview but unless one has unusual artistry in blending the above qualities into the classroom, an overdose can cause bedlam in the secondary school. The adolescent may misinterpret these qualities as boundless freedom. Of course, this does not mean to go toward the negative end of the continuum of teacher control. It does mean that the latitude for positive aspects of the emotional climate may not be as wide in the secondary school as in the elementary grades.

Fully aware that so many of the differences between counseling in the framework of this paper may be a matter of degree, it is, nevertheless, important to consider each because degree of the quality or aspect under consideration may be so slight or great as to preclude its effectiveness in counseling. Counselee responsibility also falls into this category. Robinson in his scholarly work states that "An important goal in counseling is developing willingness in the client to take responsibility for attacking his problems. That is, the client should be able to meet NEW problems on his own or at least need less help than he did before he came for counseling. Growth in such maturity might be measured by judging the degree to which the client takes on responsibility, in successive interviews, for clarifying his problems and planning what to do about them." (12:110) Counseling in the elementary school may help to give the child more self responsibility but it is certainly not of the magnitude one finds in Robinson's statement which is applicable for older youth and adults. Perhaps in the elementary years, the counselor needs to give reassurance and support, procedures which are polemic in a discussion of counseling of youth and adults.

A twelfth difference may be seen in the adult's perceptions of certain kinds of behaviors in the child which may be referred to as annoyances and which the child may or may not view as hurdles. These same kinds of behaviors in the adolescent become obstacles as they grow in proportion to the individual's fantasying about them. Thus, it becomes difficult at the child level to know whether the child will *grow out* of these annoying behaviors or *grow into* a contumacious individual. Here is but another challenge for the counselor.

At this point let us look, briefly to be sure, at what may be done to think through the counseling function in the elementary grades.

Granted that much more needs to be done at the high school level, one can safely argue that more of the adult procedures will work here and that we are lagging behind in investigating counseling for the elementary school boy or girl. Whether one accepts in full, in part or not at all, the psychoanalytic theories, one must give due consideration to the ideas presented by some of its proponents. What Slavson says in the following quotation surely has implications for counseling of children. Slavson states that, "There is a sharp difference between psychotherapy for adults and psychotherapy for children."

"The most outstanding characteristics of a child are his comparatively weak ego organization and his limited ability to deal with inner impulses and external demands. The second difference, which is a direct outgrowth of the first, is the basically narcissistic quality of the child's libido organization, his lack of ego control, hence impulsiveness, his still narcissistic character, hence self-indulgence and feelings of omnipotence. The third distinction is the surface nature of his unconscious. One is impressed with the readiness and almost complete unself-consciousness with which young children act out and speak about matters that are embarrassing to an older person. This can be attributed to the incomplete superego development, the lack of repressive forces (ego), and undeveloped sublimation channels. Finally, the child's identifications are in a fluid state." (13:143)

To me this offers a sound base for re-emphasizing the need for support, reassurance and adult initiative in helping the child. Initiative in the sense of helping the child gain a sense of direction is intended; certainly not blind submissiveness of the child. Thus, the counselor of children assumes more responsibility, not so much for the children's actions as he does for deciding the direction of what is acceptable behavior. To help the child see his purpose in what he is doing is a far better approach than to try, and that's about all one would be doing, to help him see the raison d'etre for his behavior. Dreikurs states it well when he says, "An effective discussion with the child should not be concerned with WHY the child misbehaves or fails, why he acts as he does: it should lead to an explanation of the PURPOSE for which he does it." (5:46) Dreikurs continues by emphasizing that it is more important to look at the child and what he wants—than to look at what caused this behavior. "Such interpretations of his true intentions evoke, if correct, an immediate and characteristic reaction. This automatic reaction consists of a roguish smile and a peculiar twinkle of the eyes, a so-called 'recognition reflex.' The child need not say one word, or he may even say 'no'; but his facial expression gives him away." (5:47) Although the sincere and earnest relationship is required in all counseling, it is in this recognition reflex that one may see a different action in elementary counseling than in senior high school. By the time of late adolescence, the boy or girl has learned to a more or less degree to wear the mask of personality. If the relationship exists, the teacher in his counseling function in the elementary or secondary setting may say, "I wonder whether you would like to talk more about . . .", "Could you be doing this because . . .", "Perhaps you are trying to do . . ."

As one reflects on the differences between elementary and secondary school counseling, as one tries to see several steps or ideas that might improve counseling in these boys and girls, the basic question of "WHO NEEDS COUNSELING?" arises. Do elementary teachers and secondary teachers look in similar ways upon similar kinds of students in terms of guidance help needed? Using the Robinson questionnaire WHAT SHOULD BE DONE? (11:500) and a modification of it for the elementary school child (11:501) Mangan and I decided to search for similarities and differences. A comparison of the combined participants of 222 elementary and secondary school teachers and the results by elementary and secondary school teachers were made. The teachers were from a variety of schools with a variety of cultural frameworks.

It was interesting to note that a trend existed for more secondary school teachers to recommend intensive counseling and elementary school teachers to recommend special non-conference methods out of the four categories given for rating on the questionnaires.

Each questionnaire contained 14 paragraph descriptions of 14 typical yet hypothetical pupils. The rater then indicated which of the following types of guidance might be best for each pupil:

0   Probably no need for guidance program to work with this student.

1   Routine use made of conferences and activities; nothing especially planned for student at this time.

2   Special plans made to fit this student's needs with particular

emphasis placed on non-conference personnel methods, e.g., activities, readings, change of grade, work experience, etc.

3   Special plans made to fit this student's needs with particular emphasis placed on the school providing intensive counseling help.

4   Refer the student to some agency outside of the school for help.

Full realization was made of the fact that these were severely brief character portraits.

In this paper some of the differences between elementary school and secondary school counseling have been set forth. These were differences based on the purposes of guidance.

Several basic points for a reconsideration of the elementary school counseling function were presented: (1) the need to study the theory of the ego organization of the child, (2) the need to use the procedure of explaining the "purpose" rather than the "why" of the child's behavior to the child, and (3) a look at teachers' responses to the questionnaire involving who needs what kind of guidance.

In closing let us think of Kowitz and Kowitz's statement pertinent to the topic and as given in their 1959 book, *Guidance in the Elementary Classroom*: "Although there have been a number of advances in therapy with children, few of these are within the area of counseling. The effectiveness of the counseling process with elementary school children is a field which deserves careful study and thorough research." (8:142)

BIBLIOGRAPHY

1. Adler, Alfred. *The Education of the Individual.* New York: Philosophical Library, 1958.
2. Bijou, Sidney W. "Therapeutic Techniques with Children" in L. A. Pennington and Irwin A. Berg, *An Introduction to Clinical Psychology.* New York: The Ronald Press Company, 1954, pp. 608-631.
3. Blair, Arthur W. and William H. Burton. *Growth and Development of the Pre-Adolescent.* New York: Appleton-Century-Crofts, Inc., 1951.
4. Board of Education—City of New York. *Guidance of Children in Elementary Schools.* New York: Board of Education, 1956.
5. Dreikurs, Rudolph. *Psychology in the Classroom.* New York: Harper and Brothers, 1957.
6. Farwell, Gail F. and Peters, Herman J. "Guidance: A Longitudinal and

a Differential View," *The Elementary School Journal.* Vol. 57, No. 8, May 1957, pp. 442-445.

7. Jersild, Arthur T. *The Psychology of Adolescence,* New York: McGraw-Hill Book Company, 1957.

8. Kowitz, Gerald T. and Norma G. Kowitz. *Guidance in the Elementary Classroom.* New York: McGraw-Hill Book Co., Inc., 1959.

9. Pepinsky, Harold B. and Pauline Pepinsky. *Counseling Theory and Practice.* New York: The Ronald Press Co., 1954.

10. Polster, Arthur H. "Counseling in the Elementary School" *California Journal of Elementary Education.* Vol. 4, No. 1, August, 1935, pp. 51-54.

11. Robinson, Francis P. "Guidance for All: In Principle and Practice" *The Personnel and Guidance Journal.* Vol. 31, No. 8, May, 1953, pp. 500-504.

12. Robinson, Francis P. *Principles and Procedures in Student Counseling.* New York: Harper and Brothers, 1950.

13. Slavson, S. R. *Child Psychotherapy.* New York: Columbia University Press, 1952.

14. Wells, Marian. "Counseling the Elementary School Child" *The National Elementary Principal.* Vol. 27, February, 1948, pp. 44-45.

15. WHAT IS DIFFERENT ABOUT HIGH SCHOOL COUNSELING?

Herman J. Peters and Gail F. Farwell

Counseling may be defined as a person-to-person interaction in private in which the counselor assists the counselee in adjusting to some concern or concerns. Most books concerning counseling are based upon college and/or clinical counseling situations. However, two books, one by Glenn E. Smith and the other by Hamrin and Paulson, stand out because they focus attention upon counseling in the high-school setting. The question arises as to whether the data obtained from college and clinical case studies and research yield principles and procedures which are applicable to high-school counseling. Thus, the following issues are raised as suggesting useful

Reprinted by permission of the authors and *The School Counselor*, V, No. 4 (May, 1958), 67-70. Copyright 1958 by The American School Counselor Association.

questions rather than as stating differences between high-school and college counseling. Research findings that are available to substantiate or refute any such differences are scattered, and need to be published in a more accessible form.

Some queries concerning high-school counseling are as follows: (1) Is the role of the high-school counselor less known to possible clientele than that of the counselor in a college or clinical setting? Though the students' perceptions of the role of the counselor may vary from school to school, often it seems that students perceive the counselor only as a schedule maker, program producer, attendance checker and/or yearbook advisor.

(2) Are most reported counseling studies based on counseling in well identified situations where the counseling center is identified with a more effective operating self or in the more diffuse situations found in high schools where the counseling office is identified with a smoother functioning school organization? The counselee in a college or clinical situation comes to the counselor with a purpose to change something. It is true that the counselee may not have insight into his problem, but he has faced the issue of "finding out something about or for myself." High-school students either "drop in" to visit the counselor, or they are called in for a brief clerical maneuver, more often than not for programming, rather than for a serious consideration of the development of self.

(3) Within the college or clinical setting, is counseling more significantly related to the counselee's next step in life than it is to the counselee's next step within the high-school setting? Pressures of our society grow in ever-increasing force upon the individual to set a life direction. To many college-age students there is an important need to make choices with life long implications. This results in a greater focus upon "getting started" for youth and young adults than for high school students. Thus, it would seem that counseling is seen by many college students to be necessary as compared to the "all right if you do—all right if you don't" attitude by many high school students.

(4) Does the concept of authority permeate the entire high-school schedule to a significantly greater degree than it does the college or clinical setting? One has only to compare the various facets of high-school living with similar ones at the college level to realize the more rigorous and definitive lines of adult-directed movement in high

schools as contrasted to student-directed movement in colleges. The concept of a more controlling and pervasive authority surely must permeate the total high-school atmosphere, even into the counselor's office and thus have its bearing on counseling procedures.

(5) How does the maturation level of the high-school student affect the counseling process? One might hypothesize that the immature student will see less need for counseling and will respond less favorably to any overtures to assist him in his growth toward adulthood than will the mature student. Is counseling different, at least in part, because the student hasn't yet learned sufficient knowledge to handle major changes in the direction of his behavior? Perhaps that idea is reflected in Jersild's statement, "Too frequent doses of original thinking from others restrain what lesser portion of that faculty you may possess of your own. You get entangled in another man's mind, even as you lose yourself in another man's grounds."

(6) Is there a difference in counseling because the high-school student may see a personal difficulty as an event or a series of events rather than as a pattern of living which calls for examination? An interesting experience of one of the authors was to observe seven high-school students who were in a discussion of self. These students viewed their concerns as discrete events. Even though the problems had been checked on an inventory, the students seemed to view the problems as those of the moment rather than as concerns which might be developing into a pattern. To the author, it seemed probable that here a pattern was developing.

(7) Does the high-school schedule and physical setting change the mechanics of the counseling process? Experiential evidence leads the writers to state that most high-school schedules and physical facilities negate many of the efforts of even the best trained counselors. The difficulty in scheduling appointments amid a packed academic program and a trolley car class schedule is known to many counselors. Therefore, the many time consuming procedures used in college and clinical counseling may, if attempted within the high school, add only to the counselor's frustration when he attempts to use them.

(8) Does the high-school counselor have immediate responsibility to the school where the college counselor or the counselor in a clinic may have his immediate responsibility to the counselee? The school counselor is a responsible member of the total school program. It may be argued, and properly so, that the high school counselor has

immediate responsibility to the school rather than the individual, especially in school-centered counselee problems. This may result in a much more limited range of socially acceptable choices for the student to use as a basis of adjusting to his concerns. This is in contrast to the possibility of wider choices (although each may be equally as difficult for choice as the fewer choices in high school) for the college age youth or adult.

(9) Does the school counselor have imposed upon him a limit of the kinds of counseling problems discussed in contrast to the greater freedom of college and clinic counselors? Although the limits may be more or less from one high school to another, there are the cultural taboos which make it safer to omit the consideration of some of the serious concerns of students. Too, the re-enforced experiences of students as to what one discusses "at school" almost automatically form a mental set limited to a narrow range of human concerns.

(10) Does the usual high-school counselor operate on a different professional level than the college or clinic counselor? The reader may reply that the answer is obvious. If so, then consideration should be given to the impact of professional level upon counseling approaches.

The reader is cautioned that the authors do not mean to imply that counseling should be at a lower level in high school than in a college or clinic setting. On the contrary, the authors believe that levels of competencies should be similar. However, with few exceptions, the guidance movement is still in its pioneering stages in many secondary schools and some have not yet made the discovery of an organized guidance program.

The central theme of this article is that researchers in counseling should consider the two basic questions (1) "Are there significant differences in the counseling framework in high schools as contrasted to counseling in a college or clinic setting? (2) If so, what do these differences mean in terms of counseling procedures applicable at the high-school level?" Before transposing to high-school counseling principles and procedures based upon research which has been conducted in college and clinical settings, it might be worthwhile to determine the adequacy and relevancy of such principles and procedures when applied in a high-school situation. Also, if the research reveals major differences then would it not seem likely that the guidance movement in the secondary schools would be enhanced through the application of directly relevant research findings?

16. THEORETICAL PRINCIPLES UNDERLYING THE COUNSELING PROCESS

Leona E. Tyler

Counseling is serious business. Across a counselor's desk come the aspirations and anxieties, the convictions and the difficult choices that have generated all the theories about human personality. Because this is so, a counselor needs the kind of organization that some theory of his own gives to his thinking. A theory about anything is simply a way of organizing what is known with regard to it, and a psychological theory is a way of organizing present knowledge about human nature. A counselor can scarcely avoid thinking theoretically about the human situations he encounters.

Persons in most kinds of psychological and educational work find it quite feasible to adopt a general theory that seems reasonable and stick with it, rather than to devote a large part of their own time and energy to thinking about theory. Since a laboratory scientist cannot do all possible kinds of experiments anyway, he might as well do those suggested by one theory and let someone else tackle those which an alternative theory suggests. A classroom teacher has no difficulty in setting up adequate conditions for learning on the basis of whatever learning theory she was exposed to in the course of her professional training.

THE COUNSELOR'S PERSONAL THEORY

But, for a counselor, the situation is more complex. His first responsibility is to *understand* the individuals with whom he works. Every personality has many facets. Different theories of personality

Part of a symposium on Counseling Theory and Practice, American Psychological Association, August 31, 1957. Reprinted by permission of the author and *Journal of Counseling Psychology,* V, No. 1 (Spring, 1958), 3-8.

are like spotlights focused on the individual from different directions. The same facets do not show up when one turns on the light labeled Freud that appear clearly when one throws the Rogers switch. And while Freudian concepts may enable a counselor to understand and to help Bill Amory, they may hinder him from seeing what is really the dominant factor in the life of Sarah Peele.

The counselor thus needs many different varieties of theoretical concept, but for his own confidence and peace of mind he needs to have them organized in some way. Such an organization, one's own individual personality theory, can be a dynamic, growing thing with the kind of unity that maintains itself in spite of constant modification. The cultivation of such a theory is, of course, a lifetime undertaking. Every book one reads, every client one comes to know well, adds to the complexity of its pattern.

This, then, is one counselor's selection from the dominant personality theories of our time of a few of the concepts she has found essential to her understanding of the people with whom she works, and her attempt to bring them together into an organized whole. I am not recommending this particular synthesis for anyone else because I am convinced that each person needs to produce his own. My purpose is to point the way to a sort of *theorizing* counselors can employ rather than to a sort of *theory* they should adopt.

SOURCES OF PERSONALITY THEORY

Our basic concepts about personality have come to us from many sources. We will encounter most of the essential ones if we examine what we have received from the physiological and psychological laboratories, from the psychiatric consulting room, from the field of practical activities, and from whatever place it is that the ideas of philosophers and religious leaders emanate.

The Laboratory

First let us turn to the laboratory work. Physiologists who have studied the complex organ systems of the body have had a great influence on theories of personality. A concept that has permeated all of recent psychological thinking is what is called *homeostasis,* meaning the maintenance of constant inner states—temperature, blood sugar, etc.—even in the face of drastic changes in the external environment. In the last few years, Selye and his co-workers have been sketching the outlines of a still more complicated picture that they call the *general adaptation syndrome,* meaning the body's reaction to *stress* of any kind. We are learning to think in terms of complicated dynamic structures, equilibria that maintain themselves by a constant series of delicately balanced changes. In our thinking about emotion we must consider both this complex physiological state and the mental content. They occur together. One is not prior to the other. Familiarity with these ideas makes us less prone to try to change one part of a personality, to remove a single neurotic symptom, for example, without being concerned with what happens to the rest of it.

From the psychological laboratories has come work on many research problems. Of these, learning and perception have turned out to be most relevant to counseling. If we are not too fussy about details, we can classify the theories about learning from which experiments have been generated into the *stimulus-response* theories and the *cognitive* theories.

The workers in the stimulus-response group have been most interested in the relationship of the observable end-product—what the subject does—to a variety of stimulating conditions. But attitudes, emotions, and social behavior can all be included as varieties of end-product or response. Thus it has been possible to think about personality as well as specific kinds of behavior within a stimulus-response framework. The basic problem, from this theoretical point of view, is how *habits,* or *tendencies* to respond in certain ways, are strengthened or weakened. The essential concepts are *reinforcement,* of both positive and negative varieties, *extinction,* and the *generalization* of responses to new stimulating situations.

The cognitive learning theorist is more likely to focus his attention on the internal *relationships* or organization of experience, rather than on the responses. He holds that it is the way the person sees things, consciously or unconsciously, that changes as learning proceeds, and that it is the central patterning of experience, rather than any automatic tendency, that leads to a response. Evidence for such changes in some inner structure comes most frequently in problem-solving situations when a person suddenly sees the way to a solution. The key concept is *insight*. Because counseling can be thought of as a problem-solving situation, this kind of theory has had much to contribute to our thinking.

Laboratory work on perception is closer to the work of the cognitive learning theorists than to those of the stimulus-response school. Perception *is* this process of inner organization. Experimental work in many specific areas—on illusions and on size and color constancy, for example—has shown how pervasive and universal this organizing process is. There has been recent work showing the relationships between motivational states and what is perceived in ambiguous situations, and between personality traits and general perceptual characteristics. This has made us aware of the fact that each person's world is to some extent an individual creation. I cannot look at a landscape or listen to a symphony and assume that my companion is seeing or hearing the same thing as I am. I cannot analyze a client's relationship to his family and assume that he sees it as I do. It is these concepts of the *organized* and *individual* quality of perception that counselors must incorporate in their theories.

Psychoanalysis

From the consulting room have come theories centering around the difficulties and abnormalities that arise in the course of human life. The dominant theoretical system has been Freudian psychoanalysis. It would obviously be impossible in a paper of this length even to list all the Freudian concepts that influence present-day thinking about counseling and most other things. In making a selection, I would give first place to the concept of unconscious processes. While many psychologists do not like the notion of *the* unconscious as a part of the personality and while some have been able to dispense with the whole notion, most of us who are doing counseling constantly encounter what seems to be evidence for processes that occur without the subject's awareness. Somehow our system must take these into account. The second theoretical concept I find indispensable is what Freud called *instinct,* but most psychologists would rather consider simply as *motivation.* The assumption that life is basically a dynamic process, with wishing and striving woven into its very fiber, has deeply penetrated our thinking, whether we call ourselves Freudian or not. Another concept or habit of thinking we employ constantly is that of *anxiety* and *defenses* against it. We can hardly avoid becoming very sensitive to factors that raise a person's level of anxiety and to the individual ways each person has of defending himself against such threats. Finally, the idea of the special significance for personality development of the first few years of life has become a basic principle in almost all personality theories, a principle we apply over and over again in our thinking about people's lives.

The tremendous influence of the Freudian viewpoint has perhaps led us to underestimate the theoretical contributions of non-Freudian analysts. I have found the idea of *creative, constructive* unconscious processes, emphasized by both Jung and Adler, very useful in my own thinking. The social emphasis in Adler and the neo-Freudians has much to contribute to a counselor's theory, the assumption that man is basically a social creature and that the socialization process does not proceed against nature but with it. Rank's emphasis on the will, his insistence that a person's own free choices have some effect on his personality, and that there is a need for separation and independence, represents a point of view we often take in counseling, even when it conflicts with other aspects of the general theory under which we operate.

The Social Disciplines

Next let us look at research from the field rather than the laboratory or clinic. The thinking about personality that has been done in cultural anthropology has the advantage that it is based on objective observations of people in natural settings. Under the impact of such work we have been modifying our concept of a person as a biological system affected by a social environment. We have been learning to think in terms of a larger system in which biological and social aspects are inextricably bound together. From anthropology and sociology we have also taken over the very useful concept of *social role* and the part it plays in personality and behavior.

Another kind of field work that has given us concepts we use constantly in counseling activities is the development of mental tests and their application to all sorts of problems in the selection and classification of personnel. Here the central concept that has permeated our theoretical thinking is that of personality *trait*. It implies that one aspect of personality at a time—such as intelligence, sociability, ego strength—can be considered apart from the rest and measured along some scale. The concept of *quantitative* differences in personality traits common to all has been very influential.

Philosophy and Religion

The fourth major source of theoretical ideas has been philosophical thinking. No survey of theoretical concepts we need in thinking about personality would be complete without the ideas of the great philosophers and religious leaders of all time. I would select for special comment from this great stream of thought the emphasis on the significance of the individual *soul*. We find this showing up among psychologists as emphasis on the *self* in *personality* organization and as a concern with *choice* and *freedom* and *responsibility*. As counselors we must somehow come to terms with these issues, since so much of our work has to do with the choices and decisions of our clients.

THE BASIC PRINCIPLE IS DEVELOPMENT— ONE COUNSELOR'S THEORY

With this all-too-brief survey of essential theoretical concepts, I turn to the attempt at a synthesis. For me, the basic principle out of which such a synthesis grows is that of *development*. At each moment of life, any person is in process of changing into something a little different from what he now is. The whole *pattern* is changing, and it is important to keep in mind at one time both the fact of pattern and the fact of change. What the pattern at any stage will be depends upon the previous pattern and upon the influences being brought to bear upon the individual from his present surroundings. But it depends also on his own *response*, both to what has gone on before and to the influences that are acting upon him now. A person to some extent shapes the pattern of his life by the choices and decisions he makes at successive stages. Once a choice has been made and its effects built into the developing structure, it can never be eradicated. Development is a one-way street.

Stages

Like other continuous processes, development can be split up into separate parts to facilitate its study. We can think of life as a series of stages of development. While these could be delimited in various ways, the division that seems now to be of most value to educators and counselors is based on the concept of developmental *tasks*. At each stage, certain special tasks or challenges face a person. The choices that matter most to his future are those centered around these particular tasks. With our increasing concern for the adjustment of the aged, we have come to realize that development is a lifelong process and that the later stages, like the earlier, can be marked off from one another by the developmental tasks they bring. One of the reasons I have come to prefer the term *development* to the term *growth* is because it more obviously fits all the periods of life.

Because it provides for complex, multiple causation of whatever happens in a human life, this general framework has a place for all of the separate concepts that have been stressed by the various personality theories—learning and motivation, cultural influences, individual differences, and self-determination. If a counselor adopts this general orientation, he sees his task as a process of working with nature in each individual case. He sees sensitivity as the most important asset he can have—the ability to grasp the complex pattern of each developing life and the nature of the changes that are occurring or that can occur in it. He finds a general attitude of acceptance very important also, since there is nothing to be done with the fixed aspects of any present pattern, determined as they are by factors in the unrecoverable past, except to accept them.

Learning-in-General

It has always seemed to me that so far as learning is concerned, the detailed propositions that have come from the experimentalists of either the stimulus-response or the cognitive schools are less applicable in counseling than just the general ideas. There is one thing laboratory workers do in setting up experiments that we can hardly ever do. It is to fix outcomes in advance. The first step in planning an experiment is to decide what the experimental task or problem is to be. This is the very step we cannot usually take in the counseling setting. We know that the client needs to learn something and that a learning process will certainly occur, but we have no way of knowing at the outset what it is that this person really needs to learn. Our concern has to be with the setting up of conditions favorable to *learning in general,* so that the amount contributed by this learning experience to the *total developmental process* may be as large as possible.

Development of Personal Identity

The over-all concept of development, with its application to all of life, is somewhat too broad for our purposes. All kinds of people have a part in promoting development as a whole—parents, teachers, physicians, playground supervisors, and many others. But there is one kind of development that seems to me to be the special province of counselors, although even this is certainly not their exclusive responsibility. I am thinking of the process by means of which a sense of *personal identity* grows and is maintained. Many personality theorists are talking about the self-concept. What I am calling *identity* means pretty much the same thing. I have a slight preference for it because it has a social as well as a personal reference. Identity covers what and whom one belongs to as well as what one is.

Psychologists have concerned themselves mostly with the problem of what *kind* of a self-concept each person has. They have asked him to sort cards or check adjectives in order to show what characteristics he sees himself as possessing. An increasing number of literary and philosophical writers are concerned with another question—how *firm* or *certain* is the individual's grasp of his own identity. As counselors, our methods and techniques are more suitable for helping with the first kind of question than with the second. We know how to give tests and to collect ratings and records of previous achievement and to use the information in a way that enables a person to see the pattern of his own individual personality more clearly than he did before. But how do we proceed with the person who feels lost, unattached, uncommitted—who does not know who he is? There are many such. Our theory should be able to account for such failure to grasp one's own identity, and our skills should enable us to help such people.

Limitations of Development

As I have considered this matter, the orientation I have found most helpful is to consider the whole developmental process as the actualization of potentialities. Counseling should help each person with his personal task of making potentialities into realities. But what we must recognize is that there are far fewer realities than potentialities, and that the process of self-actualization requires drastic self-limitation of some sort. This is true from the moment of conception on. The genetic potentialities in thousands of sperm cells are wasted when only one of them fertilizes an egg. At a later stage, all sorts of possibilities for personality development are ruled out by the fact that the individual spends his earliest, most formative years in a certain kind of family, in a certain geographical location, belonging to a certain kind of subculture. At still later stages, each choice that the person himself makes actualizes some possibilities but rules out many others. Thus if he commits himself to an attempt to make a career in music, and really takes it seriously, he will probably never be an athlete, although his neuromuscular structures would originally have made either line of specialization possible.

In our time, the wealth of opportunities and the many channels of communication, by means of which people are made aware of them, tend to make self-limitation especially difficult. It is true that in some cases a physical disability rules out many possibilities and determines which potentialities are to be actualized. In other cases, financial circumstances or family responsibilities delimit the area of choice. But for most adolescents or young adults, self-actualization involves a real problem of renunciation of parts of the self that can never come to fruition. It is out of this real dilemma that identity problems can easily grow.

At first glance, this may seem like a pessimistic view of development, bleaker and less appealing than many discussions of human potentialities that we hear. In practice it does not turn out to be this way. It is the richness and depth of the life that is lived within a person's distinctive pattern of internal and external limitations that really matters. And the counselor's most important job is to

help each person locate his special areas of *strength,* the most promising growth potentialities. The developmental process counseling
should try to facilitate includes acceptance of limitations, exploration of strengths, and finally choice, decision, or commitment. Just
what counseling can contribute will vary from person to person. In
some cases it may help define limitations, in others it may locate
or help the person to develop assets. In still others a little extra
courage to make a commitment and live by it is what should come
out of the counseling relationship.

Developing Identity versus Therapy

During the last few minutes I have been focusing on only some
parts of a general developmental theory which would incorporate
concepts from many theoretical sources. I have selected the parts that
seem to me to apply particularly to counseling. In doing this I have
limited the meaning of counseling to one kind of process—that of
helping a person attain a clear sense of personal identity. Such a
concept of what counseling is departs from some current usage in
that it distinguishes it from psychotherapy. Therapy is aimed essentially at *change* in developmental structures rather than at fulfillment. It should be obvious that these two things cannot always be
separated in practice. But it seems to me to add clarity to our thinking about our task when we make such a distinction on a conceptual
level.

Our job, as *counselors,* is not to remove physical and mental
handicaps or to get rid of limitations, but to find sturdy shoots that
can grow and flourish even though some of the branches of the plant
are defective. Our *acceptance of limitations* and our *respect for
strengths* go together. When we play our other roles as therapists
or as educators, we may relate ourselves to the development of the
individual in other ways. We may take action designed to repair
damage done to him in the past, to stimulate inadequate development of some stunted aspect of his personality, or to bring into his
life new kinds of knowledge and skill. I make a distinction between
counseling and these other activities, not because I would restrict
anyone's job to one of them but to enable us to decide, as we go
about our helping activities, what it is we are trying to do in each

case. It can be very confusing to a client if at the same time we try to cure him, remodel him, educate him, and still encourage him to "be himself."

To summarize, this general personality theory is centered around the concept of a complex, patterned developmental process which, for convenience, can be divided into several successive stages. *Counseling is one kind of psychological helping activity, the kind that concentrates on the growth of a clear sense of ego-identity and the willingness to make choices and commitments in accordance with it.* Remember that I am not selling this theoretical product, but rather am trying to promote do-it-yourself activity. It is out of the interchange of theoretical formulations based on unique experience that deeper, more richly patterned personality theories will come into existence.

Section Four

THE COUNSELING PROCESS

The counseling process is a dynamic and flexible process conducted in a way that is unique to the counselor. The basic feature of the process is the kind of relationship that is established between two persons: the counselee, who is a person seeking assistance either because of stress and strain or a desire to use fully his abilities and apply his aspirations, and the counselor, who is a person equipped by virtue of his professional training and personality to give assistance to the counselee. The nature of such a relationship is that the person who seeks help must feel (1) a sense of trust in the counselor, (2) that the counselor understands him, and (3) some independence in making choices and decisions. The goal of the counseling process is to attain changes of a facilitative nature in the thinking and behavior of the counselee through clarification of his self-concept.

In recent years much professional literature in the counseling field has been directed to the roles of the counselor and counselee and to the evaluation of what goes on between them. The recording of interviews has enabled the researchers to apply more scientific methods to the assessment, analysis, and description of counseling techniques and methods. The articles in this section illustrate the counseling process as seen from diverse fields or types of counseling. It is assumed that counseling of all types has an affective element and much in common. Consequently, the selection of articles in this section, while drawn from various helping professions, will illustrate

the techniques, methods, and roles involved in the counseling process. It is hoped that the high school counselor
will analyze each in terms of the realities of his work
situation.

The ideal working relationship for the counseling process is one of mutual trust and confidence. One of the best
ways to establish such a relationship is for the counselor
to find genuine interest in the counselee and to be sincere
with him. Wall believes that counselors have misused the
concept of rapport in that they speak and write of rapport as though it were a separate distinct step taken during the beginning of counseling. His point is that relationships are developed and strengthened throughout the
entirety of the counseling contact, and rapport is better
viewed as simply a descriptive adjective of the superficial
aspects of the counselee-counselor relationships.

Most counselors find themselves in accord with the
notion that both counselee and counselor attitudes are
important in counseling. The counselor's attitudes of
objectivity, warmth, involvement, and understanding toward the counselee condition the success of the counseling process. The counselor's goal in understanding the
counselee is to see things from the counselee's place, to
enter his perceptual field. He must not only understand
the counselee but must convey this understanding to the
counselee. This ability has been labeled empathy, which
has been described as the ability to feel and describe the
thoughts, actions, and feelings of others. Lifton's article
reports a study on the relationships between empathy and
sensitivity. He defines both terms and presents the instruments used in the study to assess these qualities in the
subjects under study and the results obtained. In view of
the importance of empathic ability in a counselor and
the urgent need to screen candidates for counselor training, Lifton's study assumes major importance.

Communication between the counselee and the counselor in the counseling process has long been studied.
Robinson, one of the leaders in the study of counseling
communication, suggests that the counselor make certain

estimates concerning the counselee and the field under discussion and then use these estimates to modify his approach. The counselor, by playing different roles, varying his attitudes, and by the degree of leading in his remarks, affects the outcomes of the counseling conference.

There are other forms of communication in the interview besides verbal communications. Facial expression, gestures, bodily movements, and the like convey meaning to which the counselor must be alert. Barbara points out in his article the necessity for the counselor to be tuned to the total language behavior inherent in the counseling process. Many gestures, movements, and symbolic expressions used by the counselee are helpful indicators to the insightful counselor for understanding the counselee's anxieties or emotional tensions.

Many inexperienced counselors become embarrassed when silences develop in the counseling process. The situations of silence seem long and endless but do not necessarily represent an absence of activity. The counselee may have exhausted a topic, be searching for words, or studying an idea; the counselor may be mentally organizing material. Tindall and Robinson analyzed the occurrence and the effect of pauses or silences in the counseling process. Sixty-one protocols of counseling situations conducted by twenty-two different counselors revealed 369 counselor-initiated and 285 counselee-initiated pauses. Tindall and Robinson classified each silence, the nature of it, the activity which seemed to terminate the pause, and the effects of the pause in counseling.

Gendlin's article discusses another variable of the counseling process—the variable of experiencing—that is "felt" in the immediateness of the counseling relationship. Gendlin delineates six characteristics of experiencing and then explains how the formulation of experiencing helps to establish the aim and achievement of the counselor's responses to the counselee. He cites seven studies in the field to illustrate that although experiencing is subjective, it can be operationally defined and researched.

Most writers agree that the counselor is an authority figure and that the bases of authority are to be found in the
counseling process. Such bases include the fact that the
counselee is dependent by virtue of seeking help and that
the counselor is looked upon as being knowledgeable and
able to aid the counselee. Vogel's article is a report of a
study made to determine whether or not authority was a
critical factor in the development of the relationship between the therapist and the counselee. His purpose was to
determine if authority as a personality trait affected the
attitudes of both the counselee and the therapist and
whether similarity of the trait between the two would
facilitate counseling.

The counselor who knows the degree of open-minded-
ness of his counselee to new information and experiences
is in a better position to understand him. Kemp investi-
gates whether dogmatism, the degree of open- and closed-
mindedness to new experience, affected the vocational
choices of fifty students. His study indicated that dogmatism affected the counselee's responses to vocational
interest inventories and led to their distortion or rejection
of new material.

The counselee will complete the learning process about
himself and about his particular world if there are certain
things that he feels he has to do as a result of the counseling process. Schmideberg discusses the development of
volition or goal-striving in the counseling process. She
does not believe that the removal of inhibitions in counseling will automatically lead to goal-directed behavior.
Rather, the counselor through his ethical and clinical
judgment must give guidance and use his influence to
create challenging, realistic goals within the counselee's
reach. She discusses three types of special techniques the
counselor can use to provide motivation or incentive to
the counselee to carry out positive goal action, or responsibility.

Sociologists and anthropologists have established a close
relationship between culture and personality. Since culture exerts such a molding influence on personality it
would appear that counselors should be familiar with the

cultural backgrounds of their counselees. Relatively little literature is available in the area of counseling and cultural background. The importance of knowing the cultural and societal patterns of the counselee is well illustrated in "Cultural Patterns as They Affect Psychotherapeutic Procedures." Abel stresses that the counselor must understand and be familiar with the meaning of cultural and social factors in the counselee's life in order to understand him as an individual. Included in her presentation is a discussion of the way a particular cultural background or backgrounds have (1) shaped the attitudes of individuals toward therapy, (2) entered into the causes of the individual's problem, and (3) complicated the communications between the counselee and counselor. The essential significance of cultural differences among counselees, and between the counselee and the counselor, is in its effect on communications and the understanding that can be achieved. Abel also presents three suggestions as to ways counselors can prepare themselves for working with counselees of the same, similar, or different cultural backgrounds.

One of the counselor's ethical considerations is that he shall not divulge confidential information received in the counseling process. Confidentiality of counseling interviews is a long established and generally accepted practice. It is usually agreed that confidential information may be discussed only with other professional persons concerned with the case. Ross' article deals with the modifications of absolute confidentiality when treatment is taking place in a child guidance clinic. Such modifications are necessary when the therapist shares information received from the counselee or a member of the family with other staff members who are concurrently working with a member of the counselee's family. It is assumed that the counselee is aware of the practice and knows that records are kept and accessible to staff members of the agency, but Ross believes it would be best to forego the questionable benefits of this limited confidentiality because of its stultifying effects on the counselee in the counseling interview.

17. RAPPORT: AN OUTMODED CONCEPT

Bartholomew D. Wall

In some branches of the behavioral sciences the organization of theory into an integrated whole is being delayed by the use of certain outmoded concepts. In the field of guidance and counseling the phenomenon of *rapport* constitutes such a concept. Whereas writers in related fields—clinical psychology, psychiatry, psychoanalysis and case work—have taken the long view of interpersonal relationships transpiring throughout the entire counseling contact, leaders in guidance and counseling have espoused what might be termed a segmented view of the counseling process.

Some writers in the field of guidance speak of *rapport* as though it were a separate step in the total guidance process. Jones has said in outlining the counseling procedure:

"Establish rapport. Feelings of friendliness, security and mutual confidence are essential and should be established before the serious work of the interview begins." [1]

With reference to the same general point, Robinson has stated:

"Friendly discussion or small talk often occurs at the start of a conference . . .

". . . Realizing the true nature of small talk in the beginning of a conference, the counselor can participate in it naturally and easily and then turn to the client's problems when both of them are seated and have attained an initial stage of rapport and understanding." [2]

Still other writers regard *rapport* as being no more significant

---

Reprinted by permission of the author and *Mental Hygiene,* XLII, No. 3 (July, 1958), 340-42.

[1] Arthur J. Jones, *Principles of Guidance,* New York, McGraw-Hill Book Co., 1945, 274.
[2] Francis P. Robinson, *Principles and Procedures in Student Counseling,* New York, Harper & Brothers, 1950, 149.

than "getting acquainted" in any other type of relationship situation.

Williamson and Hahn have stated:

"Establishing rapport is very much the same problem as becoming intimately acquainted with persons in other relationships of a face-to-face nature.[3]

In such statements *rapport* seems to be defined as a doorway through which both client and counselor must pass simultaneously to attain their ultimate goals. Such statements appear also to imply that *rapport* is a rather conclusive first step so far as the outcomes of guidance are concerned, as though the type of *rapport* attained predetermined subsequent action. This point of view would seem to be incompatible with the idea that relationships can be and usually are developed throughout the entire guidance contact, whether one or several interviews.

An example of the long-range view existing in related fields has to do with the mechanism of transference and with a definition of guidance which emphasizes the interpersonal relationships existing throughout the entire guidance contact.

If one accepts the mechanism of transference as a real, functioning concept, one must see *rapport* as nothing more than a descriptive adjective limited to the superficial aspects of client-counselor relationships, especially with the transference process beginning immediately with the first contact and continuing through to the end of the relationship. Sterba, Lyndon and Katz have described transference as a repetition of previously conditioned attitudes toward a significant adult in later contacts with other significant adults.[4] The most significant adults in a person's life would appear to be his parents, and the establishment of attitudes toward them would appear to play a part in the attitudes, expectancies and feelings of a person in later contacts with other key figures.[5]

---

[3] E. G. Williamson and M. E. Hahn, *Introduction to High School Counseling*, New York, McGraw-Hill Book Co., 1940, 203.

[4] Richard Sterba, Benjamin H. Lyndon and Anna Katz, *Transference in Case Work*, New York, Family Service Association of America, 1948, 16.

[5] For example, teachers, principals, counselors, policemen, supervisors on the job, etc. The attitudes expressed by the client toward the therapist are referred to as transference, and those of the therapist toward the client as counter-transference. Transference and counter-transference may be positive or negative depending upon the type of feelings expressed by the client or the therapist.

The working through of the transference by the client constitutes the backbone of the treatment relationship between the therapist and the client.[6] Fenichel has stated:

"The repetition of previously acquired attitudes toward the analyst is but one example of the most significant category of resistance, the handling of which is the core of analysis: the transference resistance." [7] And again in a recapitulation of Freud's theories:

"By 'establishment of a transference neurosis' Freud meant that the repressed infantile instinctual conflicts find their representation in the feeling relations toward the analyst." [8]

Thus an awareness of transference would seem to motivate one toward an emphasis of the total counseling relationship rather than toward any artificially segmented part of the procedure.

Most dictionaries define *rapport* as harmony, and *process* as forward movement or progress. However, when one attempts to define progress operationally one generally thinks of such on-going talents as the ability of the client to aspire to certain achievements through guidance and counseling, to assimilate certain knowledge, to make realistic decisions in keeping with that knowledge, and to initiate and sustain appropriate goal-directed action. It would appear only reasonable to include something about his ability to establish and to maintain effective interpersonal relationships, not only as an indication of progress in the interpersonal relationship of client and counselor but as an indication that the transference phenomenon had been facilitated.

Well-known writers in the field of guidance seem to feel that the following benefits will derive from an acceptance of *rapport* as a first step in the guidance procedure:

1. It enables the counselor to start out with emphasis upon first relationships, "putting the best foot forward," so to speak.
2. It enables the client to relax amidst all his problems.
3. It facilitates the ventilation of problems and feelings by the client.

---

[6] It is not suggested here that the counselor administer therapy in the medical sense, but that he see the value of understanding such mechanisms as they function within his professional frame of reference.

[7] Otto Fenichel, *Psychoanalytic Theory of Neurosis*, New York, W. W. Norton and Company, 1945, 29.

[8] *Ibid.*, 559.

4. It puts the client and the counselor together or on the same plane in seeking solutions.

Yet the writer knows of no research supporting such expectancies by experts in guidance. In addition, separating the initial phase of the guidance procedure, conceptually, by giving it a name would seem to contain several weaknesses:

1. It would seem to enhance the odds in favor of an artificial relationship between the client and the counselor, where the counselor emphasized the creation of a friendly atmosphere.
2. In terms of item #1, the counselor might be inclined to do too much of the talking, with subsequent and unwarranted structuring of guidance process (that is, blocking the transference process).
3. It might conceivably incur anxiety in the client where inconsistency in counseling techniques and pacing adversely affected the client-counselor relationship.
4. It could conceivably result in later blocks where the client was seemingly encouraged to ventilate his problems too fully, thereby developing embarrassment and accompanying defensiveness.

It would seem better for persons who wish to function in the role of guidance to take the long view of the total counseling process rather than approach it segmentally for the following reasons:

1. Segmenting the counseling procedure, even nominally, cannot help but lead to the emphasis of one "part" over the other in some cases. For proper balance it would seem more reasonable to approach the guidance task, conceptually, with a wholistic view.
2. The total process view would seem to provide a better conceptual base for consistency in the use of techniques and in pacing.
3. The total process view would appear to facilitate acceptance and awareness of the mechanism of transference.
4. The total process view would appear to preclude any feeling of artificiality during first contacts.
5. The total process view would seem to reserve to the counselor

some controls over the kinds of spontaneous outbursts which might later act to block the relationship.

In summary, the writer would like to state that the concept of *rapport* as put forth by some writers in the field of guidance seems to be misleading generally and that the theories out of which it emerged have been superseded by more pragmatic theories which emphasize the long-range or total process point of view. The counselor might more effectively concern himself with such total contact phenomenon as the mechanism of transference. It would seem that the best way to expedite the transference process would consist of dealing immediately with the problems which bring the client to the counselor in the first place, since they are of most interest and of most pressing concern to him.

18. THE ROLE OF EMPATHY AND AESTHETIC SENSITIVITY IN COUNSELING

Walter M. Lifton

This paper describes a pilot study designed to explore the relationships between empathy and sensitivity. Since both of these factors represent qualities that are difficult to measure, this study attempts to develop definitions of both empathy and aesthetic sensitivity as they bear a relationship to the role of a counselor or teacher. This study is not seen as definitive. In many ways it raises more questions than it answers. It is hoped, however, that the instrument developed and some of the significant relationships uncovered may help others interested in exploring this area.

A survey of the literature in the field of counseling strongly indicates an awareness of the crucial role empathy plays in counseling effectiveness. This concern over the role of empathy has had special meaning to people engaged in the professional training of counselors. Interest has been specifically focused on trying to select the more sensitive candidates for training. Equal interest in the past has been directed toward finding ways of predicting or measuring changes in empathic ability.

Reprinted by permission of the author and *Journal of Counseling Psychology*, V, No. 4 (Winter, 1958), 267-75.

DEFINITION OF EMPATHY

Although previous studies indicate the possibility of selecting trainees who will meet academic standards, results to date on the selection of good clinicians have been sparse. One possible reason for the lack of more definitive results has been the use of questionable techniques for the measurement of empathy. Typically, empathy has been described as putting oneself in the other person's shoes. Norman and Ainsworth (8, p. 55), in attempting to separate out empathy from projection, arrived at this definition of empathy: "An individual empathizes when he says others possess a trait in question and others actually do have it when speaking of themselves."

Operationally, many studies have attempted to measure empathy by having a person fill out an instrument. They, then, have their subjects attempt to fill out the instrument the way they believe the person to be predicted has filled out his form. Gage (4), Cronbach (5), and Hastorf and Bender (6) have described in detail the fallacies of assumed similarity and operational techniques that have been developed to factor out such elements as projection. At best the data resulting from these techniques can only reflect diagnostic accuracy rather than therapeutic skill.

Empathy, as applied to the counseling situation, and as discussed in this study, is seen as somewhat more complex. It is an interrelationship between two people and is dependent upon mutual agreement on the experience being shared. Accordingly then, empathy may be said to exist when a counselor recognizes the feeling a client presents as being the client's and not his own, and is able to communicate back to the client the same feeling so the client can recognize its similarity to the one he expressed.

If the above definition of empathy is accepted, and if the assumption that the more accurately the counselor can sense the client's idiosyncratic meaning the more empathic he can become is also accepted, it then follows that to the degree that aesthetic sensitivity reflects a person's capacity to sense nuances and shadings, it would be significantly related to empathic ability.

Definition of Aesthetic Sensitivity

Definitions of the meaning of the term "aesthetic sensitivity" have paralleled changing concepts in psychology about the nature of man. Man is seen as not only responding to stimuli but also as interpreting their meaning. This transition in meaning can be illustrated by a brief survey of the defined role of aesthetic sensitivity in music.

Earlier writers felt the aesthetic person responded to the form of the music, rather than to the imagery it produced. Lundin (7), a more recent writer in the area, describes clearly how these earlier views fitted the psychological philosophies of that era with their emphasis on the stimulus rather than the perceiver. Seeing aesthetic sensitivity as an acquired reaction, Lundin feels aesthetic skills are subject to all the principles of learning.

Present-day theories which interpret a person's response from a phenomenological point of view imply that it is impossible to separate a person's present perceptions from his past experiences and training. Seashore (10) expressed the belief that aesthetic experience comes from the meaning an object conveys to the listener. That meaning can take the form of feelings, ideas, desires, needs or emotions. The aesthetic quality of an object, therefore, becomes a function primarily of the subject's perception of and reactions to it.

For this study then, an aesthetic response is defined as one which reflects the properties of the stimulus as it causes feelings, ideas, desires, etc., to be experienced by the perceiver. The more aesthetic response is seen as one which produces a greater range and intensity of ideas and emotions in the perceiver.

The next question that arises relates to the aesthetic sensitivity to be found in counselors, psychologists, and teachers. Based upon descriptive studies of these professional groups there is evidence that there is a tendency for people in the counseling area to get high *MF* scores on the Minnesota Multiphasic Personality Inventory. These scores have been interpreted as reflecting interests in the fine arts and social relationships rather than as evidence of sexual maladjustment. Similarly, the manual for the Kuder Interest Inventory

(3), citing the study by Baas (1), suggests that counseling psychologists as a group have their highest interests in artistic and literary activities. There seems to be a basis, therefore, for believing that counselors typically like activities or interests involving aesthetic appreciation.

One of the most relevant studies suggesting the relationship between personality factors and reactions to musical stimuli can be found in the work of Cattell and Anderson (2). This study, based upon a factorial analysis of different types of musical preference, has isolated one factor which appears to be associated with emotional sensitivity. The nature of this factor, however, includes qualities beyond those defined here as involved in empathy.

Although the ultimate focus of the present research was directed toward understanding counselors, the work of Ohlsen and Schultz (9) suggested that the characteristics deemed desirable in the best teachers do not differ materially from those sought in counselors. Based upon this implied similarity, and for practical reasons, it was decided to use student teachers in music education as subjects. The twenty subjects included 11 women and 9 men.

ASSUMPTIONS

Based on the preceding discussion and for the purpose of this study it was assumed that:

1. Empathy is a two-person phenomenon, requiring communication between the people involved.
2. Aesthetic sensitivity reflects an ability to perceive shadings, nuances, associations, and emotions caused by a stimulus.
3. Aesthetic interests are typical of counselors.
4. Sensitivity to the feelings of others is professionally valuable.
5. Aesthetic and empathic skills are acquired reactions and hence are subject to the principles of learning.
6. Written responses to musical stimuli can reveal a person's aesthetic and emotional sensitivity.

Hypotheses

The study was planned to test the following hypotheses.

1. There is a significant positive relationship between a person's measured empathic ability and his measured aesthetic sensitivity.
2. There is a significant positive relationship between raters' rankings of the subjects' empathic ability and their desirability as teachers.
3. There is a significant positive relationship between raters' pre- and post-rankings of peers in the areas of teaching competence, empathic ability, and technical proficiency (ability to play a musical instrument). It was expected that in the raters' eyes the subjects would change, but that their relative standings in their group would remain constant. In other words, there is reliability of the raters' judgments over time.
4. There is a significant positive relationship between a person's measured desirability as a teacher and his measured technical skill as a musician.
5. There is a significant positive relationship between technical skill as a musician and empathic sensitivity.
6. There is a significant negative relationship between discrepancy scores on empathy obtained by taking the self-ranking and subtracting the median group ranking, and measures of aesthetic sensitivity. Since empathy is dependent upon self-acceptance this relationship is relevant.

Instruments

One of the major problems of this study was to develop valid and reliable measures of both empathy and aesthetic sensitivity. In an earlier section empathy was described as a relationship between two people. It seemed most reasonable then to attempt to obtain a measure of empathy based upon the feelings of classmates about each other. The most expedient method was to obtain either ratings or rankings of classmates on the dimensions to be explored. The use of ratings was rejected because of our inability to train subjects in the use of the instrument reliably. It was also felt that ratings might result in a clustering of scores since the general tendency toward avoiding negative evaluations would limit the real differences between subjects. By use of ranking, a forced difference between subjects could be obtained.

Questions Used in Rankings

1. One instrument developed was a series of three sheets. Each sheet contained a question which provided a basis for ranking the group. Each subject filled out sheet one before sheet two was given to him. The same procedure was followed for sheet three. In other words, no subject was able to rank his classmates the same way through set or halo, because the rankings of nineteen other classmates intervened. Each subject was asked to include himself in the ranking so that it was possible to see how closely each subject's self concept coincided with the rankings he attained from the group. Since acceptance of self was postulated as one basis for empathy the possibility of obtaining these discrepancy scores was of value.

All of the subjects ranked their classmates on the following questions both at the beginning and at the end of the semester. (Pre- and posttesting.) Question one was:

> Let's suppose that you are a coordinator of music education in a large city system. You have been given the responsibility of looking over a large number of applications which include those of all the members of this group. How would you rank them in order of preference to fill the vacancy as teacher of music on your staff?

It was assumed that ranks obtained from this question would reflect general competence and desirability as a teacher.

Question two was:

> Beginning teachers frequently feel anxious and upset about their job, their ability, and their personal problems. In selecting someone to help people look at their feelings and worries, it is important that the person be someone whom you feel is sensitive to the feelings others may have about the problems that face them. If your list of applicants included the members of the class, rank them in the order in which you would hire them.

The ranks obtained from this question were assumed to reflect a person's empathic qualities in terms of how well the rater felt accepted and understood by the subjects. It is interesting to note that during pretesting one subject questioned whether the experimenters were asking about a counselor or a teacher. This question was particularly relevant because subsequent results revealed that on pretesting the people selected as teachers were not generally seen as also empathic. This relationship shifted on posttesting.

Question three was:

> In presenting a music appreciation lesson to a general music class, you wish to have a demonstration of the ways in which music can convey feeling. If you were selecting from the members of this class persons who might be able to demonstrate this, in what order would you invite them in to perform?

When this question was first developed it was assumed that it would provide a measure of a person's aesthetic competence. Based upon students' comments and later results it is believed this question more nearly reflected a student's skill as a musician (technical musical competence). To insure that subjects had a basis for making judgments in this area, experiences were provided the subjects without their knowledge of its relationship to this study. In a course, other than the one where the research took place, students were given an assignment to perform on their instrument as if they were demonstrating to a class the musical potentials of their instrument. All subjects then had an equal opportunity to observe their classmates in this area. To translate this into counseling, it is as if people were asked to demonstrate their ability to use and identify counseling techniques, but demonstrating no relationship of their knowledge of the appropriateness of the technique at any one point in the counseling process.

2. To obtain measures of aesthetic sensitivity an instrument called the *Music Reaction Test* was developed. Based upon prior research in this area, and with the assistance of two professional music educators, four pieces of music were selected which met the following criteria: (a) The music was not to be familiar to the subjects, (b) The keys in which the music was played were not to favor either major or minor keys, (c) Each selection was to reflect different emotional intensities, (d) Any music involving words was restricted to un-

familiar tongues and scenes, and (e) All subjects were to have equal opportunity to hear the selections before recording their reactions. It was anticipated that the subjects would respond to this ambiguous situation in a fashion comparable to that found in other projective techniques. Some would describe their reactions in terms of form, content, and technique. Others would dwell on the aesthetic and sensual reactions they experienced. The scoring key was developed to quantify the degree subjects responded to either effect or content.

It is commonly accepted that people do not comfortably relate to individuals who display uncontrolled emotionality. Similarly, people do not feel understood by others who avoid emotion and stick purely to the content involved. Maximum communication (and empathy) seems to occur with people who can accept emotion but express it in a controlled fashion. By the very nature of the instructions to the subjects listening to the selections, the experimenters were in reality seeking an assessment of the emotions the subject was feeling, accepting, and was willing to let others see, too. This screening process communicated the manner in which the subjects handled and related affective experiences.

Specifically each subject was given a sheet which contained the following words at the top. "You will hear different musical selections. After each piece, please write on this sheet a statement of what the music means to you. There are no right or wrong answers. Just explain your reaction to what you have just heard."

During the initial administration the subjects' comments indicated their awareness of the projective quality of the test. One comment of interest was, "Should we write what the music expresses or the feeling it brings up in us?" It was suggested to record their reactions. This is almost as if a counselor was asking whether to respond to the content or the feelings presented by a client.

After the four selections were completed, the subjects were given the following instructions. "This time listen especially for the feelings and emotions involved." They then heard a replay of piece #1 by Prokofiev, the selection believed to hold the highest affective loading. This represented a method of determining if a changed set, caused by differing instructions, would modify the responses obtained. Each subject, therefore, provided five responses of which two were to the same selection. Subsequent treatment of the data revealed that the larger the number of statements scored the more accurate the predictions. The different instructions appeared to have little effect. Based upon these data it was possible to develop a scoring key which was tested for inter-judge reliability and against a criterion of clinical judgment.

The rank order correlation computed to estimate the reliability of the scoring method gave a Rho of .94. In order to determine if the method offered a valid means of predicting empathy, the ranked scores were correlated with the student's position (as assigned by the group) on question two (dealing with empathy). The Rho was .63 which is significant at the .005 level. This is a higher correlation than was found when only the subjective ratings were employed.

In order to determine the relationship between the clinical judgments of the test developers, as compared with the MRT score, a Rho was determined for the correlation between the ranks assigned in the clinical judgments and the ranks based on MRT scores. The hypothesis was that the two orderings should be positively significantly related since the MRT scores are assumed to be an objectification of clinical judgment. As was expected, the MRT scores correlated highly with the subjective clinical rankings (Rho = .77, significant $P = <.001$).

VALIDITY OF THE CRITERION

Probably the most crucial aspect of this study came from attempts to determine the validity of the criterion, and to discover ways of treating the data so that they reflected empathy as a relationship between two people rather than as the property of the predictor. Inspection of the raw data in this study clearly illustrated that the subjects were not equally treated by their peers. A few subjects showed consistent trends in being seen by their peers as either highly empathic or lacking this characteristic. Many showed bimodal distributions. There were a few subjects where the raters appeared unable to establish any agreement as to the subjects' empathic characteristics. Typically, this spread of rankings would cause concern over either the ability of the raters to discriminate or the reliability between the raters rating the same area.

In evaluating these data, however, based upon the definition of empathy previously established, the following questions arose. Is it not possible that we tend to accept (and hence empathize with) some people and reject others because they more or less accurately help us feel accepted? Can we not feel accepted by a person in some areas but not in others? Is it not logical then that some subjects will, in any area, have people they can empathize with *based* on their feelings about these areas in themselves? If, from a clinical basis, we give positive answers to the above questions then the validity of our criterion (since it is phenomenologically based) *cannot depend solely on consensus between judges.*

To get some possible picture of what these ideas might mean the data were treated in two ways. To establish a criterion it was decided to utilize the median score obtained from all of the rankings of a subject, including the subject's ranking of himself. The median was selected because it was felt that it, of all the measures of central tendency, would be least distorted by the distribution of scores.

To obtain a clearer picture of each subject's behavior as a judge, correlations were run of his rankings of the class on all the questions, both in pre- and posttesting. Correlations were also run between each of the questions. By this procedure it was possible to gain a measure of the ranker's implicit theory of how the questions went together. In perceptual terms, there was obtained a measure of the consistency with which each rater in the group perceived the group both from one situation (type of question) to another, and in terms of time, the consistency of each rater from the beginning of the study to the end. The correlation measure used was Rho, since the data were taken as ranks.

ALTERNATIVE BASES CONSIDERED FOR DEVELOPING A CRITERION

Several attempts were made to refine the criterion of empathic ability since the use of the median rank on question two (measuring empathy) seemed inadequate. It seemed worth determining what would occur if a more "expert" group of raters were employed.

Consequently, a group of five "expert" raters was selected from the group of twenty subjects by taking those five individuals who were themselves ranked highest for empathic ability. The rationale for this procedure was that those who were rated most highly for empathic ability would be more likely to be able to distinguish this characteristic in others, than would an unselected group of raters. The median of the ranks assigned by these five "expert" raters for each of the twenty students was then considered to be the subject's empathy rank. The MRT ranks were correlated (Rho) with this new criterion. The resulting correlation was lower than that obtained when the entire class was involved.

Another effort was made to purify the measure of empathy by attempting to use as subjects only those students who were rated with reasonable reliability by the group as a whole. The reasoning behind this procedure was the hypothesis that the empathic quality is not equally susceptible to observation and rating in all subjects; and that for a study of this nature it might be better to eliminate subjects who were not judged essentially the same by most of the group. However, there was so little agreement among the raters, on the rankings, that it was impossible to select a group of sufficient size. Even using a minimum requirement of 75 per cent agreement by judges on placement of an individual within a *two* quartile spread furnished too few subjects to study.

To digress for a moment, this problem of the nature of empathy carries fascinating implications. Are we saying then that the most empathic person should be all things to all people? Does this mean, for example, that the typical high *MF* score on the MMPI reflects the ambivalent sex role the counselor may have to play as he is perceived as a father by one client, a mother to another, etc.? Does this mean that in training counselors we are seeking to develop a neuter quality which, chameleonlike, can adapt to the client's colors and thereby help the client feel understood?

RESULTS AND CONCLUSIONS

It was the purpose of this study to check the following hypotheses:

1. There is a significant positive relationship between a person's measured empathic ability and his measured aesthetic sensitivity.

Results. Employing several different measures of empathy, in all cases tested, a relationship at the .01 level of confidence or beyond was found with the pretest of the MRT which was presumed to measure a person's aesthetic sensitivity. In no case, however, was a significant relationship (.01 to .05 level) discovered in post-testing. No satisfactory explanation is available to explain the change in relationships. Rho was .63 on pretest (.005 level) and .22 on posttest when peer group rankings were correlated with MRT scores. Other empathy measures gave lower results.

2. There is a significant positive relationship between raters' rankings of the subjects' empathic ability and their desirability as a teacher.

Results. In both pre- and post-rankings raters saw a positive relationship between empathy and desirability as a teacher. With relationships existing at .01 to .05 levels of confidence, it can be said with assurance that something during the student-teaching semester changed the subjects' attitudes towards characteristics of good teachers. There was a shift from 9 out of 20 to 16 out of 20 subjects significantly relating questions 1 and 2.

3. There is a significant positive relationship between raters' pre- and post-rankings of peers in the area of teaching competence, empathic ability, and technical musical proficiency.

Results. As a group, the subjects were highly reliable in their rankings of subjects in the three areas. They were most reliable in their rankings of their peers in technical musical proficiency with 19 out of 20 subjects demonstrating reliabilities at the .05 level or above. They were only slightly less reliable in the area of empathy with 17 out of 20 subjects demonstrating significant relationships. The lowest of the three was the area of desirability as a teacher. There, 14 out of 20 subjects provided significantly reliable results. Considering that a six-month period intervened, the reliability of the judges is rather surprising. This fact becomes of even greater interest when the lack of agreement *between* judges is explored. These results tend to confirm the idiosyncratic nature of interpersonal relationships with difference between pairs of people, but stability in each pair over time.

4. There is significant positive relationship between a person's desirability as a teacher and technical proficiency as a musician.

Results. This hypothesis was of considerable interest since many disciplines today insist that only a master technician can be a good teacher. Based upon the way the subjects in this study ranked subjects comparably in the two areas it would appear that on both pre-

and post-testing (14 and 12) the subjects saw these two areas as significantly related. This is really not surprising since we would expect the subjects to reflect the professional bias in this direction.

5. There is significant positive relationship between technical proficiency and empathic sensitivity.

Results. It was of interest to see if the stereotyped picture of the skilled artist as being skilled in expressing emotions and ideas through his medium but as inept at social skills held true for this group. The results obtained indicate that the relationship of empathy to technical skill was the lowest of all studied with only 6 subjects on pretest, and only 7 on posttest (out of 20 subjects) seeing these as being significantly related.

6. There is a significant negative relationship between discrepancy scores on empathy (self-ranking minus median group ranking) and measures of aesthetic sensitivity.

Results. In previous discussions of the relationships of empathy to acceptance of self it was suggested that the more closely a person's self-perception lined up with reality (group ranking), the more likely he would be to accept himself and the higher his empathic ability ought to be. To test this hypothesis, cumulative discrepancy scores were obtained for each subject. The scores reflected the distance between a subject's ranking of himself and the median ranking of his peers of him. These discrepancy scores were then correlated with the ranks resulting from the MRT. A Rho of .08 was obtained.

Summary

To summarize then, this study has attempted to develop definitions of empathy and aesthetic sensitivity which are consistent with clinical experience and present psychological theories.

An instrument called the *Music Reaction Test* was developed. Results from this test initially showed correlations with measures of empathy of as high as Rho = .63 which is above the .005 level of significance. These relationships did not stand up over a six-month period despite essentially little change in either the predictor or the criterion. No adequate explanation for the fact is available.

The discussion of the phenomenological nature of empathy has raised questions about the feasibility of use of a criterion whose validity is based upon high group reliability. Alternative ways of solving the selection of an appropriate criterion were explored.

In terms of the music students used as subjects, there is evidence to suggest a change in their attitude during the semester, with a growing awareness of the role of empathic skills in a good teacher. We might postulate the possibility of getting similar changes in counseling trainees.

The study also tends to focus attention on the question as to whether the arts ought to continue to stress form and content in their courses, or whether greater aesthetic sensitivity lies in freeing the artist so he can use his medium as a basis for communicating his ideas, feelings, and needs, in order that he and others can feel understood. It has also raised the question as to whether we need to develop in counselors a quality which may enable them to be all things to all people.

Received May 31, 1957.

REFERENCES

1. Baas, M. L. Kuder interest patterns of psychologists. *J. appl. Psychol.,* 1950, **34**, 115-117.
2. Cattell, R., & Anderson, Jean C. The measurement of personality and behavior disorders by the I.P.A.J. music preference test. *J. appl. Psychol.,* 1953, **37** (6) , 446-454.
3. Examiner manual. Kuder preference record. Chicago: Science Research Associates, 1954.
4. Gage, N. L. Judging interests from expressive behavior. *Psychol. Monogr.,* 1952, **66** (18), 1-20.
5. Gage, N. L., & Cronbach, Lee. Conceptual and methodological problems in interpersonal perception. *Psychol. Rev.,* 1955, **62**, 411-422.
6. Hastorf, A. H., & Bender, I. E. A caution respecting the measurement of empathic ability. *J. abnorm. soc. Psychol.,* 1952, **47**, No. 2 supplement, 574-576.
7. Lundin, R. *An objective psychology of music.* New York: Ronald Press, 1953.
8. Norman, R. D., & Ainsworth, Patricia. The relationship among projection, empathy, reality, and adjustment, operationally defined. *J. consult. Psychol.,* 1954, **18** (1), 55.
9. Ohlsen, M. M., & Schultz, R. Projective test response, patterns for best

and poorest student teachers. *Educ. psychol. Measmt.*, 1955, **15** (1), 18-27.

10. Seashore, C. *The psychology of music.* New York: McGraw-Hill, 1938.

19. THE DYNAMICS OF COMMUNICATION IN COUNSELING

Francis P. Robinson

Treatment sciences have traditionally tried to improve diagnosis so that more specific treatment procedures might be developed and used. Medicine has sought to isolate the source of a disease so that specific medicines could be discovered. Remedial workers have tried to isolate new causes of particular disabilities or to set up symptom patterns for which they could develop pragmatic treatment procedures, e.g., the use of pacing devices with slow readers. Similar attempts have been made in the area of adjustment counseling.

In addition to such improved diagnosis and treatment content, however, there is a third and somewhat neglected area that is the topic of this paper—the social psychology of the counselor-client interaction. It pertains to the optimum means of communicating those counselor orientations which help the client to discover insights into his problem and accept them. It also includes optimum means of giving treatment suggestions so they are understood and carried out. This demands more of a counselor than his being "good at heart" and using understandable language. It includes skill in expressing attitudes and ideas in light of the client's characteristics as he enters the conference and of the dynamics of the conference as it progresses. It deals, in brief, with the *when* and *how* of doing things in the conference—throwing responsibility, listening, giving information, interpreting, expressing reinforcement, leading on further with a topic, closing a conference, etc.

Medicine has little trouble in this area since diagnosis can be done with little client co-operation, treatment can be sugar-coated or in-

Address of the retiring president of the Division of Counseling Psychology of the American Psychological Association, San Francisco, September, 1955. Reprinted by permission of the author and *Journal of Counseling Psychology*, II, No. 3 (Fall, 1955), 163-69.

jected, and the necessary physiological actions demand no client effort. In the counseling field, on the other hand, all is dependent on the client continuing to be motivated, on his gaining insight into what is needed, and on his willingness to accept these points. A counselor may know the specific cause and what will remedy it, but if he cannot communicate effectively with the client, little will be gained.

The use of recorded interviews in studying client-counselor interactions originated only a little over a dozen years ago (20). However, these first efforts merely described the effect of single counselor speeches on immediate client responses (23). These studies entirely missed the important first step in counseling interaction—what *client* behavior determines or should determine counselor response. Furthermore, these early studies in using an atomistic, single speech approach and dividing interview series into fractions tended to cover up an important factor in the dynamics of communication, i.e. counselor roles (17).[1]

These early studies did show, however, that experienced counselors had little understanding of interview dynamics. That is, each counselor showed a definite pattern of response as he moved from one client to another but various counselors showed little similarity to each other (20, 22). In brief, each had a "deskside manner" based on his own experience.[2]

Within more recent years some attempts at theoretical formulations have been made in this area of interview dynamics (2, 12, 14, 25). But as yet little of this has been followed by research. In the sections which follow it is proposed to describe some characteristic dimensions of the counseling process and to note some recent research using them.

---

[1] Muthard found that both counselor and client behavior during the second half of discussing a particular topic was significantly more related to their behavior during the first half of discussing that topic than it was to their behavior during the first half of the next topic (C.R. 3.71 and 4.40). Correlations between comparable halves of fractional units showed no such differences. Something as to the nature of this factor will be brought out later in discussing "roles" (7).

[2] Counseling centers also tend to be set in their ways. Protocols obtained from different counseling centers often show local emphases in types of problems handled and in the general approaches used, e.g., some schools have only therapy cases, others have a heavy loading of study skill problems, etc. Yet early studies frequently used only locally obtained interviews. Future research studies should use a wide sampling of clients from various counseling centers. Ohio State University now has a pool of over 350 interviews from eight universities from which samplings are taken as needed.

Dimensions of the Client and the Field

Making judgments about the client and his situation are obvious first steps in counseling. While these characteristics might be categorized in various ways we have found the following outline to be helpful. Each area is thought of as varying as a dimension in a way that should affect counseling behavior.[3]

A. Dimensions of client behavior
   1. Kind of problem, e.g., skill vs. adjustment problem.
   2. Degree of motivation, e.g., from the student called in to the self-referred client who is distraught and desperate.
   3. Stage the client has reached in thinking through his problem, e.g., from the student who says, "My adviser says I have to declare my major by registration time tomorrow" to one in Pepinsky's "Lack of Assurance" category (19).
   4. Role the client expects the counselor to play, e.g., from wanting the counselor to take all responsibility to only wanting him to listen.
   5. Client proclivities, e.g., dependency attitudes, emancipative aggressions toward all adults, tendency to develop transference.

B. Dimensions of the field
   1. Validity of knowledge in the field, e.g., from advising what courses are necessary for graduation to advising on the choice of a mate.
   2. Learning theory, e.g., importance of growth factor, reinforcement, repression, etc.
   3. Counselor proclivities, e.g., projection of own needs, working in one's favorite area, effect of one's own style of counseling.

---

[3] Care must be used in interpreting the word "dimension" as used in this discussion. Certainly no aspect of counselor or client behavior can be considered as lying along a straight-line continuum nor is it as precisely measured as with a yardstick. On the other hand, a counselor can vary his behavior in many ways to adjust to the changing characteristics of his client. If the different aspects of the client's and the counselor's behavior can be described and the different ways in which each aspect may be varied can be pointed out, then such a listing of major categories and sub-categories provides a more precise means of testing the nature and effectiveness of different kinds of client-counselor interactions.

The first of these dimensions—kind of problem—has been the subject of much study. However, recent studies have shown that the usual mode of classifying problems according to the location of the frustration, e.g., home, school, vocation, etc., is not particularly helpful in determining interview content (3). In the early work at Ohio State University client problems were classified into vocational, therapy, scholastic questions, and skill categories. But no significant difference in the counselor's manner was found in the first three so these units were lumped together as *adjustment problems* in contrast to the other category of *skill problems.* [4,5] Elton found that an experienced counselor usually makes greater changes in his counseling behavior in going from a skill to an adjustment topic with a single client than he does in going from one client to another (11).

Dipboye, working independently at Missouri, sought to get at evidences of counselor style through dividing interviews into six kinds of discussion topics—test discussion, interpersonal relations, family relations, educational and vocational planning, self reference, and study skills (10). He found, however, that counselor behavior in these six units actually fell into two clusters which he tentatively labeled *cognitive* and *affective* problems. Both Elton's and Dipboye's dual classification systems have much in common. Further research will help clarify their nature and labeling.

A second major approach to studying client characteristics was carried out recently by Davis (9). He studied the reliability with which some of these client characteristics could be rated and how early in the interview this might be done. Using a sampling of forty initial interviews obtained from five universities, he had two judges independently read the protocols and rate the following four characteristics of the client: nature of problem, degree of motivation, role expected of counselor, and stage reached by the client in thinking about his problem. Ratings were made about halfway through the

---

[4] A third category, *immaturity problems,* has generally been added on logical grounds but studies of actual conference notes by Pepinsky (19) and Elton (11) show that few clients complain of such problems and so long as counselors deal primarily with areas of complaint we are not apt to get many such interview protocols to analyze.

[5] Both Bordin and Pepinsky have proposed systems of diagnostic constructs that seek to be more functional in approaching the client and his problem. The above three-fold system does not disagree with their suggestions; several of their categories are merely lumped together under *adjustment problems.*

first interview when the client seemed to have finished an initial telling about his problem (called the "transition point" by Davis) and again a month later after reading the entire first interview. He found that each of these client characteristics can be reliably rated (reliability coefficients varied from .59 to .74) and the ratings at the midway transition point were about as reliable as after reading the entire first interview.

He also found some suggestive relationships among these client characteristics, e.g., students with skill problems expected the counselor to play a more responsible role than with adjustment problems, the further the client had progressed in thinking about his problem the less active a role he expected of a counselor, degree of motivation was positively related to the stage reached by the client in thinking about his problem, but there was no relationship between motivation and role expected.

In studying the relationship of these client characteristics to counselor technique, he found that on skill problems the counselors tended to lead more and take more responsibility, but lead did not vary with the other three client characteristics. Finally, he found a high relationship, as might be expected, between degree of client motivation and working relationship in the conference ($r = .83$).

Further research work is obviously needed on these as well as other characteristics of the client. Work is needed to determine to which characteristics counselors are most sensitive and also to determine whether other important characteristics are at present being ignored by most counselors. Studies should also be made of the importance of the "field characteristics" listed above. Fiedler has indicated that experienced counselors do not let theoretical differences loom as large in determining their counseling methods as do inexperienced beginners (13). Some recent attempts to show commonalities between different theoretical approaches rather than to emphasize differences may help these beginners to obtain a better perspective here (1, 13).

DIMENSIONS OF THE COUNSELOR'S RESPONSE

Having looked at the characteristics of the client and of the area of work which should affect counseling procedures, let us now look at the ways in which a counselor may vary his procedures so as to fit sensitively these characteristics. In addition to what a counselor may do about the conference room arrangements and his own dress and manner, he may vary his manner of speaking. Since primary communication is through speech, most research has been in this area (15).

Certain general dimensions of counselor response have been emphasized in most analyses of counselor speeches, e.g., acceptance attitude, responsibility division, degree of lead, degree of interpretation, response to feeling, etc. (2, 6, 21, 24). Before discussing these dimensions, however, two findings should be noted. First, while fruitful studies can be made of each dimension, these dimensions do not encompass all aspects of counseling behavior nor are they independent of each other. In brief, the counseling interaction is complex and dynamic. For instance, Elton found a marked interaction effect in doing an analysis of variance study on the effects of topics and clients on counselor behavior (11).

The second finding concerns the part played by counselor roles in determining these dimensional behaviors. Practically all previous sociological studies of roles have dealt with large roles, e.g., as a father, a counselor, or a teacher. However, here we are interested in the subordinate roles that are used to carry out the one large role of counselor, e.g., at one moment a listener, at another a diagnostician or a tutor. A recent study by Danskin indicates that during segments of the interview a counselor shows a certain consistency in his behavior as he tries to play one or another subordinate role (7). In brief, subordinate roles of the counselor are an important determiner of other dimensions of his behavior.

Danskin selected thirty early and late interviews from the conferences of fifteen counselors. Judges, reading these interviews independently, agreed with high reliability upon the points of transition between role changes and upon the classification of these role segments among thirteen types of roles. He also found that roles frequently changed when the topic of discussion changed (71 per cent of time) but role changes also occurred within discussion topics. While counselor speeches within a single role segment varied over a wide range of lead, the role seemed an important determiner of the general level or average degree of lead used. Danskin's sample of interviews was not large enough to provide normative information about the range and use of counselor roles although he did find some indication that many counselors play a limited range of roles. We are at present making a larger normative study which will provide more complete information as to the total range of roles used in student counseling and something as to counselor differences in their use.

As noted above, particular counselor speeches within any particular role unit vary in light of immediate client behavior. It is important that the counselor be aware of the manner in which he may vary his behavior and of the effect of these changes. The following dimensions of counselor response have been useful in our research studies.

1. *Acceptance attitude.* This continuum varies from unintentional rejection (e.g., incorrect use of assurance, presenting a "silver lining" in response to a client's problem statement, pursuing the counselor's line of thought rather than the client's, etc.) through differing degrees of acceptance (i.e., differing degrees of warmth and approval indicated in response to different client ideas).

2. *Responding to the core of what the client says.* It is generally agreed that a counselor should respond to what the client is saying, but counselors occasionally fail because they do not realize how important this is or because they miss getting the core. Elton found that five experienced counselors (ten clients in thirty-four interviews) varied in responding to the core of a client's remarks from 45 to 94 per cent of the time; the median was 82 per cent (11). The rest of the time they were either responding to some secondary aspect that had been mentioned or were introducing some new aspect on their own. Some workers have suggested as a further refinement that the response should be to the feeling expressed rather than to the content (2).

3. *Division of responsibility.* Depending on the type of problem and client's stage in attacking his problem there may be varying divisions of responsibility within an interview, e.g., from the counselor's listening as a client first tells of his problem to the coach's role in tutoring on some skill. Carnes found that experienced counselors are quite flexible in shifting division of responsibility as they progress through a conference series (4). That is, if the range of responsibility taken by eight experienced counselors in discussing

many topics in thirty-two interviews is taken as a norm, it was found that a single counselor, on the average, covered over two-thirds of this total range in talking with a single client. On the other hand, counselors are not always sensitive to these conference demands—witness sudden client questions, queries as to the proposed nature of the conference, as well as other symptoms of client desire to change the division of responsibility.

4. *Degree of lead.* Others have labeled this a directiveness dimension or an interpretation dimension, but all agree that the degree to which a counselor's remarks tend to go beyond what the client has said represents a sensitive means of adjusting to moment-by-moment changes in client characteristics and is markedly affected by differences in thoeretical orientation (6, 8, 23, 24). Elton found that degree of lead showed more variation than any of the other counselor dimensions during the interview (11). Quite a bit of normative information has been reported elsewhere (21) on this dimension, but Nelson's study probably best indicates its importance (18). She found that independent judges tend to agree on the degree of lead needed after each client speech ($r = .70$) and the closeness with which the counselor actually came to this rated optimum was positively related to interview outcome ($r = .70$).

It is believed that counselors can be trained more effectively if they are made aware of the roles which they are playing and might be playing. Furthermore, awareness of the four dimensions of acceptance, core, responsibility division, and degree of lead should help in responding more sensitively to client characteristics. But additional research is obviously needed in this area.

DIMENSIONS OF OUTCOME

While client characteristics should determine counselor response the effectiveness of these counselor responses must in turn be evaluated in terms of their effect on the client's subsequent behavior. The ultimate criterion of effectiveness is the client's behavior outside of the interview, but in actual counseling the counselor cannot wait for such measures; he has to use immediate symptoms, e.g., willingness to talk, take responsibility, statements of insight, etc. These immediate symptoms have no significance unless they are related to later expected outcomes, but little research has been done in this area.[6]

What little that has been done has been mainly concerned with noting the relationship of a client's immediate behavior to his behavior later on in the interview series. Thus McCormick studied the relationship of client behavior the first time a topic was discussed with his behavior later on when the same topic recurred (16). He found that composite ratings of client growth, working relationship, and responsibility-taking made the first time a topic was discussed correlated from .81 to .91 with similar ratings made the second and third time the topic occurred. However, the correlations between the third and fourth occurrence (r = .42) was no higher than between the ratings on the first and fourth occurrence. He attributed this drop in relationship to the fact that the client by the fourth discussion period had probably gone into a new or deeper aspect of the problem and a different situation existed. Obviously additional studies are needed on the relationship of these client interview behaviors to his behavior outside the conference.

Summary

The traditional emphasis on diagnosis and treatment content has tended to ignore a study of the dynamics of communication between counselor and client—the social psychology of the interview. In outlining possible approaches to a study of these dynamics it has been suggested that the counselor ought to make certain estimates concerning (a) the client, i.e., kind of problem, degree of motivation, stage in problem, role expected of counselor, and certain client proclivities; and also concerning (b) the field under discussion, i.e.,

---

[6] Before a comparison can be made between immediate and delayed criteria, however, available tests and measures will have to be improved. In a recent study by Tindall sixteen measures of adjustment (including self evaluations, peer ratings, expert ratings, behavior sample ratings, and projective tests) were carefully administered to a population of adolescent boys; the median intercorrelation among these tests was only .23 (26)! And much of this relationship was shown to be due to the use of the same or similar judges on certain tests. A somewhat comparable study by Cattell and Saunders involving a factor analysis showed a similar lack of commonness among measures of adjustment (5).

validity of knowledge in that area, learning theory accepted, and certain counselor proclivities.

The counselor in turn is able to modify his approach to these client and field differences by playing different roles and within these roles making sensitive adjustment to moment-to-moment client changes, i.e., by varying his acceptance attitude, responding or not to the core of the client's remarks, altering the division of responsibility, and modifying the degree of lead in his remarks. Finally, it was indicated that a study of these dynamics can only be meaningful if analyzed in light of the outcomes of the conference for the client. While delayed outcomes must be the ultimate measure, actual practice calls for evaluation in light of certain immediate criteria within the interview situation, e.g., working relationship, talk ratio, responsibility taking, statements of insight, expressions of feeling, etc.

These various dimensions are obviously merely constructs of suggestive use in studying the dynamics of the interview. Other workers may find somewhat different terminology useful in describing characteristics of the interviewing process. Eventually research studies will help determine which characteristics of the counseling process are most important. In the meantime, preliminary research making use of these dimensions has provided some useful ideas about how to improve counseling. It is hoped that these ideas will be useful to others in designing research and in teaching in this neglected area of counselor-client communication.

Received February 28, 1955.

REFERENCES

1. Black, J. D. Common factors in the patient-therapist relationship in diverse psychotherapies. *J. clin. Psychol.,* 1952, **8,** 302-306.
2. Bordin, E. S. Dimensions of the counseling process. *J. clin. Psychol.,* 1948, 4, 240-244.
3. Bordin, E. S. Diagnosis in counseling and psychotherapy. *Educ. psychol. Measmt.,* 1946, **6,** 169-184.
4. Carnes, E. F. *Counselor flexibility: Its extent, and its relationship to other factors in the interview.* Unpublished doctor's dissertation, Ohio State Univer., 1949.
5. Cattell, R. B. & Saunders, D. R. Inter-relation and matching of per-

sonality factors from behavior rating, questionnaire and objective test data. *J. soc. Psychol.,* 1950, **31**, 243-260.

6. Collier, R. M. A basis for integration rather than fragmentation in psychotherapy. *J. consult. Psychol.,* 1950, **14**, 199-205.

7. Danskin, D. G. Roles played by counselors in their interviews. *J. couns. Psychol.,* 1955, **2**, 22-27.

8. Danskin, D. G., & Robinson, F. P. Difference in "degree of lead" among experienced counselors. *J. couns. Psychol.,* 1954, **1**, 78-83.

9. Davis, S. E. *An investigation of client characteristics shown in interview behavior.* Unpublished doctor's dissertation, Ohio State Univer., 1953.

10. Dipboye, W. J. Analysis of counselor style by discussion unit. *J. couns. Psychol.,* 1954, **1**, 21-26.

11. Elton, C. F. *The effect of client and topic on counselor behavior.* Unpublished doctor's dissertation, Ohio State Univer., 1951.

12. Fearing, Franklin. Toward a psychological theory of human communication. *J. Pers.,* 1953, **22**, 71-88.

13. Fiedler, F. E. Factor analysis of psychoanalytic non-directive and Adlerian therapeutic relationship. *J. consult. Psychol.,* 1951, **15**, 32-38.

14. Goldman, Leo. Counseling; content and process. *Personnel and Guid. J.,* 1954, **33**, 82-85.

15. Krim, Alaine. A study in non-verbal communications; expressive movements during interviews. *Smith Coll. Stud. Soc. Wk.,* 1953, **24**, 41-80.

16. McCormick, K. F. *A comparison of immediate and delayed criteria in counseling evaluation.* Unpublished doctor's dissertation, Ohio State Univer., 1951.

17. Muthard, J. E. The relative effectiveness of larger units used in interview analysis. *J. consult. Psychol.,* 1953, **17**, 184-188.

18. Nelson, J. A. *A study of optimum leading: Its relation to actual leading and the relation of the deviation of actual leading from optimum leading to outcomes in the counseling interview.* Master's thesis, Ohio State Univer., 1949.

19. Pepinsky, H. B. The selection and use of diagnostic categories in clinical counseling. *Appl. psychol. Monogr.,* 1948, No. 15, 140 pp.

20. Porter, E. H., Jr. The development and evaluation of a measure of counseling interview procedures. *Educ. psychol. Measmt.,* 1943, **3**, 105-126, 215-238.

21. Robinson, F. P. *Principles and procedures in student counseling.* New York: Harper, 1950.

22. Seeman, J. A study of preliminary interview methods in vocational counseling. *J. consult. Psychol.,* 1948, **12**, 321-330.

23. Snyder, W. U. An investigation of the nature of non-directive therapy. *J. gen. Psychol.,* 1945, **33**, 193-223.

24. Stone, D. R. Logical analysis of the directive, non-directive counseling continuum. *Occupations,* 1950, **28**, 295-298.
25. Sullivan, H. S. *The psychiatric interview.* New York: Norton, 1954.
26. Tindall, R. H. Relationships among indices of adjustment status. *Educ. psychol. Measmt.,* in press.

20. THE VALUE OF NON-VERBAL COMMUNICATION IN PERSONALITY UNDERSTANDING

Dominick A. Barbara, M.D.

In discussing the psychophysiological aspect and higher order of abstractions in humans in differentiation to animals, Korzybski (3) states: "It is obvious that the fundamental means which man possesses of extending his orders of abstractions indefinitely is conditioned, and consists in general in symbolism and, in particular, in *speech.* Words, considered as symbols for humans, provide us with endlessly flexible conditional semantic stimuli, which are just as 'real' and effective for man as any other powerful stimulus."

I would like to refer to "language behavior" as the totality of a person's behavioral and semantic responses at the time he speaks in any one particular speaking situation. It can be understood mostly as a dynamic process in a totally integrated individual with expressive activity observable in his (overt) behavior, such as talking, walking, sleeping, etc., plus implicit behavior (subjectively experienced), including thinking, feeling, wishing, understanding. It is the awareness of these total integrated components in action in any given situation that give meaning and direction to his behavior.

In persons with conflicting tendencies leading ultimately to conflict, we usually discover associated distortions and emotional disturbances pertaining to the process of verbalization. An individual who feels basically divided, experiences anxiety and psychic disintegration which simultaneously affect his organism as a whole. Unable to preserve enough of his "real self" to express clearly or directly the real intent of his thoughts and feelings, he becomes disorganized and reacts confusedly to this total environment. He is thus unable to

Reprinted by permission of the author and *Journal of Nervous and Mental Diseases,* **CXXIII**, No. 3 (March, 1956), 286-91.

abstract clearly or productively, with the resultant that objective reality situations become subjectively experienced with irrational fear and in abnormal proportion to their true evaluative perspective. Epictetus once said, "What disturbs and alarms man are not the things, but his opinions and fancies about the things." Finally, in the actual process of verbal communication, we will find that, instead of free-flowing spontaneous expression, a blocking, hesitant, and confused form of speech ensues. This latter word jargon with all of its neurotic attempts toward psychic-restoration (rationalization, compartmentalizing, externalizing, "bugaboo" words, distractions, etc.) includes a wide range of overt, anxious attempts on the part of the individual to remove disturbing subjective stimuli and conflicting tendencies at the time of conflict.

Consider the great deal of silent and hidden interplay of feelings, thoughts, and actions (either of a conjectured or comprehensive nature) which occurs between two or more persons in the subterranean communicative channels of language behavior. We relate a considerable portion of this data through conscious hearing, sight, touch and smell. A further portion is relayed to us in the process of intuition and through unconsciously felt perceptions. We communicate every minute of the day with others and the outside world through "speaking" gestures, peculiarities in gait and dress, a sense of touch while shaking hands, the mannerisms of another person's glance or looks, the condition and texture of his skin, the color of his eyes, his lips, his body build, and a multitude of similar bodily characteristics.

The minutest movements, states Theodor Reik (6), "accompany every process of thought; muscular twitchings in face or hands and movements of the eyes speak to us as well as words. No small power of communication is contained in a glance, a person's bearing, a bodily movement, a special way of breathing. Signals of subterranean motions and impulses are being sent silently to the region of everyday speech, gesture, and movement.

"A series of neurodynamic stimuli come to us from other people and play a part in producing our impressions, though we are not conscious of noticing them. There are certain expressive movements that we understand, without our conscious perception really being at work in that understanding. We need only think of the wide field of language. Everybody has, in addition to the characteristics we know, certain vocal modulations that do not strike us; the particular pitch and timbre of his voice, his particular speech rhythm, which we do not consciously observe. There are variations of tone, pauses, and shifted accentuation, so slight that they never reach the limits of conscious observation, nevertheless betray a great deal to us about a person. A voice that we hear, though we do not see the speaker, may sometimes tell us more about him than if we were observing him. It is not the words spoken by the voice that are of importance, but what it tells us of the speaker. Its tone comes to be more important than what it says. 'Speak, in order that I may see you,' said Socrates.

"Language—and here I do not mean only the language of words but also the inarticulated sounds, the language of the eyes and gestures—was originally an instinctive utterance. It was not until a later stage that language developed from an undifferentiated whole to a means of communication. But throughout this and other changes it has remained true to its original function, which finds expression in the inflection of the voice, in the intonation, and in other characteristics. It is probable that the language of words was a late formation, taking the place of gesture language, and it is not irrational to suppose, as that somewhat self-willed linguist, Sir Richard Paget, maintains, that the movements of the tongue originally imitated our various actions. Even where language only serves the purpose of practical communication, we hear the accompanying sounds expressive of emotion, though we may not be aware of them."

Consider the multitude of bodily expressions and behavioral gestures which give insight and understanding to psychosomatic disease. In the symbolism of symptoms, the individual unable to find an outlet for tension of emotional origin either by word or action discovers instead a means of expressing these tensions through a kind of "organ language." Unable holistically to verbalize his feelings, thoughts, or actions, either to himself (intrapsychically) or to others (interpersonally); his organism as a whole becomes threatened and the struggle toward achieving psychic-unity, self-protectiveness, and pseudo-integration is crystallized in the manner of bodily responses.

Language of the body or organ language is astonishingly well described in everyday popular phrases. We speak, for example, of not being able to "swallow" an unpleasant life situation, an insult or belittling remark; frequently a feeling of oppression in the chest

accompanied by sighing respirations in the absence of organic findings indicates that a person has a "load on his chest" that he would
like to get rid of by talking about his dilemma. Nausea usually expressed symbolically in the words "can't stomach it" represents an
attempt on the part of the individual to "vomit away" his difficulties. A common advice or warning to others who "burn up" or
"explode with anger" is "don't get your blood pressure up, take it
easy." Bodily expression in the form of fatigue is very often due to
emotional conflict which uses up so much energy that little is left
for constructive use. An ache in the arm may, for instance, sym-
bolize a defensive action against striking at someone else. Itching
with no organic basis often represents an attempt to "come alive"
or self-inflicted contempt for not being able to idealize one's self.
These and many other examples are indications in which the body
has a peculiar language of its own through which it conveys feelings
and meanings it is unable to verbalize or healthily abstract to higher
and more productive bodily levels.

In hysteria, for example, we find a dramatic form of expression of
language behavior. The hysterical person, for instance, when faced
with an unbearable or unacceptable reality, unconsciously avoids
experiencing or perceiving the same situation by resorting to symptom formation. In the chaotic attempt to avoid feeling anxiety, and
in order to "pull himself together" and restore some form of psychic
unity, the hysterical individual externalizes all of disturbing situations, thoughts or feelings associated with anxiety to his body and
to the outside and attempts to rise up into his imagination where he
creates, in a sense, a "body-image" of his own. Hysterical speechless-
ness, for instance, may represent an attempt to satisfy two conflicting
drives of a particular speaking situation: the wish to assert one's self
or express hostility openly, and the conflicting need to be accepted,
loved and thought of as being "a nice one" by his listener. The result, as one can see, leads to a state of emotional and physical stress,
inhibition, paralysis and blocking of the whole person—including
that of verbalization.

Semantically speaking, the symbol *is not* the thing symbolized. It
is also an obvious fact, in the process of verbalization, that words or
labels represent conveniences and *are not* the objects or feelings
themselves. As Korzybski (4) so clearly states, "we should carry the
labels in our pockets, so to say, as we carry our money, or checks for

hats or trunks, and not identify them 'emotionally' with what they eventually stand for, because monetary standards change, and hats and trunks get exchanged, lost or burnt. To accomplish this, we must have *objective levels,* which we may handle and carry in our pockets, and also an objective something to which we can attach the labels . . ."

What goes on in the non-verbal, silent or unspeakable levels in relation to life facts can only be differentiated in terms of our individual reactions, orientations, evaluations, etc. To begin with, whatever we perceive from our objective environment through the senses of sight, taste, smell or touch, is absolute in nature and *unspeakable.* For instance, if we take and handle an apple, we discover that the object *is not words* and that to react or arrive at some degree of evaluation, we cannot reach this level with *words alone.* To arrive at a level of awareness and realistic objectivity, we must of necessity handle, look, listen, remain silent, reflect and, in a sense, feel our way through. This "silence on the objective level" involves, to a large extent, checking many of our irrational feelings, preconceived notions, prejudices and dogmatic beliefs. Finally, what occurs is mainly an individual and personalized interpretation of an object, which is, in turn, verbalized and expressed in *one's own symbols and words.*

According to Korzybski (4), to begin with "our lives are lived *entirely* on the *un-speakable* level." We illustrate this constantly in our daily living activities such as sleeping, eating, walking, feelings, desires, pleasures and pain which *are not* words. If words are not translated into the first order unspeakable effects, with the result that we do not do something, or do not feel something, or do not learn or remember something, such words have *no effect* and become useless noises.

The problem in not being able to demonstrate the objective or unspeakable levels, in direct and absolute representations, is *not* necessarily one of inadequacy of words. We can always invent "adequate words," but even the most ideal and structurally adequate language will *not be* the things or feelings themselves. Distortions in verbalizations and language structure occur, in the main, in our reluctance to accept *what is,* and to create, because of our anxieties, conflicts and apprehensions, idealizations and magical identities with words and symbols. In our attempts to describe and verbalize our feelings, actions, beliefs and emotions as we feel they *should be* and not as they exist in *actual reality,* we of necessity are compelled to create and use a vocabulary of magic and imaginative identification, with definitely confused attitudes toward words and symbols.

To arrive at clearer understanding and the choice of a more productive language, we need more than "common sense"—which some time ago was defined by Stuart Chase as that which tells you that the world is flat. Since we live in a world where our manner of thinking and self-expression is strongly molded and influenced by such powerful mass media of communication as television, newspapers, the radio, advertising and magazines—we find little time or, in most situations, do not even care to become self-evaluative. To avoid semantic confusion, we must guard against taking what we hear from others (our teachers, preachers, politicians, salesmen, radio commentators, etc.) as being the "gospel truth." Finally, in this same context, it would prove beneficial in breaking down semantic barriers that: The symbol is *not* the thing symbolized; the word is *not* the thing; the map is *not* the territory for which it stands.

In the process of further clarification of language structure, we must stress the fact that words, as such, must be divided into two categories: a first, in the main, of descriptive, functional words; and a second, of inferential words, which involve assumptions or inferences. For instance, let's take the statement, "John did not go to work this morning." As the comment stands, it is merely descriptive of an event which may or may not have happened to an individual known as John and is in relation to certain concomitants of time and space. If we later discover that John, for some reason or another, *refused* to go to work, then it still remains a descriptive statement, and we now have more definite information and evidence of his inner state of being. Without the latter data, that is without some cognizance of John's attitudes and feelings at the time of action, we are only led to make assumptions or inferences of the facts involved. This discrimination between descriptive and inferential words is not based on any "absolute" differences but, to a large extent, is variable and depends on the context.

An inference may be defined as a statement of the unknown made on the basis of the known. We may *infer,* for instance, from such cultural externals as the pretentiousness of a person's home, automobile, or clothes, his wealth or social position; we may *infer* from the noise of a human cry that a person is in some form of danger; we may *infer* from a man's bodily configuration the nature of his work; we may *infer* from a senator's vote on an economic bill his attitude toward small or large business. These same inferences may be made on the basis of a wealth of previous experience with the subject matter, or of no experience at all. For example, the inferences the trained psychiatrist makes about the prognosis of a person's state of mental health are much more accurate and to the truth than those inferences made by the so-called "parlor analyst," who may base his facts on hearsay and irrational deductions. In short, inferences are generally statements about matters which are not directly known to the conscious mind, made on the basis of what has previously been observed, felt or experienced.

In the process of evaluating ourselves and our relationships to the world about us, we tend to rely on *words rather than facts.* The healthier and the more aware a person is, the more accurate a map he creates of himself, and the more he "knows himself," as *he is* and not as he feels he *should be.* However, to repeat, a map *is not* the territory; one's self-concept *is not* one's self. A map can never represent *all* of its territory; one's self-evaluation in and of itself *omits* certain details of one's actual self—we never know ourselves *completely.* Maps of maps of maps, and so on, can be made: one may describe oneself to oneself, and then make about oneself *any number of inferences and generalizations at higher levels of abstraction* (1).

In relating to others and in the use of our language when speaking, we express our opinions, feelings, beliefs or awareness to the degree to which our thoughts or statements are projective representations of our own inner state of being, at the particular time of expression. This process in itself is variable, flexible and is in dynamic change, from person to person, object to object, and situation to situation. Finally, in our verbal statements, we report facts in the main as they appear *to us,* in relation to our inner condition at the time, by such words as "it seems to me," "from my point of view," "as I see it, it appears thus and thus," etc. For convenience, then, we may refer to consciousness of projection as *to-me-ness* (2).

We are plagued many times today, in our everyday use of language, by the use of *is* as though it were an identity of actuality. The problem, however, is not so much one of revising the language or of eliminating some of the words since our language is so predominantly an *is* language that it would be practically impossible to speak without using the various forms of *to be*. More important is the developing of a keen awareness of projection and the developing of the consciousness that this "is" breeds false-to-fact evaluation. It would prove helpful, in order to minimize verbal confusions and daily disevaluations, to attempt to replace the use of the word *is* by such relative terms as seems, appears, looks like, may be, etc., whenever possible and to indicate to-me-ness by such expressions as "in my judgment," "in my opinion," "from where I stand," "from my particular point of view," and similarly. "But the essential thing," emphasizes Johnson (2), "is *awareness* of projection. We need not always, by any means, express this awareness in so many words out loud or in writing. We can say, 'It is a blue curtain,' or 'It is art,' and know quite clearly what we are doing."

The mechanism of unconscious projection in our everyday language can prove to have some adverse consequences unless we are consciously aware of its process. One of its first consequences is that of making judgments about "things." "Observers," writes Lee (5), "who do not know that the adjective 'is' represents projection tend to rigid and inflexible behavior on the assumption that the 'qualities' are in the object, and obviously 'what is seen is seen.' If other observers are unable to see the 'same' as I do, then they must *be* perverse, blind, or simply dumb. That is, if 'beauty' or 'ugliness' or 'hardness' or 'difficulty' (or any other 'quality') exists in 'things,' and if they are apparent to me, why do others not see and appraise them my way? Of course, the argument is phrased more subtly, but the effect is similar. And invariably, investigation of some of the assumptions of the speaker reveals that he or she ends with, 'Well, it *is* beautiful,' quite unmindful that the inside impressions only are being described . . ."

In the use of judgments, the speaker, consciously or unconsciously, projects his own inner feelings, beliefs or thoughts of approval or disapproval of the occurrences, persons, or objects he is describing. For example, in the statements, "John is a *liar*," "Jack is *cunning*," "Frank is *intelligent*," we imply that the comment as such "to be" or "is" a "fact." We express in such verbal communications a pro-jection of that which is "within ourselves," and accept it as though it were a truthful and meaningful report without too much concern for the external observation of facts or its scientific verifiability.

Still another consequence of "unconscious projection" is the pit-fall in language which occurs when impressions between different observers differ, not so much in relation to the facts at hand, but because of the use of different variable adjectives. For instance, the questions: "Was Jack Dempsey the greatest of champions or merely a good boxer in his prime and day?" "Which is the best form of relaxation, reading, golf, movies, tennis or radio?" or "Could Willy Mays outhit Ty Cobb in his prime?"—are usually aimless and fruit-less to discuss or debate. When this happens, verbal interchange between people leads to little productivity, with no settlement of the question, and with a great deal of emotional interplay which has very little connection with the issue at hand. If the insistence on "splitting hairs" persists, more and more superlative adjectives tend to be injected into the discussion, less and less agreements occur—finally leading to confusion and discord. If we could listen more (without prejudice, criticism or condemnation) and argue less (with-out flared-up emotions and fixed opinions of our own), we might then be able to communicate with each other with more meaningful purpose. The end result would also be one in which we may leave the discussion slightly better informed, slightly more aware of things, and slightly less one-sided and dogmatic than we were before the conversation began.

A second manner in which we might be able to avoid having con-flicting issues in a discussion become an argument is to move the talk from the level of judgment-making to more descriptive levels. In other words, instead of attempting to debate the issue of whether Ty Cobb or Willy Mays is the better hitter or fielder, it would prove more constructive to discuss at length the individual qualities, attri-butes or accomplished actions of either one or both the players involved. Using these extensional facts as a basis for further discus-sion, levels of agreement are more easily achieved, genuine under-standing more easily reached, and the continuation of talk on healthier planes of evaluation is more readily accessible.

SUMMARY

In order to communicate with more purpose and meaning, we of necessity should tend toward a language which is productive and understandable to both the "speaker" and the "listener." An organism which is in conflict and tends toward psychic disorganization and the formation of anxiety will concomitantly express this state of disturbance in all areas of personality, including that of verbalization. Disturbances in communication are not only expressed in terms of the spoken or written word, but in all the interplay of hidden gestures, feelings, bodily reactions, glances, etc., which are constantly going on in dynamic human beings. An awareness of both verbal and non-verbal factors is essential in order to arrive at a more complete understanding of human behavior.

Finally, something cannot exist as something else. The symbol is not the thing symbolized; neither is an object a word. In the process of evaluating ourselves and the relationship to the world about us, we unconsciously tend to project onto words rather than facts. The healthier and the more aware a person is, the more accurate a map he creates of himself, and the more realistically he sees himself, the more will he be able to verbalize facts, situations or feelings as *they are* and not as they *should be*. In conclusion, with our language as it is, we can only make verbal statements and report facts in the main as they appear *to us,* in relation *to our inner condition at the time,* and with variable terms such as "it seems to me," "from my point of view," "as I see it," "it appears thus and thus," etc.

BIBLIOGRAPHY

1. Hayakawa, S. I.: *Language in Thought and Action*. New York: Harcourt, Brace & Co., 1939.
2. Johnson, W.: *People in Quandaries*. New York: Harper & Bros., 1946.
3. Korzybski, A.: *Science and Sanity*, 3rd Edition. Lakeville, Conn.: The International Non-Aristotelian Library Publishing Co., 1950.
4. Korzybski. A.: *Science and Sanity*. Lancaster, Pa.: The Science Press Printing Co., 1933, pp. 476, 477.

5. Lee, I.: *Language Habits in Human Affairs.* New York: Harper & Bros., 1941.
6. Reik, T.: *Listening with the Third Ear.* New York: Farrar Straus, 1949.

21. THE USE OF SILENCE AS A TECHNIQUE IN COUNSELING

Ralph H. Tindall and Francis P. Robinson

INTRODUCTION

Counseling is increasingly recognized as an important method of modifying human behavior. In recent years various attempts have been made to define more objectively the various aspects of this relationship and to study the outcomes of those relationships. Much of this research has been developed at Ohio State University in connection with counseling programs described by Robinson (3) and Rogers (4). Studies by Porter (1), Raimy (2), Snyder (6), and Sherman (5) have demonstrated that it is possible to categorize the various responses and analyze their effects; these studies have shown the distribution and pattern of techniques in conferences.

A next step is an analysis of the effectiveness of particular counselor techniques. This study is an attempt to investigate one of these techniques, the pause or period of silence that occurs during the counseling situation. It is proposed to analyze these pauses or periods of silence as they occurred in transcripts of counseling situations so as to discover (1) the frequency with which silence or pause is used and (2) the effect of their use on the dynamics of the counseling situation.

METHOD

Sources of Data

At Ohio State University many conferences in connection with a how-to-study course and some in connection with therapy cases

---

Reprinted by permission of the authors and *Journal of Clinical Psychology,* III, No. 2 (April, 1947), 136-41.

have been mechanically recorded and subsequently typed. In preparing these transcripts any noticeable pause during the conference was noted. Sixty-one of these transcripts became the basic source material for this investigation. They represent the work of twenty-two different counselors who were persons with professional recognition in the counseling field or advanced graduate students with some experience in counseling. An analysis of these sixty-one transcripts revealed a total of 708 pauses. Of these pauses it was found that 369 were counselor-initiated, 285 were counselee-initiated and 54 were unclassifiable because of incomplete transcriptions due to mechanical difficulties.

Classification System

It was first necessary to construct a categorizing system that would adequately describe each pausal situation. Fifteen representative transcriptions were read and a short description of each pause was written out. These descriptions were then read and classified in similar groups. It was found possible to include all pauses in the following eight categories subsumed under the two general headings "counselee-initiated" and "counselor-initiated." These were later found to be broad enough to describe all of the pausal situations found in the entire study.

Counselee-Initiated Pauses:

I (Indecision). The counselee pauses because of emotional involvement in the topic under discussion; he is undecided as to just how to proceed, because he feels the discussion may be getting too close to his real conflicts.

N (Normal). The counselee reaches the natural, normal termination of his part of the conversation. There is rarely any degree of emotional involvement in this type of pause.

O (Organizational). The counselee pauses for the purpose of organizing what he is going to present verbally. Such a pause is usually followed by re-statement or by a more complex elaboration of the point just made.

S (Solicitation). The counselee pauses to solicit a response from the counselor. He desires approval, advice, information, or an answer to a direct question.

Counselor-Initiated Pauses:

D (Deliberate). A deliberate use of pause on the part of the counselor in an attempt to force the counselee to carry the burden of the conversation.

O (Organizational). This use of pause by the counselor corresponds to the Ce *O* pause classification.

N (Normal). This is the use of pause by the counselor as a natural termination of a particular phase of the topic under discussion.

Unclassified:

This category includes pauses where mechanical failure in the recording apparatus made it impossible to determine who initiated the pause or its nature.

The next step was to devise a system of analyzing the effects of these different types of pauses. In order to construct such a list of categories, the fifteen original transcripts were re-read and after several revisions the following list was developed. It proved adequate in describing the effects of the various types of counselee-initiated and counselor-initiated pauses in all the interviews studied.

Responsibility Assumed—Other: The responsibility for carrying forward the conversation of the conference is assumed after a pause initiated by the opposite person.

Responsibility Assumed—Self: The person who paused in his conversation reassumed the responsibility for continuance.

Cue Missed: The party not initiating the pause failed to respond to the pause, failed to take over the burden of the conversation, failed to clarify, or failed to give information.

Clarification: Following a pause either the counselee or the counselor found it necessary to elaborate, explain, or re-define because what he had said previously was not clear to the other.

Fill-in: Practically verbatim repetition while either the counselor or counselee was doing such activities as lighting a cigarette or manipulating materials used in the counseling situation. It was also found to occur in comments introduced as inconsequential asides that added little to either clarification of concepts or addition of new material for consideration.

Information Given by Counselor: The counselor either gives requested information or cites examples which form a basis for the counselee formulating an answer to his stated problem.

Information Given by Counselee: The counselee gives new information that has a bearing upon the problems under consideration

Develops Problem Statement: Either the counselor or the counselee phrases a statement of the problem which at the moment seems to be giving the counselee difficulty.

Develops Plan Statement: The counselor states a proposed plan of action for the counselee to reject or adopt, or the counselee states a plan of action that he plans to follow.

Resistance Follows: The counselee either refuses to consider further the topic under discussion or objects to the counseling situation or the counselor as such.

Subject Change Occurs: The pause is followed by a distinct subject change.

Summarization: A summary of what has gone before by either the counselee or the counselor.

Unclassifiable: Effects that could not be determined due to mechanical failure, garbled reproduction, or otherwise undeterminable effects.

TABLE 1

DISTRIBUTION OF TYPES OF PAUSES AND (BELOW THE DOUBLE LINE)
THEIR EFFECTS ON THE INTERVIEW

	Counselee					Counselor			
	I	N	O	S	Uncl	D	O	N	Totals
Pause-frequencies..........	48	109	101	27	54	109	196	64	708
Effect—totals..............	99	225	207	54	55	261	388	142	1,431
Responsibility assumed—other	20	84	0	26	0	55	0	20	205
Responsibility assumed—self..	28	25	100	1	0	49	195	40	438
Cue missed	0	0	0	1	0	40	0	0	41
Clarification	10	38	41	11	1	39	115	29	284
"Fill-in"..................	12	25	1	2	0	11	5	6	62
Information given by Cr.....	0	13	0	8	0	8	41	12	82
Information given by Ce.....	8	8	40	0	0	31	0	10	97
Develops problem statement..	10	8	17	3	1	9	10	4	62
Develops plan statement.....	4	7	6	1	0	10	10	1	39
Resistance follows...........	4	0	0	0	0	2	0	6	12
Subject change occurs.......	2	11	1	1	1	2	2	10	30
Summarization.............	1	3	0	0	0	0	9	0	13
Unclassifiable..............	0	3	1	0	52	5	1	4	66

After this categorical scheme for both frequency and effects of pauses was devised, the pauses found in the preliminary fifteen transcripts were tabulated on a chart similar to the form of Table 1. An alphabetical tabulatory scheme was used so that the effect or several effects of each frequency in the vertical categories could later be traced as to their effects. Thus, the first pause found in a transcript was labeled (a) under its proper vertical heading and also entered in its proper horizontal effect category or categories.

In order to establish some measure of reliability with which the analyst used this check list, a period of three weeks was allowed to elapse and then these same transcripts were re-read and re-categorized. During the interim some of the other forty-six transcripts in the study were read and their pauses tabulated as this activity was felt to aid in obliterating the memory effect of specific cues that influenced the original categorization. When the 112 cells of the two tabulation check lists for each of the fifteen transcripts were compared and averaged, it was found that the writer was in absolute agreement with himself 85% of the time.

RESULTS

The results from the categorization of the 708 pauses in 61 interviews are summarized in Table 1. Reading the table horizontally the first or frequency line shows the distribution of the pauses under the categories of counselee-initiated and counselor-initiated and their subheadings. Thus, there were 48 pauses of the Ce I (indecision) category, 109 pauses of the Ce N (normal) category and similarly the frequency of pause for each category described can be read. The effects are tabulated below the broken line. The next two horizontal lines show the effect of each type of pause upon the interview in terms of who carried the responsibility. Thus, it can be seen that of the 48 Ce I pauses, 20 were followed by a shift of responsibility while 28 were followed by a resumption of the responsibility by the person initiating the pause. Below the responsibility lines it is possible to read the frequency of other types of effects as they occurred following the different types of pauses.

It can be seen that the counselors were more apt to use pause than the counselees (369 times as compared to 285 times). The counselees' most frequent use of pause was as a normal termination of a topic under discussion (109 out of the 285 times) followed closely by using the pause for organization prior to verbalization (101 out of the 285 times). On the other hand the counselors were more apt to use pause for organizational purposes (196 out of the 369 times) than for any other purposes. For the total pauses studied (708) there were 1,431 effects noted; each pause tended to more than one effect. This was caused by checking (a) who assumed the responsibility where determinable and (b) other effects.

An understanding on the counselor's part of the counselee's purpose in using pauses should enable the counselor to guide the conference more intelligently. With this in mind the relation of the 285 counselee pauses to their 585 effects was analyzed. This included re-reading the original protocols as each category was studied. In the following paragraphs a few of the most significant findings are presented.

Ce I (indecision) pauses represented 17% of all counselee pauses. Responsibility for carrying the interview forward was assumed about equally thereafter (20 vs. 28). The most common effects are "fill-ins" (12 times) followed closely by clarification and developing a statement of the problem (10 times each). Re-reading the interviews showed that when the counselor waits silently, feeling that the counselee may re-assume the burden of conversation, the counselee tends to develop further a statement of his problem or to introduce new information pertinent to the interview. However, if the counselor feels it necessary to take over the responsibility, we find him most frequently filling in with inconsequential activity or clarifying significant statements already made.

The 109 Ce N (natural termination) pauses represented the counselee's most frequent usage of pause; in 84 of these instances the counselors assumed the burden of conducting the interview. When this occurred, clarification was the major effect following the pause, next most frequent was fill-in. If the counselee was allowed to re-assume the burden, the most frequent effects were introduction of new information by the counselees and clarification of statements already made.

Ce O (organization) pauses were used by the counselees 101 times. After none of these pauses did the counselors studied take over the responsibility. This type of pause was most often followed by attempts of the counselees to clarify previously made statements. The next most frequent effect was the introduction of new information by the counselees. Less frequently the counselees developed a statement of their problems and still less frequently a plan of attack upon those problems.

Ce S (solicitation) pauses were the least frequent type of pause used by the counselees. In almost every instance this type of pause demanded a taking of the responsibility by the counselor. The counselors utilized the counseling period following this type of pause to clarify statements or to introduce new information for the counselee's consideration in the solution of the problem.

Next, what are the most pertinent effects of the counselor-initiated pauses? The counselor has the opportunity to weigh the momentary counseling situation with all of its variables and decide what technique can be most profitably used for the purposes of the conference. A controlled use of silence may well be considered one of the techniques available.

Cr D (deliberate) pauses were used by the counselors 109 times out of the 369 counselor-initiated pausal situations. The counselors were successful in getting the counselees to assume the burden half the time (55 instances). When the counselees did assume the responsibility, they (in order of decreasing frequency) added new information, clarified, developed plans of action, or formulated statements of their problems. In 49 instances the counselor had to reassume the burden of responsibility. When this occurred the major effects were counselor clarification and counselor introduced fill-in. There were only two instances where the counselor's deliberate use of pause as a forcing technique resulted in counselee resistance.

Cr O (organizational) pause was the most frequent use (196 times) made of the pausal situation by the counselors studied. These were found to be followed usually by the counselors re-assuming the responsibility for carrying the conversation forward, which they did by attempting to clarify statements already made. They frequently utilized the period following such a pause to introduce new information for the counselee's consideration.

Cr N (natural termination) pauses were used the least frequently by the counselors studied. Following such a pause the counselors had to re-assume the burden of conversation twice as often as it was assumed by the counselees. When the counselors continued with the burden, the major effects were clarification, new information, and a change of subject. In the instances where the counselees assumed the responsibility, they were most likely to add new information dealing with their problems followed less frequently by an attempt to clarify their statements already made.

SUMMARY

Sixty-one counseling transcripts involving twenty-two different counselor-counselee relationships were examined to determine the frequency and effect of use of silence as a counseling technique. It was found that pauses occur frequently and can be classified as to intent and as to their varied effects upon the counseling situation. It was also demonstrated that these classifications can be made with a significant degree of reliability (85% absolute agreement).

It was found that the 285 counselee-initiated pauses studied could be classified under four major classifications in order of frequency of use: (1) pauses representing natural termination of statement, (2) pauses primarily for the purpose of mental organization prior to verbalization, (3) pauses resulting from indecision, (4) and pauses for the purpose of soliciting information from the counselor. The greatest effect of the counselees' use of pause was clarification; other effects in order were introduction of information, fill-in, statement of the problem, statement of plan of attack, a subject change, and (in rare instances) summarization and resistance.

It was found that the 369 counselor-initiated pauses could be categorized under three major headings in order of frequency of use: (1) pauses for the purpose of organization of thought prior to verbalization, (2) pauses used deliberately in an attempt to force the counselee to contribute to the counseling situation, (3) pauses used to terminate a phase in the counseling unit. Here, too, it was found that the greatest single effect upon the counseling situation was clarification. This effect was followed in order of frequency of occurrence by the introduction of new information, a statement of the problem, a fill-in, a development of plan statement, and a change of subject. Rare effects of pauses initiated by the counselor were summarization and resistance.

Counselors who become conscious of the frequency and nature of the different types of pauses can forecast, to a limited extent, the probable effect of any particular pause upon the immediate counseling situation. With such knowledge on the counselor's part it is possible to develop a greater control over the progress toward the counseling objective being sought.

REFERENCES

1. Porter, E. H., Jr. The development and evaluation of a measure of counseling interview procedures. *Educ. Psychol. Meas.,* **3,** 1943, 105-126, 215-238.
2. Raimy, V. C. *The self concept as a factor in the counseling and personality organization.* Unpublished Ph.D. Dissertation, Ohio State University, 1943.
3. Robinson, F. P. Two quarries with a single stone. *J. higher Educ.,* **16,** 1945, 201-206.
4. Rogers, C. R. Counseling and psychotherapy, New York: Houghton Mifflin, 1942.
5. Sherman, D. M. *An analysis of the dynamic relationships between counselor techniques and outcomes in larger units of the interview situation.* Unpublished Ph.D. Dissertation, Ohio State University, 1945.
6. Snyder, W. U. *An investigation of the nature of non-directive psychotherapy.* Unpublished Ph.D. Dissertation, Ohio State University, 1943.

22. EXPERIENCING: A VARIABLE IN THE PROCESS OF THERAPEUTIC CHANGE

Eugene T. Gendlin

INTRODUCTION

For many years there has been a heated discussion in psychology between those who emphasize the need for operational scientific method and those who emphasize the need for consideration of the subjective, personally important variables of human phenomena

Reprinted by permission of the author and *American Journal of Psychotherapy,* XV, No. 2 (April, 1961), 233-45.

which science too often omits. The present paper holds that both viewpoints express the need for science to move *from* naturalistic and subjective observation of important human phenomena *to* operationally defined observations of these phenomena.

The purpose of theory is to lead to hypotheses and operationally defined observations which test hypotheses. It is the contention of this paper that theory which conceptualizes subjective observations can lead to operational hypotheses and research. Operationally defined observation is the *aim,* not the *start* of theory. The theory of experiencing, here presented, starts with subjective and naturalistic observation. It attempts to formulate theoretical concepts which lead to operational research categories. Operational and objective standards of science should be applied to the research procedures that result from theory, not to the naturalistic observations from which theory must start. If the start and the outcome of theory are confused, observations of central variables of human behavior will be kept out of science on the grounds that such observations are subjective. The present paper formulates six theoretical propositions which refer to a subjective process: "experiencing." The paper will attempt to show that a theory which formulates concepts referring to a subjective process can lead to objective operational research.

I. The Experience Process

Therapeutic change may be viewed as an outcome or as a process. Outcome is the difference between personality measures before and after psychotherapy. A good deal of theory and research has been devoted to the outcome of psychotherapy. By "process," on the other hand, I mean an ongoing flow of events that occurs continuously in the individual. Outcome differences are the result of an ongoing process of therapy. Very little theory and research has so far dealt with this process.

In this paper I will discuss one variable of the process of therapy. I will call that variable "experiencing."

Let me begin my delineation of the variable "experiencing" by discussing two of its characteristics: (1) Experiencing is *felt,* rather than thought, known, or verbalized. (2) Experiencing occurs in the *immediate* present. It is not generalized attributes of a person such as traits, complexes, or dispositions. Rather, experiencing is what a person feels here and now, in this moment. Experiencing is a changing flow of feeling which makes it possible for every individual to feel something in any given moment. I would like to discuss these two characteristics of experiencing together:

(1) *Experiencing is a process of feeling*
(2) *Experiencing occurs in the immediate present*

When therapists discuss cases, they use rough metaphoric terms to refer to a feeling process. They often say that they observe clients "emotionally absorbing something," or "working through," or "feeling through." The therapeutic process is observed to involve not only concepts, but also a feeling process, which I would like to call "experiencing."

Freud relates how he discovered that it was not sufficient for therapy to arrive at an accurate diagnosis. The diagnosis had to be communicated to the patient. Then, the patient still had to be brought to understand and accept it. But even then, the patient often accepted the diagnosis more as a matter of courtesy for the doctor, or as a matter of intellectual insight, without genuine emotional change.

> The ego still finds it difficult to nullify its repressions, even after it has resolved to give up its resistances, and we have designated the phase of strenuous effort which follows upon this laudable resolution as the period of "working through" (1).

Genuine psychotherapy began at this point, that is to say, at the point of going beyond the intellectual approach by helping the patient to an *immediate, present experiencing* of his problems. Even though the problems may concern events which occurred early in life, therapeutic change in these problems requires a present *experiencing*, that is to say a *present feeling process*. Freud achieved this present immediacy by discovering manifestations of the patient's problems in the present moment of the relationship between doctor and patient. In this way the patient could be helped to grapple with his problems on an emotional level and in the *immediate present*.

From this discussion by Freud we may formulate the two characteristics of experiencing stated above: (1) experiencing is a process of feeling rather than intellectual understanding; (2) experiencing is a process which occurs in the immediate present of the therapy hour.

(3) *Experiencing is a direct referent*

Let me now add a third characteristic: Experiencing can be *directly referred to* by an individual as a felt datum in his own phenomenal field. Very frequently, during therapy hours, clients may be observed to refer directly to their experiencing. Experiencing itself is, of course, private and unobservable. However, gestures, tone of voice, manner of expression, as well as the context of what is said are often observable indications of direct reference to experiencing. Certain characteristic forms of verbal expression are also observable indices of direct reference to experiencing. When a client refers directly to his experiencing, he is likely to use some demonstrative pronouns like "this" or "it" or "that all tied-up feeling." His verbal expressions indicate that he is pointing to a felt datum within himself. Let me cite some common observations from therapy hours in which experiencing is directly referred to.

Clients frequently speak of feeling something without knowing what it is they feel. Both client and counselor call such a feeling "this feeling" and continue to communicate about it although neither person knows just what that feeling is. At such times, both persons directly refer to the client's ongoing experiencing. They do so without a conceptualization of what the client refers to. The symbols used (such as the term "this") do not conceptualize. They do not formulate anything. They only point. Such symbols are neither accurate nor inaccurate. They convey no information about the feeling, they only refer to it. I am giving the name "direct reference" to such pointing to present experiencing.

Direct reference may also occur when client and counselor do know what the feeling is but nevertheless need to *refer directly* to the experiencing and not to the conceptualization. For example: "I have *known* all along that I feel this way, but I am amazed at *how strongly* I do feel that."

Let me cite another, similar case where direct reference to experiencing is necessary even though an accurate conceptualization is also present. A client has all along asserted something about himself, for example, "I am afraid of being rejected." After many hours of therapy he comes upon the feelings which make this so. He discovers anew that he is afraid of being rejected. Usually he is then somewhat troubled by the fact that the feelings are new, different, amazing, yet no better words exist for them than the old, trite, "I am afraid of being rejected." The client then struggles to communicate to the counselor that now he "really" feels it, that the concepts are old but the experiencing is *new.*

Direct reference to experiencing is also noticeable in many clients' reports about their experiencing between therapy sessions. Clients often report being "disturbed," "unsettled," a "churning," a "something going on in them" but they may or may not know what it is.

In these observations it is clear that the client is referring to something other than conceptualizations. He is referring directly to his present *experiencing.*

(4) *Experiencing guides conceptualization*

A fourth characteristic of experiencing lies in the client's use of it to guide him toward increasingly accurate conceptualizations. A client may feel a feeling and refer to it for quite some time before attempting a formation of it in terms of concepts. When he has attempted such a first formulation he often considers what he has just said and then feels: "yes, that's it!" or, "no, that isn't quite it." Often he does not know how what is said differs from what he feels, but he knows it differs. In these examples it is clear that the client refers directly to his experiencing, and is checking his first rough conceptual formulations against his present experiencing. In this way present experiencing guides conceptualizations.

So far, I have said about experiencing that it is felt and occurs in the immediate present, that the individual refers directly to it as a datum in his own phenomenal field, and that he guides his conceptual formulations by such direct reference.

(5) *Experiencing is implicitly meaningful*

The fact that direct reference to experiencing can guide conceptualization, implies a fifth characteristic of experiencing: It is implicitly meaningful. The implicit meaning is only felt, and may not become explicit until later. Yet this implicit meaning can guide conceptualization.

Here is something we call a "feeling," something felt in a physical sense, yet later on the individual will say that certain *concepts* now accurately represent that *feeling*. The feeling, he will say, *was* such and so all along, but he didn't know it. He only felt it. He felt it in such a unique and specific way that he could gradually, by directly referring to it, arrive at concepts for it. That is to say, the feeling was implicitly meaningful. It had a meaning which was distinguishably different from other feelings and meanings, but its meaning was felt rather than known in explicit symbols.

If I may speak of "felt meaning," I am of course using the term "meaning" in a very special sense. Such "meaning," is somewhat different from the sense in which concepts or words have meaning. Here is an example of the difference. *One* concept or *one* word has a univocal single meaning, whereas *one* feeling often implicitly contains very many different conceptual meanings. Like a dream symbol, *one* felt datum may give rise to a great many complex conceptualizations. A client in therapy can work with one felt referent which implicitly contains very many complex meanings that may become conceptualized only much later.

The following is an example of how felt *implicit* meaning becomes conceptualized.

A person may say "I have to go to a meeting tonight, but for some reason I don't want to go." Now, from this verbal content *we* have no way of getting at why he doesn't want to go. Only *he* has a way of getting at the feelings and this way lies through direct reference to his present experiencing about it. As he refers directly to his present experiencing he may say, "Well, I don't know *what it is,* but I sure don't want to go." He may continue to refer to his present experiencing and it may change even without further conceptual formulation. Or, as he continues to refer to it, he may say, "H-mm, I don't want to go because Mr. X will be there and he will argue with me and I hate that." This verbal content will have arisen for him from a direct reference—a direct grappling with his present experiencing. Nor is this all the meaning that might emerge as he grapples with his present experiencing. A little later he may say, "Oh, it isn't that I hate arguing with Mr. X; actually I love to argue with him, but I'm afraid he will make fun of me when I get excited in arguing." In this example, the individual forms concepts on the basis of direct references to his experiencing. He is not simply using certain concepts which accurately say something about him. He is not deducing from his behavior that he is afraid of being ridiculed. Rather he forms the conceptualizations on the basis of direct reference to present experiencing.

As he refers directly to the felt datum from which all these verbalizations spring, he finds new aspects which he can now differentiate, all of which were implicitly contained in his not wanting to go to the meeting. He may all the while be feeling intensely and working with his fear of being ridiculed and his feelings of inadequacy. A book might be written about all the meanings which are implicitly contained in this one datum of directly referred to experiencing with which he is now working. Although not conceptualized, all these meanings may be in the process of changing. Such meanings are felt as a single "this way I feel"; the implicit meanings can be complex, multiple, and can contain all sorts of perceptions and differentiations of circumstances, past and present. Thus, present experiencing is an implicitly meaningful felt datum.

(6) *Experiencing is a preconceptual organismic process*

I would like to distinguish implicit felt meaning from what is usually called "unconscious," or "denied to awareness." Implicit meaning is often unconceptualized in awareness. However, the experiencing of the felt datum is conscious. Only because it is conscious can the client feel it, refer to it, talk about it, attempt to conceptualize it, and check the accuracy of his conceptualizations against it. The implicit meaning of experiencing is felt in awareness, although the many complex meanings of one such feeling may not have been conceptualized before.

The many implicit meanings of a moment's experiencing are not already conceptual and then repressed. Rather, we must consider these meanings to be preconceptual, aware but as yet undifferentiated.

Preconceptual events in the organism can have meaning, because all organismic events occur in organized patterns of interaction in the biologic and interpersonal environments. In this way, as Harry Stack Sullivan (2) points out, "all human experience is symbolic." The complex organization of the organism is partly biologic and partly interpersonal. It exists at birth but it is also modified by subsequent conditioning and learning. Thus any event of the organism is symbolic of its organized interrelations with other events and processes of life and interaction. Hence one such event can implicitly represent—or mean—many complex aspects of many other events. Hence the directly felt data of present experiencing have implicit preconceptual meaning.

The process of therapeutic changing involves this directly felt, implicitly meaningful organismic experiencing. In the therapeutic process, certain few differentiated meanings do play an important role. However, a vital role is played also by organismic processes, as these are at any given moment felt. They constitute a present inner datum, a direct referent. Change in therapy does not concern only those few conceptual meanings which the individual thinks or puts into words. Therapeutic change occurs as a result of a process in which implicit meanings are in awareness, and are intensely felt, directly referred to, and changed, without ever being put into words. Thus the process of therapy involves experiencing.

The characteristics of experiencing which I have mentioned are: (1) Experiencing is a process of *feeling* (2) occurring in the *immediate* present. (3) Clients can *refer directly* to experiencing. (4) In forming conceptualizations, clients are *guided* by experiencing. First rough conceptualizations can be checked against direct reference to experiencing. (5) Experiencing has *implicit meanings*. (6) These are preconceptual. Experiencing is a concrete *organismic* process, felt in awareness.

II. Therapeutic Responses

If it is true that therapists observe and talk about the function of what I am calling *experiencing* in therapy, then this formulation of experiencing should help state the aim of therapeutic *responses* and should help explain how therapeutic responses *achieve* their aim. Let me attempt to discuss the aim and the effect of two kinds of therapeutic responses in terms of the function of experiencing in the therapy process.

I will try to show that both client-centered responses and interpretations can be described in a way which makes them seem effective, or they can be described so as to seem ineffective. I will try to show that when therapeutic responses are said to be effective, it is because they are said to maximize the role of experiencing in the therapeutic process.

Client-centered responses are sometimes described as mere repetitions of what the client says. According to this description, the therapist adds nothing to what the client says. Such a description makes client-centered responses appear shallow. Client-centered therapists do not merely repeat. But since they also wish to emphasize that they do not interpret, it is difficult to formulate just what they really do. Applying what I have said about experiencing, I believe it would be true to say that a good client-centered response formulates the *felt, implicit* meaning of the client's present experiencing. The client-centered response at its best formulates something which is not yet fully formulated, or fully conceptualized. It formulates what the client is aware of, but not conceptually or verbally aware of. It formulates the meaning which the client has been trying to get at by various different verbalizations. In short, I believe that the optimal client-centered response attempts to refer to, and to formulate, the client's present felt experiencing. It thereby helps the client formulate it, and refer directly to it, so that better and more differentiated conceptualizations can be worked for, and so that he can feel his present feeling more deeply and intensely.

I have tried to contrast a shallow and inadequate description of the client-centered response with what I believe is an accurate description. This accurate description requires the notion of experiencing as an aware, felt, and implicitly meaningful direct referent.

Let me attempt the same kind of contrast in the case of interpretation. A poor and shallow description of interpretation, I believe, would be that interpretation explains to the patient something of which he is himself unaware. He is unaware of the matter, presumably because his defenses make direct awareness impossible. Therefore, the patient can profit from such an interpretation only in an intellectual sense. The mere concept does not overcome the emotional defenses. Hence the patient goes home with only a concept. Instead of helping the patient, the therapist leaves him to grapple with the emotions and defenses by himself.

Obviously this describes interpretive therapy as it stood previous to Freud's discovery that intellectual insight is not enough. An effective interpretation must somehow help the patient deal with the inner experiencing to which the interpretation refers. How does it help him to cope with the experiencing? Fenichel (3), in *The Psychoanalytic Theory of the Neurosis,* says:

> Since interpretation means helping something unconscious become
> conscious by naming it at the moment it is striving to break
> through, effective interpretations can be given only at one specific
> point, namely, where the patient's immediate interest is momen-
> tarily centered.

In other words, an effective interpretation is one which refers to
just that datum on which the patient's interest is centered, or, as I
would put it, an effective interpretation refers to the present experiencing to which the patient just now directly refers. Also, an effective interpretation names or tries to conceptualize the *implicit*
meaning which, although *now being felt* and now striving to break
through, has not quite fully broken through yet.

I have tried to show that when therapeutic methods are oversimplified and criticized, they are usually portrayed just so as to omit
experiencing. This makes them appear purely conceptual. Client-
centered responses can be oversimplified as mere repetitions of the
client's concepts. Interpretations can be oversimplified as mere in-
tellectualizations. On the other hand, these responses are said to be
effective when they are said to enhance the role of experiencing in
the therapeutic process. They refer to the individual's present experiencing. They attempt to name accurately what he is aware of
and feels, but has not fully conceptualized. They help the individual
refer to a present inner datum which, although felt in awareness, is
not conceptually known.

I believe that when these kinds of therapeutic responses achieve
their aim, they are in practice quite similar to each other. Let me
now try to describe such a response in words which do not belong to
any one orientation. An effective therapeutic response refers to what
the individual is now aware of. However, it does not refer simply to
his words or thoughts. Rather, it refers to the present felt datum, his
present experiencing. Presumably, the individual's words and gestures are attempts to express, imply, get at, this present felt datum.
The response will not always be able to state it accurately, but it can
always refer to it. Even before it becomes clear just what the implicit
meaning of a present experiencing is, both persons can refer to it,
both persons can call it "this feeling which is so and so," or "this
whole problem with your mother," or, "what you are trying to get
at seems to be somewhat scary," or similar words which obviously

refer to *this* in the individual, to which he now directly refers. An effective therapeutic response thus aims to refer directly and to help the individual refer directly, to his present experiencing. Such a response aids him to feel this present experiencing more intensely, to grapple with it, face it, tolerate it, and work it through. Such a response helps him to put the implicit meaning of his experiencing into concepts which accurately state it.

It is clear that the therapist's responses, when they refer to and name present experiencing, are not theoretical deductions about the client. Rather, they refer to an implicit meaning of which the client is now directly aware and which he communicates by implication. When responses refer to and name experiencing, they have "depth," because what the client now feels is often much more than his words explicitly state. It is a kind of depth, all of which is in the client's awareness, but in a felt, rather than a conceptual form.

I have tried to give a theoretical formulation of the role of experiencing in the process of therapy, and to show how this role of experiencing is implied in the aim of effective therapeutic responses.

III. Research

I would like now to turn to the operational indices which have so far been used to test hypotheses concerning experiencing. The studies I will cite are not presented as research reports. They are intended to illustrate that although the theory of experiencing formulates subjective phenomena, it leads to operational research employing commonly known techniques and instruments.

The instruments used are those which have been developed during the last ten years in order to measure outcomes of psychotherapy. In addition to personality measures they include Q sorts, rating scales and other ways of quantifying the subjective aspects of psychotherapy. Although these instruments are used in new ways, their basic operational character is not altered by the theory of experiencing.

Indices of experiencing are observed by counselors. Thus one avenue of research uses counselor rating scales concerning their observations of clients during therapy. Scores on these scales are then correlated with other measures. Another avenue of research is the client's own quantified report of his experiencing on a Q sort consisting of descriptions of therapy experiences. A third avenue is a classification of verbalizations on tape recordings of therapy hours. Indices of experiencing found on the tapes can be correlated with measures of personality change.

The basic hypothesis derived from the theory is: the greater the role played by experiencing during the therapy hours, the greater will be the therapeutic change and the successful outcome of therapy. Change and outcome are measured by traditional personality measures, such as the TAT, Rorschach, or MMPI, and by counselor success ratings after therapy. The role played by experiencing during therapy has been measured in terms of operational indices of three of the mentioned characteristics of experiencing:

(a) immediacy of feeling (characteristic 2) as contrasted with postponed affect.

(b) direct reference to directly felt data (characteristic 3) as contrasted with external or cognitive content.

(c) feelings which are not yet understood but which guide the individual's formation of new concepts about himself (characteristic 4).

In each of the following research projects the hypothesis is that the amount of therapeutic change will correlate with the degree to which an operational index of a characteristic of experiencing is observed during therapy.

(a) *Immediacy of experiencing:* In a study by Gendlin, Jenney, and Shlien (4) counselors quantified their observations of clients during therapy by marking several rating scales with a range of 1-9. These ratings were then correlated with the clients' success ratings. It was found that success ratings did *not* correlate at all with those scales which concerned verbal content. It made no difference whether clients chiefly talked about past or present events. On the other hand, success ratings correlated with a rating scale of immediacy. Success ratings went to those clients who were observed, during therapy, as most often expressing feelings directly and with *immediacy,* rather than merely talking *about* feelings.

Immediacy of experiencing is also measured by Rogers' Process Scale (5, 6). A part of that scale rates tape-recorded interview material on a continuum between the poles of "remoteness from experiencing" and "experiencing in the immediate present . . . as a clear and usable referent."

(b) *Direct reference to experiencing:* Direct reference to experiencing is being measured by Zimring who devised a classification system of clients' verbalizations. The classes include direct reference to presently felt but not cognitively known data as well as other types of reference. The classification system is applied to tape-recorded therapy interviews, and can be correlated with measures of personality change to test the prediction that those clients who show the most indices of direct reference will show the greatest therapeutic change.

(c) *Feelings guiding concept formation:* A Q-sort was devised to measure the degree to which a client's experiencing during therapy guides his formations of concepts. The Q-sort consisted of 32 cards containing statements which describe experiences that many clients have during therapy hours. Each statement describes an experience involving strong feelings that are not yet understood, or efforts to understand puzzling present feelings during therapy. The Q-sort was administered to clients during and after therapy. Preliminary findings show that success ratings by counselors correlate significantly with client's scores on this Q-sort. The finding is a preliminary indication that clients succeed in therapy if they often experience immediately present feelings which they do not as yet understand.

Rating scales, Q-sorts and classifications of verbal responses used by counselors, clients, and judges can define quantitative operational formulations of the characteristics of experiencing. Thus, although theoretically the term experiencing refers to the *subjective* feeling process privately referred to by the individual, the theory leads to operational hypotheses which can be tested by quantitative objective observation.

This paper introduces some of the theoretical concepts (7) of the continuing research on experiencing. Many of the basic concepts were originated and developed in collaboration with Fred M. Zimring (8). The whole approach was developed from the work of Carl R. Rogers.

These beginnings of research show that it is possible to measure the relationship between the outcome of therapy and indices of experiencing as it functions in the process of therapy. Thus operational research is possible concerning the function of experiencing in the process of therapy.

SUMMARY

Experiencing is a variable of the process of therapeutic changing. Experiencing is a process of feeling, rather than concepts. It occurs in the immediate present and can be directly referred to by an individual as a felt datum in his phenomenal field. Experiencing guides the client's conceptualizations, and has implicit meaning which is organismic and preconceptual. Change occurs in therapy even before the client has accurate concepts to represent the feelings to which he directly refers. Experiencing is in awareness, but is felt rather than known conceptually. Experiencing can implicitly have a great many complex meanings, all of which can be in the process of changing even while they are being directly referred to as some one "this way I feel."

When therapeutic responses, both client-centered and interpretive, are said to be effective, it is because they are said to enhance the function of experiencing in therapy.

Operational research has begun to test the importance of the function of experiencing in therapeutic change by correlating observable indices of experiencing with other measures of therapy.

BIBLIOGRAPHY

1. Freud, S. *The Problem of Anxiety*. W. W. Norton, New York, 1936, p. 105.
2. Sullivan, H. S. *The Interpersonal Theory of Psychiatry*. W. W. Norton, New York, 1953, p. 186.
3. Fenichel, O. *The Psychoanalytic Theory of the Neuroses*. W. W. Norton, New York, 1945.
4. Gendlin, E., Jenney, R., and Shlien, J. Counselor Ratings of Process and Outcomes in Client-Centered Therapy. *Report to the American Psychological Association Convention,* 1956.
5. Rogers, C. R. A Process Conception of Psychotherapy. *Am. Psychologist.* 13: 142, 1958.
6. Walker, A., Rogers, C., and Rablen, R. Development and Application of a Scale to Measure Process Changes in Psychotherapy. *Report to the American Psychological Association Convention,* Washington, D. C., 1958.

7. Gendlin, E. *Experiencing and the Creation of Meaning.* The Free Press (in press).
8. Gendlin, E., and Zimring, F. The Qualities or Dimensions of Experiencing and Their Change, *Counseling Center Discussion Papers.* 1: 3, 1955.

23. AUTHORITARIANISM IN THE THERAPEUTIC RELATIONSHIP [1]

John L. Vogel

This study was concerned with the therapist, the patient, and their relationship in psychotherapy. It dealt with authoritarianism as a personality trait in each of the individuals, and tested for associations between authoritarianism as a trait, attitude, and behavior. A major hypothesis of this study was that the peculiar interaction of authoritarianism in therapist and patient would be crucial to the development of the therapeutic relationship. Although this study did concern itself with authoritarianism, this trait was not necessarily thought to be the most basic or critical aspect of the therapeutic relationship. It was selected for study here to demonstrate the importance of considering the personality, needs, and motives of therapist *and* patient, as they interact in the therapeutic relationship.

Of the many personality variables that might be studied in this manner, the writer chose to consider authoritarianism, as delineated in the major work on *The Authoritarian Personality* (Adorno, Frenkel-Brunswik, Levinson, & Sanford, 1950). It was thought that the patient population of any clinic might not be as individualistic, equalitarian, and self-actualizing as some writers seemed to assume. Further, even a generally equalitarian patient may develop authoritarian expectations about psychotherapy from his experience with other professions. For the therapist, we know that there is a wide range of therapeutic behavior in terms of training and orientation, to say nothing of the range of attitudes and needs they may have.

Reprinted by permission of the author and *Journal of Consulting Psychology,* XXV, No. 2 (April, 1961), 102-8.

[1] Based on a doctoral dissertation submitted to the University of Chicago, 1959. The writer is indebted to Donald W. Fiske, Desmond S. Cartwright, and Ralph W. Heine for their encouragement and help.

Authoritarianism, then, was thought to be one of the trait dimensions relevant to patient and therapist roles.

A major issue which still surrounds authoritarianism as measured by the F Scale refers to the question of its behavioral implications and correlates. Titus and Hollander (1957) raise serious questions about the relationship between authoritarian attitudes and behavior. They urge special caution where interpersonal behavioral implications are to be drawn. Christie, on the other hand, makes a strong case for congruency of F Scale scores and predicted behavior, citing four studies in support of his position (Christie & Jahoda, 1954, p. 145). As a test of the question, this study hypothesized that authoritarianism, as a trait of therapists and patients, would find expression in their attitudes toward psychotherapy and their behavior in therapy.

The second basic hypothesis of this study follows from the argument that a similarity of personality traits in patient and therapist tends to facilitate the relationship. Barron's thesis (1950) seems to be the first study to consider both patient and therapist variables in an experimental approach to the therapeutic relationship. Axelrod (1951) argued and found partial support for the hypothesis that progress in therapy was more likely when the personalities of patients and therapists were similar than when they were dissimilar. Underlying this hypothesis was the theory that

> the presence of an emotional identification or empathy between patient and therapist, springing from common emotional experience and manifested more or less by a similarity of personalities, is a condition favorable for the successful development of the therapeutic process (pp. 4-5).

Studies by Bown (1954), Hiler (1958), Libo (1957), and Ashby, Ford, Guerney, and Guerney (1957) are pertinent considerations of this question. Although the evidence is something less than substantial, there does seem to be a line of thought suggesting that there is an interaction between the personality traits of therapist and patient, and that generally a similarity of traits tends to facilitate the relationship. This position receives some support from studies in the fields of leadership and education (Goldberg & Stern, 1952; Haythorn, Haefner, Langham, Couch, & Carter, 1956; Jones, 1954; Sanford, 1950). The second basic hypothesis of this study states that a similarity of therapist and patient along the trait dimension of authoritarianism—equalitarianism is related to the establishment of successful or good therapeutic relationships.

Sanford (1956) raises some question about whether authoritarian patients, without reference to therapist traits, may not have real difficulty forming therapeutic relations with any therapist. He is rather blunt on this point, writing:

> The person high on F rarely seeks, but rather resists the idea of psychotherapy; and once a start has been made, the technical problems are trying (p. 313).

Sanford then goes on to note a study by Freeman and Sweet (1954) in which they offered evidence that patients with many features of the F pattern actually respond better in certain forms of group therapy than they do in individual therapy. This argument, obviously, refers to patient traits only. As a more parsimonious explanation of therapeutic failure the question merits testing and forms a specific hypothesis of this study.

Method

Instruments

The California F Scale as a measure of authoritarianism was taken directly from Forms 45 and 40 as published by Adorno et al. (1950). One item: "It is best to use some prewar authorities in Germany to keep order and prevent chaos," was omitted as untimely and probably ambiguous to most subjects. Scores were derived in the conventional manner. Responses from -3 to $+3$ were converted to positive scores ranging from 1 to 7, with no response scored as 4. The sum of scores for the 29 items was used for tests of hypotheses in this study.

The Authoritarian–Equalitarian Therapy sort (designated as AET) was especially developed for this study. A 40-item card sort was constructed containing 20 items reliably prejudged as descriptive of an authoritarian therapy relationship, and 20 items similarly prejudged as descriptive of an equalitarian therapy relationship. By verbal instruction the subjects were asked to sort the 40 items in 8 piles of 5 items each. The piles were numbered from

1 to 8, pile Number 1 designated as "Least True or False," pile Number 8 as "Most True." Patients were asked to sort the 40 items to indicate "which of these things you would like to have be most true and which of these things you would like to have be least true, or even false, about the relationship between you and your doctor (therapist, counselor)." Therapists were given essentially similar instructions with added emphasis on the expression of "own opinions" rather than what they had been taught or had read. Each item was scored according to the pile number in which it was placed. The scores for the 20 authoritarian items were summed for each subject and designated the AET score, with a possible range from 50 to 130. For each patient-therapist pair an AET Discrepancy Score was computed by summing the squares of the score differences over the 40 items. This Discrepancy Score is, of course, a negative function of the correlation between patient and therapist sorts. The Discrepancy Score was considered an adequate representation of similarity and differences of patient and therapist attitudes toward therapy along the specific dimension of authoritarian-equalitarian attitudes and behaviors.

A Therapist Rating Scale was developed, drawing heavily from an instrument developed at the University of Chicago Counseling Center (Rogers & Dymond, 1954, p. 101) and currently in use there. Several items of the original form were omitted to produce a shorter rating blank. A new item was introduced in which the therapist was asked to rate the "quality of the relationship," thus: "Does this seem to be a 'good' and effective therapeutic relationship? How do you estimate the quality of the therapeutic relationship between yourself and this patient?" (nine-point scale from "poor" to "good"). The rater's estimate of patient satisfaction in the relationship was retained in its original form, thus: "Estimate the patient's feeling about the relationship" (nine-point scale from "strongly dissatisfied" to "extremely satisfied"). Only these two items are utilized in the present study.

The formation of successful or better therapeutic relationships as a criterion was assumed to be directly related to the various types of criteria employed in other studies, but it was thought to have a specific pertinence of its own, as elemental or more basic. It seemed reasonable to attempt a direct measure of the quality of the relationship. It was assumed that the quality of the relationship is largely determined and may be evaluated in the very early contacts of patient and therapist. Although a rating of patient satisfaction may not be one of the essential goals of psychotherapy and may not be directly related to the quality of the relationship, it was thought to be a useful supplementary criterion measure. No matter how good the quality of the relationship may appear to the therapist or judges, the degree of patient satisfaction with its implications for continuance in therapy or premature termination may be a crucial evaluation.

An Observer Rating Scale was developed for the use of judges in rating patient and therapist behaviors as observed on short recorded segments of therapy. Items 1 and 2 provided estimates of the quality of the relationship and patient satisfaction, and were identical in form to the items described above. In Item 3 the therapist's behavior in the recorded segment was rated on five dimensions: aggressive–submissive, directive–nondirective, highly anxious–low anxiety, dominating–equalitarian, and rigid–flexible. In Item 4 the patient's behavior was rated on these five dimensions: aggressive–submissive, dependent–self-sufficient, highly anxious–low anxiety, conventional–individualistic, and rigid–flexible. From the many qualities and behaviors attributed to authoritarians in the literature, these five in each case were selected as being both relevant and ratable. In Item 5 the judge was asked to rate the behavior of the therapist along the single dimension of authoritarian–equalitarian on a nine-point scale. In Item 6 a distinction was made between dominant and submissive types of authoritarian behavior by the patient. Dominant behavior was defined by aggressive active authoritarian behavior, while submissive behavior was defined by passivity or deference, expecting or seeking authoritarian behavior by the other. Although dominant and submissive authoritarian behaviors were thought to be dynamically related, it seemed plausible to consider the two aspects mutually exclusive in any short sample of behavior. Thus, a V-shaped scale was used, with equalitarian at the apex and authoritarian–dominant and authoritarian–submissive at each of the two extensions, each on a nine-point scale. The judge was asked to select the aspect most prominent in the given segment and make a rating on the selected scale.

Samples

The subjects were drawn from two clinic populations. Those designated as Group A include treatment cases in the Psychiatry Clinic of Albert Merritt Billings Hospital, University of Chicago. Senior medical students are required, as part of their training in psychiatry, to treat in psychotherapy one selected patient who has been referred to the clinic. It should be noted that these students had little training and no prior experience in psychotherapy. All patients were told that their treatment would be limited to 18 weeks' duration, after which they would be either terminated or referred elsewhere. The present sample is composed of patients and therapists drawn from this program during two successive quarters. Of the 35 patients originally tested for this study, 1 was eliminated because of a suggested organic involvement, 1 for an alleged inability to read, and 1 patient who failed to keep the first and subsequent therapy appointments. The remaining sample of 32 cases included 15 males and 17 females, with a mean age of 38 years, ranging from 23 to 68 years.

The subjects designated as Group B were drawn from the client population of the University of Chicago Counseling Center. Clients are normally assigned to therapists on the basis of therapist availability, and clients who agree to participate in research studies are then randomly assigned to projects in progress at that time. The present sample includes 30 cases assigned to the writer's project over a 6-month period. The therapists in this group included three staff members with extensive experience, seven staff members with some or considerable experience, and seven students in training who were seeing their first or second cases. The client population included 16 males and 14 females, with a mean age of 27 years, ranging from 19 to 43 years.

The population in Group A includes 32 patients and 32 therapists, each patient seeing a different therapist. In Group B, the population includes 30 clients and 17 therapists, several therapists treating more than one client in this sample.

Collection of Data

Patients and therapists were seen prior to their first therapeutic interview and were asked to complete the F Scale and AET sort. After the second therapeutic interview, the therapist completed the Therapist Rating Scale.

Observer ratings were made on Group A only. Recordings of the first interview were retained, and 5-minute segments were selected from the beginning and ending of each interview. These segments were rerecorded in random order, with at least five other segments between the two segments of any given interview. Two judges (the writer and another graduate student of psychology, both with training and experience in psychotherapy) rated each segment on the Observer Rating Scale. Thus, for each case there were four ratings: beginning and ending segments by each of two judges. One recording was inaudible and tests based on judges' ratings will be drawn from an N of 31. Reliability of judges' ratings was tested on each of the 14 scales of the rating form. The two judges' summed ratings (beginning plus ending segments) were significantly correlated on 10 of the 14 (9 at the .01 level, 1 at the .05 level: $r = .38$). Only these 10 items were utilized in this study. It is striking that the four items on which the judges were not in agreement all dealt with patient traits.

RESULTS

Authoritarianism, as a personality trait of the therapist, was hypothesized to be significantly related to his description of the ideal therapeutic relationship in terms of directive, paternalistic, and nurturant qualities. Full scale scores on the F Scale were compared to AET scores. For the 32 therapists in Group A the Pearson r correlation was .03, a clearly nonsignificant result. For Group B, with 17 therapists, the Pearson r correlation was .62, significant at the .01 level.

It was predicted that therapists characterized by authoritarianism would tend to show more authoritarian behavior in their therapy than those characterized as equalitarian. The Observer Rating Scales were utilized here. The 31 therapists were dichotomized on the basis of their F Scale scores, 16 low and 15 high. Results in tests of this hypothesis may be summarized as follows: (*a*) On a global behavioral rating of authoritarian–equalitarian the high F scorers were rated significantly more authoritarian than low F scorers. (*b*) Although high and low F scorers did not differ on the full scale dimension of aggressive–submissive, they did differ on their deviation from "appropriate" mid-point behavior, i.e., high scorers were given more extreme ratings on this dimension. (*c*) High scorers were rated as more directive, anxious, and dominating than low scorers, but not significantly so. (*d*) Behavior of high scorers was rated as significantly more rigid than that of low scorers.

Authoritarianism, as a personality trait of the patient, was hypothesized to be significantly related to his description of the ideal or preferred therapeutic relationship in terms of directive, paternalistic, and nurturant qualities. Full scores on the F Scale were compared to AET scores. The 32 patients in Group A showed a Pearson r correlation of .34, significant at the .05 level. In Group B, with 30 patients, the Pearson r correlation was .38, significant at the .05 level.

It was predicted that patients characterized by authoritarianism would tend to show more authoritarian behavior in their therapy than those characterized as equalitarian. The Observer Rating Scales were utilized here: a global rating of patient behavior on a nine-point scale and a rating on patient aggression. As a test of this hypothesis the 31 cases were dichotomized on the basis of the patient's F Scale score, 15 low and 16 high. On the global rating of patient behavior the difference between low and high scorers was not significant. The two groups did not differ on the full scale dimension of aggressive–submissive. High scoring patients did show the larger deviation from "appropriate" mid-point behavior as predicted, but the difference between groups was not significant.

In line with the argument of Sanford, discussed above, it was predicted that patients who are characterized as equalitarian will tend to form better therapeutic relationships than those characterized as authoritarian. In Group A, the hypothesis was tested against four criterion measures: the therapist's rating of the quality of the relationship, therapist's estimate of patient satisfaction, judges' composite rating of the quality of the relationship, and the judges' composite estimate of patient satisfaction. The differences between low and high scoring patients on the therapist ratings were not significant. The differences on judges' ratings were both in the predicted direction. Judges rated the quality of the relationship significantly ($t = 2.50$, $p < .01$) higher for the group of low F scorers, and the estimate of patient satisfaction was slightly higher for this group but not significantly so. In Group B the hypothesis was tested against two criterion measures, the therapist's rating of the relationship and his estimate of patient satisfaction. Differences between low and high scorers were not significant.

The last three hypotheses were developed from the argument that similarity of patient and therapist personalities facilitates the development of good therapeutic relationships. It was hypothesized that patients characterized by authoritarian traits would tend to form better therapeutic relationships with therapists characterized as authoritarian than with those characterized as equalitarian. For a test of this and the following hypothesis the dichotomies between high and low scorers in patient and therapist groups were retained. First, each of the patients characterized as authoritarian was considered with his respective therapist. Mean criterion ratings are shown in Table 1. In Group A the hypothesis was tested against the

TABLE 1

MEAN CRITERION RATINGS ON AUTHORITARIAN AND EQUALITARIAN GROUPS OF PATIENTS WITH THEIR RESPECTIVE AUTHORITARIAN AND EQUALITARIAN THERAPISTS

	CRITERION					
	Group A				Group B	
	Therapist Rating		Observer Rating		Therapist Rating	
	QR[a]	PS	QR	PS	QR	PS
Authoritarian Patients						
Authoritarian Therapist	5.89	6.11	3.44	4.95	5.80	6.20
Equalitarian Therapist	7.14	6.71	4.14	5.57	5.00	5.25
Equalitarian Patients						
Equalitarian Therapist	5.89	5.55	5.39	5.97	5.70	5.40
Authoritarian Therapist	6.00	6.14	4.38	4.75	6.28	6.86*

[a] QR = Quality of Relationship, PS = Patient Satisfaction.

* Difference significant at .05 level, in a direction opposite to that predicted.

four criterion measures listed above. All differences were nonsignificant. In Group B the hypothesis was tested against the two criterion measures listed above. Both differences were nonsignificant.

Secondly, it was hypothesized that patients characterized by equalitarian traits would tend to form better therapeutic relationships with therapists characterized as equalitarian than with those characterized as authoritarian. Each of the patients characterized as equalitarian was considered with his respective therapist. Mean criterion ratings are shown in Table 1. For Group A, on the four criterion measures, all differences were nonsignificant. In Group B both therapist ratings were in a direction opposite to that predicted, with the difference on rated patient satisfaction significant at the .05 level.

In the last hypothesis, therapist and patient descriptions of ideal or preferred therapy conditions (AET) were utilized. Discrepancy Scores for each case were computed as previously described. These scores were dichotomized in terms of low and high discrepancy. It was predicted that the quality of the therapeutic relationship would

TABLE 2

MEAN CRITERION RATINGS ON CASES WITH HIGH AND LOW DISCREPANCY BETWEEN THERAPIST AND PATIENT AET SORTS

	CRITERION					
	Group A				Group B	
	Therapist Rating		Observer Rating		Therapist Rating	
Patient Group	QR[a]	PS	QR	PS	QR	PS
High Discrepancy	6.06	6.00	4.16	5.12	5.00	5.53
Low Discrepancy	6.31	6.19	4.55	5.58	6.33*	6.13

[a] QR = Quality of Relationship, PS = Patient Satisfaction.
* Difference significant at .05 level.

be related to the degree of discrepancy between patient and therapist expectations of authoritarian attitudes and behavior in therapy. Mean criterion ratings of low and high discrepancy groups are shown in Table 2. Although only one of the differences was statistically significant, low discrepancy cases received higher ratings on all criterion measures in both groups.

DISCUSSION

The failure to find a relationship between F Scale scores and attitudes toward therapy in the therapist population of Group A may be related to the nature of the F Scale items and the students' reaction to them. It has been said that authoritarian people as measured by the scale agree more with authoritative statements; and that, therefore, a portion of the discriminatory power of the F scale derives from its form, rather than its content (Leavitt, Hax, & Roche, 1955, p. 221).

The very authoritative tone of the statements in the F Scale, referred to as a form characteristic, may, however, operate with reactive effect on some subjects. Several of the therapists (who, it will be recalled, were senior medical students) commented on the stringent wording of the statements. One student commented that: "In medical school one of the first things you learn is to suspect any statement with 'always' or 'never' in it." These are not individuals who are rigidly or self-consciously equalitarian, but rather students trained to be critically sensitive to the literal meaning of words, and to hold in suspicion all authoritative sounding statements. The form component may, in such cases, have an inhibitory, and thus invalidating, effect.

Since therapists' scores on the F Scale do correlate quite well with their rated behavior in therapy it may be more reasonable to view their F Scale scores as a relatively reliable representation of authoritarianism as a personality trait and to re-evaluate their expression of attitudes toward therapy. It is well to remember that this population of therapists is composed of students with no experience and very little training in psychotherapy. They probably had few consciously developed attitudes toward therapy. By contrast, the therapists in Group B, with more training and experience in therapy, do show a consistency between personality trait and therapy attitudes. It may be proposed that one of the consequences of training and experience is the increased congruence of therapist traits and attitudes, a greater consistency between the personality of the therapist and his consciously held and expressed attitudes toward therapy. Whether such congruency is an effect of training or experience, or both, could and should be tested.

It was noted that the judges rated the quality of the relationship significantly higher for the patient group of low F scorers, while differences between therapist ratings were not significant. It may be that this reflects some differences in conception of the "good patient" role, and differences in what constitutes a "good and effective therapeutic relationship." Some differences in perspective between therapist and judges may also be operative here.

The finding that the rated quality of the relationship is related to the degree of similarity of patient and therapist descriptions of a preferred relationship on items specifically defining authoritarianism tends to support the second basic hypothesis of this study. The quality of the relationship and an estimate of patient satisfaction in the early interviews appear to be somewhat predictable. To say this in another way: there does seem to be some pretherapy data from which we could anticipate good or poor, satisfying or unsatisfying, therapeutic relationships.

An observation may be made on the failure to find a relationship between the criterion and similarity on F Scale scores. Dichotomizing cases at the mean F Scale score for the group is probably too gross a division. For individuals not scoring in the extreme, high or low, authoritarianism is probably not the most crucial trait. The writer would speculate that for these individuals there are other traits, attitudes, and needs which play a more crucial role in determining the quality of their interpersonal relationships.

It may also be observed that attitude items, the AET sort, have a greater immediacy or relevance to the therapy situation than F Scale items. Many AET items refer to attitudes or behaviors which are very soon conspicuous by their presence or absence. By contrast, the F Scale measures a more fundamental trait which may not express itself so immediately or directly. In spite of the careful manner in which the AET items were developed, it may be that the sort contains several items of serious import to the development of the relationship, but not heavily loaded with authoritarianism. The method of deriving the Discrepancy Score, by summing the squares of the pile number differences over all items, gives an equal impact to all items.

This discussion should not, however, obscure the finding that similar attitudes of therapist and patient toward therapy were related to better therapy relationships. We are still some way from the point at which we can "match" patient and therapist to maximize success in therapy. As a therapist, the writer doubts that research of this kind will ever take all of the "mystery" and the essentially personal quality out of psychotherapy. Research may, however, help us to avoid the more blatant difficulties, and thus permit the more individual aspects of psychotherapy to operate more effectively.

Summary

It was predicted that authoritarianism, as a personality trait of therapist and patient, would be reflected in their attitudes toward therapy and in their therapeutic behavior. Secondly, it was hypothesized that authoritarianism and equalitarianism, as interacting personality traits of therapist and patient, would have specified effects upon the quality of the relationship established.

A total of 62 patients and 49 therapists in two clinic populations completed the California F Scale and a specially devised instrument in which they described the ideal or preferred therapeutic relationship. After the second interview these therapists completed a scale containing two criterion items: a rating of the quality of the relationship and an estimate of patient satisfaction with the relationship. In one of the two clinic settings, two 5-minute segments were selected from each of the first interview recordings. For each segment, two judges rated the two criterion items and specific and general traits referring to authoritarian behavior on the part of the therapist and patient.

Authoritarianism (as measured by the F Scale) was found to be related to authoritarian attitudes toward therapy in both patient populations and in one of the two therapist populations. The hypothesis that authoritarianism, as measured by the F Scale, would be related to authoritarian behavior in therapy was supported for the therapist population, but not for the patients. A test of the hypothesis that equalitarian patients would form better therapeutic relationships than authoritarian patients gave equivocal results. The second basic hypothesis, that similarity of therapist and patient on the specific dimension of authoritarian–equalitarian would tend to facilitate the relationship, was not supported. There was, however, an association between criterion ratings and the amount of discrepancy between therapist and patient descriptions of the ideal or preferred relationship on items related to authoritarianism.

References

Adorno, T. W., Frenkel-Brunswik, Else, Levinson, D. J., & Sanford, R. N. *The authoritarian personality.* New York: Harper, 1950.

Ashby, J. D., Ford, D. H., Guerney, B. G., Jr., & Guerney, Louise F. Effects on clients of a reflective and a leading type of psychotherapy. *Psychol. Monogr.,* 1957, **71** (24, Whole No. 453).

Axelrod, J. An evaluation of the effect on progress in psychotherapy of similarities and differences between the personality of patients and their therapists. Unpublished doctoral dissertation, New York University, 1951.

Barron, F. X. Psychotherapy as a special case of personal interaction: Prediction of its outcome. Unpublished doctoral dissertation, University of California, 1950.

Bown, O. H. An investigation of the therapeutic relationship in client-centered psychotherapy. Unpublished doctoral dissertation, University of Chicago, 1954.

Christie, R., & Jahoda, M. (Eds.) *Studies in the scope and method of the authoritarian personality.* Glencoe, Ill.: Free Press, 1954.

Freeman, M., & Sweet, B. A theoretical formulation of some features of group psychotherapy and its implications for selection of patients. *Int. J. group Psychother.,* 1954, **4,** 355-368.

Goldberg, S., & Stern, G. The authoritarian personality and education. *Amer. Psychologist,* 1952, **7,** 375. (Abstract)

Haythorn, W., Haefner, D., Langham, P., Couch, A., & Carter, L. The effects of varying combinations of authoritarian and equalitarian leaders and followers. *J. abnorm. soc. Psychol.,* 1956, **53,** 210-219.

Hiler, E. W. An analysis of patient-therapist compatibility. *J. consult. Psychol.,* 1958, **22,** 341-347.

Jones, E. E. Authoritarianism as a determinant of first-impression formation. *J. Pers.,* 1954, **23,** 107-127.

Leavitt, H. J., Hax, H., & Roche, J. H. "Authoritarianism" and agreement with things authoritative. *J. Psychol.,* 1955, **40,** 215-221.

Libo, L. M. The projective expression of patient-therapist attraction. *J. clin. Psychol.,* 1957, **13,** 33-36.

Rogers, C. R., & Dymond, Rosalind F. (Eds.) *Psychotherapy and personality change.* Chicago: Univer. Chicago Press, 1954.

Sanford, F. H. *Authoritarianism and leadership.* Philadelphia: Institute for Research in Human Relations, 1950.

Sanford, N. The approach of the authoritarian personality. In J. L.

McCary (Ed.), *Psychology of personality: Six modern approaches.* New York: Logos, 1956, Pp. 253-319.

Titus, H. E., & Hollander, E. P. The California F Scale in psychological research: 1950-1955. *Psychol. Bull.,* 1957, **54,** 47-64.

24. DOGMATISM IN VOCATIONAL CHOICE

C. Gratton Kemp

Years ago the counselor assumed that the choices checked on a vocational interest inventory directly reflected the counselee's actual interest in occupations. More recently he has been informed that items of vocational interest may be preferred or ignored for reasons other than interest per se. Writers have warned that certain inventories are subject to distortion.[1]

DISTORTION OF RESPONSES

Why do students fake responses? Why do they try to make inventories come out the way they want? It is likely that the feelings and attitudes of the student influence the character of his response to the test items. And there probably is a relationship between the student's reaction to new experience and his response to items on an inventory.

To gain some understanding of the student's reaction to new experience the Dogmatism Scale Form E[2] was administered to a sample of 104 college students. This scale, developed and standardized by Milton Rokeach was designed to measure the degree of openness or closedness of the mind to new experience.

His research led him to the conclusion that the closed-minded or high dogmatic rejects, distorts or narrows new experience to make

---

Reprinted by permission of the author and *Vocational Guidance Quarterly,* IX, No. 1 (Autumn, 1960), 43-46.

---

[1] Donald E. Super, *Appraising Vocational Fitness,* New York, Harper and Brothers, 1949, 416.

[2] Milton Rokeach, *The Open and Closed Mind,* New York, Basic Books, 1960, 71-80.

it conform to his preformed value system. Whereas the open-minded or low dogmatic is more inclined to recognize, analyze, and evaluate new experience without distortion and narrowing.

The results of this scale indicated that 25 students were low in dogmatism or open-minded and 25 were high in dogmatism or closed-minded. Would their responses be significantly different?

EXPERIMENT IN DISTORTION

The sample (50 students, 42 male and 8 female) were majoring in human relations in preparation for positions as boy scout executives, and YMCA or YWCA directors. Many had chosen this major through the encouragement of members of these professions in their home localities and some anticipated returning upon graduation to work with these leaders.

To what degree did the influence of these interested persons affect the thinking of the students? Did they respond according to their feelings or to the way they thought these persons would like them to respond? To assess the degree of their identification, each student was asked what persons outside his family were most influential in his life.

To provide some indication of their vocational interests each student was administered the Kuder Vocational Interest CH and the Strong Vocational Interest Blank. Since the Kuder is known to be subject to distortion, it was hoped that using both inventories would gain more reliable knowledge of their interests and secure, as well, evidence as to the degree of distortion by either or both groups.

A PICTURE EMERGES

On the basis of the theory it was hypothesized that the high and low in dogmatism would respond differently. To the question, "What other persons influenced your development?" only two (or 8%) of the low in dogmatism specified one or a few persons; five (or 20%) mentioned a number of persons with no special emphasis, and 18 (or 72%) made a general response, no reference to any individual or group.

On the other hand, fifteen (or 60%) of the 25 in the high dogmatic group, specified one or a few persons, generally a boy scout executive or a Y director; eight a number of persons, no emphasis on any; and two a general response, no reference to any individual group. The difference between the two groups was significant at the one per cent level.

This striking difference was convincing evidence that the high identified with authority figures, whereas the low did not. It was later found that this strong identification affected responses made on the vocational interest inventories.

The results on the Kuder indicated the low in dogmatism had widespread interests. Each of the ten areas was represented, areas nine (Social Service), and five (Persuasive) received fewer choices than several others.

Whereas for the high in dogmatism only eight areas were represented, areas nine (Social Service) and five (Persuasive) received the greatest number of choices. Such a difference between the two groups becomes significant, since the Kuder is subject to distortion[3] and the students knew that these "Social Workers" were high in the Social and Persuasive areas.

Consider also the fact that the results were used for counseling with reference to the wisdom of the student's choice of major, and it is reasonable to assume that the "high" in dogmatism distorted their responses on the Kuder to correspond to the interests held by the Boy Scout Executive, other authority figure in the local home communities, with whom they had identified.

The results of the Strong Vocational Interest Blank suggested an entirely different situation. The high dogmatic group expressed interest in 20 vocations as compared with 27 by the low dogmatic group. The high group had a total of 82 choices or 3.20 per capita, whereas the low group had a total of 108 or 4.32 per capita. It is apparent that the high group had more and different interests than they indicated by their choices on the Kuder.

Some Conclusions

Those high in dogmatism or closed-minded distort their responses more than the low or open-minded on standardized measures of in-

---

[3] *Ibid.* Super.

terest. Apparently they are more ready to act in accordance with
the expectancies of an authority figure than to endanger the modification of their thinking by a true confrontal of experience.

In contrast the low in dogmatic appear to be more independent,
more confident, to identify to a lesser degree and are more ready to
examine new experience.

The degree of closed-mindedness apparently affects the student's
performances on vocational interest inventories.

COUNSELING IMPLICATIONS

The counselor who knows the degree of closed-mindedness of his
counselees is in a much better position to understand them. The
greater the degree of closed-mindedness, the higher is the expect-
ancy of distortion, narrowing or rejection of new information.
Those students who require more time and assistance if they are to
benefit from vocational testing and counseling can be tentatively
identified and their responses can be anticipated. With experience
the counselor may be able to develop approaches and methods to
increase his effectiveness in assisting the highly dogmatic.

25. A MAJOR TASK OF THERAPY: DEVELOPING VOLITION AND PURPOSE

Melitta Schmideberg, M.D.

All poor functioning is to some degree a disturbance of volition;
such disturbances frequently dominate the clinical picture. Even
when patients complain about unhappy feelings, these may not be
altogether irrational, but the result of poor functioning.

The trend in modern psychotherapy is to look at pathologic
phenomena and dynamic factors essentially from the viewpoint of
emotions; for example indecision is usually seen as a painful sen-

Reprinted by permission of the author and *American Journal of Psychotherapy*, XV, No. 2 (April, 1961), 251-59.

sation rather than as a disturbance of will.* Another trend, originating with Freud (1), is to regard all painful emotions, such as guilt and anxiety, as the main causes of pathology and to assume that disturbances of volition are essentially due to irrational anxiety, and can be cured by making this anxiety conscious. This view, while not altogether wrong, is one-sided. To balance it we must study volitional phenomena in their own terms of reference (2).

Volition is the sum total of our conscious goal-directed strivings, aided by unconscious mechanisms. It is the ability to act toward a chosen goal in spite of obstacles. We are more aware of the dramatic quality of volition if there is a struggle; actually, however, if there is success without struggle volition has proved more effective (3).

How Volition Is Developed

Volition, like other mental or bodily faculties, can be developed by training, repetition of effort, suitable identifications, and example. It rarely consists of a single immediately successful attempt, but in repeated and sustained efforts with many setbacks and failures, implying a constant realization of limitations, repeated attempts to desensitize the individual to the painfulness of failure, the narcissistic hurts involved, the resentment elicited. Past successes are a source of courage to go on; so are identifications with those who have struggled and overcome their early failures.

(a) Identification

Persons more successful provide a source of incentive, identification, challenge, and goal; the less effective ones, a sense of what to avoid as well as a temporary sense of superiority. To continue to exert himself, a person needs the right balance between discouragement (the awareness of limitations) and encouragement (the hope of success).

---

* It is indicative that the comprehensive *American Handbook of Psychiatry*, containing 100 articles of about 1½ million words, lists "volition" and "will" in the subject index only under the following headings: *Volitional action:* brain reflexes and; choice in; cortical motor apparatus for; disintegration of in senile dementia; impairment of in brain damage; reduction in. *Will:* capacity to; catatonia and; and "moral defectiveness" and; schizophrenia and.

Because it is necessary to identify with other people's initiative, the children of weak parents have a harder task. Sometimes strong parents may crush their children, but often they enable them, by means of identification and defiance, to become strong. Psychiatrists who are too detached and inactive do not offer the patient the opportunity to develop volition by identification.

(b) *Pressure*

Pressure or criticism, either from the environment or the psychiatrist, does not necessarily interfere with the development of independent volition. It does so only if spontaneous efforts are too frequently crushed. Too little outside pressure often causes poor will power; too much pressure may lead to hopelessness or defiance, or both. A combination of positive and negative incentives is necessary.

(c) *Approbation*

Some confidence and hope of success is necessary to induce people to exert themselves, but overpraising is bad because it dulls the incentive; a person must be aware of his ignorance and mind it sufficiently to be ready to make the effort to learn. Also, undue encouragement leaves the person unprepared for the unavoidable failures and the painfulness of the effort involved, and he becomes discouraged when he discovers that the discrepancy between his expectations and the actuality is too great (4). Many sport instructors maneuver this situation effectively by first giving the pupil the feeling that he does well, so that he has the incentive to continue, and as soon as he does a bit better, they begin to correct him and give him increasingly harder tasks.

THE NORMAL CHAIN

Volition consists of an interlocking chain of reactions: (1) selection of goal; (2) awareness and anticipation of success having a strong enough feeling tone to act as an incentive, combined with the negative incentive of refusing to tolerate failure; (3) deciding upon the best means of achieving the goal (it is here that judgment, values, and reality sense enter); (4) the exertion of volition.

These processes always involve a complexity and a multitude of incentives and counterforces as well as a multiplicity of goals: facing and overcoming initial setbacks and failures; repetition of efforts and perseverance; mental reactions to anticipated consequences; actual consequences; a multitude of reactions to these consequences.

Normally, volition develops through overcoming situations of obstacle. The basic normal conflicts within every individual are: (1) between inertia and action; (2) between anti-social or unorganized activity, and social activity; (3) having to choose between multiple goals and multiple means. It is the task of upbringing and education to establish, develop, and guide these processes, to socialize the child by creating and teaching him to choose goals, conditioning him to positive and negative incentives, and linking them to desirable and undesirable behavior. The child partly complies and partly fights this process. His personality is the outcome of the struggle. Actually there are many struggles in the same person, and many outcomes of these struggles, concerning different areas.

DISTURBANCES OF THE NORMAL CHAIN

All disturbances can be related to the outcome of struggles over socialization. As a result, some parts of the chain may not develop in a desirable manner and some may break after they have been established. Even "normal environment," may not have succeeded in overcoming reluctance to social behavior. Special circumstances may aggravate the problem: conflicting parents and authority, the absence of strength and guidance, hopelessly high or too diffuse goals.

A disturbance may affect any of the links of the chain. The normal sequence of incentive-volition-activity-goal may have been interrupted at any point and these interruptions are related to the struggle over socialization. The task of therapy is to re-establish these links, to lessen the factors that deter the patient from exercising his volition, to make the adjustment more attractive. Poor incentives, wrong choice of, or contradictory goals, or wrong means of achieving his goals, are some of the inhibiting factors involved.

(a) *Are All Disturbances Neurotic?*

It is essential to distinguish between functional and neurotic disturbances. Usually there is a combination of both these factors, and poorly functioning patients should be handled on both levels.

The current assumption that the mere highlighting of the neurotic element and discovering its unconscious reasons will automatically remedy the disturbance implies that man is a rational animal who, even untrained and unguided, will act rationally. This unfortunately is not the case. Granted that unconscious factors inhibit proper functioning, most patients still suffer not only from being hampered, but also from the failure of having acquired and developed skills, organized thinking, planning, and so on. Thus, hand in hand with release of crippling inhibitions, poorly developed functions must be developed.

(b) *Interrelation Between Emotion and Volition*

Although reason guides us, rational considerations are often insufficient to make us act, unless they have sufficient emotional quality, both positive and negative. Thus, emotions are levers for volition and action and therefore can not be studied or influenced, except in context.

In general, the positive value of painful emotions has been underestimated by both modern psychiatry and education. Though some painful emotions are paralyzing—for example, hopelessness and despair—not all painful emotions are necessarily irrational and harmful, and even irrational feelings help people to act rationally if they are linked right. Anxiety, guilt, shame, remorse often act as strong socializing forces and incentives toward achievement (6). Only if excessive or misdirected do they inhibit the individual.

The analysis of painful emotions in terms of the patient's past experience is usually insufficient, especially if it is taken out of the context of his behavior, past or present. It is harmful if the incentive-function of the emotion gets blunted. Rarely can a painful emotion be cured by insight alone. The patient's behavior and reactions must be changed, and this in turn will influence his way of feeling.

Aims of Therapy

Having accepted the sobering fact that a mere removal of inhibitions does not automatically lead to rational behavior and good functioning, it follows that the therapist, in order to be effective, must give guidance, whether he takes open responsibility or does it by implication (7). Ethics and clinical judgment determine how much influence the therapist should use, but the issue cannot be ignored. Patients are, to a varying degree, confused in their purpose, have no purpose, or the wrong purpose.

Therapy, while strengthening volition, should attempt to integrate, modify, and even create realistic goals which are challenging, yet within the patient's reach. Therapy should distinguish between realistic goals and fantasy. A realistic goal is something within the patient's reach, something at which he is seriously aiming, not merely a passing fancy; the criterion is whether he is willing to work toward this goal, make efforts and sacrifices. These differences should be made clear to the patient.

Therapeutic Dependency Is a Legitimate Tool

As a reaction to old-fashioned authoritative psychiatry, most modern psychiatrists are reluctant to establish influence and dependence or to admit openly to their responsibility and authority. But as long as the dependence is used constructively and effectively for therapeutic purposes, it helps in the long run to make the patient independent. The patient becomes independent by learning to function better and finding his satisfactions outside the therapeutic situation. Excessive dependence on the therapist or others is the result of malfunctioning, but if a good therapeutic relation is established, the wish to gain the approval of the therapist becomes a powerful incentive and therapeutic tool.

It is often claimed that advice was ineffective or suggestion short-lasting and therefore should not have been given. However, the fact that the patient did not act on the advice does not mean that he cannot be influenced; in most cases, it means that the therapist had no influence over him, gave him advice that was, at least in the patient's present situation, or frame of mind, impracticable, or that it was not put forward forcefully or skillfully enough.

By common consent, identification with the therapist is an important therapeutic tool. But if the therapist fails to show initiative, zest, or is reluctant to take responsibility, this is bound to have a bad effect on a weak-willed patient, in particular if the therapist makes the patient "delay decisions until the analysis has progressed further."

The ideal of the modern psychiatrist is to be an oversophisticated introvert, concentrating on understanding and not on acting, and since he is dealing essentially with patients from a protected environment, he is under no serious pressure to develop therapeutic initiative and resourcefulness in the patient. Moreover, he even feels guilty about such initiative in his attempts to be "objective" and "scientific" and often tends to analyze with some misgivings his unconscious motives for therapeutic initiative.

Some psychiatrists take it too much for granted that the patient regards their detachment and inactivity as indications of sympathy. Often he does not, as evidenced by the fact that the patient gets more upset as he continues therapy. But even if he feels reassured by the doctor's sympathy, this is no therapeutic aim. It helps to tide him over the immediate unhappiness and may aid in cementing a therapeutic relation, which, however, is valuable only if it serves to normalize the patient, and this happens if he is made to function normally in an increasing number of areas.

SPECIAL TECHNIQUES

Linking Incentives to the Patient's Preoccupation

Frequently the incentives are too weak, or the individual is not willing to, or not used to, exerting himself. What motivates one person may leave another cold. The one is motivated by social feelings or pity, the other one not; some will do anything for money, others are ruled by anxiety. To motivate a patient we must look not just for what would seem most desirable objectively, but what is of immediate concern to the patient. Most patients will agree in general terms as to the direction in which they should improve and even on the steps to be taken, but such knowledge rarely motivates the patients sufficiently to change. Being able to link a course of action or a change of attitude to an immediate preoccupation is usually more effective. In the second interview, I told a woman in her forties who was worried by her "hot flashes" that satisfactory sex life is likely to diminish them, and this made her resume sexual relations with her husband.

Incidentally, in therapy I do not want to motivate the patient merely in the direction and for the purpose I suggest, but I use the incentives that motivate him and the course of action or behavior he accepts as desirable for "slipping in" others that I consider therapeutically desirable. In the above-mentioned case I was not primarily concerned with diminishing the patient's hot flashes, her main concern, but with improving her relationship to her husband. Had I brought up this relationship, she would have resented it as she had many grievances against him, so I did not discuss it. But it was evident that a better sex life would improve both partners' attitudes to each other, and that this would be of therapeutic value.

Negative Incentives

For every positive incentive there are many negative ones; everything the patient wants to do is strengthened by knowing the consequences of his not doing it, the realistic effects on his situation, on his feelings of self-esteem. Skillful use of relatively unrewarding goals, first as alternative, then as negative incentive, can be a very valuable technique.

I interviewed a patient who had had many, many years of therapy with a number of psychiatrists, with dubious results. He came to me in a terrible depressed state. It took some time to discover his financial situation, which was deplorable. I pointed out to him that he could not have self-esteem as long as he was supported by his girl friend. He claimed that he could not get a job in his profession. After discussing this problem rationally he agreed to take a job in a factory or a hamburger haven if within a month he could not get a job in his profession. Within two weeks he had a job as a commercial artist.

Insight

The danger of stressing insight, unconscious motivation, and the past, is that it often distracts the patient and even the therapist from concentrating on realistic consequences, on purpose, and the future. Some patients are only too ready to use motivational "insight" as an excuse for not acting. Often free associations into causes are nothing but the ruminations, grievances, and self-accusations of the neurotic or depressed; to encourage them only makes the patient more abnormal and inactive.

For insight to be effective, it must be turned into a negative or positive incentive. Understanding the past is bound to evoke feelings, to help make the patient clarify what he does or what he does not want, should or should not do. Combining it with other incentives, fears, hopes, desires, it can be a useful tool.

Going from Goal to Goal

One of the major reasons for failure of volition is in the choice and attitude toward goals. Sometimes even remarkably intelligent persons select goals that are utterly fantastic for them, or select so many goals that they cannot possibly accomplish anything. At the same time, they tend to belittle the goals that are within their reach. It is important, therefore, to get them started in doing something constructive, no matter how modest. Sometimes it can be stressed that this is a partial goal, a stepping stone for other things (if the patient is not too frightened). Once a goal is accomplished, it should be turned into an incentive for new and more rewarding goals. By going from goal to goal, the patient achieves more and more satisfaction; at the same time he gets a more realistic picture of his abilities and limitations.

A schizophrenic in his late twenties in a delusional state was unable to hold his job and I prevailed on his father to let him study instead. But as he improved, I tried to get him to take a part-time job; whenever he ran short of money I dwelt on all the things he could be doing, and how easily he could make some extra money; at the same time I stressed how much better he was now, how much less strain a job would be to him, that since he was so intelligent (this was his special ambition), studying really was nothing to him; then I proceeded to tell him how to go about getting a job, and once he got it I gave him praise and encouragement.

Of course the patient knew as well as I that he could make money by taking a part-time job, but he was afraid to do so because his last job had been a failure, and he was reluctant to work because he had a negative attitude and the job would involve him in human situations. I could prevail upon him because at that moment he was already better—it is important to choose the right moment for pressure—and he had an attachment to me and some trust in my judgment that he was better. Also, one of the reasons he did not want to have a job was that this ran counter to his ideas of grandeur. My whole course of action rested upon my clinical judgment that he was sufficiently improved, or else he could not have held the job; and after a while, his work gave him a great deal of satisfaction. After many vicissitudes, he gradually began to study seriously and he has since succeeded in getting a Master of Arts in mathematics and holding good jobs.

SUMMARY

Some people succeed at too great a cost, some don't succeed, or suffer too much in trying to adjust. The aim of therapy is to get the patient to function and adjust socially, at not too great a cost. The therapist should work with the entire chain of the patient's responses, the inertia of his volition, the unreality of his goals, as well as his emotions. He should try to transform a weak chain with unrealistic goals into a strong chain with better ones.

Reality should be brought to bear on his feelings of omnipotence and wish for unlimited possibilities which so often hide the hopeless feeling that he cannot do anything at all well. Once the patient carries out a positive action, no matter how small, it can be used as an incentive for a better goal. By going from more modest to more fruitful goals in a realistic way, the patient will more and more get a feeling of strength, will be able to shoulder more responsibility, and will feel more independent as a result.

Since there is no reason to believe that a patient can spontaneously unfold in the right direction without guidance or pressure on the part of his environment or the therapist, the latter cannot remain nondirective or "objectively" detached, but should take a strong position on the side of health and act as the patient's reality sense organ, until the patient himself becomes able to cope with life.

BIBLIOGRAPHY

1. Freud, S. *Inhibitions, Symptoms and Anxiety.* Hogarth Press, London, 1936.
2. James, William. *The Principles of Psychology.* Dover Publications, New York, 1950.
3. Hobb, D. O. *The Organization of Behavior.* Wiley, New York, 1939.
4. Schmideberg, Melitta. Tolerance in Upbringing and Its Abuses. *Internat. J. Social Psychiatry.* 5: 2, 1959.
5. ———— Treating the Unwilling Patient. *British Journal of Delinquency,* 9: 117, 1958.
6. ———— Principles of Psychotherapy. *Contemp. Psychol.,* 2: 186, 1960.
7. ———— Making the Patient Aware. *Crime and Delinquency,* 6: 225, 1960.
8. ———— Values and Goals in Psychotherapy. *Psychiatric Quart.,* 32: 233, 1958.

26. CULTURAL PATTERNS AS THEY AFFECT PSYCHOTHERAPEUTIC PROCEDURES

Theodora M. Abel

At the present time there is an extensive literature on the subject of culture and personality and on the effect specific forms of child rearing have on the characteristic modes of behavior of the adult in a given society. As Kardiner (11) has stated: "It is important to know the culture in which the individual lives because everything he tells us is attuned to its values and emphases." But in spite of all that has been and is being written on the role of cultural patterns on character formation, we often overlook these patterns in our psychotherapeutic practices. We pay little attention to interpreting the thoughts,

Reprinted by permission of the author and *American Journal of Psychotherapy,* X, No. 4 (October, 1956), 728-39.

feelings and behavior of a patient as being manifestations of or deviations from the cultural regularities of his particular social milieu. This is understandable since the training of the psychoanalyst and psychotherapist has largely been that of assessing a patient's personality in such dichotomies as healthy and neurotic, or neurotic and psychotic; as based on reality factors or on fantasy; as indicators of ego strength or weakness; or as defenses against anxiety, and so forth. Transference phenomena are viewed as the patient's unrealistic struggle with a parent surrogate, and countertransference is interpreted as traces of the therapist's unresolved familial conflicts. In addition, we go about trying to effect a characterological change in the patient by helping him achieve more satisfying interpersonal relationships. None of these procedures and goals would we suggest changing. We only want to indicate that it can be helpful for the psychotherapist to include in his armamentarium knowledge of cultural patterns and ability to perceive cultural variables; to appraise the ways in which particular patterns may influence the patient's thoughts, feelings and actions; and to judge when it is timely to give the patient an interpretation of these patterns (16).

We should like to cover the following points in our discussion of the subject of this paper, cultural patterns and psychotherapy: first, attitudes toward treatment and therapist; second, estimation of and attitudes toward type and degree of disturbance; third, some of the ways in which cultural patterns may enter covertly and overtly into the communications between patient and therapist; and fourth, instances in which cultural patterns may affect transference and counter-transference.

1. Attitudes Toward Treatment and Therapist

The attitudes of various cultural groups towards psychotherapy and therapist have not been systematically studied. We do know, however, that the more highly educated individuals usually seek psychotherapeutic help and generally those with some sufficient income to pay for therapy. Psychotherapy also is available at the present time only in certain urban areas in the United States, in a few of the larger cities, in V.A. installations and some social agen-

cies. Certain religious groups are less likely to encourage psychotherapy than others. According to Tsung Yi-Lin (17), among the
Chinese there seems to be greater tolerance of deviant behavior in
the family than in many other cultural groups. Psychoanalysis and
psychotherapy, where available, are likely to be considered as acceptable forms of treatment among the more educated Jews. This is due
most likely to the larger number of Jewish therapists available, and
to the Jewish reverence for the learned man, the doctor, whose word
is respected.

Françoise Dolto (5), a French child analyst, has written about
attitudes toward therapy in her article on French and American
children. In the first place, she stresses the point that the American
children she has seen do not seem to distrust adults as much as do
French children. The French child is much more on his guard
against adults, particularly a doctor. American children, in spite
of their neurotic difficulties, do succeed in enjoying life in the
presence of an adult. The French child enjoys life more easily with
other children. This difference is understandable since in America
the position is taken that childhood is the time to enjoy yourself;
that it is time enough to be serious when you grow up. The French
position is that only when you grow up can you really enjoy yourself;
childhood is the time to learn to grow up, to be serious, to be reasonable, and to prepare for the future (13).

Dolto goes on to say that there is a great difference between
French and American mothers in their acceptance of therapy for
children. French mothers take the view that the doctor does *not*
know best, mother knows best. They go to the analyst as they go to
a physician to get a diagnosis but they are sceptical of the cure pre-
scribed. The American mother, on the other hand, is likely to doubt
her methods of bringing up the child and to rely on the analyst. The
French mother has no such doubts.

All of us in our practice have to deal with patients' attitudes
toward the therapist. We often have to cope with attitudes toward
our sex, age, discipline, analytic orientation and personal idiosyncrasies. We frequently have the experience of dealing with religious
affiliations. Patients may say they chose a particular therapist because of his background with the remark, "he will understand me,
and my problems." Other patients choose a therapist from a different background than their own, as they feel the therapist will

allow them to do things disapproved by the regularities of their own cultural group (for example, sexual freedom). Patients soon discover that the similar or different background of the therapist is not so important but they do appreciate an understanding on the part of the therapist of what their particular background might be.

In establishing a working relation it is quite important for the therapist to be aware of the covert communications of the patient, communications that may be culturally oriented. For example, one Jewish patient I had came into therapy because overtly he said he wanted to work with a psychologist. He was a graduate student in psychology and hoped one day to take post-doctoral training in psychotherapy. He thought the therapist would understand his struggles for the Ph.D. and would probably guide him in his professional life as well as in his emotional difficulties. One day the patient was telling about how his father had wanted him to be a doctor and how his studying psychology was only second best. Then he said, "but you are a psychologist," meaning presumably that the psychotherapist was a second best. We discussed then the possibility that he covertly felt like his father, that an M.D is the most learned man. He said he had not been aware at all of taking covertly the Jewish point about the M.D. being a learned and more respected person but he realized this was correct.

2. ESTIMATION OF AND ATTITUDES TOWARD TYPE AND DEGREE OF DISTURBANCE

We have been trained to evaluate or to understand an evaluation of the type and degree of disturbance in a patient; that he is suffering from a particular psychosis; that he is a latent schizophrenic but with strong defenses; that he is a psychoneurotic with phobias, or a personality disorder with passive aggressive components, or a sociopath. We take very little into account the cultural background of the patient and its possible connection with the particular disorder he exhibits, although the need to do so has been often pointed out, particularly by Chess, Clark and Thomas (4) in their discussion of Negro children treated by white therapists. They have indicated the importance of making a cultural evaluation of the patient as part of the total evaluation for diagnosis and treatment planning. But as

Marvin Opler has indicated in his article on Cultural Perspectives in Mental Health (14), it is hard to make such evaluation for our cultural information is meager and we have only scratched the surface anyway. Opler goes on to say that we do not have systematic knowledge, for instance, of the kinds of material a specific cultural group represses. Does a group project or introject particular targets? What does it use for sublimations? These questions and many more need to be answered before we can estimate thoroughly the whole area of quality and quantity of disturbance in different cultural and socioeconomic groups.[1] We do, of course, have a good deal of unorganized and scattered bits of information about deviant behavior in different groups. For example, we would be genuinely surprised, I think, if a Jewish patient has as his chief complaint *chronic alcoholism*. If the patient was Irish we would not be so surprised (1). In the third session I had with a Chinese patient, who found it hard to talk to me, I was amazed that he told freely of a dream in which *he saw himself as a child playing on the floor by a bed. In the bed were the therapist and her husband. As he played he urinated on the floor.* His association with the dream was that he was enjoying himself. My first interpretation of the dream (not told to the patient) was that here was an hostile act, expressed by urinating where he was not supposed to and doing it so near the therapist who was not paying attention to him but was with her husband. Then I remembered that toilet training in China proceeds very gradually for the young child, and that the child is treated permissively. Wetting on the floor in a small child would not result in a reprimand nor lead to his feeling of shame and subsequently of guilt. The dream seemed to show this. In the dream the patient enjoyed himself. I took this partly as a positive transference phenomenon. The patient subsequently had many dreams showing anger toward the therapist, but urinating was not the means of expressing hostility. Also, without taking the cultural point into account, I could probably have felt that the patient must be quite sick to come out so early in therapy with a dream about urination and be able to report this so freely and with no feeling of shame (American position about urination).

---

[1] It is hoped that as a result of the psychosomatic studies now going on among different cultures, and as a result of the Yorkville study of mental health as well as other studies, some of them under the auspices of the World Federation for Mental Health, we can begin to accumulate more concrete material that can be used to evaluate cultural points in diagnosis and treatment.

The anthropologist, John Gillen (15), has given an example of how a doctor from the North misinterpreted the communications of a patient from a southern rural community. This patient was talking out loud to Jesus, telling him all her troubles. The doctor interpreted this behavior as disorganization of the personality and classified her as a schizophrenic. Actually, the patient came from a religious sect where everyone talked aloud to Jesus when he was in trouble. The patient had been abandoned by her husband and was in economic difficulties. She had come to the clinic in despair, but actually was not suffering from anything more than a situational neurosis.

3. Some Ways in Which Cultural Patterns Enter into the Communications Between Patient and Therapist and How These May Be Handled

At the 1955 meeting of the American Orthopsychiatric Association Mildred Burgum (3) read a paper on the subject of values and some technical problems in psychotherapy. She showed the extent to which value judgments enter into the whole process of therapy and how the present-day techniques of supportive, re-educative and re-constructive psychotherapy consist of a series of values expressed both by the patient and the therapist in the communications that go on between them. As I see it, many of these values reflect the cultural regularities in the background of the patient and therapist and the new cultural patterns different from the original ones that they, patient and therapist, have decided to adopt.

For example, a young Jewish girl of 25 comes in one day with a dream about *candles burning in her mother's home. It was Friday night and she lit the candles. For once her married sisters who were present were not making disparaging remarks. The patient felt the atmosphere was pleasant and that her friends, including the therapist, might have been present. All of a sudden she felt something was wrong and she blew out the candles and woke up.* The patient associated with the dream only the wish that home could be pleasant like that. She never lit candles, her mother did. She was ashamed of her home and of all the bickering. Then she said, "Well, I guess I should tell you about the candles. Did you ever hear of how they are lit Friday nights?" The patient felt that being non-Jewish I had never heard of Jewish customs. The patient then said she felt she blew out the candles because I (the therapist) would have been ashamed of her home, that I was siding with her desire to leave home and live in an apartment with another girl, that I wanted her to better herself socially. It took some time before the patient understood that she projected onto the therapist her own wishes to leave home and "better herself," as she said it. The patient was also accusing the therapist of not appreciating the values her home might represent, such as candles and warmth, and of siding with values against her cultural background where it was considered outrageous for a girl to leave home before she married, that if she did so she was just a "loose" girl.

What was done in therapy at this point was to review the position of the patient's family toward a girl not being married at 25, and one who decided to leave home although the mother threatened to get sicker if she did. This was clarified as a Jewish old-world point that the mother threatens to get sick and die if the child does not obey her. We discussed the fact that to leave home and live with another girl was not at all against the culture of a big city and did not brand her as wicked. It was a matter of choice. She could live at home if she chose, but by leaving home she might find it easier to have some life of her own, some privacy, and she might also be able to have a happier relationship with her family whenever she went home for a visit. Only six months later after the patient left home were we able to go into the psychodynamics of why she felt so badly in relation to men. By clarifying the cultural points first it made it easier for the particular patient not to use cultural points as defenses or as resistance to getting at her other problems.

In his book on *Social Science and Psychotherapy for Children,* Pollak (15) and his collaborators have given some excellent examples of taking into account cultural points. Pollak gave an instance of how a thirteen-year-old boy, whose parents were Chassidic Jews, was determined to talk to the rabbi daily as did his parents. However, he insisted on going at an early hour in the morning which upset the routine of the household. Here the boy was using a cultural regularity in a way to annoy his parents the most.

The problems arising from cultural points do not take place only in the early stages of therapy. I had one patient where after two years in therapy interpretation centering about a cultural point came up which helped him over a final hump in his recovery. This patient was a young thirty-year-old male who had been unable to get a job and had a very restricted social life because of his anxieties. After two years his difficulties were largely over, he had started to work in a good position, had gone to quite a few parties and was going steady with a girl. He was thinking seriously of marrying her. He came in one day saying the girl had told him what her financial assets were and had asked about his. He said, "It took me a year to tell you my income although I never have told you specifically (he had inherited quite a little money) but somehow I was shocked by Nancy." Then I thought of his cultural background, brought up in a Protestant puritanic home, with a mother who was overshadowed by two 19th-century maiden aunts who ruled the home and a father who kept his business affairs to himself. All I said to the patient was, "You were thinking that Nancy was not quite a lady, a lady never talks of personal money matters; whom does that remind you of?" The patient then laughed and said, "Gee, I thought I had shed those old girls long ago. I've got to watch my step or they'll creep up on me. In fact, today, I expected you to be shocked by Nancy's disclosures."

4. Ways in Which Cultural Patterns Can Affect Transference and Counter-Transference Phenomena

We can detect cultural patterns in the verbal and non-verbal communications between patient and therapist both when the therapist and patient have dissimilar or similar cultural backgrounds. These patterns may play a large or only a minor role in the relationship. It is particularly important for the therapist to be aware of these patterns under conditions where transference and counter-transference phenomena occur.

In her paper on values referred to earlier, Mildred Burgum gives an excellent instance of transference where a cultural point was used as an attack by the patient on the therapist as a defense against feelings of worthlessness. A non-Jewish patient hummed a bit of a tune from a Jewish ritual in a mocking tone to her Jewish therapist who picked up the point. The patient said she had been thinking "Jew." As it turned out the patient had been in the room prior to the therapist and had been reading a personal letter of the therapist's she had seen on a desk. The patient felt very guilty and thought the therapist would be very displeased with her (presumably as had authority figures in her life). Here the cultural point only played a small role, for the large therapeutic task was to work with the patient's misconceptions of the nature of self-assertion and her relationship to other people. However, taking up the cultural point showed the patient that the therapist was aware of what she was doing and was willing and interested to explore with her, her thoughts and feelings, and to see what it was that led to this form of hostility.

In working with Chinese patients it has not always been so easy to pick up the cultural points which might influence the transference. In working with my Chinese patients I was aware that I might represent for them a large number of individuals in their lives since they came usually from multiple family units in China. One Chinese patient treated me deferentially but with masked hostility. He would try to please and then would clam up or talk in an incomprehensible way. I felt some of his difficulty was his dealing with a "foreign devil," and a woman, but he could not express just what he felt. After a year and a half in therapy the patient ventured the suggestion that the therapist had changed. He said, "I saw you coming down the stairs and you walked *feminine*." He continued that I had always up till then walked *masculine,* but I now took smaller steps. Since this patient had told me how he had hated his grandfather's concubine who was bossy, I suggested maybe he had seen me as this concubine. He said "Yes, square shoulders like her but—" he hesitated; somehow I did not fit into the picture. The concubine was Chinese and a member of the household, I was not. The next week the patient dreamed *he was at home in China. In the room among others was a woman who was a distant relative, but poor.* She frequently came to spend a day and was treated partly as servant, partly as relative. When asked to associate with this dream the patient remained silent. He said he had no associations and could not understand why this relative had been brought in. I suggested that maybe she reminded him of me, that he had finally brought me into his home but at the same time I was in an inferior position, someone there to serve and to receive money. He laughed and said all of a sudden he felt fine. From then on therapy proceeded much more easily. Using in his dream a cultural point about such a poor relative who is treated menially (a common occurrence in China), he was able to work out much better his relationship to the therapist.

But progress in therapy with this patient had been slowed up by the therapist's being mistaken about a cultural point. Often I could not understand the patient even when I asked him to talk slowly. I assumed this was due to the difficulty he had in pronouncing English. Occasionally he spoke more clearly, especially when he felt at ease. I finally asked him if he was understood when he talked Chinese. He said not always, that his friends complained that when he was upset he could not be understood. Here was an emotional problem that a cultural interpretation had masked. In several months I had felt his difficulty was his limited inability to pronounce certain letters. The therapist had been brought up on the stereotype of Chinese mispronunciations of English.

Pollak (15, pp. 114-116) has given an instance of how a little girl was not able to get into a positive transference relationship with her therapist for as long as three years because the therapist did not understand the cultural points the child was trying to communicate. For instance, the child incessantly wanted to play mother and have the therapist play *bad child* who insisted on drinking milk for her lunch. The therapist tried to introduce a new game of blocks but the little girl seemed afraid to play. A new therapist took the cue that this child came from a Kosher home and was trying to work out her difficulties through Jewish practices. The therapist was thus able to play the game of milk with the child which endeared her to the child and together they worked out what it was the little girl was trying to communicate. She was trying to say that she could not always be a good Jew for she could not honor her father and mother —honoring them meant accepting their yelling and hitting.

A young therapist I was supervising had quite a little trouble working out his counter-transference with a white patient who was married to a Negro. This girl had been a year with a therapist in another city. The first therapist took the position that inter-racial marriages could not work out in the United States and told the patient so. The patient left him because she wanted her marriage to work out. The new therapist took the overt position that he could not pass judgment on the marriage because he knew very little about it. But he found himself siding with the patient whenever she expressed feelings of wanting to leave her husband. He suspected he was attracted to her and was siding with her against the hostile reactions of her husband. One day I asked him how he felt about inter-racial marriages anyway. He answered, "They could work out in other countries, say France, but not in the United States." Then he realized what position he had been taking and that he had compensated for his disapproval by siding with the girl. So he told the girl that in general he did not think a marriage such as hers could work out but that he was willing to look at it from all angles. From there on treatment proceeded much more smoothly.

Becoming overly interested in a patient and his life experience has been a problem many therapists have had to face. Freud himself is said to have transferred an Egyptologist who was a patient of his because he, Freud, became engrossed in what the patient had to say about ancient Egypt.

George Devereux (6) has written about the problems arising when the therapist analyzes a patient from a culture very different from his own and when research was one of the motivations of the therapist. He speaks of the legitimate resentment the patient feels in the therapist who is treating him more as an informant than as a patient. This was the case with my first Chinese patient. In some early session with this patient I would ask questions which turned out to be more useful for adding to my own knowledge about the Chinese family than to understand the patient's particular problems. At this time the patient had a dream in which *he was arrested in Peking and was being questioned by a communist general. Some money had to be paid out and the general asked too many questions —all about America.* Realistically this patient did have a conflict about remaining in America or returning to China but I felt the matter of too many questions and the exchange of money gave some hint of what I had been doing. Devereux refers to a similar situation. He had an American Indian as a patient. This patient dreamed *some people met him and asked him if he was an Indian. He resented the fact that he was not even asked his name.* The therapist took this as a warning about his over-eagerness to gather cultural material.

Conclusion

In this presentation I have tried to show the importance of looking for cultural patterns that may be causing a patient to resist therapy, to distort some of his actions and reactions in the world around him, and to limit his possibilities for leading a richer and fuller life. The cultural patterns of the therapist and his lack of understanding of the cultural patterns of the patient may limit his grasp of the therapeutic process. Cultural patterns, of course, do by no means need to have exclusively a negative influence. The values a patient and therapist set on achieving a goal of healthier and happier living for the patient are themselves patterns. How to achieve these goals or what factors including cultural patterns prevent or slow up the achieving of these goals are the task of the therapist.

Devereux has stated that he hopes some day that a satisfactory technique of cross-cultural psychotherapy may be worked out but that in the meantime he suggests the therapist has the job of taking a genuine interest in the cultural background of the patient and must try to understand the patient's productions in terms of his own culture (6). I feel this needs to be done not only in inter-cultural therapy but in intra-cultural therapy where the patient and therapist come from the same background. Cultural patterns need to be pointed out in cases where they seem to be operating as we said, disadvantageously. There are occasions where it is well for the therapist to indicate the positive aspects in cultural patterns. To do so he needs to be aware of what they are.

In conclusion, I should like to suggest three ways in which psychotherapists could prepare themselves for working with their patients whether of the same, or different cultural backgrounds than their own, whether the difference is national, religious, or socio-economic. *Firstly,* I think therapists need some formal training in cultural anthropology so that they will understand what cultural regularities of thoughts, feelings and actions occur in a given group, particularly, in the cultural groups with which they will be working. *Secondly,* I feel it would be helpful for therapists to become more keenly aware of their own cultural background. This could be brought about either by having the therapist write his own cultural autobiography and discuss it with a cultural anthropologist, or

288   *The Counseling Process*

by his participating in some form of group psychotherapy where a cultural anthropologist is present to point out cultural points. In the *third* place, I think it would be valuable for therapists to do some research or at least give some thought to the role cultural regularities play in the therapeutic process and when interpretations of cultural patterns are indicated. If these suggestions are carried out I feel we should then have a more thorough and systematic body of knowledge about cultural patterns as they enter into psychothera-peutic procedures.

BIBLIOGRAPHY

1. Bales, R. F.: "Cultural Differences in Rates of Alcoholism." *Quart. J. Studies on Alcohol,* 6: 480-493, 1946.
2. Benedict, Ruth: *Patterns of Culture.* Houghton-Mifflin, New York, 1934.
3. Burgum, Mildred: *Some Technical Problems in the Role of Values in Psychotherapy.* Read at Annual Meeting of American Orthopsychiatric Assoc., 1955.
4. Chess, S., K. B. Clark, and A. Thomas: "The Importance of Cultural Evaluation in Psychiatric Diagnosis and Treatment." *Psychiat. Quart.,* 27: 102-114, 1953.
5. Dolto, Françoise: *French and American Children as Seen by a French Child Analyst.* Margaret Mead and Martha Wolfenstein, "Childhood in Contemporary Cultures," 408-423, University of Chicago Press, Chicago, 1955.
6. Devereux, George: "Cultural Factors in Psychoanalytic Therapy." Reprinted from *Journal of the Amer. Psychoanalytic Assoc.,* Vol. 1, #4, by Devereux Schools, Devon, Pa.
7. Ginsberg, S. W.: "The Impact of the Social Worker's Cultural Structure on Social Therapy." *Social Casework,* 32: 319-325, 1951.
8. Gioseffi, Wm.: "The Relationship of Culture to the Principles of Casework." *Social Casework,* 32: 190-196, 1951.
9. Green, Arnold W.: "Social Values and Psychotherapy." *J. Personality,* 14: 199-227, 1945-46.
10. Henry, Jules, and Joan W. Boggs: "Child Rearing, Culture and the Natural World." *Psychiatry,* 15: 261-271, 1952.
11. Kardiner, Abraham: *The Psychological Frontiers of Society.* Columbia University Press, New York, 1945.

12. Kluckholm, C., and Henry A. Murray (Eds.): *Personality in Nature, Society and Culture.* Alfred A. Knopf, New York, 1949.

13. Metraux, Rhoda, and Margaret Mead: *Themes in French Culture.* Hoover Institute Studies Series D, Communities No. 1, Stanford University Press, Stanford, 1954.

14. Opler, M. K.: "Cultural Perspectives in Mental Health Research." *Amer. J. Orthopsychiatry,* 25: 51-59, 1955.

15. Pollak, Otto, and collaborators: *Social Science and Psychotherapy for Children.* Russell Sage Foundation, New York, 1952.

16. Savitz, Harry Austryn: "The Cultural Background of the Patient as Part of the Physician's Armamentarium." *J. Abnorm. and Soc.,* 47: 245-254, 1952.

17. Tsung-yi, Lin: "A Study of the Incidence of Mental Disorder in Chinese and Other Cultures." *Psychiatry,* 4: 313-336, 1951.

18. Wolfenstein, Martha: "Some Variants in Moral Training of Children." *Psychoanalytic Study of the Child,* 5: 310-328, 1950.

27. CONFIDENTIALITY IN CHILD GUIDANCE TREATMENT

Alan O. Ross

The confidentiality of psychotherapeutic interviews is a well-established and generally accepted principle. Inherited from medicine on its ethical basis, practical considerations have made it a virtual *sine qua non* in psychiatry. Without the assurance that his communications will be held in the strictest confidence, no patient would feel free to divulge the highly personal material which needs to be verbalized if treatment is to be effective. In the psychotherapy of adults the therapist will usually assure his patient during the first interview of the confidential nature of treatment. In the rare case where it may appear therapeutically necessary to diverge from this

Reprinted by permission of the author, Alan O. Ross, Pittsburgh Child Guidance Center and University of Pittsburgh; *Mental Hygiene,* XLII, No. 1 (January, 1958), 60-66; and Grune & Stratton, Inc. The material contained in this article appears with only minor changes in Dr. Ross' book, *The Practice of Clinical Child Psychology* (New York: Grune & Stratton, Inc., 1959), pp. 79-86.

principle, the conscientious therapist will attempt to obtain the patient's specific concurrence before revealing material obtained during treatment to an outsider. This rare instance where confidentiality thus becomes relative instead of remaining absolute is usually one involving an acute danger to the life of the patient or of others.

The concept of absolute confidentiality also becomes slightly modified when treatment takes place not in individual practice but in a clinic or training setting where the need to discuss case material with supervisors or other members of the clinic staff brings third parties indirectly into the therapist-patient relationship. In a clinic, these third parties also include clerical personnel responsible for record-keeping and the confidential relationship thus obtains between the patient and "the Clinic" as a professional institution. The primary ethical responsibility for confidentiality rests at all times with the therapist. Whenever treatment takes place under these circumstances, the patient should be made aware that the principle of confidentiality is being extended to include other, indirectly involved individuals.

The practical need for assuring the patient of the confidentiality of his communications, important in the treatment of adults, becomes crucial in the treatment of children. Most children, and particularly those being treated for emotionl disturbances, have had important experiences which they entrusted to or shared with one adult, who promptly revealed the information to another, to the embarrassment and chagrin of the child. A neighbor, observing the child in some "forbidden" activity and rushing to tell his mother; mother telling father of the child's misdeeds; or parents sharing a laugh over something "funny" the child said or did, are frequent childhood experiences. Often, too, a child may have worked up courage to make known to his mother an important question or a confidential experience, only to have the mother share the material with the father or another adult in the most casual manner. From such situations many children generalize that adults cannot be trusted and when a therapist first enters the picture he is usually viewed as just another adult, in alliance against the child.

The initial experience in a child guidance clinic contact tends to reinforce this idea, which is compounded by generalizations stemming from visits to the pediatrician or family physician. The parents usually contact the clinic before bringing in the child, who then comes to a place which is strange to him but familiar to his parent. In most instances the parents are unable to prepare the child adequately for his visit to the clinic, for no matter how well preparation was rehearsed with the parents during the initial contact it frequently becomes distorted or omitted entirely because of the parents' own anxiety and conflict about the visit.

The child, arriving at the clinic anxious and confused, has nothing but his own generalizations about doctors and adults by which to order this new experience conceptually. Being responsible for bringing the child to the clinic and having obvious familiarity with the physical layout and the receptionist, the mother is viewed by the child as having "the inside track" in the clinic—apparently being in conspiracy with all the other adults inhabiting the place. Assuming that the child is first undergoing an evaluation, as is usual at most clinics, he will at this point be seen by an adult who will either want to "play and talk" with him or give him psychological tests. It is unlikely that this contact will do much to change the attitude with which the child came to the clinic. He will undoubtedly assume (and usually correctly) that the "doctor" talked to his mother before he saw the child, thus getting her side of the story, and that he is going to talk to her again afterwards to tell her what he "found out" about the child. Everything that happens would appear to be for the mother and against the child.

As stated earlier, confidentiality cannot be absolute in a child guidance clinic because information received from the patient must be shared with other staff members. The team approach in which mother and child are treated by different individuals requires that the two therapists involved in a given case frequently and regularly exchange information relevant to that particular family. This exchange of information may be oral or written (through the medium of the case record) and it may take place in an informal discussion between the two therapists or in the setting of a staff conference, where the information is shared with yet other professional persons. This is a modification of absolute confidentiality, discussed earlier, and the patient is entitled to know that this condition obtains and that it is in the best interest of treatment progress. The adult members of a family in treatment will usually accept this relatively easily, and if any doubts about the confidential nature of communications should later on disrupt the treatment relationship, they can be worked through like any other resistance mechanism.

In the case of the child, however, the situation is somewhat complicated, for he may be expected to find it more difficult to conceptualize the nature of the therapeutic team operation. If, following evaluation, the child is taken into treatment, the therapist will have to establish a relationship of confidence and trust within which treatment can become possible. This task is complicated by the child's attitude of not trusting adults in general and the people at the clinic in particular. Again, as at the time of the first contact, the child is brought to the clinic by the mother, and although she is not in the same room, her physical presence in the building continues to make the child suspect that she will find out anything he may do or say. The question of confidentiality of the relationship thus becomes of paramount importance. The therapist will want to explore the child's feelings and thoughts about his coming to the clinic during the first treatment sessions. He will want to discuss what sort of a place the clinic is, what will and what will not happen to the child, and what he can and cannot do. As part of this general introduction to treatment the question of confidentiality should be taken up, but what and how should the child be told about it?

A statement, such as "Everything you do and say in your hour with me is strictly between the two of us and I won't tell your mother about it," is obviously incomplete but anything more than this raises a great many problems. If one adds "While you are playing and talking with me, your mother will be talking to her social worker and the social worker and I will be talking with each other from time to time so that we can all help you better," one tends to lend support to the child's initial suspicion that his mother will hear about what he says and does in his treatment session. It would thus be necessary to add a specific assurance that neither the therapist nor the mother's worker will tell the mother anything about what goes on in the child's hours. Unfortunately, even this extended statement fails to cover every potential situation. What if the therapist becomes convinced that a child is serious about a threat to commit suicide or that a 5-year-old actually plans to run away from home? Most therapists would feel obliged to inform the mother or another responsible adult so that this potential danger can be averted. At the same time, they would probably inform the child of their intention of doing so, trying to obtain the child's agreement but taking the required step with or without his concurrence. Does this mean that one should refer to such a contingency at the time confidentiality is taken up at the beginning of the child's treatment? One might say that one won't inform the mother of anything the child does or says unless one had first talked to the child about one's intentions. This is an innocuous enough statement for most adults, but a child with limited abstract ability and only a vague concept of the future might easily find this confusing. He may well attend solely to that part of the statement referring to telling the mother, using it to confirm his suspicion and disregarding the qualifying clause altogether. It would thus seem best to keep the statement in its simplest form at the beginning of treatment, adding modifications at a later time when a relationship has been established and any resulting confusion can be more readily resolved.

The problem of assuring the child of the confidentiality of his therapeutic sessions seems complicated enough even in situations where therapists sincerely have no intention of communicating the child's material to the mother except in the most crucial situations involving the child's safety. While most therapists subscribe to this concept of confidentiality some advocate a further modification which might be called "limited confidentiality." Faced with the apparent lack of progress and productivity in the child's sessions and stymied in their indirect attempts to focus on an area in which they know the child to be holding back, they are sometimes inclined to introduce material obtained from the mother's hours directly in order to elicit movement on the part of the child. At the same time they will usually insist that nothing the child produces shall be transmitted to the mother. The principle involved has sometimes been referred to as "one-way communication" and introduces a critical complication. Limited confidentiality requires that one announce to the mother at the beginning of treatment that some of the material she brings to her worker will be used by the child's therapist in his treatment of the child. Since the time element does not make it feasible to obtain the mother's consent each time some of her material is to be used in this manner, the decision as to what is and what is not to be treated confidentially must, of necessity, be left to the child therapist's discretion and thus becomes arbitrary. If this were not so, at least two weeks would pass under a conventional once-a-week treatment schedule before the child's therapist could utilize a specific piece of information.

An example will help to clarify this: In a given week the mother tells her worker that the child has begun to refuse to go to school. In conference following this session, the child's therapist learns of this and decides that he would like to use this fact with the child, who has failed to mention it himself. The worker would now have to clear this with the mother in the subsequent week and to transmit the mother's reply to the therapist, who then raises the issue with the child in the third week.

The first problem arising out of an acceptance of limited confidentiality as a working principle has to do with the mother's reaction. Even though she may accept the rationale that this approach is therapeutically advantageous, the realization that some of the things she reveals to her worker are going to find their way to the child in some form or other may well result in her being less than frank in her treatment session. Not only may she fear that the child, in turn, might wish to talk about a topic with her before she is ready to accept such discussion without embarrassment or uneasiness, but she may also fear that the child might reveal to outsiders or the father something she does not wish to become known. Because of these concerns, many mothers will shy away from revealing sensitive material unless they are fully convinced that the information will remain, if not with the worker, then at least among the professional clinic staff.

The second, and it would seem more serious, complication arises out of the child's awareness that he can find out some of the things his mother talks about in her sessions. This makes it very difficult to convince a disturbed child that communication of this nature really goes in only one direction. If he can find out things his mother says to her worker, how can he be sure that his mother will not also find out things he tells his therapist? A complicated statement, such as "Your mother will not find out what you say or do in your hours, but sometimes, when I think it will help you, I will introduce in your hours with me things your mother tells her social worker," cannot possibly be very convincing, no matter how simplified the wording. The realization that therapy material is carried back and forth plays into and tends to confirm the child's suspicion that the therapist cannot be trusted, and may well represent a major obstacle to treatment progress. It is highly probable that the apparent advantage gained by using the mother's material in the child's hours is vitiated by the reinforcement this lends to both the mother's and the child's resistances. For this reason it would seem advisable to carry out treatment in a setting where only information the child himself feels free to introduce is used in his treatment sessions.

A different aspect of the problem of confidentiality is that involving direct contact between the child's therapist and the mother. In the individual practice of psychotherapy it is generally accepted usage that the therapist either occasionally or regularly interviews one of the child's parents. The fact that treatment can be carried out under these circumstances would seem to demonstrate that this approach does not make treatment impossible, but one of the reasons the child guidance team approach was evolved is that such contact makes treatment more difficult because it interferes with the therapist-child relationship in many cases. That this is being recognized by therapists in individual practice is demonstrated by the recent trend of having social workers, charged with the responsibility of maintaining contact with parents, collaborate with private practitioners. In spite of the obvious advantages the team approach lends in the separation of treatment functions and the concomitant greater ease with which the child can be convinced of the trustworthiness of his therapist, there exists an occasional urge on the part of some child therapists to short-circuit the team and talk directly with the mother. When this urge becomes translated into action, it demonstrates a lack of confidence in the team partner who is thus shunted aside and a failure to appreciate and accept the principle of the team approach. In addition, it tends to disrupt the social worker's treatment of the mother; but worse than this, it jeopardizes the relationship between therapist and child. Knowing, as he ought to, that his therapist talks to his mother, the child cannot but assume that he is the topic of discussion and to fear that his therapist will not only divulge information obtained from him but also hear the mother's version of his behavior outside the clinic. Avoiding the treatment disrupting reaction which must follow this reasoning on the part of the child seems well worth relying on the social worker for interpreting to, and gathering relevant information from, the mother.

The therapist's urge for direct communication with the mother has its counterpart in the mother's desire to talk directly to the child's therapist. It was pointed out earlier that the child comes to the clinic with certain preconceptions carried over from his experience with pediatricians and other physicians. It must be remembered that the mother, too, tries to order the new and threatening experience of coming to a child guidance clinic in terms of something she is familiar with, and thus tends to generalize from taking the child to a pediatrician to taking him to a "psychiatric doctor." In all the old situations she has known the physician examined the child, nearly always in her presence, and then told her of his findings and recommendations. In a child guidance clinic, however, she is suddenly excluded from the "examination" and has the recommendations interpreted to her by someone who has never talked to the child. Many mothers will react to this exclusion with resentment and a negative attitude toward the interpretations of the clinic's findings. If the recommendations are unwelcome and threatening, as statements of the child's disturbance and need for treatment invariably are, the mother may well refuse to accept them and fail to follow through on any treatment plan offered.

To avoid this reaction, many clinics are making it a practice to have the person who saw the child during diagnostic study join the mother's worker in interpreting the results of an evaluation. This not only places the weight of the doctor's prestige behind the statements made but it also enables the mother to ask specific questions of the person who has first-hand familiarity with the child. While this practice has undoubted advantages, it should be remembered that if the individual who saw the child during study is assigned the case for therapy, this direct contact with the mother may place him at a handicap in establishing a treatment relationship. For the child must feel that the only reason the therapist talks with him again is to "find out more things" in order to communicate them to the mother. The advantages gained from direct interpretation to the mother should always be weighed against the possible disadvantages such contact represents in the treatment situation.

Unfortunately, the disadvantages are not confined to the initial phase of treatment. Having once had direct contact with the child's therapist, the mother may expect that she can continue to talk to him directly. As pointed out earlier, any contact between the child's therapist and the mother during treatment is deleterious to the therapist's relationship with the child, but as treatment takes its slow and lengthy course many mothers will continue to want to know "what the doctor found out." This is why some mothers will try to buttonhole the therapist in the waiting room to ask him "how Johnny is doing." The mother's worker must be constantly aware of her patient's need to know what progress, if any, is being made with the child, so that she can interpret therapeutic principles to her and satisfy her legitimate desire to know what is going on. This means that the nature of treatment in general, and the practice of the team approach in particular, must be brought up again and again, and any attempt on the part of the mother to communicate directly with her child's therapist should be viewed not only as a failure to make this interpretation meaningful and acceptable but also as an indication of a weakness in the worker-patient relationship.

Unable to learn from the child's therapist "what he found out," and not satisfied with the worker's generalized statements about treatment progress, some mothers will attempt to elicit from the child information about the content of his hours with his therapist. This "pumping" frequently occurs soon after the hour, usually on the way home from the clinic and takes the form of such questions as "What did you and your doctor talk about today?" or "What did you do today?" While these queries would seem to reflect only casual interest (parents often ask their children what they did in school that day), they have a deeper meaning and can seriously hamper treatment progress. Such inquiries may indicate that the mother cannot permit the child to be close to anyone but her, so that her questions are attempts to insinuate herself into the child-therapist relationship. Again, "pumping" may reflect the mother's concern that the child will "tell on her," will reveal aspects of her life or of her relationship to the child about which she feels guilty. By asking him questions, she may unconsciously be trying to sabotage the child's treatment and this is exactly the result that these questions tend to bring about. Knowing that after each hour he may have to "report" to the mother on what he did or said, the child will soon censor his productions, the effect being the same as if the treatment hour were conducted with the mother present in the room.

Whenever either the child's or the mother's therapist discovers that the mother tries to "pump" the child in this manner, it will have to be taken up with the mother in order to try and have her desist. It may, in fact, be desirable to cover this point with all parents in one of the first treatment hours, possibly at the time the topic of confidentiality of interview content is dealt with, since many parents find it difficult to understand that the child is entitled to the privacy of his treatment hours and even more difficult to accept their exclusion from the therapist-child relationship.

Child guidance treatment is a costly procedure because of the duplication of professional services, nearly every case involving at least two staff members. This expenditure of money and time has proved worth while because it provides both parent and child with his own therapist, thus avoiding the treatment-retarding complications which often result when both members of a family are treated by the same person. Therapists in individual practice, who have to work with both parent and child, have to deal with these complications during treatment, thus spending valuable time on a problem which therapy itself creates and which the team approach is ideally suited to avoid. From the point of view here represented, this major advantage of the team approach over individual practice is vitiated when contacts between child therapist and parent are permitted or when the principle of limited confidentiality is accepted.

It would therefore seem generally best to forego the questionable benefits of limited confidentiality, operating instead within a framework where nothing either parent or child reveals in his hours is directly introduced into the other's treatment, and where contact between the child's therapist and the parent is held to an absolute minimum. In this manner optimal use can be made of the unique opportunities the child guidance team approach presents for the treatment of emotional disturbances of children.

Section Five

GROUP METHODS IN COUNSELING

One of the problems which faces the school, public or private, is the rapid increase in school population. How to handle more pupils is a major concern of administrators, instructional staff, and guidance workers. For guidance workers the problem is even more critical because the focus of their activities is the individual and because it seems unlikely that the expansion of counseling services will keep pace with population growth. Thus, more pupils in school result in less time for the counselor to spend with individual students. Group methods have been proposed as one answer to this dilemma. But the use of group techniques to better understand and aid the individual is a difficult challenge in itself. Jenkins suggests in his article on using group procedures that counselors "go beyond individual techniques and explore the possibilities of group techniques to see if they would be helpful in making some of the changes which seem needed in the pupils."

Even if all counselors were operating in situations where the recommended 250 or 300 to 1 pupil/counselor ratio were in effect, it would be difficult for them to spend much time with each student. One solution to this problem is given by Froehlich, who points out that it may be possible for the counselor to work with several counselees at the same time if the counselees manifest at least one common problem. From the results of his study of the effectiveness of "multiple counseling," Froehlich suggests that counseling need not be individual. The reader should ask whether or not he could utilize group processes as aids to individual improvement.

As suggested earlier, the question the counselor should ask is: "How can group methods enable me to work with an individual more effectively?" If group procedures do not help the counselor become more effective, it would be better not to use them.

Three articles of this section present some results of group methods which were used in school settings and which may help the reader better judge the potential for his own particular use. Broedel provides an interesting study of the use of group processes for counseling gifted underachieving adolescents. It should be noted that one reason for utilizing this technique is that adolescents are "genuinely reassured when they discover that their peers have problems similar to their own." In this way the counselee is supported by the knowledge that he is not alone against the world. Many times this thought does not occur to the counselee when he has only the "adult" counselor for an ally.

Mercer's article points out that the overcrowding which is present in many schools makes it difficult to deal with student problems on an individual basis. After identifying a group of pupils who had a problem in common, it was feasible to experiment with group procedures as a means of aiding in the solution of the problem. An interesting point illustrated by this study is that the group, as originally formed, was too large and that readjusting the size seemed to make the group process workable and profitable. This illustrates the need for evaluation and careful examination of the techniques and procedures used to determine if they are really of help to the student.

Richards' article supports the utilization of group techniques when they help the counselor better understand and work with the pupil. She lists a number of group activities which have been helpful in her school. This list may provide a base on which the counselor can begin to examine the possibility of group methods in his situation. Richards concludes that these "many group guidance activities are very helpful and free more of the counselor's time for those with deep seated problems."

The reader is cautioned against either a complete acceptance or rejection of the concept and techniques of group procedures. Each situation demands careful evaluation as to which methods and processes are appropriate. If group procedures seem to be indicated as potentially helpful the counselor should attempt to use them. It is important, however, that a thorough examination of the process in the situation be made in order to ascertain the reasonableness of employing such methods.

Above all, the counselor should bear in mind that the dignity and worth of the individual is the primary consideration in all counseling and guidance activities. If any process, whether group or individual, does not provide increased opportunity for the individual, it should be replaced by a more meaningful technique which will aid the growth of the person toward maturity. The articles in this section provide the bases for each counselor to begin an investigation into group methods. The outcomes can be fruitful only if evaluation by the counselor demonstrates whether the procedure is effective and indicates direction for future activity.

28. COUNSELING THROUGH GROUP ACTIVITIES

David H. Jenkins

Before we go into the problems of group counseling let us consider for a moment a story about Mr. X and what this hypothetical
Mr. X did in developing his counseling program.

Mr. X had been facing some difficulties in counseling his students.
He was finding, for instance, that although John and he had held
some excellent interviews, and John had gained some insight, there
was still not the change in his behavior that was desired. The counseling relationship was fine, but no change happened. With some
other boys he was having difficulty getting any kind of relationship
established—they just didn't want any help from an adult. And
other problems were similar. There seemed to be so much to be
done, so many counseling contacts that needed to be made, and Mr.
X just didn't have enough time to see everyone who needed to be
seen.

To make a long hypothetical story a short one, Mr. X got the idea
of working through small groups to help meet these problems. To
prepare himself for this kind of technique he studied about groups
and got some good training in the necessary skills of working with
groups. He knew that training in methods of being a good group
leader was as necessary as it was in methods of being a good interviewer. Then he went to work.

Mr. X persuaded six or eight boys whom he had been counseling
to meet together. He suggested to them that they might like to start
a "Human Relations Club" in which they could work together on
problems of how to get along with people better. The boys were
dubious at first—the idea sounded all right, but they hadn't been
too happy in some of their school clubs with adult leaders. Well,
they finally gave it a try. So Mr. X and the boys settled down to-

Reprinted by permission of the author and *Clearing House,* XXIII, No.
8 (April, 1949), 488-93.

gether to see what they could get out of such an activity. There were some difficult moments in the process, but as we look in on them several meetings later this is what we might observe:

The boys and Mr. X are sitting informally together having a discussion. They seem to be talking about something that happened in a class that morning. The discussion seems friendly and interested, with the boys doing most of the talking. There doesn't seem to be any argument—they seem to know what they are talking about and where they want to go in their discussion.

One of them says, "I can't quite get the idea of what happened. Why don't John and Mack act it out for us exactly as they remember it happening, then we can all talk about it better?" The group agrees. John becomes the teacher, Mack remains himself, and they act out what happened. As soon as they finish the boys begin to analyze the situation as they saw it, trying to figure out why it happened as it did. Then they begin to suggest to Mack things he might have done differently so the teacher wouldn't have become angry. Soon Mack says, "Let me try that idea out."

John becomes the teacher again, acting as he felt the teacher would act, and they start the same scene over. This time Mack tries the new idea and finds the teacher responding quite differently. The boys now feel that it is a good idea, and they discuss for a few minutes why it worked and what it might mean. Then they decide to try this idea out during the next few days and report back to the group how it actually worked. That way they can tell what changes they may want to make to improve the idea.

Now it's about time for them to end their meeting. Someone says, "Time's about up—let's take a look at our meeting today." And here they call on the member who has been acting as their group observer to lead them in a discussion of how good they thought this meeting was in comparison with the earlier meetings and why. The observer suggests some of the problems which he felt had prevented this meeting from being as effective as it could have been. With this lead-off, the members criticize and evaluate one another's behavior as group members as well as their own, and make suggestions as to what each needs to do to improve future meetings. Today Mr. X and Bill are given special attention because they got into a little argument over a point instead of trying to clear it up cooperatively.

Mr. X has been in the group, participating like any of the other members. His suggestions are considered along with those of the other members and rejected just about as often as those of anyone else. But he has built a good group here. It's quite amazing, but the leader and the boys keep talking about "we" and "us," not "you" and "I." They seem to have a real appreciation of one another even though they were rather direct in some of their criticisms. They have learned how much they can gain from sharing their feelings and ideas together.

Now, Mr. X looks at counseling in this way: He feels that the purpose of counseling is to initiate and encourage *change* in the pupil. This may be a change in the way he behaves in the class or corridor, or it may be a change in his attitudes toward school in general and toward study. It may also include changes in the way he looks at the people around him—whether he sees them as being friendly and helpful or as hostile. So Mr. X was willing to go beyond individual techniques and explore the possibilities of group techniques to see if they would be helpful in making some of the changes which seemed needed in the pupils.

Here are four questions for which Mr. X felt he needed answers before using group techniques:

1. What values does a group situation offer for counseling, that is, for stimulating changed behavior or attitudes in the pupil?
2. What is the nature of the group that can supply the best counseling situation and how may it be built?
3. What are some group-counseling techniques one might use?
4. Where can this kind of group be found, or built, within the school curriculum?

Let us turn to Mr. X's first question, "What values does the group situation offer toward inducing change in a pupil?"

First, participation in a healthy group supplies a *supportive relationship* to the student. He is given a membership in a group and now belongs to something. This very fact of belonging may be a partial solution for some unadjusted students, giving them some feeling of acceptance by others. It may remove others from a feeling of "being alone in a hostile world" to, at the very least, being together with a few others, "all of us against a hostile world." At least a small part of the world is no longer hostile to this individual and this process may continue to expand.

In the second place, the group offers a *sharing experience,* the group correlate, perhaps, of rapport. This, in a group, differs from the individual counseling situation for it offers a *two-way sharing,* a mutual interchange of problems with other group members.

At least four results seem possible from this sharing experience. Each student begins to see that other students have problems too, he is no longer "different" because of his problem, and this may relieve some of his anxiety. Also, he begins to see other members as a resource for help in diagnosing his problem, in giving insight, and in suggesting possible changes or solutions. Moreover, by sharing, he learns that it is acceptable behavior to discuss problems, and he learns how to consider his own problems more objectively. He finds it no longer necessary to contain his new problems within himself. His response to a new problem can become a reason *for* group contact rather than a reason for cutting himself off from groups. Finally, he finds that, in return for the assistance he is given by the group, he can make valuable contributions toward helping someone else with another problem.

A third value is that group experience will permit the group members to see that problems of getting along with people are *two-way problems.* They can begin to learn that the group, itself, may need to change its behavior and attitudes toward the student as much as he needs to change his behavior toward the group. This insight undoubtedly accelerates the individual adjustment. A simple example of this is presented by a pupil with a speech difficulty which is aggravated by group laughter. As the group comes to understand this reaction they can understand that they must help in meeting the problem by avoiding laughter at an inappropriate time so that this student can begin to work out a desirable adjustment.

A final major value is that a group situation is one in which *changed behavior can be practiced.* With a group oriented to the adjustment problems of its members, it can give attention to improving the relationships in its own group. Learning can begin "at home" in a "real life" learning situation.

We saw how Mr. X's group evaluated their own group and their own behavior. This was learning by immediate experience. In addition, practice can be carried on to improve the techniques of "getting along better together," at little emotional loss or cost in a supportive, sharing group. Practice can be play-acted (role-played) without strong emotion. Failures in practice are not disastrous—they can be occasions for trying it a different way and seeing how it works. Actual success in practice can also demonstrate that *change is possible.* "It *can* be done differently, because I practiced it that way."

Now, to meet Mr. X's second question, "What is the nature of the group that can supply these values?" let us list several of the more important qualities:

1. It must be a group that has a feeling of control over its own destiny; it is not dominated by outgroup members nor subject to arbitrary control. Here is a big problem in a school system.
2. It is a group that accepts each member as a person. It may not approve of what an individual does, but it does not reject him, only his behavior.
3. It has a feeling of common purpose. It knows why it is together and where it wants to go.
4. It gives its members a sense of progress and of satisfaction.

   These qualities are found in a basically democratic group which is composed of interdependent, but independent, persons.

How, then, can such a group be built?

Mr. X knew, in planning for his club, that what he did during the first few meetings would be crucial. He felt that his job would be mainly to stimulate the boys and extend the limited thinking of the group to new possibilities for consideration and action. Decisions, however, would have to be left to the group. For a while, he knew, it would be difficult for the boys to make adequate decisions for themselves as they, like most students, had had very little experience of that nature. But they must learn by doing.

Mr. X also knew the cost of arbitrary action on his part would be the death of the group. The values by which the group acted would have to be those of the boys. To assume anything else would be unrealistic. If he wished these values to change, he would have to help the group get appropriate experience as a basis for that change, and let the changes grow out of that experience. It would have to become clearly understood by the boys that he did *not* have all the answers and that his ideas were only to be considered along with those of the other members. Finally, his constant aim was to train the group to become independent of his leadership but interdependent on one another. These are some of the approaches that help this kind of group to develop.

"What are some techniques which can be used effectively in such groups?"

The use of role-playing has been found to be very effective in groups which were concerned with both adjustment and human-relations problems. This technique is a modification of psychodrama in which group members assume the roles of whatever characters are involved in the problem and then enact the situation. Using this technique to present a past event, rather than attempting to describe it verbally, gives a common basis for discussion not possible by the verbal method. One is able to observe, in watching the portrayal, the emotional content of the behavior and much of the actual behavior which is often omitted by a person who attempts to describe a situation in which he has been a participant.

Role-playing also finds, in addition, a valuable place in the actual practice of new techniques in human-relations problems. A situation can be replayed several times with one member trying out different kinds of behavior to evaluate their relative effectiveness. Once selected, this new behavior can actually be repeated until the individual gains confidence in his ability to handle it in a new situation.

A second method, one that is implied in the previous paragraph, is that of experimentation. This is the building of a scientific approach in the group toward problems of human relationships. As a method it is represented by a willingness to analyze a problem and try various solutions to it, experimenting to see how the solutions actually work. Confidence in their own problem-solving ability is gained by group members who have carried through successfully the experimental approach.

Good discussion method is the third technique for use in these groups. Discussion is the usual procedure in a group situation, but often it becomes a frustrating experience. The problem for the leader, then, is learning how to lead the group so that all members can participate in an efficient group-thinking process. This requires real practice and training which most of us have not had. Research is beginning to point the way more clearly in this area and to demonstrate that efficient discussion method is a powerful tool for both individual and group change.

For final consideration is the use of the combined procedures of observation, feedback, and evaluation. These three go hand in hand, and have proved to be very fruitful both in obtaining modification in the behavior of individuals and in improving the ability of the group to think effectively together.

The job of observer is usually performed by a member of the group who takes as his task watching the group during a discussion period. During this time he notes the kinds of difficulty which impede the group's progress, the conflict in which members participate, and the points of efficient action. At an appropriate time during the meeting, usually near the end, he presents some of his observations to the group, acting as a mirror by which the group can see itself functioning. This latter is the process of feedback. Evaluation enters almost immediately when the group begins to discuss why they behaved as they did and to suggest what changes they may wish to make in the future.

It is the usual practice in most groups, of course, for a member to express his dissatisfactions about a discussion meeting to someone privately or to keep them to himself. Keeping this important information away from the group prevents any successful modification of its own actions. The procedures just described supply a method by which that very important information can be presented for the group discussion and analysis which serve as a basis for change.

These four techniques, Mr. X found, gave him some of the tools which he needed to make his experiment in group counseling successful.

Now, let us turn to the final question Mr. X poses, "Where can this kind of group be built within the school curriculum?" The kind of group Mr. X developed, a special club activity concerned with problems of adjustment, is one resource which might be incorporated into the school program quite readily. This method would mean that the counselor could handle six or eight students at a time rather than have separate interviews with them. Thus, not only would the time-per-student efficiency of the counselor be increased, but the values which the group situation has to offer for many kinds of adjustment problems could be added. For some of these problems the group situation may be far more therapeutic than the environment of the individual interview. In such a club the purpose would simply be to learn "how to get along with other people better," a purpose embracing many problems of adjustment.

Two other opportunities for group counseling already exist in the school program. The classroom itself can be a basic group for change in student behavior, that is, for counseling. We well understand that each experience the child has during his day has some effect on his adjustment. If his adjustment pattern is ineffective, his experiences in the classroom will either reinforce his poor adjustment, or they will encourage new adjustment. It seems quite evident that the classroom is usually *not* neutral in its effects upon the pupil's adjustment. Thus, the better the classroom becomes as a group in which change toward better behavior is possible, the better it becomes a "counseling situation."

Here one should not be limited to the concept of every teacher being a counselor to the individual pupil. The stress, instead, needs to be placed on the responsibility of the teacher as a *group leader,* which, in fact, he is. The class-teacher relation is a group-leader situation. But rarely have we been concerned with making the teacher at the same time a good group leader! And so our classroom groups are often poor, immature groups, with all the symptoms of aggression, frustration, and lack of purpose and motivation which are characteristic of poor groups. More adjustment problems are probably aggravated by the classroom than are alleviated.

A somewhat similar condition is present in most extracurricular activity groups. Rarely have the students been given the experience and training to be good group members. They may often have more chance to take the initiative in such groups than they have in the classroom, but they are not given opportunities to learn the skills of working with other people successfully and efficiently. Of course, most of us find ourselves in a similar fix, and so we struggle along with less than satisfactory patterns of adjustment to other people.

One wonders whether we ask ourselves often enough about adjustive experiences in school. There seems to be a gap in present thinking about schools—we have teachers who are concerned with the imparting of knowledge and skills to classes and with seeing that the classroom is a good "learning situation." We have, also, counselors who are interested and concerned with the individual adjustment problems of students and who are very careful to see that their own contacts with a student are good counseling situations. But who looks at the classroom itself to see if it is a good situation for adjustment? Isn't that a gap that needs to be filled if our schools are actually to offer a realistic learning experience for the "whole child"?

Here is a possibility: Why couldn't the counselor, who is the specialist in problems of individual adjustment, become the resource person for the teachers in matters of making their classrooms good places for adjustment? This would mean that the counselor would not only need to be skilled in techniques of individual contacts with students, but he would also need to become skilled in the techniques of group leadership and group behavior. Here is a chance to develop a program of "preventive counseling."

This suggestion would mean that the classroom group atmosphere and the club atmosphere and the student council atmosphere would all be the concern of the counselor, and he would be called upon to advise the teachers and student leaders in ways and means of improving them. Solving the problems in the classroom *before* they arise seems much more efficient than having to attempt a cure after the problem has become acute. Preventive counseling seems as sensible as preventive medicine.

SUGGESTED REFERENCES

Elliott, Harrison Sacket. *The Process of Group Thinking*. New York: Association Press, 1928.

Hendry, C., Lippitt, R. and Zander, A. "Reality Practice as Educational Method," *Psychodrama Monographs,* No. 9. New York: Beacon House, 1944.

Jaques, Elliott, Ed. "Social Therapy." *Journal of Social Issues,* Spring 1947.

29. MUST COUNSELING BE INDIVIDUAL?

Clifford P. Froehlich[1]

Traditionally, definitions of counseling have stated or implied that the individual interview was THE *modus operandi* of counseling. This position has been challenged by the writer and others

Reprinted by permission of Mrs. Clifford P. Froehlich and *Educational and Psychological Measurement*, XVIII, No. 4 (Winter, 1958), 681-89.

[1] The writer is indebted to Mr. Shepard Insel, Director, Student Personnel Services and Research, Sequoia Senior High School District, California, for his assistance in gathering data for this study.

who, from their own experience, have felt that the group approach was a potentially effective avenue to counseling objectives. The writer coined the term "multiple counseling" to designate a procedure in which a counselor works simultaneously with several counselees manifesting symptoms of at least one problem in common. The details of the multiple counseling approach have been reported elsewhere (4, 5). To date, the relative effectiveness of multiple and individual counseling has been largely a matter of conjecture. Bilovsky (1), reported a comparison of individual and group counseling, but the data were not reported in a manner which yielded clearcut evidence of counseling effectiveness. Driver (3), and Peres (7), also presented research on the effectiveness of multiple counseling, but they did not compare it with individual counseling. It is the purpose of this study to do so.

The most difficult task confronting the person who wishes to evaluate counseling is the selection of a criterion, because there is none about which it is feasible to collect data and which has been widely accepted by counselors. The major criterion in this study, therefore, was not selected because of its general acceptance; rather, it was chosen because, from the writer's orientation, it reflects a logical outcome of counseling, and because it is being used in a series of studies of which this is one.

The criterion was agreement between self-rating and test scores. Both pre-counseling and post-counseling ratings are compared with test scores. Application of the criterion assumes that a person should learn about himself during counseling. If he does, presumably his self ratings should be in closer agreement with his tested abilities after counseling than before.

The students used as subjects in this study were seniors in a large California high school. The problem they had in common was an indicated desire for more information about themselves in order to make post-high-school plans. The students participated in the testing and counseling program voluntarily; part of the testing was done outside of school hours. The decision regarding which students were provided with individual counseling and which had multiple counseling was made arbitrarily and was influenced primarily by practical consideration of scheduling. Seventeen students were counseled individually, and 25 were counseled in small groups of four to six students.

In this study, self-ratings were obtained by asking students to rate themselves before counseling and again after counseling. Each subject rated himself on a five point scale in each of the areas measured by the *Differential Aptitude Tests;* these areas are listed in Table 2. In order to facilitate statistical treatment of the data, each step on the rating scale was assigned a numerical value from one through five; the highest rating was assigned five; the next highest, four; and so on. Because the extreme steps contained so few cases, they were combined with adjacent steps when the data were processed. That is, ratings of one were combined with ratings of two, and ratings of five were combined with ratings of four. Hence, for each subject there were eight pre-counseling ratings and eight post-counseling ratings distributed on a three-step scale: the first step which was given a value of two included ratings of one and two, the next step with a value of three contained only ratings of three, and the last step with a value of four included ratings of four and five.

In addition to rating himself before and after counseling, each student completed the *Differential Aptitude Test* battery. The scores on this test were converted to centile ranks and were then assigned numerical values of two, three, or four in a manner similar to the assignment of numerical values to the rating scale steps. Centile ranks of 76 or above were assigned a value of four, ranks from 25 through 75 were given the value of three, and ranks below 25 were classified as two. As a result, each student had a rated-test-score value of two, three, or four for each of the eight areas of the *Differential Aptitude Test.* Throughout the remainder of this report, the phrase "test score" is used to refer to rated-test-score value obtained in the manner just described.

THE FINDINGS

The data in Table 1 summarize the agreement between ratings and test scores for all eight areas taken together. The first category indicates the total number of ratings that were the same as the corresponding test score both before and after counseling. In other words, the rating was correct before counseling. Hence, no change in rating was required to bring it into agreement with the corresponding test score. The post-counseling rating was the same as the pre-counseling rating; therefore, it also agreed with the test score. Of the 336 ratings available, 126, or 38 per cent required no change. The counseling objective in this case was merely one of confirming the counselee's original rating.

The second category of Table 1 contains those pre-counseling ratings which were not in agreement with test scores before counseling but the corresponding post-counseling ratings were in agreement. Such a change in ratings reflects a desired outcome of counseling if it is assumed that correctness of ratings is related in a meaningful way to self-concept and this in turn to choices which might be made by the counselee. Sixty-five, or 19 per cent of all ratings were of this type.

In the third classification are those post-counseling ratings which were the same as corresponding pre-counseling ratings neither of which agreed with its test-score counterpart. These were 80 such ratings, 24 per cent of the total. Essentially, counseling in this instance was ineffective.

The final category contains cases in which the first rating was not the same as the second rating and neither the first nor second rating agreed with the rated test score. Persons whose ratings fell into this category may be considered counseling failures according to the criterion applied in this study. There were 65 ratings of this type, 19 per cent of the total.

The distributions of agreement of ratings and test scores by categories for individual and multiple counseling reported in Table 1 were tested by chi-square to see if the hypothesis that they came from the same population was tenable. It must be remembered that for chi-square to be an appropriate test in this instance the independence of the entries in the cells of Table 1 had to be assumed. (6, 8) On this assumption chi-square was found to be 3.032, which is not statistically significant. Hence, it was concluded that no difference in the effectiveness of counseling methods as judged by the agreement criterion used in this study was revealed by the data in Table 1. This finding is negative in the sense that the superiority of either individual or multiple counseling is not demonstrated. Because it was believed that the assumption or method of treating the data may have not revealed differences further analyses were made.

The criterion was applied to the data in another manner. This was done by comparing the number of ratings which agreed with

TABLE 1

AGREEMENT OF RATINGS AND TEST SCORES BEFORE AND AFTER COUNSELING
BY TWO METHODS OF COUNSELING

Categories of Agreement	Individual counseling	Multiple counseling	Total by category
Pre- and post-counseling ratings both agree with test score (no change, none required)	48	78	126
Pre-counseling rating not in agreement with test, but post-counseling rating agreed (correct change)	27	38	65
Pre- and post-counseling ratings agree with each other, but not with test score (no change, one required)	29	51	80
Pre- and post-counseling do not agree with each other; the post-counseling rating does not agree with test score (incorrect change)	32	33	65
Total ratings (8 times number of subjects)	136	200	xxx

test scores before counseling with the number which agreed after counseling. The results of this comparison are reported in percentage form in Table 2. The first row of this table indicates that 59 per cent of the pre-counseling ratings of verbal reasoning agreed with test scores and 71 per cent of the post-counseling ratings agreed. Comparable figures for multiple counseling are 64 and 68, respectively. Succeeding rows in this table, with few exceptions, reveal substantially the same picture, a slightly higher percentage of agreement for post-counseling ratings than for pre-counseling ratings. Albeit, when a test of significance was applied, none of the differences between the pre- and post-counseling percentage of agreement was statistically significant.

The number of agreements upon which the percentages in Table 2 are based, were summed for all areas of the test. The resulting totals and corresponding percentages are presented in Table 3.

The significance of the difference between the percentage of ratings in agreement with tests before individual counseling and the percentage after counseling was found to be at .10 level. In contrast, the comparable difference for the multiple counseled group was significant at the .008 level. After multiple counseling the subjects in this study apparently brought their ratings into closer agreement

TABLE 2

PERCENTAGE OF RATINGS IN AGREEMENT WITH TEST SCORE

D.A.T. Area	INDIVIDUAL COUNSELING		MULTIPLE COUNSELING	
	Pre-counseling rating	Post-counseling rating	Pre-counseling rating	Post-counseling rating
Verbal reasoning	59	71	64	68
Numerical reasoning	53	53	48	76
Abstract reasoning	59	76	60	56
Space relations	47	59	36	52
Mechanical reasoning	59	35	48	72
Clerical speed and accuracy	47	47	44	48
Spelling	41	47	60	76
Sentences	35	65	52	60

with their scores than before counseling. Individual counseling appears not to have influenced self rating in a significant way.

Another approach to evaluation of the data was made through the use of an index number which reflected relative agreement between an individual's test score and his rating. Preliminary to computing this index, a numerical value was assigned to each rating and test score in the manner previously described. The pre-counseling-agreement index was computed by subtracting the test-score value from the pre-counseling-rating value and adding a constant of five to eliminate negative numbers and summing these figures for the

TABLE 3

AGREEMENT BETWEEN TEST SCORES AND ALL RATINGS FOR INDIVIDUAL AND MULTIPLE COUNSELED GROUP

	INDIVIDUAL		MULTIPLE	
	Number	Per cent[a]	Number	Per cent[b]
Pre-counseling rating	68	50	103	52
Post-counseling rating	77	57	127	64

[a] Based on N = 136 ratings, 8 for each of 17 individuals before and after counseling.

[b] Based on N = 200 ratings, 8 for each of 25 individuals before and after counseling.

eight areas for each individual. The process is illustrated by the following data concerning one student:

	D.A.T. Areas							
	1	2	3	4	5	6	7	8
Pre-counseling-rating value	3	4	2	3	4	3	4	2
Test-score value	2	3	3	3	4	3	2	2
Rating value less score value plus constant of five	6	6	4	5	5	5	7	5

In the first column the result of the subtraction of the test-score value from the pre-counseling-rating value and the addition of a constant of five was six, shown in the last row. When all of the eight figures in the last row were added, the total was found to be 43, his pre-counseling-agreement index. The post-counseling-agreement index was computed in a similar manner except that post-counseling ratings were used. The mean and standard deviation for pre-counseling and for post-counseling indices for the individual counseled group and for the multiple counseled group were computed, the resulting statistics are reported in Table 4. When the significance of

TABLE 4

MEANS, STANDARD DEVIATIONS, AND *t*-RATIOS BETWEEN
MEANS OF TOTAL AGREEMENT INDICES

	INDIVIDUAL COUNSELED		MULTIPLE COUNSELED		t between means in same row
	Mean	Standard Deviation	Mean	Standard Deviation	
Pre-counseling index	39.8	3.18	41.2	2.72	1.44
Post-counseling index	40.7	3.84	41.0	2.79	.27
t between means in same column	1.10		.29		

the differences between the means in Table 4 was evaluated by the t-ratio, none was found to be significant. The conclusions based on this method of analysis must be stated in negative terms: neither individual nor multiple counseling appeared to affect the means of the agreement indices. Likewise, the means of the individual and multiple groups are essentially the same.

The agreement index has a definite shortcoming in that the effect of ratings which were too high in terms of corresponding test score could be cancelled out by low ratings. The net result is an obliteration of the individual's variability of agreement between his ratings and score. Cronbach and Gleser (2) have discussed a mehod of profile analysis which overcomes this limitation. The method defines similarity between profiles in terms of the linear distance between the respective points on the profiles being compared. The eight pre-counseling ratings were treated as one profile, the post-counseling ratings as another, and the test scores as the third. A pre-counseling-profile-agreement score was computed by the formula (rating value–score value).[2] The method of computation is illustrated by the data for the student who was used to illustrate the computation of the agreement index.

| | D.A.T. Areas | | | | | | | |
	1	2	3	4	5	6	7	8
Pre-counseling rating value	3	4	2	3	4	3	4	2
Test-score value	2	3	3	3	4	3	2	2
Rating value minus score value	1	1	−1	0	0	0	2	0
(Rating value minus score value)^2	1	1	1	0	0	0	4	0

In the first column, the test-score value has been subtracted from the pre-counseling-rating value, the difference was one, the square of this was one, as shown in the third and fourth rows, respectively. The figures in the last row were added, their total, seven, is the pre-counseling-profile-agreement score. In a like manner, the post-counseling-profile-agreement scores were computed. The mean and standard deviation of the pre- and post-counseling-profile-agreement scores for the individual counseled group and for the multiple counseled group were obtained and are shown in Table 5. The difference between the mean of the pre-counseling-profile-agreement scores and the mean of the post-counseling-profile-agreement scores for the multiple counseled group is significant at the .05 level, no other difference between the means in Table 5 is significant. This analysis of the data appears to favor the conclusion that multiple counseling is more effective in terms of the criterion than is individual counseling. These data also point out that the individual and multiple counseled were very similar both before and after counseling.

TABLE 5

MEANS, STANDARD DEVIATIONS, AND *t*-RATIOS BETWEEN
MEANS OF PROFILE-AGREEMENT SCORES

	INDIVIDUAL COUNSELED (N = 17)		MULTIPLE COUNSELED (N = 25)		*t*-ratio between means in same row
	Mean	S.D.	Mean	S.D.	
Pre-counseling-profile score	2.176	.859	2.284	.514	.452
Post-counseling-profile score	2.146	.992	1.992	.338	.592
t-ratio between means in same column	.136		2.584		

In addition to the criterion described, a supplementary criterion based on counselee rating of counselor helpfulness was also used. Counselees rated on a five-point scale the amount of help they thought they had received from the counselor. This criterion was used to determine if the counselees would be more favorably impressed by an individual interview than by the group situation. Some counselors believe that because a counselee gets individual attention in a private interview a situation is created in which he feels comfortable and is helped thereby to move toward counseling objectives. On the other hand, these counselors view the group situation as threatening and productive of negative attitudes toward the process. After the ratings were converted to numerical values in the manner previously described, the mean of the individual counseled group was found to be 4.06 and the standard deviation equaled .56. The multiple counseled group was found to have a mean of 3.94, the standard deviation was .68. A t-test of the difference between means revealed that it was not statistically significant. The subjects in both groups were apparently not different in their evaluation of their counselor's helpfulness.

DISCUSSION

Of course, like other studies of counseling effectiveness the criteria used in this study may be questioned because they do not indicate what actions the counselee took as a result of counseling. But if self-knowledge is a necessary prelude to intelligent planning and doing, then the self-rating criterion has the endorsement of a logical approach.

The writer recognizes the limitations imposed upon the conclusions by the smallness of the sample, the use of a single test, and similar shortcomings. Nevertheless, the data presented in this report point to one major conclusion: Insofar as the criteria used in this study reflect desirable counseling outcomes, the findings do not support the claim that counseling must be individual.

REFERENCES

1. Bilovsky, David and others. "Individual and Group Counseling." *Personnel and Guidance Journal,* XXXI (1953), 363-365.
2. Cronbach, Lee J. and Gleser, Goldine C. "Assessing Similarity between Profiles." *Psychological Bulletin,* L (1953), 456-473.
3. Driver, H. I. "Small Group Discussion." *Personnel and Guidance Journal,* XXXI (1952), 173-175.
4. Froehlich, C. P. *Multiple Counseling—A Research Proposal.* Berkeley: School of Education, University of California, no date, 7 p. mimeo.
5. Hoppock, Robert. *Group Guidance: Principles, Techniques, and Evaluation.* New York: McGraw-Hill, 1950.
6. Lewis, Don and Burke, C. J. "The Use and Misuse of the Chi-square Test. *Psychological Bulletin,* XLVI (1949), 433-489.
7. Peres, H. "An Investigation of Nondirective Group Therapy. *Journal of Consulting Psychology,* XI (1947), 159-172.
8. Peters, Charles C. "The Misuse of Chi-square—A Reply to Lewis and Burke." *Psychological Bulletin,* XLVII (1950), 331-337.

30. THE EFFECTS OF GROUP COUNSELING ON GIFTED UNDERACHIEVING ADOLESCENTS

John Broedel, Merle Ohlsen, Fred Proff, and Charles Southard[1]

Counseling psychologists operating in schools have become increasingly interested in group counseling. Accompanying this interest, however, is an appalling lack of experimental evidence to support training practices, utilization of staff, and the application of therapeutic techniques in groups (Ohlsen, Proff & Roeber, 1956). These conditions, combined with an interest in gifted youth, led several of us at the University of Illinois to undertake a long-range project to investigate the application of group counseling[2] in treating gifted youth. The present paper is a partial report of a study growing out of the first phase of this project. It is concerned with the extent to which group counseling improves the mental health and academic performance of gifted underachieving adolescents.

Group counseling is particularly appropriate for adolescents. So often they are made to feel that they are culprits, and that whatever the difficulty is they are the ones who should be expected to change their behavior (Berman, 1954). Most also believe that few adults will listen to them and try to understand them; many question whether adults can understand them. On the other hand, they believe that their peers can and want to understand them. Because they often use peers as models and they want to win peers' ac-

---

Reprinted by permission of the authors and *Journal of Counseling Psychology,* VII, No. 3 (Fall, 1960), 163-70.

---

[1] This study was conducted in Evanston Township High School. Funds for the initial phase of this project were provided by Evanston Township High School, College of Education at the University of Illinois, and the University of Illinois Research Board. Funds for the second phase of this project were provided by U. S. Office of Education under the provisions of Public Law 531, 83rd congress. The writers are indebted to the following school counselors who served on the two four-man observer teams: Edward Adamek, Jean Cantelope, Floyd Cummings, Edward Curry, Barbara Garrison, Colleen Karavites, Joseph Kanitzi, and Marilyn Meyers and to the assistant superintendent, Lloyd McLeary, and the television engineer, Frank Bullard.

[2] The authors use the terms counseling and psychotherapy to describe the same process. However, they prefer the term group counseling to indicate that clients within the normal range of adjustment were treated in a non-medical setting.

ceptance, adolescents appreciate the opportunity to exchange ideas with peers in a permissive and accepting group. Inasmuch as they are struggling for independence from adults, they also prefer peers' assistance in solving their problems. Moreover, they are genuinely reassured when they discover that their peers have problems similar to their own. Ackerman (1955) reported that while members of a counseling group, adolescents not only came to feel better understood by others, but that they also learned to empathize with others and to increase their tolerance for others' idiosyncrasies.

THE PROBLEM

The previous paragraph makes the case for treating adolescents in groups. To the extent that underachieving gifted adolescents are like other adolescents it applies to them too. Gifted underachieving adolescents have a number of unique characteristics that makes group treatment especially appropriate for them. Shaw and Grubb (1958), Gowan (1955), and Kirk (1952) found underachievers to be hostile. Gowan also described them as indifferent to their responsibilities, unsociable, self-sufficient, and hard to reach and Shaw and Grubb reported that others' demands on them for better quality of work tended to produce negative results.

Generally, these descriptions agreed with our observers' descriptions of our clients. Our observers also concluded that most of our clients questioned whether they were gifted. Apparently they felt that academic promise had been used against them so often that many of them had to deny it. In other words, these youths are not the type that one would expect to seek counseling. Furthermore, when caused to look at their problems, one would expect them to deny that they had problems and to withdraw from counseling. Supporting evidence for the previous point is reported by Katz, Ohlsen and Proff (1959). From Caplan's (1957), Gersten's (1951) and Paster's (1944) work with hostile people and Ackerman's (1955) and Berman's (1954) experiences with adolescents, *we concluded that group counseling would increase our clients' acceptance of themselves and improve their ability to relate to others.* We also assumed that these changes were necessary conditions for motivating them to accept and to use their untapped resources.

METHOD

This study was conducted in a four-year high school which provided better than average counseling services. In short, this was not a setting in which one would expect any added personal attention, regardless of type, to account for client improvement.

The counseling was provided in an ordinary classroom which was furnished with movable arm chairs. These were arranged in a circle. Three microphones were placed in the center of the circle. Two remote-controlled television cameras were mounted on opposite walls. Usually one or the other kept the entire group in view. The other was focused on behavior which was judged to be clinically significant. All the counseling sessions for all four groups were, with subjects' awareness, electrically recorded and observed by four-man observer teams by closed-circuit television. The two groups which were treated last also were kinescoped. For these latter groups, the observer teams received the same stimuli which were recorded on kinescopes. An experienced clinician decided what video material should be sent to the observer teams and be recorded on kinescopes.

The sample was composed of ninth grade students who as eighth graders ranked in the top ten per cent of their class on the California Test of Mental Maturity and at the ninth decile or below, in terms of their grade-point average earned in the eighth grade. Of the 34 pupils identified by this method, 29 actually participated in group counseling. The parents of one child refused to grant permission for their child to participate. For another, his mother asked that he be dropped from the project because his work improved significantly during the first six weeks grading period. Scheduling problems prevented the other three from participating in counseling.

Originally the entire population of 34 was divided into four groups—assigning proportionate numbers of boys and girls to each group by random numbers. The 29 who actually participated in the project were divided into two experimental and two control groups as follows: E_1—2 girls and 4 boys; E_2—3 girls and 5 boys; C_1—2 girls and 6 boys; and C_2—2 girls and 5 boys.

After the sample had been selected, every prospective client was interviewed for three purposes: (a) to acquaint him with what he might expect from group counseling and to inform him what would be expected from him; (b) to answer his questions about the experience, and (c) to appraise the seriousness of each client's problems. This was followed by a meeting of the parents where the project was described in detail, their questions were answered, and written permissions for pupil participation were obtained. Though the investigators stressed the point that they wanted only those pupils who themselves recognized the value of group counseling and elected to participate, they learned from the pupils' comments during counseling that every counseling group except C_1 contained some pupils who participated as a consequence of parental pressure.

While E_1 and E_2 were counseled C_1 and C_2 served as the control groups. Following the post-testing, group counseling was provided for C_1 and C_2 by the same counselor. These latter clients were used as their own control for the purpose of evaluating growth during two periods: the second period in which they received counseling and the first when they served as control groups for themselves as well as E_1 and E_2.

During the first treatment period, clients were excused from their study halls for counseling. Each group met for one class period twice each week for eight weeks.

An effort also was made to control the educational and guidance experiences during the experimental period. In most instances the members of one experimental group and one control group were assigned to the same sections for English, social studies, study hall, and homeroom. The same was done for the other experimental group and control group. During the course of the experiment, none of these pupils were referred either for assistance with study skills or for counseling.

Originally the plan called for the members of the control group also to be excused from study hall and to be assigned some special activity while the members of the experimental groups were in group counseling. None of the activities suggested for the control groups met the criteria defined by the school administration: an educational experience that is sufficiently worthwhile to justify excusing the pupils from a study period.

Growth of clients was evaluated and compared with members of the control groups in terms of three variables: (a) academic performance as measured by the California Achievement Test Battery and grade point averages earned in high school; (b) acceptance of self and of others as revealed in responses to the Picture Story Test; and (c) behaviors in interpersonal relationships reported on the Behavior Inventory by the pupils themselves and such significant others as the members of each observer team, the clients' parents, and the counselor.

RESULTS

Originally these were two separate studies: the first dealt with the results obtained from E_1 and E_2 and the second with results obtained from C_1 and C_2. Except for those instances in which the t-test was used, the same statistical tests were used in both studies. In the latter the t-test for correlated means was used in certain instances to determine whether chance could account for differences between pre- and post scores during treatment period and control period. In each instance the E_1 and E_2 data will be presented first.

Acceptance of Self and Others

Attitudes of acceptance of self and of others were evaluated by content analysis of clients' written responses to the Picture Story Test. Five pictures were selected for the test: Card 1 of the Michigan Picture Story Test; Card 2 of Murray's TAT; and Cards 1, 4, and 5 of Alexander and Cronbach's adaptation of the TAT.

The scoring procedure devised by Ohlsen and Schultz (1955) was used to classify the clients' responses. For our purposes here 20 questions were used in the content analysis. In each instance the story was read with a particular question in mind and when the client discussed the content of the question either a positive or negative sign was assigned to that content. Each client's score was the algebraic sum of these signed numbers (not more than 1 for each question) for the 20 questions on all five pictures. Actually, by the very nature of the questions two subscores (one for acceptance of self and one for acceptance of others) and a total score was obtained.

For E_1 and E_2 the mean gain in acceptance of self and of others was significantly greater than the mean gain demonstrated by their control groups over the pre- to post-testing period. In stories elicited in response to the Picture Story Test, the clients, after group counseling, demonstrated an increased ability to project affectivity into their stories. Not only was more affect introduced into the stories, but Identification Figures as well as others were described in more positive terms than previously. In stories produced after counseling, clients also tended increasingly to depict Identification Figures as demonstrating more warmth and affection for others, as well as being more willing recipients of affection.

With only one exception, an inspection of the scores for C_1 and C_2 also showed increased acceptance of self and of others. However, these differences were not significant. On the other hand, it should be noted that while these same students were serving as their own controls, and waiting for counseling, most of their scores shifted in the opposite direction. Moreover, clinical evaluations of the members of C_1 clearly suggested for three clients increased acceptance of others, for three clients increased acceptance of self, and for two clients substantial improvement in their total scores. In C_2, which was judged by observers to be unproductive (Katz, Ohlsen & Proff, 1959), substantial improvements were noted for one client on self score, for three clients on acceptance of others' scores, and for three clients on their total scores.

Unfortunately, a problem arose in the administration of the follow-up testing which could have invalidated the responses. Therefore, they were not scored. Nevertheless, even a cursory analysis of these data suggested that the gains achieved were maintained.

Academic Performance

Grades were given every six weeks. The school used five numerical grades in addition to the F which was given as the failing grade. Since 1 was the top grade, an F was assigned a value of 6. Gain in academic performance, therefore, was demonstrated by a decrease in grade-point average.

Group counseling was begun for E_1 and E_2 immediately following the first grading period. The second grading period occurred during the experimental period and the third occurred four weeks after the termination of counseling (counseling was terminated for E_1 and E_2 just prior to Christmas vacation).

While some improvement was demonstrated between the first and third grading periods by control subjects, experimental subjects' grades grew gradually worse. The differences between the mean grade-point average earned by experimental subjects at the first grading period and that earned at the third was equal to .54. The comparable difference for control subjects was equal to .26. The discrepancy between these two differences was demonstrated by an analysis of variance test to be significant at the .05 level. Changes in the second semester grades for E_1 and E_2 also were compared with the grades they earned prior to counseling. None of these differences was significant. Though there was a slight improvement in grades between the third and fourth grading periods, this improvement was not maintained. Despite their giftedness, and their increased acceptance of self and of others, they failed to improve their grades significantly even in the eighteen-month follow-up.

For C_1 and C_2 counseling began just one week before the third grading period. No significant improvement in grade point average was obtained. However, it is interesting to note that when one compares grades earned in ninth grade with those earned in the tenth grade, these clients improved their grades every grading period except one.

With reference to improvement in scores on the California Achievement Test Battery, we found that whereas the scores for E_1 and E_2 decreased slightly during the treatment period, their control groups remained almost constant. However, analysis of variance tests indicated that these differences could be accounted for by chance. On the other hand, when we compared pre-, post-, and four-month follow-up performance for E_1 and E_2, we found that the difference between the mean raw scores earned at each of the three testing periods was significant at the .01 level. Thus, the impaired performance on this standardized test was only a temporary effect. A further statistical analysis indicated that there was no point in giving this achievement test again in the eighteen-month follow-up—the form of the test used lacked adequate ceiling for these clients to make further significant improvements in their scores.

Interpersonal Relationships

The Behavior Inventory was designed for this study to ascertain the ways in which subjects perceived their own behavior and the ways in which the subject's behavior was perceived by others. The instrument was a forced-choice rating schedule consisting of 66 pairs of statements describing 12 classifications of behavior.

A Rank Profile of Behavior was obtained for each record by ordering the behaviors in terms of the frequency with which each of the twelve behaviors was selected by the rater as more typical of a subject than another. Although the Rank Profiles provided summary descriptions of subjects' behavior, a criterion was needed with which the profiles could be evaluated quantitatively. A Model of Adjustment was constructed to serve this purpose.

The combined judgments of 13 counseling psychologists were utilized in formulating the Model of Adjustment. These psychologists were provided with comprehensive definitions of the 12 classes of behavior included on the Behavior Inventory. They were then instructed to think of some individual they knew or had known who came closest to approaching their concept of the ideally adjusted person and to describe that person by ranking the twelve behaviors in terms of the extent to which each was characteristic of him. The 13 sets of ranks obtained from the psychologists yielded a coefficient of concordance of .82 which was demonstrated by an F test to be significant at the .01 point. In the computation of the W coefficient, the mean rank of each behavior was determined; it provided the basis for establishing the order of the behaviors in the Model of Adjustment.

Three of the behaviors had a mean rank of six when rounded to to the nearest whole number, so the 12 behaviors were reduced to ten ranks in the model. The order given the classes of behavior in the Model of Adjustment was as follows:

1. Behavior indicates acceptance of self
2. Behavior indicates acceptance of others
3. Gives information
4. Gives action-oriented suggestions
5. Agrees with others
6. Gives opinions
7. Asks for information
8. Asks for opinions
9. Disagrees with others
10. Asks for action-oriented suggestions
11. Behavior indicative of rejection of others
12. Behavior indicative of rejection of self

The clients' parents, members of the observing teams, and the counselor provided their judgments of clients' behavior on the Behavior Inventory both before and after the counseling period. The behavior of clients was quantitatively expressed by computing rank correlation coefficients r' between the Model of Adjustment and each Rank Profile obtained from judges' responses to the Behavior Inventory. To ascertain whether judges perceived positive changes in client behavior after group counseling, each r' coefficient resulting from a single judge's precounseling description of a subject with the Model of Adjustment was compared with the r' obtained from the same judge's description of that client after counseling. The significance of the differences between such pairs of r' coefficients was determined by making Fisher z' transformations.

A total of eighty-five pair of r' coefficients was obtained for E_1 and E_2. In only 8 of the 85 were the r' coefficients based on a description of precounseling behavior more highly correlated with the Model of Adjustment than the r' coefficients based on postcounseling data. In none of the 8 cases were the differences significant at the .05 level. The remaining 77 pair of r' coefficients indicated cases where judges reported clients as acting in a manner more congruent with the Model of Adjustment after counseling than before. In 41 of these 77 cases the improvement was demonstrated to be statistically significant: 18 at the .01 level; 23 others at the .05 level. It was concluded, therefore, that behavioral changes were manifested by clients participating in group counseling and these changes were in a healthy direction.

The clients' perceptions of their own behavior before and after counseling were obtained by use of a self-report form of the Behavior Inventory. The method for determining differences between pre- and post-testing was the same as that used in evaluating changes in behavioral descriptions provided by parents, observer teams, and the counselor. No significant changes in the clients' reported perceptions of their own behavior were revealed.

Unlike the precounseling ratings of others, clients from E_1 and E_2 described themselves before counseling in a way that indicated moderate to high correlation with the Model of Adjustment. While not significant at the .05 level, 8 of the 14 clients described themselves in a more negative manner after participating in group counseling. These less idealized self-reports obtained after counseling more closely concurred with the descriptions made by others than did the precounseling self-reports. If, as seems likely, others were more objective and less biased in their ratings than clients themselves, it is suggested that the self-reports obtained after counseling were more reality-oriented than the initial self-reports. Further investigation would be required to determine whether group counseling does result, in fact, in participants formulating more accurate perceptions of their own behavior and/or are more able, because of reduced anxiety, to admit to others those aspects of themselves of which they are acutely aware but reluctant to admit to others.

Analysis of the data collected during the eighteen-month follow-up indicated that little change occurred during the period between the first follow-up four months after termination of counseling and the last. The descriptions of subjects' behavior by parents remained significantly more positive than precounseling ratings, but the clients' own descriptions of themselves still showed no significant changes.

Those who observed C_1 and C_2 by closed-circuit television agreed that the members of C_1 improved, but that C_2 did not improve significantly. These conclusions also were supported by the rank order correlation with the Model of Adjustment. Inasmuch as kinescopes also were made of these two groups, it was possible to have four postdoctoral research associates use a revised form of the Behavior Inventory to re-appraise the growth achieved by these two groups of clients. The differences in their descriptions of these clients revealed that the members of C_1 made significant growth. Every one of these observers of the kinescopes reported changes, based upon independent judgments, which were significant at the .07 level or better. For C_2 three of the four judges reported no significant changes in clients' behavior between the beginning and termination of counseling. The fourth judge reported changes in the clients' behavior which could be accounted for by chance only seven times in a hundred.

The data obtained from self-reports failed to indicate significant improvement in interpersonal behavior for either C_1 or C_2. However, certain individuals from both noted significant changes in their own behavior. For example, one client from C_2 noted significant improvement within his behavior between pre- and post-testing and two other clients noted significant improvement between pre- and follow-up testing.

DISCUSSION

Shaw and Grubb (1958) were right when they said that under-achievement is not a surface phenomenon which is easily modified. Though three of the four groups (E_1, E_2, and C_1) were judged to have made significant growth, we concluded that it is expecting too much to complete treatment for this type of client within the eight-week period.

Results obtained with C_2 were disappointing. However, this was not a surprise. From the beginning the group showed little promise for growth. This nontherapeutic climate was created largely by two hostile boys who consistently attacked those who tried to make the group therapeutic. Their influence on this group, and on each other, and the ways in which the counselor attempted to cope with them is discussed in a paper by Katz, Ohlsen, and Proff (1959).

Two interesting sidelights are worth noting: (a) certain clients may impede or inhibit the therapeutic process for others and still profit from counseling themselves; and (1954) group counseling, in contrast to individual counseling, affords an opportunity for non-verbalizers to participate vicariously through the verbalizations of others, and thereby achieve significant growth.

Picture Story Test protocols, as well as the opinions of members of the observer teams, indicated that prior to counseling the under-achievers had negative attitudes toward themselves and others which would have interfered with any program specifically designed to help them improve their academic efficiency.

Although this study failed to produce evidence that group counseling will improve underachievers' academic performance in school, it may nevertheless make it possible for improved scholastic performance to be attained. Further investigation is needed to determine whether the replacement of negative attitudes by attitudes of acceptance of self and of others permits the underachiever to benefit from a remedial program specifically designed to help him improve his academic efficiency and his study skills.

Had not the Picture Story Test and other indicators pointed to an increased acceptance of self and of others in experimental subjects, the negative movement in school grades might have been interpreted as an indication that the subjects had in fact become more self-rejecting. The occurrence of growth in acceptance of self and of others accompanied by poorer achievement, however, deserves special consideration. Initial retardation in school performance may have been a result of increased independence and assertiveness, both products of increased acceptance of self. Since participation was the parents' idea for some, it was not necessarily an indication that the underachievers saw their performance as a serious problem. The underachievers' new sense of well-being after counseling may have been directed to areas more important to them. These perhaps caused them to focus more of their energy on interpersonal relationships, which had not been satisfactory to them in the past, to such an extent that they gave less attention to their academic work.

It also can be hypothesized that increased assertiveness and independence in students who have already created problems in the classroom may not have been recognized by the teachers as an indication of growth. Teachers were perhaps as baffled as the parent who noted, "A manner of conversation has developed among him and his friends to say the most horrible things and insults to one another —and nobody seems to resent it!" If a failure to understand changes in behavior was communicated by the teachers to the underachiever, it would create feelings of rejection in the student, which, in turn, would result in increased hostility toward the teacher. Implicit in this proposed explanation is the further suggestion that group counseling *per se* is not adequate in bringing about better school performance unless it is accompanied by closer cooperation between the counseling staff and the teaching faculty in order to achieve in teachers greater awareness of the needs and dynamics operating in the underachieving group and to interpret for them the changes which they may observe in the classroom.

Finally, we should like to give our clinical explanations of what we think happened to our clients. With varying degrees of depth each client discovered: (a) that expressing his own real feelings about people, things, and ideas helped him to understand himself and the forces that disturbed him; (b) that at least one adult could accept him and that this adult, the counselor, wanted to understand him; (c) that his peers had problems too; (d) that, in spite of his faults which his peers wanted to help him correct, his peers could accept him; (e) that he was capable of understanding, accepting, and helping others; and (f) that he could learn to trust others. When a client discovered that others accepted him, he found that he could better accept others, and eventually, that he could better accept himself. After he began to accept himself, then, and only then, could he accept the fact that he was gifted, and make plans which required him to use his great potentialities. All of this takes time—these changes come ever so gradually—yet they must precede substantial improvement in grades. What is more, each client must learn to live with his new self, communicate this new self to important others, and teach these important others to understand, to accept, and to live with the new self. For example, it is difficult for the average teacher to believe that these hostile and uncooperative students have really changed and for the distressed parents to believe that these youngsters are willing to take responsibility for their work, and without nagging.

SUMMARY

Four groups of underachieving ninth graders were treated in small groups. All of the sessions were electrically recorded for the four groups; kinescopes were made of all 16 sessions for each of two groups. Growth of clients was evaluated in terms of grades earned, scores on an achievement test battery, responses to a Picture Story Test, and observations made by the clients, their parents, and the members of observer teams.

We concluded that three of the four groups achieved significant growth. Positive changes in clients were noted in improved scores on the achievement test, increased acceptance of self and of others, and improved ability to relate to peers, siblings, and parents.

Received August 17, 1959.

REFERENCES

Ackerman, N. W. Group psychotherapy with a mixed group of adolescents. *Internat. J. group Psychother.,* 1955, **5**, 249-260.

Berman, S. Psychotherapeutic techniques with adolescents. *Amer. J. Orthopsychiat.,* 1954, **24**, 238-244.

Broedel, J. W. The effects of group counseling on academic performance and mental health of underachieving gifted adolescents. Unpublished doctoral dissertation, Univer. of Illinois, 1958.

Caplan, S. W. The effect of group counseling on junior high school boys' concepts of themselves in school. *J. counsel. psychol.,* 1957, **4**, 124-128.

Gersten, C. An experimental evaluation of group therapy with juvenile delinquents. *Internat. J. group Psychother.,* 1951, **1**, 311-318.

Gowan, J. The underachieving gifted child—A problem for everyone. *J. except. child.,* 1955, **21**, 247-249.

Katz, Evelyn W., Ohlsen, M. M., & Proff, F. C. An analysis through use of kinescopes of the interpersonal behavior of adolescents in group counseling. *J. coll. student Personnel,* 1959, **1**, 2-10.

Kirk, Barbara. Test versus academic performance in malfunctioning students. *J. consult. Psychol.,* 1952, **16**, 213-216.

Ohlsen, M. M., & Schultz, R. E. Projective test response patterns for best and poorest student teachers. *Educ. psychol. Meast,* 1955, **15**, 18-27.

Ohlsen, M. M., Proff, F. C., & Roeber, E. C. Counseling and adjustment *Rev. educ. Res.,* 1956, **26**, 292-307.

Paster, S. Group psychotherapy in an army general hospital. *Ment. Hygiene,* 1944, **28**, 529-536.

Shaw, M. C., & Grubb, J. Hostility and able high school underachievers. *J. counsel. Psychol.,* 1958, **5**, 263-266.

31. MULTIPLE COUNSELING AT THE ELEMENTARY SCHOOL LEVEL

Bertha W. Mercer

School #228 in Baltimore, the school in which the author has served as counselor for the past six and one-half years, is somewhat

Reprinted by permission of the author and *The School Counselor,* VI, No. 1 (October, 1958), 12-14. Copyright 1958 by The American School Counselor Association.

unique in that it has twice as many intermediate pupils as primary. This situation is the result of overcrowding in the nearby, low-income housing project. Since the project school can accommodate only the children in the first four grades, their fifth and sixth graders come to #228 by bus. In this situation the counselor's work, for the most part, has been concerned with children in the second term of the sixth grade, the 6A's.

During the study of the 6A records preparatory to making class studies, the counselor was concerned over the poor attendance of many of the children. Some had missed more than twenty-five days in each of the three preceding terms. Some action seemed indicated and so, in February 1955, the following project was started. The thirty-two children having the poorest attendance for the three preceding terms were interviewed individually early in the term. Attention was directed to absence and, in many cases, children themselves were able to relate the drop in achievement to poor attendance. All agreed to take part in the group program for the rest of the term. Each home was visited by the counselor who explained the proposed activity and invited parental cooperation. In one case a parent agreed to change her hours of work in order to relieve her daughter of the responsibilitiy of getting the younger children off to school.

The children concerned met as a group for the first time the third week of March. Each child was given a graph showing his attendance for the past three terms and also a small folder for his daily record. During the discussion of plans, children were encouraged to talk about the things that made them miss time from school. The five most common ones were: (1) oversleeping because of lack of parental interest or planning; (2) going places with parents when fathers' shifts changed and they were at home during the day; (3) minding younger children while mother went out; (4) lack of lunches; and (5) lack of suitable clothing.

Ways of overcoming these difficulties were discussed and approved by the group. As a tentative goal, each child agreed to try to equal or better by one day the poorest record on his graph.

During the remainder of the term the group met for half an hour each Friday immediately following the noon recess. A quick showing of hands indicated those who had been present three, four or five days respectively. Those with perfect attendance were praised for their efforts and the others encouraged to try again the next week. Absent members were visited by the other children whenever possible. A stockpile of usable clothing, collected in the school, was given to those who needed it. In one instance the counselor packed an extra lunch for a child to tide him over until the arrival of the family welfare check. Interest increased and teachers commented on the improved attendance of several club members. On the last Friday of the term attendance totals were entered on the graphs and outlined in gayly colored stars. The group closed the program by signing the counselor's large autograph folder. Final results of the activity are: 2 children transferred to other schools; 7 children showed no gain in attendance; 2 children achieved the tentative goal set in the initial meeting, that of equaling the record of their poorest term's attendance; 2 children gained 1 day; 1 child gained 2 days; 1 child gained 6 days; 2 children gained 7 days; 1 child gained 8 days; 1 child gained 8½ days; 1 child gained 11 days; 1 child gained 14 days; 1 child gained 16 days; 1 child gained 18 days; 1 child gained 18½ days; 1 child gained 20 days; 1 child gained 20½ days; 1 child gained 21 days; 1 child gained 21½ days; 2 children gained 22½ days; 1 child gained 26 days; 1 child gained 28 days.

In reviewing the program, the counselor felt that a smaller group would probably be better. Consequently, when a similar project was undertaken the following term, this group was limited to twenty-five children. An innovation that proved quite popular with the group was the introduction of a secret code number. Each child was assigned an identification code composed of the initials of the club, the teacher's initial and the child's number on the counselor's weekly record, thus: AC W 16 meant Attendance Club, Mr. Wilson's class plus his number. Each child entered his code number under the corner of his daily attendance folder out of sight. As the counselor's record passed around the group each child having perfect attendance for the week indicated it by placing a metallic star after his code number. The children's daily records were collected periodically and checked against the teachers' roll books. The low incidence of error attested to the honesty and sincerity of the group.

As to the final results, actual days gained remained at about the same level as for the previous group. The counselor felt, however, that there had been more growth evidenced in members of the group than before. The informality possible only in the smaller one resulted in getting to know each other better and seemed to pave the way for more lasting improvement. Since the children concerned are now attending junior high school in the annex on the third floor of School #228, it has been possible for the counselor to keep in touch with some of them. In several instances there has been evidence of real gain. One 7B student asked for a folder to continue her weekly attendance record. Another makes a point of stopping in once a month to report her progress.

As to the future of the project, if the school should ever return to a normal situation with primary and intermediate departments about equal, the counselor hopes to begin with the fourth grade, carry out a similar undertaking through the sixth or possibly on through the first year of junior high school, working out necessary details with their counselor. It may well be that with earlier identification and sustained interest, these irregular attendants might be helped to move over into the ranks of the regulars.

32. GROUP COUNSELING AT THE JUNIOR HIGH LEVEL

Clara Richards

Like all educational institutions we find at Horace Mann not enough counselor hours to meet the needs. One effective means of compensating for this condition has been the use of many types of group counseling. Our concept is in harmony with the expression of Willey and Andrew: "Guidance is assistance made available by competent counselors to an individual of any age to help him direct his own life, develop his own decisions, and carry his own burdens. Guidance involves personal help given by someone. This help may be given to individuals in a group or directly to the individual alone." *

Each year we find new avenues in guidance to explore. We feel

---

Reprinted by permission of the author and *The School Counselor,* V, No. 3 (March, 1958), 47, 59 ff. Copyright 1958 by The American School Counselor Association.

---

* Roy DeVerl Willey and Dean C. Andrew, *Modern Methods and Techniques in Guidance,* New York, Harpers and Brothers, p. 17.

our approach this year has been most rewarding. In May of 1957, two of our mathematics teachers accepted an invitation of the counselor to make a counseling survey of 108 students—38 algebra and 70 mathematics students. This included an equal distribution of above average, average, and below average students. The results of the survey follows:

1. Do you feel that you have been adequately informed as to the purposes of counseling and the services a counselor performs?

No	*? or doubtful*	*Yes*
22	3	55

2. Have there been any instances in your school life in which you feel you needed the help of a counselor and were not able to obtain this service?

No	*? or doubtful*	*Yes*
56	1	21 (Some mentioned not private enough place.)

3. What suggestions would you have for improving the counseling services provided by your school?

1. Give counselor more time and help.	11
2. Have more counselors.	25
3. Have separate places for boys and girls and counselors of both sexes.	16
4. Make room, private place or better place.	10
5. Make more private appointments with students.	5
6. More time for student to be with counselor.	5
7. Not bother with my business.	1
8. Make counselor more known around school.	7
9. Counseling service good as is.	35

4. How do you feel adequate counseling can be of service to you?

1. Help me out of trouble.	9
2. Let me talk about my problems.	11
3. Give me information on what I need or want to know.	3
4. Give me someone to go to.	4
5. Help with solving my problems.	17
6. Just be there for emergencies.	1
7. Occupational help and work permits are needed.	22
8. Help me to understand.	9

9. Help in school program choices and problems.   17
10. Help me with study problems.   3
11. Help me to get along with others.   2
12. *Yes,* it will just help.   19
13. *No,* it will not help.   2

This year the counselor has three small rooms made from one large room thus securing privacy in a temporary way. A project to help all with more understanding of counselor service and other hints for personal happiness was accomplished by student group reports to all advisory groups.

The counselor contacted a former student, a junior in a near-by high school, to see if she would like to chairman a project for ninth home room groups. She was delighted and selected two sophomores to work with her. They all worked diligently and discussed their plans with the counselor in after school conferences. Their subject was, "Hints to Ninth Graders to Make High School Tops." They divided the topic as follows: (A) Participation in social life and activities; (B) Personality growth and choice of friends; and (C) Scholastic success, attitudes, and study habits. The committee of three gave talks and answered questions in each ninth grade home room. For the seventh and eight grade home rooms, a home room one grade above was chosen to do the project. Delbert Fowler and his eighth graders did committee work (interviews with principal, nurse, and counselor) for one month to prepare a six panel report to the seventh graders on the topic—*Understandings, Records, and Persons I should have been better acquainted with as a Seventh Grader.* Reinald Stelter and his ninth grade home room did the same project for all eighth grade home rooms. The students did a complete orientation of responsibilities and services of the complete school personnel. They explained all forms and records used in the school, indicating the value of each individual building his history card the way he really wanted to advertise himself. They made a series of charts and posters to illustrate their talks.

SUMMARY

This project has worked successfully. In viewing the growth of those participating, it seems their service gave them more strength than the students receiving the service. It was the touch of personal worth that was so valuable. Mr. Fowler, the teacher working with the eighth advisory, said, "I didn't know a home room group could work so hard, organize so well, and delve so deep in problems as this group has. It has been a thrilling experience."

Other group activities have been effective in our school. These are: (1) Daily home room guidance periods with optional projects, outlines, and reading suggestions, given by the counselor; (2) Parent, teacher, counselor, student, and principal, as needed conferences; (3) Discussion groups of active social participating students with those finding social adjustment difficult; (4) Small common health problem groups (such as obese students) ; (5) Student leaders and officers with inactive students; and (6) Counselor and new student groups, etc. These many group guidance activities are very helpful and free more of the counselor's time for those with deep seated problems.

Section Six

VALUES IN THE COUNSELING PROCESS

The counselor's value system has been given more and more consideration in analyses of the counseling process. This has resulted both from a philosophical consideration and an operational concern. The maturation of the profession of counseling and guidance has been another prime factor in the counselor's concern for the influence of his value system. The articles in this part of the text offer carefully considered ideas about the impact of a counselor's values on the counseling process.

It has been recognized in recent literature that the value structure of the individual counselor has direct effect on the counseling process. It is imperative that the counselor be aware of the effects of his value system on his relationship with the counselee in the counseling interview.

Mowrer brings focus to the discussion of values in his provocative and controversial article on the relationship of psychology and religion. The interrelationship of the physical and psychological make-up of man is presented with the suggestion that the time has come for the theologian and the psychologist to seek further, in cooperation, to discover the basis of this relationship.

In recent years there has been discussed the concept of the neutrality of the counselor. Browning and Peters support the position that it is not possible for the counselor to be truly neutral, but that instead he must be able to recognize his own philosophical biases and thus study their effects upon the counseling relationship.

345

In like manner, Smith and Williamson both recognize the importance of the counselor value system in its effect upon the counseling process. Smith is particularly concerned over (1) the lack of adequate research in the development of value understandings and (2) the general lack of professional attention to the effect of values in the training of the school counselor.

In general, there appears to be some basic agreement in these samples of the literature as to the effect of counselor values on the counseling relationship. The writers emphasize the need for a more adequate understanding of personal values on the part of the counselors. It appears that such understanding may come only from the closer and deeper look of research at factors involved.

Smith notes that most textbooks on counseling, psychotherapy, and the counseling process contain only minimal discussion of the problem of values. However, since a counselor's values affect the principles from which he operates in the counseling process, problems are likely to arise if he has neglected his philosophy of life. Thus, it is necessary that each counselor candidate give careful consideration to the important role of "Counselor Values."

33. SOME PHILOSOPHICAL PROBLEMS
IN PSYCHOLOGICAL COUNSELING

O. Hobart Mowrer[1, 2]

Is mind designed to serve the body or is body designed to serve the mind? During the last half century, assent has been so nearly universally given by psychologists to the first of these possibilities that the alternative view has hardly been considered at all.

But there are signs that all is not well with psychology, either as science or as profession, and that we may need to re-examine some of our most basic assumptions. Ask a representative sample of bright, young clinical psychologists who got their doctorate degrees at our best universities four or five years ago and who have since been on the clinical firing line, ask them what they now think of their training in light of their attempts to make application thereof. Without bitterness, self-pity, or even undue pessimism, they commonly express doubts of the most profound and far-reaching nature. They question both the instruments and the categories of diagnosis; they feel that the rationale and results of psychotherapy and counseling

Reprinted by permission of the author; *Journal of Counseling Psychology,* IV, No. 2 (Summer, 1957), 103-11; and D. Van Nostrand Company, Inc. This article also appears in Dr. Mowrer's book, *The Crisis in Psychiatry and Religion* (Princeton, N.J.: D. Van Nostrand Company, Inc., 1961).

[1] This paper, under a different title ("A practical, contemporary aspect of the mind-body problem"), was read at the Eighth Annual Institute in Psychiatry and Neurology held, under the auspices of the Veterans Administration, in North Little Rock, Arkansas (March, 1956). Since then a number of other papers in which the conventional presuppositions of psychiatry and clinical psychology are re-examined have come to the writer's attention and are listed here (2, 5, 11, 13, 15, 17, 24, 25, 26, 27, 29, 31, and 32) for the reader's convenience. Although these papers do not by any means present the same alternative point of view, they are unanimous in calling for a re-appraisal of the philosophical premises on which contemporary psychotherapy, counseling, and even diagnosis are predicated.

[2] This is a significant and competently written paper on a controversial subject. You, the reader, may agree or disagree but you will be shaken a bit in your usual comfortable orbit of thinking. Or at least this was the experience of three members of the editorial staff who read the ms. *Ed.*

are uncertain; and they divergently evaluate the significance of recent contributions to psychology as a science.

Or, listen to what some of our elder statesmen have to say in this connection. In 1955 the American Psychiatric Association sponsored an all-day symposium, by psychiatrists and psychologists, on psychotherapy—later published in book form under the title, *Progress in Psychotherapy* (Fromm-Reichmann and Moreno, 9). Here are some of the comments made on this occasion:

> Psychiatry has a great need for a clear and rational understanding of the process of recovery. . . . Hypotheses we have, . . . but none has gained that degree of validation which should serve to command general acceptance in the medical profession as a well-established theory (p. 62, Whitehorn).
>
> Psychotherapy has many more variants than psychoanalysis and what constitutes psychotherapy, and what does not, is even less clear than what is, or is not, psychoanalysis. . . . The time has come to investigate not the differences but the similarities, and to formulate common denominators among the bewildering array of different methods and procedures (pp. 72-73, Hoch).
>
> It is discontent which drives me in my approach to this problem. Only a few years ago (although it seems a long time in my life as a psychoanalyst) I harbored the comforting expectation that increasing analytic sophistication and experience would yield a higher percentage of therapeutic successes. . . . My reluctant impression is that this hope has not been realized (p. 87). I am impatient with any propagandish approach to the problem from any point of view. We have no right to be for or against anything in this field. We have a right only to the most complete humility—humility that says we still know practically nothing about many important elements either in the neurotic process or in the psychotherapeutic process (p. 101, Kubie).
>
> Psychotherapy is today in a state of disarray, almost exactly as it was two hundred years ago (p. 108). At this stage we seem to be fighting each other to attain some sort of theoretic throne, and we often forget that that throne is as unsteady as a three-legged chair (p. 110, Zilboorg).

Or, take still a different sort of evidence that we have failed to meet manifest social need in this connection. One of the most remarkable and unanticipated developments on the whole contemporary human scene is the extent to which religious leaders are thinking about and actively working at the problem of personality disorder. Books on religion and pastoral counseling are being published at an unprecedented rate, and if one takes the trouble to examine them, one finds that they are often extraordinarily thoughtful, informed, and creative. "Mental Health" is a common pulpit topic; and to the twin concepts of "Sin and Salvation" has been added, "and Sanity." Moreover, and even more remarkable, it seems that the profession of psychiatry is now beginning to think in a new way about the role of religion in mental health and illness: witness the just-published book by Viktor Frankl of Vienna (7) and by the English psychiatrist, Ernest White (30). For similar trends in this country, see *The Church and Mental Health* (Maves, 18) and *Ministry and Medicine in Human Relations* (Galdston, 10). And the same trend is also conspicuous in *Progress in Psychotherapy* (Fromm-Reichmann and Moreno, 9).

Granted, then, the reality of psychology's ailment, what precisely is the diagnosis, what the remedy?

The "Biologizing" of American Psychology

The writer has just read Boring's paper (3) on "The influence of evolutionary theory upon American psychological thought." It is most suggestive. Boring begins by noting a paradox, that in the latter part of the nineteenth century, American psychologists were busy ostensibly imitating and importing one kind of psychology from Germany while, almost unwittingly, creating something very different. This was Functionalism and, a little later, Behaviorism. Here Darwinian thought was the touchstone. Says Boring:

> To his thinking about psychology Dewey brought the concept of functional use for the events of the mind, and thus, closely related to functional use, the notion of functional activity. The way to express this matter is to say that both consciousness and activity function *for* the organism—the use of consciousness is to produce activity which "saves" the organism. That is the essential tenet of the Chicago school of functional psychology which Dewey started, and which Angell carried on. In the doctrine of this school behavior and physiology and conscious states are mixed in with each other because they are unified, not by their essential natures, but

by their common aim for the survival and use of the organism
(p. 277).

Boring then goes on to say that, in his judgment (Watson to the
contrary), Behaviorism was a direct outgrowth "of Dewey's functionalism and of Cattell's capacity psychology. . . . Watson's view
was essentially American, a psychology consistent with the [pioneer
and democratic] belief in necessity of struggle for survival" (p. 288).
Radical Behaviorism is today antiquated, on two scores. (a) Its
adherents, in the pursuit of their own objectives, have found it increasingly necessary to make use of "intervening variables." And
(b) the spread of interest in clinical psychology has, again of necessity, focused interest upon mind rather than upon body, upon disturbances of consciousness rather than upon questions of biological
adaptation. As Boring observes:

> Behaviorism was itself too unsophisticated to last. It has now
> given place to positivism or operationism or whatever one prefers
> to call the newest psychological objectivism. The operationist
> argues that all the data of psychology, including the data of con-
> sciousness, are to be defined by the operations which are used to
> observe them. You can know nothing more about mind than you
> can find in the evidence for the existence of mind. This movement
> gets its sophistication from the logical positivism of the Vienna
> Circle and from the operational physics of P. W. Bridgman, but
> this is not the place for its full consideration. It is sufficient here
> to point out that the epistemology of operationism was already
> implicit in the faiths of behaviorism, functional and capacity
> psychology, the basic American psychological faith (p. 288) .

It is not the purpose of the present paper to suggest that this faith,
this "basic American psychological faith," has been completely mis-
placed or entirely unfruitful. The present author has spent the past
several months reviewing the research and theoretical literature to
which this faith has given rise in the field of learning; the results
are undeniably impressive. The question is whether this faith is as
broad, as inclusive, as far-reaching as it ought to be.

> Functional psychology becomes the study of the organism in use.
> Functional psychology is thus practical through and through in the
> way that Darwin's theory was the greatest practical theory of living
> that has ever been put forth (Boring, 3, p. 277).

Here, then, is the crux of the issue. Is it indeed true that mind is designed to serve the body (which is presumably what is meant here by "practicality")? Or is there a reciprocal relationship of some sort, in which the body must become obedient, even subservient to mind? One hesitates to ask this question because of its clearly anachronistic ring. Religion has always insisted that soul is more important than body, that the flesh should be subjugated by the spirit. And the "old psychology," against which Functionalism and Behaviorism were so strenuously—and not without reason—rebelling, was based upon presuppositions closely akin to those of theology. Boring calls attention to "the influence of seventeenth century theology upon Descartes, an influence abetted by language." In French *l'ame,* he notes, may be interpreted either as *mind* or *soul,* and the same is true of the German word, *Seele.* Since one does not attribute a "soul" to animals, there was, then, a tendency to deprive them of "mind" (and consciousness) as well.

> The Darwinian theory, on the contrary, asserted the existence of continuity between man and animals, continuity in all respects, mental as well as physical, since man is believed to be derived from animals by continuous change (Boring, 3, pp. 284-285).

There is no doubt that much has been accomplished by the Darwinian, the organic, the mechanistic approach to mind. Many things of a psychological nature are now clearly and systematically understood in objective terms which were simply given, seemingly unanalyzable, in a psychology which made conscious experience all important. And with the physical models and thought modes provided by modern servo theory, it seems that we have by no means yet fully exploited or exhausted what can be done along these lines. But we must return to the thesis that all is not well with contemporary psychological science. To assume otherwise, in face of the manifest realities, is hazardous—and a betrayal of the ideals of science itself.

BIOLOGICAL VS PSYCHOLOGICAL SURVIVAL

The fact, the decidedly inconvenient but seemingly inescapable fact, is that man must be concerned with the struggle for *psycho-*

logical survival, as well as with physical, organic, bodily survival. Indeed, he has already succeeded so well in the latter respect that his very success now constitutes one of our most pressing dilemmas (waning natural resources and a world population that is increasing at the net rate of 75,000 persons per day). But in the struggle for psychological survival, we seem to be groping for first principles. Whether, in absolute terms, there is more "mental disease" in this country than formerly is perhaps open to question; but relatively— relative, that is, to physical illness and incapacity—psychological and emotional disorders are so clearly in the lead that it is now trite to refer to them as "the nation's number-one health problem," the *plague* of modern times.

We have remarked upon the considered skepticism and disillusionment of our bright young men in clinical psychology. And we have also seen what some of our more mature writers have to say about the field of psychotherapy. Moreover, under the urgency of the growing popular demand that "something must be done," men in positions of responsibility and public trust have openly declared that if a new "breakthrough" does not soon come in the field of mental health, they will be forced, by the very nature of their social obligations, to start supporting research and training outside the acknowledged professions of psychiatry, clinical psychology, social work, and psychiatric nursing—not, perhaps, with much conviction from sheer desperation.[3]

The professions just mentioned have, by and large, pinned their hopes to psychoanalysis. This body of theory and practice needs no criticism here; the logic of events seems to be making purely verbal objections gratuitous. While the present writer has previously joined in the attack upon psychoanalysis, he now has no zest for further criticism. If one can correctly interpret the course of on-going developments, they clearly signify the failure of this movement, leaving one only to say, perhaps, "More's the pity. Things would have been so much simpler, so much easier if Freud had only been right!"

---

[3] Since the above was written, the National Institute of Mental Health (of the U. S. Public Health Service) has approved several "pilot study" grants for training of personnel in psychopharmacology, neurophysiology, sociology, theology, and other "peripheral" professions.

Note also the work of the newly established Joint Commission on Mental Illness and Health.

But if reality is not as he thought, then the sooner and more completely we recognize his errors the better.

We need hardly remind ourselves that Freud was strongly influenced by the same forces that shaped the "new psychology" in America. We know, by his own repeated statement, that as a youth Freud read and greatly admired Darwin, and the influence is evident: For Freud, neurosis was the result of cultural (moral, religious) interference with normal physiological (instinctual) processes. The mind, if dominated by certain mistaken social values, may cease to serve the body and obstruct its functions. The body then protests and retaliates. *That* is "neurosis," and the crux of Freudian psychopathology. Here we see Functionalism and Scientific Materialism applied to Twentieth-Century man's most pressing problem. Are they indeed so eminently practical? Are they really the greatest "theory of living that has ever been set forth"?

Let us not sell them short. Functionalism and Scientific Materialism provided the intellectual climate and basic premises which have made possible unprecedented advances in our knowledge of animal behavior and have laid the foundation for attacking some distinctively human problems—for example, the psychology of language—with new insights and confidence. Perhaps we merely lack patience. Give them time and opportunity to demonstrate their ultimate potency. Indirect report has it that one of the few remaining extreme Behaviorists has recently begun researches with severely disturbed psychiatric patients and that the therapeutic results already obtained are remarkable. All power to this project. But sanguine hopes were expressed decades ago for what the New Psychology would do for the field of mental hygiene (Angell, 1). It has not, sad to say, borne the hoped-for fruit. Let no hunch go neglected here. But neither history nor the contemporary scene provides grounds for much confidence that the solution, if solution there be, lies in that direction.

The Need for a Truly Mental Hygiene

Is it, then, improper to explore the possibility that the body must serve the mind, as well as mind serve the body? While mind presumably evolved because, as Boring observes, it "saves" the body, yet once evolved it appears that mind has its own special needs, its own conditions for survival, *its own hygiene and culture.* And we must then ask, How and in what sense the body can serve and "save" *the mind?*

For psychologists, this is a dangerous question to consider; for if it is answered at all affirmatively—if we conclude that body must serve mind, it brings us immediately into a domain where we are by no means authorities, but rank amateurs. Religion has steadfastly said, save in its weaker moments, that conduct must be guided by the needs of the spirit as well as those of the body. And some of the best minds of all ages have devoted themselves to working out patterns and precepts of conduct which are "holy" (integrative, redemptive, health-giving, therapeutic). Here, not only are we psychologists relatively uninformed; we have sat, alas, in the seat of scorn and have barriers of pride and deep bias to overcome before we can become even apt students, much less teachers and trustworthy leaders in this area.

Let it be at once granted that religion has sometimes taken an extreme and indefensible position in this connection. Sometimes it has said that not only must the body be subservient to mind and soul; the body must also be despised and continually chastized. No greater or more clarion voice ever cried out against this perversion than that of Martin Luther. Said he:

> No Christian should despise his position and life if he is living in accordance with the word of God, but should say, "I believe in Jesus Christ, and do so as the ten commandments teach, and pray that our dear Lord God may help me thus to do." That is a right holy life, and cannot be made holier even if one fast himself to death. . . .

Huss has been burned, but not the truth with him (Stuber, 28, p. 213).

Although Luther successfully launched the Protestant Reformation, the philosophy of asceticism is still alive within but under debate by the Roman Church. Goldbrunner (12), an ordained priest and scholar well known in Europe, has recently stated the growing sentiment within the Church *against* asceticism, in a most interesting and energetic manner. But we need not here pursue his argument in detail. Asceticism is clearly in retreat. Moreover, it is not indigenous to or an intrinsic part of the Christian "way" or life style. The founder of the movement did not say, Do not eat at all. He even taught his students and followers to give thanks for their "daily bread." But he did insist that man *does not live by bread alone.* And he spoke of a more abundant life, a life of the spirit, which was to be achieved by relatedness, reconciliation, fellowship—with man and God. What does it profit a man, he asked, if he gain the whole world but lose his mind, his soul? Truly a life with a permanently disordered mind ("unredeemed soul") is a "life worse than death." In insanity there is physical, biological survival; a compassionate society sees to that. But to what avail?

It has been common for us objectivists to psychologize religion, to write about the "psychology *of* religion." And Freud (8), as we know, went a step further and reduced it to a form of psychopathology, often relatively benign but sometimes thoroughly malignant. How helpful, how constructive, how genuinely scientific have such forays been? Psychoanalysis as a movement is in trouble. Church attendance in this country, by contrast, is rapidly increasing, well beyond population growth. In other words, Freud's "reality principle" appears to be doing less well than the "illusion" with such an unpromising future. Perhaps Freud was still, in one sense, right: maybe he was wrong only in his estimate of man's growing capacity to live *without* illusion. Or, can it be that he himself misperceived "reality"?

Under the sway of Darwinian thought, we practical, functional, behavioristic psychologists have tended to dismiss religion as irrelevant to both the scientific and human enterprise; or, with Freud, to regard it as actively inimical to soundness of body and mind alike. We have analyzed, psychologized, pathologized religion, ignoring the possibility that it is, in and of itself, a *psych*ology, *soul*ology of the profoundest sort. By our own stated premises, our science is a species, a derivative of biology, physiology, even physics. Religion represents man's attempt, through the ages, to meet mind on its own terms. Can this be a truer, more genuine psychology than our own?

How to decide? The antiquity and continued vitality of religious thought and action may be said to bear upon the question. Freud argued to the contrary. It was something, he said, that had simply become lodged, adventitiously, in man's "unconscious" and was perpetuated like some congenital physical weakness or disorder. But contemporaneous, as well as historical, evidence suggests that religion, as an institution, has survived for the reason that it often has unique *psychological survival value* for the individual. That it gave early Christians the capacity to handle not only the ordinary conflicts and tensions of life but enabled them to persevere in the face of and eventually to overcome the most powerful political opposition on the face of the earth is established history. And in our own time the evidence from case histories of "brain washing" successfully withstood on religious grounds is steadily growing (see, for example, Perkins, 22).

The English psychiatrist Ernest White (30, p. 11) takes this position:

> One often finds that questions do not admit of a clear answer because the assumptions on which they rest are false. For example, after an address had been given on the subject of Psychology and Religion, a member of the audience asked why it was that so many more neurotic people were found inside the churches as compared with people outside. Now it is not possible to answer such a question unless it has been first demonstrated by special investigation that there are in fact more neurotics in proportion among churchgoers than among the general population. As far as I know, no such investigation has been made.

Preliminary attempts, apparently not known to White, have been made in this country to get empirical evidence on this point, with results that give church members a comparatively clean bill of emotional health (Link, Chap. 1 and p. 99, 16). But much more searching study of the issue, at the empirical level, is obviously needed. From one point of view, no neurotic individuals at all should be found in a church-going population. If religion offers an assured salvation, this might seem to follow axiomatically. But it would be absurd to condemn hospitals, as institutions of physical remediation, because one finds so many *sick* people in them. The appeal of religious institutions has always been addressed to "poor, sick soul," and Christ himself said that he did not come to call the righteous. Hence, a study which would be faithful to both sides of the argument needs to be carefully interpreted, as well as meticuously impartial.

Common Ground: The Study of Interpersonal and Group Relationships

It has already been noted that psychologists, for reasons given, have been hard to interest in religious psychology, as opposed to objective psychology and psychoanalysis. Indeed, as Roberts (24) has observed, "A psychologist who is suspected of being religious is at once under suspicion of scientific incompetence," although the same suspicion does not attach itself to a physicist, a chemist, or an engineer. But there are signs of change. A number of national organizations (typified by the National Academy of Religion and Mental Health) have recently sprung up with the avowed purpose of unifying, or at least relating, psychology, psychiatry, and religion; and, within the American Psychological Association itself, there is now a "special interest group" in this area which has held meetings at our two most recent conventions.

Perhaps most auspicious of all is the fact that so many psychologists are now turning their research interests toward problems which have long been of concern to religious and church leaders, notably problems having to do with social affiliation and what Foote and Cottrell (6) have aptly termed *interpersonal competence*. Here it is inevitable that psychologists should encounter many of the same realities as have interested religious thinkers and practitioners throughout history. This point is well illustrated in a paper recently published by Corsini and Rosenberg (4). These writers did a sort of informal factor analysis of the contents of some 300 contemporary books and articles on the subject of group psychotherapy and emerged with "ten classes of mechanisms" commonly emphasized therein.

All of these mechanisms, or principles, need not be considered here; but the two which head Corsini and Rosenberg's list are these:

> *Acceptance.* This statistically most frequent concept was taken to mean respect for and sympathy with the individual. Acceptance implies belongingness, a warm, friendly, comfortable feeling in the group.
> *Altruism.* Closely related to acceptance but in addition involving wanting to do something for others is the mechanism of

altruism. The essence of this mechanism is the desire to help others
(4).

Are these two mechanisms so salient because the authors of the
works thus analyzed have a basically religious orientation? Or have
the authors, with an initially neutral or perhaps even unsympathetic
attitude, empirically rediscovered the therapeutic potency of "fellowship" and "charity"?

Whatever the answer to this question, the fact stands out that,
increasingly, psychologists are joining psychiatrists and clergymen
in looking for both the cause and cure of personality difficulties in
the social, interpersonal, moral, or "spiritual" realm. But what of
those most welcome advances recently made in drug therapy? As
May (19) has cogently observed, these drugs—merciful as they are
for use with persons in terror states and agitations—leave essentially
untouched the problem of prevention and personality reorganization.

In our neighbor discipline, Sociology, there has long been a
tendency to view mind, or "self," as much more of a *social* than
biological phenomenon. Here the influence of Mead (20) is already
strong, and becoming increasingly so. Thus the confluence of
thought noted above gains yet another tributary.

The centrality of religious tradition and practice is obvious here.
But there was a manifest difficulty. Let one highly placed within
organized religion, itself, speak on this score. Says Rev. James A.
Pike, Dean of the Episcopal Cathedral of St. John the Divine, in
New York:

> The Biblical writers are, by and large, short on concepts, long
> on concern as to the human situation. The early Church carried
> this tradition forward: the articles of the Creeds are not just in-
> tellectual speculations. They are affirmations wrought out in the
> fire of personal and corporate experience and found to be abid-
> ing answers to perennial questions which affect the nature and
> direction of human life under God (23, p. 6).

The Biblical writers emphasize, not "theory," but *testimony*.
Make an "investment," "experiment," "try it" say characters in
Lloyd Douglas' novels. Or, in Pike's own colorful phrase, in order
to find out you have to "bet your life." *Prove* all things, said the

Apostle, Paul.[4] Perhaps psychologists can ultimately help provide a clearer, more naturalistic, more rational explanation and understanding of these pragmatic varieties. This would be an undertaking of first-rate importance and magnitude. But before psychologists and religionists can thus creatively collaborate, both must change from what they have earlier been. Contemporary religious writers now seem increasingly aware of errors into which religion fell during the nineteenth century. One of these errors was obstinacy in accepting the clear evidence for organic evolution. But ever more grievous, perhaps, was a later willingness to go *too far* in accepting the psychological view of man seemingly dictated by evolutionary considerations. In the introduction to Alexander Miller's recent book, *The renewal of man,* Reinhold Niebuhr (21) has said:

> Christianity has tried rather too desperately to accommodate itself to modernity. In its desperation it frequently sacrificed just those points in the Christian Gospel which would throw light on mysteries which modern learning left obscure (p. 8).
>
> The present age, though incredulous toward the chief affirmations of this faith, is bound to find it more relevant than previous ages, which conceived their own schemes of salvation. Our age is the inheritor of the confusion and the evil which proceeded precisely from these schemes of salvation (p. 9).

There are many indications, over and beyond those cited in this paper, that we are now well into a religious reformation comparable in scope and significance to that of four hundred years ago. Institutionalized religion had stagnated. Within the past century, science in general and biological science in particular, threatened its very life. Now religion appears to be recovering and, in that process, has gained new vitality and validity. What are the implications of this unexpected turn of events for psychology? Although we may feel uncertain of the answer, we cannot complacently ignore the question.

SUMMARY

There is clear indication that the theory of organic evolution has profoundly and pervasively influenced American psychology during

---

[4] Walters (29) has pertinently observed that Freud, while condemning religion, took the same position in holding that no one could properly evaluate or criticize psychoanalysis who had not himself had such an experience.

the past three-quarters of a century. Mind, rather than being something to be studied in its own right, has been conceived as "an organ of adaptation," an appendage of the body instrumental to the achievement of bodily ends.

Thanks to the stance of the "New Psychology" (Functionalism, Behaviorism), it has proved possible, for the first time, to develop a systematic, essentially objective understanding of many basic psychological processes. Behavior theory is now a relatively unified assembly of fact and principle which commands respect in any scientific company.

Nor was the influence of Darwinian thought restricted to psychology in this country. Equally potent was its impact upon Freud and the school of psychopathology which he founded. Here the "neuroses," both mild and severe, were seen as springing from the fact that the mind, under the sway of unfortunate or misdirected *social* experience, has, in effect, *turned against* the body and is no longer ministering to its needs.

But there is increasing evidence that neither the original Freudian formulation nor its attempted restatement in terms of contemporary behavior theory gives us the answer to some of man's most profound, and uniquely human, problems. Today we are probing the future (through research) and searching the past, through historical studies, for leads to a better and psychologically more abundant life. What do we find? Growing indication that the *human mind, in its towering complexity, long ago reached the point where it has its own special conditions for "survival,"* conditions which are not only different from those of physical comfort and well being but which may on occasion be in conflict therewith. Both ongoing researches and a re-examination of history point to the conclusion that religious precepts and practices, over the centuries, have grown up largely in response to man's unique psychological needs and that there are insights and prescriptions for action here which contemporary man may, with profit, reconsider.

Such a reconsideration seems now to be well under way, mainly by theologians, naturally enough, but also, and to a surprising degree, by psychiatrists. Psychologists, in their increasing interest in group psychotherapy, are also showing a new awareness of social values; and several interprofessional groups have recently been formed for a concerted confrontation of the problem at the level of research and practice.

The burden of the present paper is that it will greatly hasten this readjustment if we can succeed in seeing the proper relationship between man's needs for physical and *psychological* survival and can transcend the tacit assumption that mind is merely servant of the body and that, if it serves this master well, it will itself necessarily prosper. Long ago we were reminded that man does not live by bread alone; and it is none too early for us to turn our attention to the identification and better understanding of this "something more."

Received July 7, 1956.

REFERENCES

1. Angell, J. R. The province of functional psychology. *Psychol. Rev.,* 1907, **14**, 61-91.

2. Blake, J. A. Happiness versus reality. *Understanding the child,* 1955, **24**, 44-45 and 59.

3. Boring, E. G. The influence of evolutionary theory upon American psychological thought. In Stow Persons (Ed.), *Evolutionary thought in America,* Cambridge, Mass.: Yale Univer. Press, 1950.

4. Corsini, R. J., & Rosenberg, Bina. Mechanisms of group psychotherapy: Processes and dynamics. *J. abnorm. soc. Psychol.,* 1955, **51**, 406-409.

5. Fingarette, H. Psychoanalytic perspectives on moral guilt and responsibility: A re-evaluation. *Psychoanal.,* 1955, **4**, 46-66.

6. Foote, N. N., & Cottrell, L. S., Jr. *Identity and interpersonal competence: A new direction in family research.* Chicago: Univer. of Chicago Press, 1955.

7. Frankl, V. *The doctor and the soul.* New York: Alfred Knopf. 1955.

8. Freud, S. *The future of an illusion* (W. D. Robinson-Scott, trans.) London: Hogarth Press.

9. Fromm-Reichmann, Frieda, & Moreno, J. L. *Progress in psychotherapy,* New York: Grune & Stratton, 1956.

10. Galdston, I. *Ministry and medicine in human relations.* New York: International Univer. Press, 1955.

11. Gallagher, J. J. Rejecting parents? *Exceptional Child,* 1956, **22**, 273-276.

12. Goldbrunner, J. *Holiness is wholeness.* New York: Pantheon Books, 1955.

13. Hobbs, N. Curing unreason by reason: a review. *Contemporary Psychol.,* 1956, **1,** 44-45.

14. Jung, C. G. *Answer to Job.* (R. F. C. Hull, trans.) New York: Pastoral Psychology Book Club, 1955.

15. Lifton, W. M. Counseling and the religious view of man. *Personnel & Guid. J.,* 953, **31,** 366-367.

16. Link, H. C. *Return to religion.* New York: Macmillan Co., 1936.

17. Maslow, A. H. Defense and growth. *Merrill-Palmer quart.,* 1956, **3,** 36-47.

18. Maves, P. B. (Ed.) *The church and mental health.* New York: Charles Scribner's Sons, 1953.

19. May, R. Toward a science of man. (Unpublished manuscript) 1955.

20. Mead, G. H. *Mind, self, and society.* Chicago: Univer. of Chicago Press, 1934.

21. Miller, A. In R. Niebuhr (Ed.), *The renewal of man.* New York: Doubleday, 1955.

22. Perkins, Sara E. My 4½ years in a Chinese Communist prison. *Presbyterian Life,* Feb. 18, 1956, pp. 8-12.

23. Pike, J. A. *Beyond anxiety.* New York: Charles Scribner's Sons, 1954.

24. Roberts. W. H. Psychologists are getting religion. *The Dalhousie Rev.* (Nova Scotia), 1956, **36,** 14-27.

25. Schneiderman, L. Anxiety and social sensitivity. *J. Psychol.,* 1954, **37,** 271-277.

26. Shoben, E. J., Jr. Work, love and maturity. *Personnel & Guid. J.,* 1956, **34,** 326-332.

27. Shoben, E. J., Jr. Anxiety vs immaturity in neurosis and its treatment. *Amer. J. Orthopsychiat.,* 1955, **25,** 71-80.

28. Stuber, S. I. *The Christian reader.* New York: Association Press, 1952.

29. Walters, O. S. Freud, his philosophy of life. *His—Magazine of campus Christian living,* 1955, **16,** 8-11.

30. White, E. *Christian life and the unconscious.* New York: Harper & Bros., 1955.

31. White, R. W. The dangers of social adjustment. *The medical Pr.,* 1952, **228,** July 2, pp. 9-15.

32. Williamson, E. G. Counseling in developing self-confidence. *Personnel & Guid. J.,* 1956, **34,** 398-404.

34. ON THE PHILOSOPHICAL NEUTRALITY OF COUNSELORS

Robert L. Browning and Herman J. Peters

There appears to be an urgent demand among guidance counselors for a clarification of the relationship between the counselor's basic philosophy and his counseling procedures. Can a counselor remain philosophically neutral, on the one hand, and should the counselor do so, on the other hand. Is Vordenberg's dictum true that "Regardless of the kind of personal philosophy evolved by the counselor, it must surely affect the techniques he uses and the evaluation of the effectiveness of his work?" (16:440)

I. DEMANDS FOR THE CONSIDERATION OF THE INFLUENCE OF PHILOSOPHY OF COUNSELING

After giving a survey of the inadequacies of the current attempts to develop a philosophical foundation and direction for guidance, Donald Walker and Herbert Peiffer issue a call to action. They say, ". . . we would urge close and careful attention to the problems of the goals of counseling, both at the general theoretical level and as they affect the progress of the individual counseling case. . . . We are handicapped by the fact that in psychotherapy we are, to some extent, the victims of our disease orientation, our bias against value judgments and our contradictory cultural goals." (17:209) Mathewson says that the old myth of economic man is inadequate. He says, "A new myth may be forming; we cannot tell what it may be and perhaps we cannot hasten its formation, or even consciously affect its form. But unless we wish to take a completely passive position in the determination of our national destiny, it seems necessary to think about and to choose between alternative sets of social and moral values, especially in the education and guidance of our youth." (9:26)

Reprinted by permission of the authors and *Educational Theory*, X, No. 2 (April, 1960), 142-47.

Arbuckle compares the counselor and the surgeon, saying that the philosophy of the surgeon may have very little effect on the recovery or death of a patient. "The attitude and the philosophy of the counselor, however, are all important and in any research it is difficult to keep such an inconsistent factor consistent." (2) In Arbuckle's thinking the personnel point of view must include a consideration of every aspect in the development of the student—". . . his intellect, his emotions, his physical being, his moral values, his skills and aptitudes, his means of recreation, his esthetic and religious values, his social adjustment, and his environmental situation." (3:3) This is a big order! The fulfillment of such a goal in guidance is greatly complicated by the fact that the counselor, in dealing with the counselee's development along such broad lines, is confused about whether or not his own loyalties, his own philosophy of life, should be shared, or whether, in fact, he can keep himself from sharing it!

> Counseling involves the interaction of two personalities through the medium of speech and other symbolic behavior. It is reasonable to suppose, therefore, that the structure of each of these personalities will have a marked influence on the interaction. It may be hypothesized further that the ways in which the personality structure of each of the counseling participants is symbolized in the speech of the interview will also have a marked effect upon the interaction.
>
> If it is true that the counselor's personality influences the direction, course, and outcome of the counseling interaction, it might be profitable to speculate about the kinds of counselor personality traits which are likely to facilitate counseling and those which are not.

Strang states,

> The counselor should be himself but not impose himself. He should be genuine and sincere. He is likely to fail if he tries to play a role that is not natural for him. If a person cannot risk being himself in the counseling relationship, he should not try to be a counselor. Moreover, he is consciously or unconsciously influenced by his theory of counseling; his attitude toward school policies, his outlook on life, his attitude toward people. In short, his counseling is an expression of his personality, not merely a technic applied at will. (14)

Pepinsky and Pepinsky, writing in 1954, state,

> There is no denying that the counselor's behavior, also, is sub-
> ject to change as a function of his experience in working with
> clients. (11:173)

A little later under this same topic, "The Primary Function of
Interaction," they go on to say,

> Indeed, the more closely we examine the counselor's motives,
> the more they become suspect! It appears to be, at best, nonsense
> and, at worst, a delusion to try to maintain that the counselor does
> or ought to leave his own needs parked outside the door while he
> interviews a client. We can state only that the explicit function of
> the counseling relationship—to help the client to change—should
> not be interfered with or destroyed. (11:74)

Perhaps the greatest single influence on counselors to be philosophically neutral has come from the work of Carl Rogers. His nondirective theory of psychotherapy was built on the belief that man
could be trusted to work his way through to insights and new
orientation if he could have a genuinely permissive relationship
with the counselor in which he could open his inner life to himself
and the helping person. Early research by Rogers led him to state
that, "One can read through a complete recorded case or listen to it,
without finding more than a half dozen instances in which the
therapist's views on any point are evident. . . . One could not determine his diagnostic views, his standards of behavior, his social
class." (12:358) Rogers did not, at that time, comment on the effect
of the half dozen times and the absolute inevitability of such sharing
of values. More recently, but only after a number of years of general confusion about the issue, has he addressed himself more directly to this pressing concern. In 1957, he said, in answer to certain
articles challenging his position, that, "One cannot engage in psychotherapy without giving operational evidence of an underlying
value orientation and view of human nature. It is definitely prefera-
ble, in my opinion, that such underlying views be open and explicit,
rather than covert and implicit." (13:199) Rogers' insistence upon
as much neutrality as possible has been a helpful research technique
and allowed him and his associates to see deeply into the inner
dynamics of the self. From his research there is ample evidence that
the self, when free from threat or attack, is able to consider "hitherto

rejected perceptions, to make new differentiations and to reintegrate the self in such a way as to include them." (12:365) Rogers' method seems honestly to help the person change. ". . . as changes occur in the perception of self and in the perception of reality, changes occur in the behavior." (12:363) The fact that persons often integrate their lives on levels that are not ultimately satisfactory but which only give the illusion of well-being must now be faced by Rogers and others.

II. ATTEMPTS TO CLARIFY THE RELATIONSHIP OF BASIC PHILOSOPHY TO COUNSELING

One of the most powerful attempts to do away with philosophical relativism has been made by the humanistic psychotherapist and author, Erich Fromm, in his several writings, especially in *The Sane Society*. Fromm seeks to establish a solid foundation for the development of mental health for all men in whatever society. He observes that man has not only physiological and anatomical commonalities but that he is governed universally by certain basic psychic factors as well. His system of right and wrong is therefore built squarely upon whether or not man as man, in his essential being, is having his basic human needs fulfilled.

Fromm's inclusion in his list of basic needs of the necessity for a "frame of orientation and devotion" has led him to be most sympathetic toward the insights of the great religions and philosophies of the past and present. He is sensitive also to the moral standards propagated in our varying societies, because he believes that whole cultures can become full of *defects* which can and do tend to make men mentally ill. Societal arrangements, therefore, often must be changed before man's needs can be met. This observation forces counselors to be concerned with social, political, and religious philosophies which have created and are sustaining, often, such unhealthy social structures.

Fromm's theory is an attempt to build on what man's needs are *objectively* and not on what man *feels* his needs to be. This concept challenges in many ways the goal of non-directive counseling which tends to center on the process of man's expression of his inner feelings of need without reference to the fact that such needs are often a result of cultural defects which will not and cannot bring ultimate health to the client. This is true because of the very nature of his human condition, and the breadth of his needs which are in the area of ultimate loyalties and basic, undergirding frames of orientation, about which most counselors feel insecure and from which discussions they tend to steer clear!

A similar trend to that of Fromm's can be seen in the writings of Kurt Lewin. He stated as far back as 1935 that, "The individual psychical experiences, the actions and emotions, purposes, wishes and hopes, are rather embedded in quite definite psychical structures, spheres of the personality, and whole process." (8:54)

Also to be found in Fromm and Lewin thought is an emphasis on man's freedom and the necessity to broaden the range of that freedom in psychotherapy as well as in intelligent political action. Lewin observed that often the individual area of freedom is very small due to the vectors and forces in his field of psychic experience, built on past identifications, inhibitions and loyalties. Yet, this freedom existed. Man as man had qualities beyond the realm of the animal. Therapy should help man use his freedom to find the paths to growth, and to overcome the psychic barriers.

One of the most dramatic and controversial attempts to deal with the question of philosophy in psychotherapy has been made by Dr. Viktor E. Frankl, the Director of the Neurological Polyclinic in Vienna and a Professor of Psychiatry at the University of Vienna. Frankl's point of view grows out of the emphasis in existentialist philosophy on man's actual conditions of existence. Man in his essence is endowed with certain capacities for freedom, for decision making, for determining his destiny. Man is a responsible being with the power to transcend his own situation and to prophesy the results of his decisions. His intellectual powers and his psychic powers are qualitatively different than other animals. Frankl joins Fromm, at this point, in that he is seeking to analyze man's basic need for a value system on which he can base his decisions, as a result of which he will increase his freedom and his meaning.

He recognizes the significance of both individual psychology, stemming from Adler, and psychoanalysis, stemming from Freud. He maintains, however, that psychotherapy will be incomplete until man has a "psychotherapy of the mind" which deals with philosophical issues. Differing with Freud and others, he says, "The individual's philosophical attitude is part and parcel of his psychological one and emerges in every case." (6:34) He also believes, against the stream of thought in psychotherapy, that, "In no case should the intellectual problems of a person be written off as a 'symptom.'" (6:33)

Frankl honestly discusses the many profound problems related to his point of view, and pushes ahead, along with Fromm, to establish certain fundamental values inherent in man's situation. And yet, he maintains that existential analysis must not interfere with the ranking of values. ". . . what values he elects is and remains the patient's own affair. Existential analysis must not be concerned with what the patient decides for, what goals he sets himself, but only that he decides at all. . . . The physician should never be allowed to take over the patient's responsibility; he must never permit that responsibility to be shifted to himself; he must never anticipate decisions or impose them upon the patient. His job is to make it possible for the patient to reach decisions; he must endow the patient with the capacity for deciding." (6:270)

Such a view has been given great impetus by the philosophical writings of Martin Buber. Buber's philosophy urges man to relationships of trust with other men—very much like that between the counselor and the client in a permissive setting; and yet, he believes that real trust must allow and encourage honest *dialogue* between both parties. When there is a real meeting of persons (Buber describes this meeting in terms of an I—Thou relationship —very similar to Schweitzer's "reverence for life" concept) each person is bringing his full self to the dialogue. He must "be willing . . . to say what is really in his mind about the subject of conversation. And that means further that on each occasion he makes the contribution of his spirit without reduction and without shifting ground." (4:112)

Dialogue on a philosophical level, on the level of the quest for ultimate meaning, is a basic need for every human being. The counselor must be sensitive, nevertheless, to the existential situation in which the client finds himself at any given time.

Gordon Allport emphasizes the profundity of this renewed interest in studying the basic conditions of man's existence. He says, "Existentialism calls for a doctrine of an active intellect, for more emphasis upon propriate functions, including self-objectification and oriented becoming. In particular it calls for a wider and fresher view of anxiety, of courage, and of freedom. (1:80) Allport stresses the fact that Freud and his followers have dealt mostly with the anxiety in man aroused by feelings of guilt and fear of punishment and not at all the anxiety which comes from a fear of *nonbeing* (death—either actual or psychological, in the Buber sense of being not in relation; not affirmed and confirmed by others).

Allport believes that the consideration of philosophical matters has been greatly de-emphasized in counseling, to the detriment of our whole concept of personality structure. Philosophic and religious decisions have to do with what he terms *Intentional Characteristics* which become a part of the personality. He believes that, "Intentional characteristics represent above all else the individual's primary modes of addressing himself to the future. As such they select stimuli, guide inhibitions and choices, and have much to do with the process of adult becoming. Relatively few theories of personality recognize the pre-emptive importance of intentional characteristics." (1:89)

So, we are seeing a powerful movement within the guidance field, psychotherapy, philosophy, theology, and psychology for a deeper view of man's problems of existence, his wide and deep needs, his essential freedom of being, and his finite situation which forces him to go beyond knowledge to an ultimate devotion—built on faith (not an irrational faith, but faith, nonetheless).

Buber, in his William Alanson White Lectures given at the Washington School of Psychiatry, says that the counselor or educator "cannot wish to impose himself, for he believes in the effect of the actualizing forces. . . . The propagandist who imposes himself, does not really believe even in his own cause, for he does not trust it to attain the effect of its own power, without his special methods." (4:111) While Buber believes so strongly in the power of honest meeting between persons in an I—Thou relationship of mutual trust and confirmation, even with differences of loyalties, he is very *cautious about the right of the psychotherapist* to embark upon a "treatment of the essential in man." He agrees with the late Viktor von Weizsaecker who said that it is not the privilege of the therapist or counselor to deal with the final destiny of man.

Returning to the area of guidance and student personnel services, it is becoming equally well established that basic educational philosophy does inevitably influence the procedures of the guidance counselor. If he is thoroughly pragmatic in his orientation he will probably be inclined to play down or ignore the importance of religious or metaphysical beliefs that the student brings to the counseling situation. He may feel that value judgments must be left out of the considerations. Of course, with this Pragmatic Philosophy which seems on the surface to be a neutral position, goes a basic commitment just as much so as the student may have, with his religious commitment. It seems to us that considerations of ultimate values cannot be avoided by the counselor as a person, and that he must operate from some philosophical point of view—some form of Idealism, Realism (Christian or otherwise), Pragmatism, Naturalism, or Existentialism (again religious or otherwise).

It seems imperative that guidance counselors and educators must join other leaders in education, psychology, psychotherapy, philosophy and religion in doing basic research in this field.

In this spirit of scientific inquiry (even with its obvious limitations in the area of ultimate values) and also in the spirit of dialogue (with free discussion of important questions related to man's basic needs and his basic conditions of existence) we should proceed to clarify and come to decisions about the foundation and goals of counseling.

Recently, Williamson has stated that, "I have further argued for making explicit our own value orientations as individual counselors, not in order that we may adopt a counselor's orthodox creed, but rather that we may responsibly give societal and moral direction to our individual work in terms of the explicitly desired goals chosen by our student clients." (19:528)

When guidance counselors, psychotherapists, or religious counselors admit that they are not philosophically neutral, then we will be able to study more systematically the effect of our philosophical loyalties upon our counseling.

BIBLIOGRAPHY

1. Allport, Gordon W. *Becoming: Basic Considerations For a Psychology of Personality.* Yale University Press. 1955.
2. Arbuckle, Dugald S. *Student Personnel Services in Higher Education.* McGraw-Hill. N. Y. 1953.
3. Arbuckle, Dugald S. *Teacher Counseling.* Addison-Wesley Press. Cambridge, Mass.
4. Buber, Martin. "William Alanson White Memorial Lectures." *Psychiatry* No. 20, No. 2, May 1957.
5. Buber, Martin. "The Teacher and Teaching"—compiled by Dr. Ross Snyder, Univ. of Chicago. Unpublished form.
6. Frankl, Viktor E. *The Doctor and the Soul.* Alfred Knopf. N. Y. 1955.
7. Fromm, Erich. *The Sane Society.* Rinehart & Co. N. Y. 1955.
8. Lewin, Kurt. *A Dynamic Theory of Personality.* McGraw-Hill Co. New York. 1935.
9. Mathewson, Robert H. *Guidance Policy and Practice.* Harper and Bros. New York. 1955.
10. Oates, Wayne E. *The Religious Dimensions of Personality.* Assoc. Press. N. Y. 1957.
11. Pepinsky, Harold B. and Pepinsky, Pauline N. *Counseling: Theory and Practice.* New York: The Ronald Press Company. 1954.
12. Rogers, Carl. Some Observations on the Organization of Personality." *The American Psychologist.* Vol. 2. 1947.
13. Rogers, Carl. "A Note on the Nature of Man." *Journal of Counseling Psychology.* Vol. 4. No. 3. 1957.
14. Strang, Ruth. *The Role of the Teacher in Personnel Work.* 4th ed. 1953.
15. Tillich, Paul. *Systematic Theology.* Vol. 1. University of Chicago Press. 1952.
16. Vordenberg, Wesley. "The Impact of Personal Philosophies on Counseling." *The Personnel and Guidance Journal.* XXXI. April 1953.
17. Walker, Donald and Peiffer, Herbert. "The Goals of Counseling." *Journal of Counseling Psychology.* Vol. 4. No. 3. 1957.
18. Weitz, Henry. "Counseling as a Function of the Counselor's Personality." *The Personnel and Guidance Journal.* Vol. XXXV. No. 5. January 1957.
19. Williamson, Edmond G. "Value Orientation in Counseling." *The Personnel and Guidance Journal.* XXXVI. April 1958.

35. VALUE SYSTEMS AND THE THERAPEUTIC INTERVIEW

David Wayne Smith

The Importance of Value Systems in Therapy

There seems to be a rather well defined, yet seldom discussed, need for counselors and guidance workers to devote considerable attention to the *value system* inter-play and conflict functioning within the boundaries of the therapeutic interview.

In play-backs of therapeutic interviews, for example, Rogers (3) recognized evidences of the value system of the individual. Such evidences seemed to appear in what the counselees perceived as "good" or "bad," "right" or "wrong," "satisfactory" or "unsatisfactory." Rogers indicated this aspect of therapy to be one not frequently discussed, and thus barely touched from a research point of view.

Definition

The *value system* of the individual is best described as a multifactor spiral or behavioral bias which molds and dominates the decision making power of the particular person. Various external forces are constantly influencing the developing value system of the individual, and include: cultural background, educational level, economic security, family's religion, social status, varying community forces, and family ties.

It has also been demonstrated that the innate nature of the individual will affect every phase of his behavior. Studies have shown adolescents, for example, to express great concern over such matters as underweight or overweight, physical stature, and appearance. (1)

Reprinted by permission of the author and *The School Counselor*, VII, No. 2 (December, 1959), 23-28. Copyright 1959 by The American School Counselor Association.

WHAT ARE VALUES?

Values seem to depend for stability or instability on beliefs. Individual beliefs are of two origins: in reference to what is or was; and to what ought to be or ought to have been. The first of these is usually referred to as *facts;* the second as valuations, judgements, or opinions.

Individuals develop values according to the rules of conduct in a given society. These rules are most generally accepted to involve the two kinds of beliefs previously discussed. Because of the peculiar values of the people who make up our society, and the tendency for persons to be more uninformed, there is often a great deal of conflict existent in any given culture. Human conduct is therefore occasionally illogical, causing individuals to make decisions based on uncritical thinking.

THE MEANINGS AND FUNCTIONS OF A VALUE SYSTEM

A value system is often referred to as an interdependent, mutually adjusted, and consistent set of rules. This, of course, represents an ideal, and because of the crush of living amidst the complexities of culture, no rules of conduct of any actual culture have ever conformed exactly to this ideal. According to Smith, Stanley, and Shores, (4) the functions of the value system are: (1) It supplies the individual with a sense of purpose and direction; (2) It gives the group a common orientation and supplies the basis of individual action and of unified, collective action; (3) It serves as the basis of judging the behavior of individuals; (4) It enables the individual to know what to expect of others as well as how to conduct himself; and (5) It fixes the sense of right and wrong, fair and foul, desirable and undesirable, moral and immoral.

The value system serves these functions only to the degree that its rules are mutually adjusted and compatible. If new rules are introduced that are in direct contrast to the old ones, and a *conflict* is thereby evoked, future behavior may be marked by confusion and conflict.

Early in the therapeutic process the person is observed living largely by values he has introjected from others, from his personal cultural environment. Rogers (3) has given some examples of the values stated or implied by clients and has placed in parenthesis the source of these values.

> "I should never be angry at anyone" (because my parents and church regard anger as wrong).
>
> "I should always be a loving mother" (because any other attitude is unacceptable in my middle class group).
>
> "I should be successful in my courses" (because my parents count on my success).
>
> "I have no homosexual impulses, which is very bad" (according to our whole culture).
>
> "I should be sexless" (because my mother seems to regard sex as wicked and out of place for any right-minded person).
>
> "I should be completely casual about sex behavior" (because my sophisticated friends have this attitude).

Development of a *stable* system of values seems to depend largely on the kinds of choices the individual is able to make. The nature of these is also extremely important to the future adjustment of the person. This process can also be observed in therapeutic interviews, since "as therapy progresses, the client comes to realize the dimensions of the standards governing his behavior, reaching a point in the process where he can actually see the forces shaping his life." (3)

VALUE SYSTEMS AND SECURITY

Assessment of the individual's decision making ability reveals considerable reliance on that which will guarantee protection to his security. And, since persons tend to be most secure in what is most intimately theirs—such as body, ideas, and family—the expression of this security through the various roles one chooses to assume in a complex living situation could well reflect *clues* to the individual's value system.

These diverse personifications, functioning within the individual, also specify the virtues, feeling, attitudes, and personality traits proper to the particular value system. Rogers (3) has observed that as therapy progresses the client comes to realize that he has not been his real self; and tends to be less and less satisfied with his situation. Rogers has observed a period of apparent confusion and uncertainty wherein the client attempts to relinquish *introjected* values. Also, a certain sense of insecurity in having no basis for judging what is "good" or "bad," "right" or "wrong."

IMPLICATIONS FOR COUNSELING

Where the counselor seeks to control the introjection of his own value system into the therapeutic process, every reasonable attempt must be made to understand this phenomenon, and the needs and values promoting this kind of behavior. Thus, when the high school youngster announces to the counselor his plans to leave school in order to enter the armed forces, the counselor needs to exercise considerable caution in order to avoid a *fixed* response, since this decision could very well reflect a conflict between the values of the counselor and those of the counselee.

A Case in Point: The case of Larry seems to reflect, at least to some extent, the counselor's failure to consider the value system of the counselee. Larry had been referred to the counselor because of his apparent failure in commercial mathematics. The following was the counselor's summary of the interview with the boy.

> Following a brief introductory exchange, Larry states he does not like Miss Bates, his mathematics teacher. She fails to put across the subject, and he blames his failure in math on the fact that he does not like her. In spite of this conflict with Miss Bates, Larry feels that he gets along all right with his other instructors.
>
> Larry's scholastic record is not impressive. He has several grades of 5 (failure). His test scores of mental ability put him at about the 45th percentile. As to the future, he says he thinks he will attend the University. I doubt whether he has actually *thought* about it. There is little evidence to indicate this lad has given any thought at all to the future. When I asked him about possible alternative plans for his future, he was very vague. He stated he might try some kind of mechanical work. He is in the Naval Reserve and may enter the regular Navy.
>
> When it was apparent that he had no definite ideas about entering the world of work, I asked him if he thought he could carry university level courses in light of his mediocre high school record.

He stated that he hadn't thought about it, but supposed he should. When asked what his goals were in terms of college, he said he didn't know, and wondered if I had any suggestions. I asked him if he had looked at the University catalogue. When he replied that he had not, I advised him to look at the catalogue in order to see what interested him, and also told him he could get a personal copy, or find one in the school library.

I asked him what he would like to be doing five years hence provided everything went as he liked. To this question he was momentarily taken back, and it was obvious he had not looked that far into the future.

The unskillful handling of this interview reflects the counselor's tendency to assume a *judicial* attitude, not giving the counselee any responsibility to express his concepts, ideas, and feelings. The counselor's failure to construct a *permissive* atmosphere was also a violation of a basic therapeutic principle.

Interpretation of human behavior can be based on three factors: *goal*, or what a person wants or intends to do; *confronting situation*, or what he will be likely to meet in proceeding toward the attainment of the goal; and *insight*, the way he sees or sizes up the situation which confronts him. A deeper appreciation of value system interplay and conflict seems to stem from a better understanding of the *cues* observed by the counselor in the behavioral process. Insight into the counselee's goal directed efforts depends largely upon the counselor's willingness to develop an empathic feeling for the counselee's *plight*. The counselor must seek to construct an environment that will help the counselee to increase his self-percepts. The effect of such a climate might well lead to a more systematic release of the individual's perceptions in the satisfaction of his most pressing needs or goals. The counselee must not see a personal threat to his self-concept in the therapeutic interview.

Since individuals are known to respond to certain *cues* in the expressions of the feelings of others, in a therapeutic interview this principle will involve the counselor. In considering the needs and values which seasoned the high school youngster's decision to leave school in favor of the military service, the counselor must and often rather quickly, be able to explore alternative possibilities within the cognitive framework of the counselee's decision making powers.

This will also be true in the case of the boy who thought his failure in mathematics stemmed from his dislike for the teacher.

The counselor's failure to consider the numerous feasible perceptual factors inherent in a counselee's decisions, increases all too often his tendency to accept the counselee's judgment only in so far as it seems to parallel his own. There would be greater evidences of this in those cases were the therapeutic process to extend beyond a single interview. Hypothetically, then, as the counselee's problem takes on increased dimensions and becomes more complex, there is a corresponding need for the counselor to exert a good deal of caution in order to be able to more adequately handle the phenomenon of value system conflict and interplay.

In actual practice, many counselors fail to consider the power of their own *goal-directed* behavior to unduly influence the direction of the interview. Such practices minimize the chances for effective therapeutic counseling. Such blunders also run the risk of slanting the content of the counseling process to a point where it becomes *counselor-centered,* resulting in a loss of perspective.

METHODS FOR APPRAISING VALUE SYSTEMS IN COUNSELORS

It might prove helpful were those engaged in the selection and training of counselors to find some method or technique for value system appraisal. The development of such devices might serve to increase the insight of both the selector and the selectee into the desirability of the prospective counselor continuing in training.

Checklists. In an attempt to determine types of errors most likely to be made by beginning counselors, Robinson (2) designed a checklist. Robinson discovered that the beginning counselor's biggest difficulty seems to be a tendency to take too much responsibility. Other ranking obstacles were: not giving the counselee responsibility; talking too much; asking too many questions; being judicial; being authoritarian; and engaging in too much structuring. Beginning counselors often "get involved," possibly feeling that it will be a reflection on their ability if they do not produce results.

Tape Recorder. Careful consideration should be given to the tape recorder and its value as a selection and training device. The assessment of the individual's concepts, ideas, and feelings during the course of the interview is extremely difficult, particularly to the unskilled counselor. A permanent taped record permits a review of the influences which shaped the decision-making powers of the individual during the course of the therapeutic interview. Rogers (3) has attested the merits of the tape recorder, and its use can be extremely valuable for class purposes. In the play-back of an interview, either with the trainee or the class, such factors as interplay, conflict, direction, dominance, and other reflections become rather apparent.

Use of the tape recorder as a training device has many additional advantages, and frequent users have expressed a good deal of satisfaction with its flexibility, adaptability, and all around good results. Recording tape is also rather inexpensive, durable, and can be used over and over again with little if any loss in quality.

Conclusions

The dearth of research and the failure of texts to adequately treat the subject of value system interplay and conflict, leaves much to be desired. Counselor trainers must seek to develop devices to them in the training of counselors to more adequately with the problem of conflict and interplay. Since there are no short-cut scales or superficial standardized tests available for assessing the person's value system, the guidance worker faces an extremely difficult task.

Bibliography

1. Elias, L. J., "High School Youth Look At Their Problems" *Agricultural Experimental Station Publication,* State College of Washington, 1947.
2. Robinson, Francis P., *Principles and Procedures in Student Counseling,* Harper & Brothers Publishing Company, 1950, pp. 155-160.
3. Rogers, Carl, *Client-Centered Therapy,* Houghton-Mifflin Company, New York, 1951, pp. 149-151.
4. Smith, B. O., Stanley, William O., and Shores, J. Harlan, *Fundamentals of Curriculum Development,* New York, World Book Company, 1950, Part I, pp. 88-90.

36. VALUE COMMITMENTS AND COUNSELING

E. G. Williamson

As counterpoint for my discussion of some aspects of value commitment to be achieved through counseling relationships, I want to make two relevant points. First, I am a practical administrator, dedicated to the improvement of program content and techniques of varied services for students. But I am also increasingly motivated to explore the relevancy to such a program of services of consciously determined end-goals that are moral and societal in direction and force. In contrast, as I will argue, the development of counseling in American schools has centered largely, if not exclusively, upon the vocational development of the individual. While this is all to the good, I believe it is now high time that we expand the content and emphases of our counseling to embrace additional objectives, thereby immediately involving the counselor in students' efforts to select and attach themselves to value commitments which give direction and force to their lives, especially at the crucial stages of early development.

A second counterpoint does not vibrate in the same phase with the first one. Nevertheless, it is a hard fact that the climate of opinion surrounding public education today is not always sympathetic and hopeful as to the relevance of counseling in the educational enterprise. We are accustomed now to the public acceptance, pioneered by Mr. Conant, concerning the strategic importance of counseling for certain phases of the national emergency. But there are critics on the left who thunder and hiss in ways which are not only irritating but perhaps undermining of public confidence in our efforts. Howard Mumford Jones (8) is one such who has characterized guidance services in American education in these words:

Reprinted by permission of the author and *Teachers College Record*, LXII, No. 8 (May, 1961), 602-8.

Portions of this paper were used in an address to a conference in Chicago, Ill., during September, 1959, of Directors of Guidance Institutes sponsored by the US Office of Education under the National Defense Education Act.

> Today we do not cut the leading strings, we merely lengthen them.
> It is not true that an American lad cannot make a significant mis-
> take . . . but it is true to say that an entire battery of adjustors
> is happily at work to see that his mistakes shall never, never harm
> him.

SOME HISTORY

My use of these two points as counterpoint will be evident as my
discussion proceeds. Let me first characterize briefly the short history
of counseling and guidance in our high schools and colleges. In 1909,
Frank Parsons published the first systematic treatment of organized
counseling as we now know it in American schools. Possibly because
of his civic and political mindedness and possibly because of his
interest in unemployed youth, he centered his organized system of
counseling largely upon the choice of an occupation through analysis and comparison of capabilities and opportunities. The strategic
importance of finding the "correct" occupation lay in its prevention
of discouragement and failure in subsequent work. His famous
formulation still stands today as the basic framework of much of
our thinking: (a) Analyze your capabilities; (b) analyze the opportunities and requirements of work, and (c) compare the two sets of
information.

Subsequently, Kitson centered upon simplification of the first step,
a self-analysis or diagnosis of interests and capabilities through self-
appraisal. Elsewhere and meanwhile, since World War I, other psychologists have been busily constructing objective tests designed to
appraise capabilities, techniques not available to Parsons and his
immediate followers. Parallel efforts were also made to define the
requirements of various types of work in the same units of capabilities as were measured by objective tests, thus describing jobs in
terms of required capabilities as a method of making information
readily available for Parson's comparisons of two basic sets of information.

At the present time, Super (16) and Roe (14) are each adding
further refinements to the counseling process of comparing two sets
of information. Super is defining the third step (comparison) in

terms of states of development as the individual seeks to find a role in the world of work congenial and appropriate to his self-concept of capabilities and aspirations. Roe is applying certain psychoanalytic concepts to the choice process and to the search for a proper occupational fitting. Roe's formulation particularly is readily recognized as an extension and adaptation of Parson's formulation in terms of a psychoanalytic elaboration of the role of man's psychological "needs" in determining the type of work and the type of adult living that an individual chooses. To adopt for our use Wheelis's (19) title, counseling is a way of facilitating man's quest for identity, his striving for self-understanding and the expression of his aspirations. Such borrowing of concepts from the psychotherapist adds ideas of drive and dynamism to the aptitudes and abilities which the psychologist identifies through objective tests.

And currently, counseling is being further modified by borrowing other techniques and concepts from psychotherapy in establishing types of interview relationships quite different from those of decades ago, in which an inventory and assessment of the individual's capabilities were reported to him so that he might better understand what he was capable of doing before he chose a life objective. The counseling interview, generally rather than only in psychotherapy, is now perceived as a type of human relationship (warm, friendly, empathic), through which a person learns to perceive himself as he actually is and to live with and accept himself with all his faults and shortcomings as well as his positive capabilities and potentialities. Thus, his comprehension of himself is enlarged and made more accurate and more useful.

Still another modification of Parson's formulation is evident today. Through an interdisciplinary approach to appraising man, we are learning new insights from cultural anthropology, sociology, and other social sciencies. As Herberg (6) says, we now see that "the human self emerges only in community and has no real existence apart from it"; only through interdependence and one's social relationships is the full individual developed. Not by isolated individualism, but through interdependency in the human community does an individual achieve full understanding and optimum development.

THE PROBLEM OF INFLUENCE

Against this background, Conant's (1) support of the concept of guidance, however welcome as encouraging acceptance, seems undesirably centered (although not exclusively so) on the strategic role of counselors in identifying those students who possess high academic talent. Somehow or other, we are now expected to use counseling methods for the purpose of enrolling students in the difficult academic subjects of high school, including languages and sciences, with the expectation that these students will then be stimulated to enroll in college to fulfill the societal objective of increasing trained manpower of high intellectual capacities. The over-riding societal need and crisis today seems to be Conant's justification for using counselors for such a purpose. In other words, our momentous conflict with Russia, with the possibility if not probability of nuclear warfare, is held to justify assignment to the counselor of this kind of "recruiting" function for those specialties needed in that conflict.

Now there are certain aspects of this assignment which have a bearing on the topic of counseling and value commitment. For example, freedom of choice as a part of American democratic education has been a cardinal doctrine of the American pattern of counseling, as opposed to the method of sheer assignment as practiced in some countries and during certain periods of economic development, and in contrast with the still earlier system of the "inheritance" of one's occupational choice from one's parents. To be sure, I do not read Mr. Conant's statements in any respect as advocating a denial of this freedom of choice. Nevertheless, in the stress of the years ahead, counselors will be evaluated in terms of the expectation that a higher percentage of students of high ability will enroll in the more difficult college preparatory subjects. And it is to safeguard them from such a crude evaluation that I wish to restate certain aspects of the counselors' role in the cultivation of value commitments on the part of students.

I believe that there are legitimate, proper, and sound ways for counselors to "influence," *but not to determine,* the value commitments adopted by students, included those involved in choosing to enroll in colleges. I shall proceed on this line of reasoning. I am using the term *value commitments* rather loosely to indicate those principles, interests, beliefs, and guidelines which influence an individual's behavior over his developmental span of life. In his recent book, *The Stages of Economic Growth,* Walt Whitman Rostow (15) refers to a similar concept of the function of choices in the broader society:

> The process of growth poses for men and society certain problems and possibilities from which they must choose, and modern history can be viewed as the consequences of choices made by various societies at various stages of growth.

Since society's choices are those made by man, our own use of this concept in exploring the choices made in and through counseling relationships closely resembles that of Rostow.

THE COMMITMENTS

The value commitments "chosen" by an individual at different stages of development are not "rules of conduct" in the narrow sense, but rather in the sense of large-scale philosophic guidelines and emphases.[1] They are not so much a moral code or a set of prohibitions, but seminal concepts and goals and the larger value systems that one almost unconsciously develops through living and—sometimes—through critical thinking.

I need not argue that counselors are not by any means "neutral"— nor have they ever been—with respect to the pattern or content of their students' development. We have had some ill-informed discussion of the supposed neutrality of the counselor, but careful analysis reveals that counselors do influence students, as do parents and teachers, with respect to the kinds of lives they live. But for the counselor, it is a broad based pattern of influence, and by no means does it interfere with the right of the student to choose his own life style and pattern. Let me further illustrate the concept of values

---

[1] While I am not clear in my understanding of the role in counseling relationships of religious, theological, and ethical beliefs, I do *not* believe that counseling is equivalent to or identical with evangelism or a search for adherents to such systematized and ordered beliefs which express and are the formulations of value commitments.

that lies behind my discussion. Harold Taylor (18) referred to value commitments, some of which no doubt eventuate from counseling relationships:

> The desire to become intellectually independent, socially useful, informed, mature, and sensitive to aesthetic values . . . is seldom an aim which the student consciously holds. It is the function of the educator to help the student to develop those qualities, whether or not he first comes to college to achieve them. Otherwise, we have the constant reflection in our institutions of the value patterns of the society in which they exist.

A second illustration of the type of value commitments I consider relevant to counseling is contained in a statement by the British scientist, Karl Pearson (11), a half century ago: "the first demand of the state upon the individual is not for self-sacrifice, but for self-development." For many decades, this philosophic value system centered counselors' attention upon the realization or actualization of the individual's potentiality. But Jacob's (7) recent studies indicated a blind spot in this philosophic system in that concentration of the individual upon developing his own potentiality could, and in many cases did, encourage and aid him in developing "unabashed self-centeredness." Kinkead (9) identified a second example of the destructive effects of too much self-centeredness in the case of the defecting G.I. prisoners in North Korean prison camps. To be sure, not all forms of self-centeredness are necessarily "bad," although I would remind you of Herberg's contention that "personality develops only in community." On the other hand, we don't want to become the Organization Man in the pattern of the Soviet requirement that "one of the main responsibilities of the group leader in the Soviet Union is to see to it that his pupils become good members of the collective" (4).

While we wish to avoid too much togetherness, which stifles individuality, we also seek to avoid that form of extreme individualism which leads to deterioration of society and the loss of full development for all its members. John Dewey stated the proposition of *dual,* as opposed to antagonistic, obligations in these words: "If democracy has moral and ideal meaning, it is that a social return be demanded from all and that opportunity for development of distinctive capacities be afforded all" (2).

We hope and confidently expect, therefore, that the counseling relationship will contribute to that self-fulfillment which also embraces a measure of aid to others. The technique and process of these dual value commitments are as yet largely unexplored, in part because of our tradition in counseling of avoiding any imposition of value commitments upon the individual.

SOVEREIGNTY OF REASON

But a second type of value commitment to be achieved through the counseling relationship is perhaps more readily acceptable, especially to counselors with a sensitive desire to avoid interference with the individual's self-development. This value commitment pervades the entire educational enterprise. For centuries Western education has presupposed the value commitment of students to the sovereignty of reason. Muller (10) has defined the role of this commitment in these words:

> A rational person is not merely one who has good habits or right principles, but one who knows what he believes and assumes the intellectual and moral responsibilities of his beliefs.

How can the counseling process and the counseling relationship influence students to believe in and to practice the sovereignty of reason? One prior step is clear: Counselors must themselves be perceived as deeply committed to the intellectual goals of the school. We are appropriately reminded by the Carnegie Trustees (3) that "all high performance takes place in a framework of expectation—particularly in youth. . . . At every level we must create the framework of expectations within which young people will come to assume that high performance is an important goal." And the Trustees conclude, "The schools can do much to create the context of values in which intellectual achievement is valued."

But, to our dismay, the Trustees express a doubtful opinion concerning counselors:

> It is unfortunately true that some who prepare for careers as school counselors have little in the way of intellectual interests . . . and we see that sometimes in college there was too little training to

stimulate that interest. It is all too easy for such individuals to devote their time to the social work aspects of the job, to the "problem child," and to the child with non-academic interests. These
are important parts of any counselor's work, but they must not
crowd out attention to the academically talented student.

These are indeed critical characterizations of counselors. We need
to ask if they are justified by counseling practices. May it not be
true that in our understandable and sympathetic concern for the
affective development of students and their healthy participation
in activities that we have underemphasized things intellectual? I, for
one, have found in the literature of counseling very, very little reference to intellectualism and to the sovereignty of reason. And, in fact,
I can buttress my argument that the two dominant emphases of
counseling in the last half century have been vocational choice and
preparation, on the one hand, and the development of normal affect
on the other. Perhaps this is but a reflection of the *Zeitgeist* of
American culture with its dominant emphasis upon material success
and "pleasurism." Whatever the fact, our students, I believe, deserve
special encouragement from both teachers and counselors within a
climate of respect for things intellectual. Surely, this is a value
commitment that we can morally suggest to students for their
evaluation and commitment. Surely, as counselors in educational institutions, we can not hesitate to "influence" students to commit
themselves to a value system in which the intellectual life is dominant. And as educators, we must not be "neutral" about the value
of rationality and the intellect.

VALUES AND GROWTH

For me, the fear of imposition, with its associated posture of neutrality, about student value commitments is a false fear. If it is
ethical to use counseling methods to induce students to want to live
a life of rationality and to use whatever academic abilities they
possess, then it is also ethical to induce students to want to live a
life of "good" conduct rather than a life of delinquency. The moral
principle and the ethics of counseling are identical in the two different situations. But since counselors are academic in their philosophic outlook, they are hesitant to impose upon students behavior-

influencing values associated with conduct, although they rarely hesitate to persuade students to expect high intellectual attainments of themselves. But I, for one, believe that, as educators, we counselors must re-examine our counseling relationships to make certain that we are using those relationships to encourage students to pursue excellence (13) in *all* things, in *all* aspects of their lives. Harold Taylor (17) said that "by and large, students do the things that are expected of them." I believe that if we come to expect "good" behavior and high intellectual excellence on the part of students, most of them will live up to such expectations.

In short, the value commitments that are legitimately objectives of counseling in an educational institution are the full dimensions of human beings. Gould (5) characterized this function of education itself in these words:

> We must have institutions which will hunger after the answers to the Socratic questions of life, the truly crucial questions which ask again and again what is *Good* and *True* and *Beautiful* and *Just* and *Pious*. . . . Out of such answers develop the quality and pattern of man's life and his dignity as a human being.

Like all generalized ideals, the vagueness of these permits diversity of individualized application in patterns of attainment or the concrete details of living. They are not narrow, parochial, and stifling dogma; they are, rather, growth-producing incentives in the development of human potentiality.

Although we have concentrated for the past half century on this fulfillment of the individual's potentiality, we have not covered the full range of that potentiality as charted in the Rockefeller Report (13):

> We believe that man—by virtue of his humanity—should live in the light of reason, exercise the right of moral responsibility, and be free to develop to the full the talents that are in him.

Similarly, President Pusey's (12) characterization of this high mission of influencing the value commitments of students is congenially stated in these words: "The teacher's special job is to nurture in young people the desire to extend themselves, and to help them, with their minds and wills, to grow beyond competence into full humanity."

Concern for others, the pursuit of excellence in all things, the sovereignty of rationality, and the search for full humanity certainly offer a wide exploration of value commitments to be achieved through the counseling relationship. I believe that the future counselor will explore such a broadening enlargement of his functions and will reappraise his usefulness in the student's search for full humanity, for becoming a human being in his rich potentiality. I believe, also, that we will add to the search for job competence and the full understanding of one's self-concept a full commitment to value systems which are growth producing, both to the individual and to his associates, as an additional dimension of the adequate personality. Lastly, it seems to me that, if we are to enlarge the functions of guidance in the *student's* search beyond competence for full humanity, then we counselors must re-examine our own lives to make certain that we, too, are engaged in a life-long quest for the same goal.

REFERENCES

1. Conant, J. B. *The modern American high school.* New York: McGraw-Hill, 1959.
2. Dewey, J. Why he selected democracy and America. In Burnett, W. (Ed.) *This is my best.* New York: Dial Press, 1942.
3. *Education of the academically talented.* New York: Carnegie Foundation for the Advancement of Teaching, 1959.
4. Gass, Gertrude Z. The foreign scene in guidance: H. Guidance in Russia. *Personnel Guid. J.,* 1959, **38,** 34-39.
5. Gould, S. B. *Knowledge is not enough: Views of higher education.* Yellow Springs, Ohio: Antioch Press, 1959.
6. Herberg, W. Freud, religion, and social reality. *Commentary.* 1957, **23,** 277-84.
7. Jacob, P. *Changing values in college.* New York: Harper, 1957.
8. Jones, H. M. Undergraduate on apron strings. *Atlantic Mon.,* 1955, **196,** 45-48.
9. Kinkead, E. *In every war but one.* New York: Norton, 1959.
10. Muller, H. J. *The uses of the past.* New York: Mentor Books, 1952.
11. Pearson, K. *The grammar of science.* London: Adam and Charles Black, 1892.
12. Pusey, N. M. The exploding world of education. *Fortune,* 1955, **52,** 96-7.

13. *Pursuit of excellence: Education and the future of America.* Special Studies Project Report No. 5. Rockefeller Brothers Fund. Garden City, N. Y.: Doubleday, 1958.

14. Roe, Anne. *The psychology of occupations.* New York: Wiley, 1956.

15. Rostow, W. W. *The stages of economic growth.* New York: Cambridge Univer. Press, 1960.

16. Super, D. E. *The psychology of careers.* New York: Harper, 1957.

17. Taylor, H. *Essays in teaching.* New York: Harper, 1950.

18. Taylor, H. On the report of the President's commission. *Amer. Scholar,* 1949, **18,** 33-49.

19. Wheelis, A. *The quest for identity.* New York: Norton, 1958.

Section Seven

EVALUATION AND RESEARCH

The study of counseling may proceed singularly or simultaneously on intuitive, experiential, and statistical-experimental lines. When a study is concerned with a specific counseling service or bureau and with assessment in terms of ends theory, the study is usually categorized as *evaluation*. The term *research* seems to be applied to studies of counseling when means theories and the general body of knowledge concerning counseling are the objects of investigation. Obviously, there is no clear-cut distinction between evaluation and research; both have been represented by articles included in this section.

As Thorne suggests in the lead article, there is much to be said in favor of studying the individual case in the building of logically compact, internally consistent theories of counseling. But when these intuitive case methods are used to the exclusion of external validation, counseling practice approaches "charlatanism." Thorne's insightful and incisive examination of the psychoanalytically-oriented psychotherapies, counselee-centered counseling, eclectic (directive) counseling, and disciplinary counseling should serve as an excellent prelude to the remainder of the section.

In addition to the problems of sampling and the dilemma of uniqueness, the development of adequate criterion measures is a persistent problem in researching counseling. Singer and Stefflre's analysis of one criterion, the "self estimate," suggests the problematic nature of one commonly accepted measure of counseling progress.

Not only does this article raise questions concerning the criterion itself but also about those distortions of outcomes which may accrue from statistical treatment and limitations of research design.

In evaluating a counseling service, O'Dea and Zeran used several procedures based upon a polling of opinion of seventy-one prominent members of Division 17 of the American Psychological Association. This procedure represents a departure from the usual practice of developing criterion variables which arise directly from the purposes of the counseling agency. Nonetheless it is interesting to note that the three foremost criteria, based upon the polling of opinion were: (1) counselee satisfaction, (2) counselee understanding of test data, and (3) before and after measures of personality and adjustment. On completing such a self study as this, the problem of the evaluator often becomes "are the criteria to be rejected or is the agency to be modified?"

Merenda and Rothney's outcomes research concerning counseling has been underway for some years. Their findings, although they may be the basis for some optimism concerning the values of counseling, should be interpreted with some caution. The adequacy of design and the standard of 100 per cent follow-up are commendatory; the note of caution is in order because of the absence of evidence concerning the relationship of process variables to the outcomes being investigated. Although this criticism might be leveled at any evaluation which does not study process-outcomes relationships, it seems particularly critical when the counseling being studied falls into the somewhat nebulous category, eclectic.

In conclusion, it should be noted that research about counseling is beset by many problems and limitations; among them are: the restrictions of time and finance, sampling limitations, inadequacy of criteria, the dilemma of uniqueness, and difficulties in instrumentation. None of these limitations is so formidable as to preclude the undertaking of research and evaluation in the public school. As Peters and Mueller point out, there is an increase in research at the secondary school level. Peters and Mueller's review of research also implies that the complexity of the counseling interaction may dictate research which is complex and multi-variant in design.

37. CRITIQUE OF RECENT DEVELOPMENTS IN PERSONALITY COUNSELING THEORY

Frederick C. Thorne

INTRODUCTION

The progress of science would be expedited greatly if the originators of significant contributions would make periodic progress reports concerning their latest thinking about recent developments related to theoretical systems. Much speculative controversy could have been avoided if Freud, Adler, John B. Watson and other theorizers had issued periodic statements bringing their latest viewpoints up-to-date publicly, and particularly where important revisions of earlier viewpoints had occurred. These comments are particularly true of the field of psychotherapy where there is great need for systematically relating and validating a large number of theoretical contributions which too often have not been assimilated into the body of scientifically established facts but have become the foundations of isolated schools or systems. The purpose of this article is to present a critique of personality counseling theory bringing up-to-date our most recent thinking on the subject.

GENERAL REMARKS CONCERNING THEORIZING AND SYSTEM-BUILDING

No one would voluntarily restrict creative theorizing which may supply hypothetical models for lucrative research design. There are definite dangers, however, in applied fields such as psychotherapy when theorizing and system-building far outstrip anything which has been established scientifically so that unvalidated theories are

Reprinted by permission of the author and *Journal of Clinical Psychology*, XIII, No. 3 (July, 1957), 234-44.

given large scale clinical application. It must be emphasized that in psychodiagnosis and psychotherapy, unproven theories and unvalidated practices are in current use far more widely than in any other clinical field. Unlike modern medicine in which schools and cults are practically extinct and where the subject matters consist largely of what has been established scientifically, in the field of psychotherapy we find a large number of competing theoretical systems and schools all being widely applied in the almost complete absence of validation and standardization.

Theory-centeredness may lead to metaphysical and dialectic confusion which actually impedes the forward progress of science. One example of such tendencies exists in the current contents of many psychoanalytic and psychiatric journals of which a formal analysis of topics and methods reveals that 80-90% of the articles are purely speculative or anecdotal in contrast with a content of about 80 or 90% of experimental-statistical studies in basic-science oriented psychological journals. Unending speculative controversy goes on concerning the theoretical implications of even chance remarks made by Freud and other "authorities." The situation is comparable to the centuries-long speculations of the greatest minds of ancient times concerning the nature of the human circulatory system which was settled forever by Harvey's simple empiric observation of the direction of blood flow in the veins by compressing and then releasing pressure on a vein on the back of the hand. The attempt to validate theories *logically* by constructing supposedly comprehensive and consistent systems is obsolete in an era when experimental-statistical validation is possible. It is regrettable that so much time is being currently spent in the attempt to secure respectability for unvalidated clinical methods by relating them to theories which have some systematic prestige.

PSYCHOANALYTICALLY-ORIENTED PSYCHOTHERAPIES

Psychoanalytically-oriented practices probably have the largest current following and prestige in the fields of counseling and psychotherapy, particularly in educational institutions and clinics which are administered by psychoanalysts. Since 1945, the psychiatry departments of several major universities have been taken over by psychoanalysts and we have reports from such installations or cities that personnel without psychoanalytic training find it difficult to obtain or retain appointments.

There is little evidence that basic science psychology is either well understood or utilized in many psychoanalytic centers. Indeed, a large portion of the time of many analysts is devoted to the training of other analysts in the same unvalidated methods, which condition may continue to exist as long as it is necessary to obtain such qualifications to gain local professional recognition.

This phenomenon of the contemporary prestige of psychoanalysis exists in spite of the fact that today, more than 50 years after the appearance of Freud's basic theories, there is still no adequate experimental-statistical validation of the system either in whole or part. While psychoanalytic formulations may receive empiric validation in individual cases, there is little acceptable evidence that they may be universally applied to all persons at all times. Without in any way disparaging the brilliance of Freud's contributions or minimizing their importance as clarifying certain classes of behavior data, there is still room for sound skepticism concerning current practices of projecting psychoanalytic interpretations on all case materials. In personal observations of psychoanalytic approaches (as well as many others), we have frequently noted therapists displaying considerable intellectual ingenuity trying to match standard theoretical interpretations to samples of behavior data but without much apparent awareness of the evident invalidity of such practices. This constitutes an example of extreme directiveness in which the therapist projects diagnoses and interpretations uncritically whether they fit or not. Our conclusion concerning psychoanalytic approaches must be that this method is essentially intuitive, anecdotal, empiric and unvalidated in its present stage of evolution since there is a dearth of experimental-statistical data. Individual applications, no matter how brilliant and productive, are at present empiric and intuitive. A great deal of the difficulty will be obviated, undoubtedly, as the phenomena uncovered by the psychoanalytic method are integrated and interpreted in terms of basic science psychology. Expediently, however, we will all go on making psychoanalytic interpretations until some better methods become available, but dangers can be minimized if greater criticality and caution are used.

Similar comments apply to projective techniques based largely on

Freudian interpretations. Many clinicians go to extremes in applying projective interpretations to all behaviors ranging from global integrations down to the most incidental mannerisms. Such methods would not be too objectionable if diagnoses were properly qualified with limiting statements indicating their hypothetical and essentially unvalidated nature, but they become grossly unscientific and bordering on charlatanism when stated with absolute positivity which rules out the consideration of other possibilities. It would be wise not to forget the lessons taught by the fate of the early methods of Freudian dream interpretation. While dreams may have symbolic significance, their latent meanings only can be understood in terms of the dynamics of the individual case to which an universal dream vocabulary or symbolism can rarely be applied. It is unwise to apply projective interpretations unless there is definite evidence that projective mechanisms indeed are operating.

CLIENT-CENTERED COUNSELING

Nondirective, client-centered methods of personality counseling have reached a stage of empiric validation where they are now widely accepted as a valuable part of our personality counseling armamentarium *within the limits of their indications and contraindications.* Utilized with clients who are motivated to understand and change themselves, and who have sufficient personality resources to work through to their own solutions once emotional blocks have been resolved, nondirective methods permit the client to reach his own solutions with maximum freedom. They are also valuable in many other clinical situations where acceptance, permissiveness and reflection of feelings facilitate the building of rapport, lead to more complete self-expression, and encourage the development of initiative and responsibility in solving one's own problems. When such methods are utilized within their indications and contraindications, along with such other more active methods as may be indicated, and without making excessive claims for their achievements unsupported by actual research results, there can be no quarrel with their use.

Although it is too early to make a definitive statement, evidence appears to be accumulating that use of the nondirective approach is indicated more positively with "ego-negative" persons who are dissatisfied with themselves and anxious to change, and may be contra-indicated with "ego-positive" persons who are satisfied with themselves and have no insight into the fact of maladjustment or the desirability of changing. Negative self-regarding attitudes, at least when not on an obsessive or psychotic basis, tend to motivate the client to face problems and work out solutions, and a minimum of therapist activity is indicated, at least until such time as direct intervention is proven more efficient. In our experience, the nondirective approach tends to fail or reach an impasse with self-satisfied clients who either see nothing wrong or who do not want to change. This includes the large group of psychoneurotic persons whose unconscious defenses may resist even massive intervention.

Much of the dissatisfaction and published criticism of nondirectivism appear to have been stimulated more by the way in which such methods have been presented or advocated rather than with the techniques themselves. If nondirectivism had been advanced as simply a promising group of new methods to be integrated with older methods according to their indications and contraindications, it probably would have been widely accepted without controversy. However, the active promotion of the client-centered principle as the basis for a new and inclusive school of theory and practice, often advocated somewhat uncritically as a new panacea suitable for all clinical situations, and even as a philosophy for the conduct of all human affairs, has stimulated critical reactions which have sought to cut the new movement down to size and integrate its contributions into existing knowledge. The efforts of nondirectivism to erect a theoretical rationale in support of its empiric achievements often have led to the making of claims which did not seem validated by actual research findings. Finally, the tendency of some nondirectivists to refer to themselves and act as if they were the exclusive proprietors of a new school whose methods would soon make obsolete all older techniques has quite understandably stimulated criticism from those who believe that all new findings must be integrated into basic science knowledge and methods.

More than ten years ago, this writer published a critique (10) of nondirective methods of counseling and psychotherapy motivated by our concern over the apparent failure of this new school to incorporate certain standard principles of objective methodology in research and clinical approaches. A restatement of our basic criticisms in 1957 would point up five major defects of research design which seriously vitiate the conclusions which can be drawn from most of the research to date.

(a) The persistent failure of nondirectivists to recognize the importance of valid diagnosis in all scientific case study, and particularly in research design, makes it impossible to evaluate clinical claims and research results.

(b) The failure to attempt to identify all pertinent variables diagnostically has made it impossible to utilize standard research designs involving use of equated samples, rigorous identification and manipulation of dependent and independent variables, and the objectification of all factors and steps known to be involved.

(c) The failure to control, or otherwise partial out, the effects of other therapeutic factors (such as suggestion, catharsis, desensitization, etc.), which are known to be operating, makes it impossible to draw any valid conclusions as to what is actually occurring in nondirective therapy.

(d) The failure to check conclusions drawn from phenomenological data obtained from the client (or inferred by the therapist) with actual objective measurements of known factors or status may result in serious misinterpretations of the realities of the therapeutic situation.

(e) Even if positive therapeutic results are demonstrable using nondirective methods, it still remains to be proven that such effects could not have been achieved just as well or even more expeditiously with other methods.

In conclusion, then, the failure to rigorously identify, diagnose and control all factors known to be operating in psychotherapy has seriously invalidated much of recent research on nondirective methods. We are not told whether the subjects are normal or abnormal, the nature and pathogenicity in terms of actual case history findings of the factors being therapized, and we are not convinced that the postulated factors actually explain the results obtained. In other words, most of the factors which we need to know about have been left undifferentiated and uncontrolled. In effect, it appears that nondirectivism postulates one standard diagnosis for all clients, namely that emotional factors blocking growth are the most important cause of all disorder, hence diagnosis is not necessary and only one standard method (nondirectivism) is indicated.

The most prominent success of client-centered methodological research has been in objectively demonstrating the actual operations which take place in this method. Nondirectivism has made a very great contribution in developing passive methods of counseling emphasizing acceptance, permissiveness, reflection and clarification of feelings, and placing the responsibility upon the client for working out his own problem solutions. Conversely, the dangers of crude directiveness, counselor-centeredness, and the invalid projection of interpretations upon the client's behavior are all better understood as a result of insistence on the client-centered principle. The issue still remains, however, concerning indications and contraindications for use of nondirective methods with different types of clients, pathological processes, degrees of pathogenicity and other factors determining outcomes.

Proponents of nondirectivism have been less successful in trying to construct a systematic theoretical rationale for their viewpoint. It appears that Rogers' earliest contributions were developed by intuitive-empiric methods, interpreted at first (4) in terms of somewhat mystical concepts of self-realization and growth, and more recently developed in terms of a thoroughgoing phenomenological approach. (5) While such preoccupation with the self-concept and other phenomenological data as experienced by the subject himself and understood empathically by the therapist is very intriguing and commendable in itself, considerable criticism may be directed toward the attempt to construct a complete system on such a limited approach. Even more caution should be invoked in evaluating claims by nondirectivists for unique processes and results from their methods, particularly when it is known that all therapeutic methods have their successes. Before we can ascribe much validity to claims made, for example, from changes on Q sorts given pre- and post-client-centered therapy, it will be necessary to obtain comparable Q sorts from clients treated with Couéism, Christian Science, Dianetics, psychoanalysis and many types of directive methods (all of which have very enthusiastic clients and practitioners). It may be that certain standard factors underly all these methods and that specific philosophical rationales are superfluous. Snyder recognizes this dilemma when he states that "Perhaps it doesn't make very much difference which philosophies guide a therapist's work." (9) While it is interesting to attempt to trace the philosophical antecedents of recent theoretical developments as when Walker (16) perceives Freud as the intellectual disciple of Augustine, and Rogers the intellectual descendent of Jesus, Confucius or Rousseau, there are dangers in implying that psychoanalysis or nondirectivism have some face validity from being related to such respected authorities. Similar comments apply to the currently popular practice of using laudatory or discriminatory designations to categorize accepted or rejected concepts as when Snyder (9) categorizes neofundamentalism, scholasticism, behaviorism, psychobiology, learning theory and directive counseling as being "authoritarian," while nondirectivism is identified with "self-actualism" or "self-determinism," idealism, democratic government, humanism, progressive education, hormic psychology and phenomenology. Such a dichotomy is purely arbitrary and probably artifactual, and even worse are the self-reflexive connotations of the term "authoritarian" as interpreted against the recent associative contexts of Fascism, Communism, regimentation and exploitation as contrasted with other possible connotations involving such positive contexts as love, protection, paternalism, guidance, help and wise counseling. The use of such self-reflexive terms in purportedly scientific communications is very undesirable.

While we would defend to the end the right of Carl R. Rogers (5) to expound his own philosophical queries and experiences in relation to problems of science and phenomenology, we must insist that the evidential value of such observations must be rigorously evaluated by scientific methods before being accepted as anything but expressions of personal opinion and faith. The quandaries of Rogers in relation to "Persons or Science" (5) appear to be rationalizations of the deficiencies of his ideological approach. Rogers' rejection of diagnosis as a basic method of research and of clinical practice has seriously limited the scope of his whole approach, and his failure to modify his position, to publicly indicate the limitations and contraindications of nondirectivism, or to discuss their integration with older methods, may actually inhibit the acceptance of the whole movement. Snyder appears to admit this in his somewhat despairing comment of a "pox on both sides" as he concludes that "as long as Rogers cares and the Freudians care, both seem to be meeting the needs of clients." (9)

Actually, the defects of the research design under which most nondirective research has been done could be avoided by the simple procedure of having some independent authority select and thoroughly study samples of cases before submitting them for nondirective treatment. This device would simultaneously objectify the nature of the case materials while at the same time free the client-centered therapist from introducing any sort of diagnostic procedure during his case handling. After the termination of therapy, the independent authority could again study the cases for the presence and nature of any changes occurring from therapy. Such results could then be compared with other samples treated by other standard methods, and the data subjected to factor analysis to discover any common factors underlying all methods.

Eclectic Counseling

The eclectic method of selecting appropriate theories and methods to fit the indications and contraindications of each individual case has long been the standard procedure in the older clinical sciences such as medicine. In personal reaction to the seeming one-sidedness of nondirective and psychoanalytic approaches, publication of a series of articles on directive therapy was begun in 1945 and later expanded into a systematic textbook. (12) Our adoption of the term *directive* was intended only to emphasize the existence of a large number of therapeutic methods (including nondirectivism) within the larger framework of all that was known about influencing personality. Our use of this term was *not* intended to imply any preference for any special group of methods or philosophical viewpoint, and we regret that many readers immediately projected many unintended meanings which now we do not wish to be identified with. The term *eclectic* would have been more accurate semantically and, by 1948, we specifically attempted to limit the term *directive* to the systematic attempt to use all methods of therapy eclectically based on a formal plan for the identification and modification of etiologic factors in maladjustment. (11) Now, we prefer to abandon all terms such as *directive, nondirective, psychoanalytic,* etc., as tending to create artificial continua and semantic artifacts, and instead to substitute operational descriptions and nomenclature for the dynamics of any method. The term *eclectic* has value only to differentiate an approach which refuses to subscribe to any one operational viewpoint or method, and becomes entirely objectionable if given self-reflexive connotations such as "authoritarian."

The eclectic approach to scientific case handling basically depends upon adequate diagnosis as the cornerstone of all case handling in order to identify etiologic causes and apply appropriate therapeutic methods according to their indications and contraindications. Currently, the most important theoretical issue in personality counseling and, indeed, all psychotherapy, is the matter of the relation of diagnosis to valid therapy. Far from attempting to establish any new school or system based on "directive" methods, our sole purpose has been to emphasize the importance of diagnosis as the cornerstone underlying the rationale for knowing the indications and contraindications of *all* known methods utilized without systematic bias of any kind. Frankly, we have been very much disturbed over the past few years by the discovery that many teachers and clinicians have entirely misunderstood our fundamental theoretical position which stresses a thorough-going basic-science-oriented eclecticism by erroneously identifying us with directivism as a method or end in itself. Our original selection of the term "directive psychotherapy" was intended only to emphasize that an important group of methods exists in contrast to nondirectivism, and it was not intended to identify a new school or system. Now the need for emphasizing such a difference has long since passed, and we would prefer to use the term directive only to indicate one end of a continuum of passivity *vs.* activity in the therapist. In our own practice, we try to be passive or active according to the indications of the situation rather than following any ideological bias.

One of the criticisms advanced, particularly by nondirectivists, against eclecticism in its present status of development, relates to the voluminous research which has been accumulated by special schools in contrast with the meagre or nonexistent research output achieved by the exponents of eclecticism. Such criticisms have been directed against eclectic or directive counseling as where Shoben says that "Thorne is unable to escape an authoritarian tone that could not be challenged in itself if it were buttressed either by experimental evidence or convincing case material." (8, p. 43) and which comment has appeared repeatedly in many forms. Such a criticism appears to reflect a lack of understanding concerning the differing problems and responsibilities placed upon those who accept eclecticism in contrast with those who support more limited special methods. Our original aim in attempting to compile a unified systematic approach to diagnosis and therapy was to attempt to gather in one place all that was scientifically valid and fairly well accepted from all sources or schools, both clinical and experimental-statistical, eclectically. We have never made any claims for any of these methods beyond what had been advanced in the literature or appeared valid in terms of personal clinical experience. We submit that this was all that could be accomplished at time and place, and we make no special claims for any superiority of any of these methods beyond what has been empirically established. Our role was simply to attempt an integration of all that seemed to be accepted in terms of the accumulated clinical experience of our generation and without favor or prejudice for any method beyond the known indications and contraindications as currently understood. This task of attempting to integrate, in one internally-consistent presentation, the accumulated experience of clinical science is in itself so gigantic as to preclude any personal research attack upon the vast number of problems and methods, and certainly beyond our personal resources which have been invested maximally in the attempt to integrate existing research interpretively. We can only state, then, that our conclusions represent only the concentrate of human knowledge at time and place as we have interpreted it. We feel that there is a definite need not only for researchers who can provide valid data but also for global interpreters who must attempt to relate the many disparate findings which are in themselves more or less meaningless until oriented in some master frame of reference.

Any deficiencies of eclecticism or directivism simply reflect either (a) the relatively primitive state of human knowledge concerning these methods, or (b) the inadequacies of breadth of viewpoint among those who attempt an integrative interpretation. To the degree which eclecticism is able to integrate *all* operational methods and findings available at time and place, it appears to us that it must represent the last word concerning what we can validly understand and apply in practice. We may accept, as a basic premise, the axiom that clinical methods are simply individual applications (within the limits of validity of clinical judgment) of basic science experimental-statistical methods and data. We seek to protect the validity of our judgments and conclusions by rigorously seeking to discriminate cause-effect relationships by the most advanced diagnostic methods. We submit that this is all which can be done for time and place within any clinical orientation. Eclectic methodology is so diverse and complex that a general advance on all fronts simultaneously can come only very gradually and certainly beyond the scope of any one person or generation to advance them very markedly. In spite of this admitted deficiency based on the primitive status of existing knowledge, we can be assured of some degree of face, content, empirical and factorial validity by constantly seeking to relate our practices to the most advanced basic science thinking of time and place.

In contrast, the proponents of special methods have a particular obligation to demonstrate that new ingredients have been added over and above existing knowledge. Considering the impressive basic science advances of the last century, both by science in general and by special schools, the burden of the proof rests upon proponents of new schools to show where and how they have advanced human knowledge beyond merely introducing new terms or rehashing the known. Modern medicine for example, has reached a status of solid basic science achievement where we can expect new discoveries in special areas by experimental-statistical methods, but we do not anticipate any revolutionary philosophical advances which will change our basic methods of scientific discovery or thinking. Science supercedes schools of philosophy or metaphysics as soon as it accumulates sufficient objective knowledge in any field to provide valid bases for clinical applications. We believe that clinical psychological science has already achieved such a solid basic science foundation of proven facts as to make obsolete the need for metaphysical theorizing and special schools. If new advances are made, they must be integrated into the broad foundation of scientific knowledge rather than being offered as revolutionary panaceas to replace all that is eclectically known.

Eclecticism in clinical practice is always held back in situations where students are trained in only one method, and are either oblivious of other methods or insecure in their application. Until such time as students are provided training experiences with all known operational methods of diagnosis and therapy, it is evident that their capacity or competence in applying all known methods eclectically will be limited. The need to build up one's confidence clinically by becoming a "master" in some specific school, such as nondirectivism or psychoanalysis, disappears as personal competence with all known methods broadens and one is sustained by the knowledge that one knows all there is to know for time and place, *i.e.,* broad scientific knowledge and clinical competence reduce the need for speculative theorizing.

DISCIPLINARY COUNSELING

Williamson and Foley (17) have presented a detailed reporting of the use of "counseling" in the disciplinary management of student conduct problems as developed since 1941 in the office of the dean of students at the University of Minnesota. Although the authors evidently are aware of the classically *therapeutic* basic role of personality counseling, and repeatedly emphasize the rehabilitational and reeducative objectives of their program, it becomes immediately apparent that the term "management" would be a much more realistic designation of their methods of case handling than is the term "counseling." Although in defining their concept of the role of counseling in student discipline, the authors are careful to structure their activities as not being authoritarian, regulatory or punitive, an analysis of their outline of case handling methods and the actual transcripts of individual cases indicates that their activities are conducted within a plainly authoritarian judgmental framework which can hardly be perceived as anything else by the students. In spite of what Williamson and Foley theorize the situation to involve, the critical element in categorizing the nature of the situation must be in terms of what the subjects of the counseling perceive it to be. In discussing their procedures of disciplinary counseling, their schematic outline (7, p. 61) includes such steps as (a) making of charges against the student, (b) compulsory interviewing for counseling purposes, (c) reporting and review by a disciplinary committee in a face-to-face situation with the student, and (d) disciplinary action by the committee involving the imposition of further regulatory actions upon the student. Whatever the professed intentions of the disciplinary committee, the execution of its functions in such a framework cannot avoid the connotation of a judgmental, regulatory and, perhaps, punitive orientation to case handling as the whole situation is perceived by the student from the implications of what goes on. That many students may, indeed, perceive the situation as basically judgmental and punitive is clearly evident in the case of Milton Reed (7, p. 229) where not only the accused but also two friends openly profess their fears that unreasonable judgments and/or punishments are going to be administered.

In our opinion, no method of case handling deserves to be designated as counseling unless *healing* is the basic and primary objective beyond which all other considerations are secondary. In order to retain its basically therapeutic functions, the counseling situation must be thoroughly safeguarded to preserve its purpose of being the one place (in addition to psychiatry) where a person may frankly discuss his problems in a completely healing atmosphere unthreatened by any question of judgment or punishment. We are in agreement with Rogers (4) in his contention that any other structuring of the situation destroys the therapeutic context.

Implicit in the approach of Williamson and Foley is the questionable assumption that misbehavior is classifiable into voluntary and involuntary types for which discipline and therapy are the solutions respectively. While the authors recognize that immaturity and personality deviations may interact with unhealthy environmental forces to produce misconduct, the installation of such complicated judicial machinery and practices only succeeds in advancing the implication that we are really dealing with deliberate misbehavior, bordering on criminality, and which can be handled best by punitive procedures progressively applied until the miscreant sees the light and voluntarily controls himself better. We must insist that such methods of case handling are more properly designated as management and do not qualify as counseling because the basic operational framework is not primarily therapeutic but rather is regulatory and administrative. This is not to imply that counseling cannot be carried on within disciplinary or administrative auspices where the healing motive is primary and disposition is secondary. *We would prefer to base all counseling on the postulate that all misbehavior reflects immaturity, personality deviation or personality reactions to situations, reflecting various degrees of lack of control, and arising etiologically in the domain of psychopathology.* From such a viewpoint, all disciplinary problems should be handled within a completely therapeutic frame of reference, only being referred for regulatory action in the event of the breakdown of therapeutic progress and poor prognosis. The authorities could take notice of misconduct by anonymous comments on the situation, clearly indicating its position that such behavior must be the result of unhealthy thinking, and further indicating that gross regulatory methods would be enforced only in the event of the breakdown of rehabilitation.

There is serious question whether disciplinary counseling as practiced in the case of Janet Larson (7, p. 261) may be actually untherapeutic and dangerous to the health of the subjects concerned. We can think of few situations more traumatic and guilt-productive than for students to be detected in the act of sex intercourse in the bushes by the university watchman and such detection is usually punishment enough. Psychiatrically, there is great danger of the girl (at least) developing incapacitating mortification and guilt reactions which may lead to life-long neuroticism and frigidity. When this student was interrogated by F. L. Crane in the presence of John D. Foley on July 22, 1945 in great detail concerning what took place, the circumstances of the interview indicate that it was conducted somewhat like a third degree solely for the purpose of securing a signed confession and with nothing therapeutic taking place. Further, on July 23, the accused Janet Larson and William Burton were called before the faculty disciplinary committee and interrogated together about their marriage intentions, guilt reactions and penitent attitudes. The trend of the questioning seemed to hint that the university would be satisfied if the couple married (shot gun influence?) but it actually did not accomplish this purpose, perhaps because Burton was led to admit previous intercourse before Miss Larson and also did not seem completely enthusiastic about marriage. The most therapeutic action taken was the decision of the disciplinary committee to put the students on probation while continuing at the university. It is interesting to note that on May 11, 1946, counselor G. E. K. spontaneously notes that Miss Larson no longer has "a vivacious, energetic enthusiasm" in her manner but has changed to "quiet winsomeness," which might be interpreted as reflecting deep anxiety or guilt. In any case, a perusal of the case record reveals no evidence of therapeutic counseling but only the administrative details of handling student misbehavior.

An analysis of the entire 15 cases cited as examples of disciplinary counseling reveals that the counselor activity seems to consist in acting as the representative of university authority in identifying alleged misbehavior, identifying the students involved, obtaining signed confessions before witnesses, conducting judicial hearings, and later advising the student how to behave in order to stay out of trouble again. While some secondary therapeutic results may be achieved where leniency, tolerance and patience may operate to keep the student in the university until he can learn to handle objective behaviors more adaptively, there is little evidence either that the primary emphasis is therapeutic or that modern counseling methods have been used under maximally effective conditions to secure deep personality changes.

DIFFERENT OPERATIONAL APPROACHES

Order may be brought into the current confusion of competing psychotherapies by reducing or translating each approach to its lowest operational common denominator. As pointed out elsewhere (13, p. 138), behavior analysis may be attempted from the operational viewpoints of instinct theory, perceptual field theory, learning theory, motivation theory or the psychology of the emotions. Each diverse approach utilizes its own operational levels of personality study and achieves its own distinctive results which may reflect determination by general, group or specific factors. Clinicians trained primarily in one operational approach tend to have trouble comprehending the methods and results from other operational approaches. The advantage of a thoroughgoing operational approach is that it permits the study of raw behavior data directly and with the formulation of diagnostic impressions *inductively* to fit the individual case with the progressive interpretation of data. The problem is to construct a theory to fit the case inductively rather than trying to apply theories deductively. Operationism renders unnecessary undue speculation and theorizing if carried out in sufficient detail to uncover the major etiologic factors in each case.

The fact that many methods appear to produce results can only have two possible explanations. Either similar dynamic factors are operating in diverse methods, or there is more than one method for achieving the same specific goals. For example, as pointed out by Snyder (8, p. 92), perhaps a theory of psychotherapy does little more than to inspire the therapist with confidence which is transmitted to the client and becomes the basis of a relationship which shows the client that "somebody" cares. Or perhaps suggestion effects and emotional release are enough to help most clients. Or perhaps merely doing something until time and nature heal is enough. Such important questions can only be solved with a research design complex enough to identify and control all relevant variables. In the meantime, symposia on perceptual field theory or learning theory in relation to psychotherapy may be very valuable in casting light on what these various operational approaches may contribute but it should not be expected that any one operational approach can provide the complete answer. Combs (2) may be correct in concluding that traditional learning theories offer little towards the improvement of counseling (that is, beyond the general recognition that all therapy involves learning according to well-known psychological laws), but we feel that he is overoptimistic in assuming that all behavior is a function of the field of perception at the moment of behaving so that the process of counseling becomes one of altering perceptions in desired directions. Shaw (6) apparently takes a much more valid position (in agreement with our eclectic viewpoint) that varied conditions of learning in persons may produce a variety of etiologic factors operating on many levels of personality integration. We agree with Shoben (7) that contemporary learning theories are most interested in *principles* of learning while the clinician must attempt, as we have also previously pointed out, to (a) establish suitable conditions so that learning can take place, and then (b) to actually introduce new conditionings in more healthy directions. (14, p. 278) Our own detailed viewpoint is that personality integration *may* be organized by many levels of factors, which may be perceptual, learned, motivational, affective or instinctive, operating at various levels of generality or specificity, and each requiring their own particular operational methods for diagnosis or treatment. (15, p. 14-15) It will probably require complex experiments of factor analytic design to differentiate prototypical patterns of syndrome organization.

SEMANTIC PROBLEMS

A most urgent problem in the whole field of diagnosis and therapy concerns the early adoption of a uniform and universal system of nomenclature so that the coordinates and boundaries of psychological space may become standardized. Every few months some authority launches a new theory replete with its own distinctive terminology which usually is not related to the coordinates of accepted knowledge. Two recent examples of such system-building with difficult new terminologies are Allport's event-structure theory (1) and J. G. Miller's general behavior systems theory (3), both of which will require long intensive study to become proficient with and simply to master the terms with any facility. And even after the new terminology is mastered, there still remains the problem of relating the new contributions to existing knowledge to discover whether or not the new formulation makes any distinctive contribution. There is great need for the profession to adopt a standard nomenclature with a universal index of factors to be measured. The most promising beginnings in this direction have been made by the factor analysts who are working towards standard methods for labelling and mapping new factors in their space-time dimensions, and we have personally adopted standard terminology in our approach to psychological examining. Semantic chaos will result from the multiplication of new theories and systems unless standard nomenclature is uniformly adopted to relate new developments to existing coordinates. In our own editorial work, we uniformly reject papers introducing new and esoteric terminology unless it can be clearly shown that such refinements are needed to describe genuinely new developments. As matters now stand, students entering the field must spend entirely unreasonable amounts of time trying to master the babel of conflicting terminologies.

PREDICTIONS FOR THE FUTURE

The most urgent theoretical question in personality counseling and, indeed, all psychotherapy, is the matter of the relation of diagnosis to valid therapy. Currently, it is fashionable in some circles to ignore problems of diagnosis or to categorize such interests as authoritarian. (8, p. 43) It is a basic postulate of all scientific method to attempt to discover the nature and etiology of all variables determining a natural occurrence, *i.e.*, to identify causes and effects. Without in any way attempting to defend the inadequacies of current diagnostic methods and systems, we cannot see how any progress can be made in understanding causation or rationally manipulating determinants unless a diagnosis is made of all antecedents leading to consequences. Our opinion is that advances in psychotherapy must depend on more valid diagnosis and to this end we have evolved a systematic method (15) for evaluating all factors known to organize personality integration. We emphatically reject the hypothesis that psychotherapy is in any way different from other clinical science in the sense of it being possible to dispense with diagnosis in scientific case handling. This has nothing to do with any philosophic bias but is a tenet of scientific method.

Within this general basic science orientation, we may predict future developments in the issues which are now so controversial. We predict that the current heavy investment of time and energy in speculative theorizing and system-building will be supplanted by a consistent effort to relate all knowledge and new developments in terms of a standard nomenclature and universal index of factors and results. We predict that exclusive preoccupation with special operational approaches such as perception or learning theory will be replaced by a broader eclectic utilization of all available operational approaches according to the indications and contraindications of time and place. We predict that nondirectivism (and all other special therapies) will be demoted from their current status as mutually exclusive systems to take their proper places as limited technical advances integrated into a broad diagnostic-therapeutic armamentarium applied eclectically, without special bias or preference for specific tools. We predict that much of psychoanalytic speculation and dialectics will be abandoned, either because ultimately proven to be unvalidatable or more parsimoniously explained in terms of basic science concepts, and leaving a residual of fact which can be integrated into basic science knowledge in the proper places. We predict that all clinicians will accept ultimately the absolute essentiality of diagnostic thinking and will cease to seek short-cuts motivated by current deficiencies. In other words, we reaffirm our belief in the ultimate victory of scientific methodology in proving its capability of dealing with all psychological problems without recourse to less rigorous philosophizing and speculation.

We cannot escape the fact that all natural phenomena reflect the operation of laws which determine causes and effects. If we are to understand and manipulate these causes and effects with maximum efficiency, then we must recognize the various categories of action imperatives involved in the concept of "ought." Elsewhere (14), we have explored the implications of the psychology of "ought" for social planning in general, and individual efficiency in particular, with special reference to what can be accomplished in diagnosis and therapy. We insist that all this can be accomplished within the orientation of eclecticism. We hope that adherents of various special positions will cease projecting various characterizations upon each other and will work in common to discover and control the actual etiologic factors which must be operating.

REFERENCES

1. Allport, F. H. *Theories of Perception and the Concept of Structure.* New York: Wiley, 1955.
2. Combs, A. W. Counseling as a learning process. *J. counsel. Psychol.,* 1954, **I,** 31-36.
3. Miller, J. G. General behavior systems theory and summary. *J. counsel. Psychol.,* 1956, **3,** 120-124.
4. Rogers, C. R. *Counseling and Psychotherapy.* Boston: Houghton-Mifflin, 1942.
5. Rogers, C. R. Persons or Science? A Philosophical Question. *Amer. Psychol.,* 1955, **10,** 267-278.
6. Shaw, F. J. Counseling from the standpoint of an *"Interactive Conceptualist." J. counsel. Psychol.,* 1954, **1,** 36-42.
7. Shoben, E. J., Jr. Introduction: Behavior Theories and a Counseling Case. *J. counsel. Psychol.* 1956, **3,** 107-108.
8. Shoben, E. J., Jr. The mosaic for psychotherapy. *Contemporary Psychol.,* 1956, **1,** 42-44.
9. Snyder, W. U. Comment. *J. counsel. Psychol.,* 1956, **3,** 91-92.
10. Thorne, F. C. A critique of nondirective methods of psychotherapy. *J. abn. soc. Psychol.,* 1944, **39,** 459-470.
11. Thorne, F. C. Principles of directive counseling and psychotherapy. *Amer. Psychologist,* 1948, **3,** 160-166.
12. Thorne, F. C. *Principles of Personality Counseling.* Brandon, Vt.: Journal of Clinical Psychology, 1950.
13. Thorne, F. C. Operational concepts in clinical psychology and medicine. *J. clin. Psychol.,* 1953, **9,** 137-142.
14. Thorne, F. C. Directive psychotherapy: Theory, practice and social implications. *J. clin. Psychol.,* 1953, **9,** 267-280.

15. Thorne, F. C. *Principles of Psychological Examining.* Brandon, Vt.: Journal of Clinical Psychology, 1955.
16. Walker, D. E. Carl Rogers and the Nature of Man. *J. counsel. Psychol.,* 1956, **3**, 89-91.
17. Williamson, E. G. and Foley, J. D. *Counseling and Discipline.* New York: McGraw-Hill, 1949.

38. ANALYSIS OF THE SELF-ESTIMATE IN THE EVALUATION OF COUNSELING

Stanley L. Singer and Buford Stefflre

One of the foremost problems in vocational and educational counseling is to assist the client in arriving at a realistic appraisal of his own abilities, interests, personality, and other characteristics which are pertinent to long-term vocational and personal adjustment. In measuring the extent to which this aspect of counseling is successful, one approach has been to utilize the technique of "self-estimate." The self-estimate technique involves the client's judgment of his position compared with others on various factors and may also be referred to as self-rating, self-knowledge, or self-evaluation. This paper explores and illustrates one method of using such self-estimates in research on counseling in order to point out some objections to the statistical approach previously used in self-estimate studies.

Russell (4) summarizes the earlier studies on self-estimate techniques by stating that the approach needs both "further investigation and extreme caution in its application." Most of the studies in Russell's review made use of correlation. Generally, relationships were determined among such factors as subject's ratings, test scores, teachers' ratings, and peer ratings.

Johnson (3) explored the self-estimate approach with adults using both correlation techniques and tests of significance between means on measures of intelligence, interest, and personality. Subjects rated themselves before counseling, immediately after counseling, and

Reprinted by permission of the authors and *Journal of Counseling Psychology,* I, No. 4 (Winter, 1954), 252-55.

one month after counseling. In general he found that vocational counseling significantly increased the accuracy of self-knowledge.

Froehlich and Moser (2) reported a study which was designed to ascertain the accuracy with which counselees could recall test-score information which they learned during counseling. High school students were counseled, and after counseling were asked to recall the test score information. The resulting correlations between "actual" and "remembered" scores were then calculated and found to be statistically significant "but low enough to indicate marked differences between actual and recalled test percentiles."

Berdie (1) reported an attempt to determine the degree to which changes in self-ratings of abilities, measured interests, and measured personality characteristics would reflect results of counseling. An experimental group and a control group rated themselves before testing. The experimental group then received counseling and six months after counseling both groups again rated themselves on the factors enumerated above. Comparisons were made between the correlation of the second rating and the test scores and the correlation of the first rating and the test scores. Very few significant changes were found.

The present paper presents a variant of the methodological approaches used in previous studies in the belief that the use of correlation techniques to measure the degree of retention of information gleaned during the counseling process is inappropriate. Obtaining a correlation between pre-counseling self-estimates and test scores and post-counseling self-estimates and test scores does not reveal the relevant information to permit an evaluation of counseling. Such a correlation provides no recognition of the discrepancies between the first rating and actual score as compared with the discrepancies between the second rating and actual score. What we really want to find out in using the self-estimate technique is whether the individual's self-estimate deviates less from his actual score after counseling than it did before.

The example in Table 1 indicates how a high correlation between the post-counseling rating and actual score might bear no resemblance to the extent to which information was retained. Table 1 indicates that the discrepancy between the pre-counseling ratings and actual scores was less than the discrepancy between the post-counseling ratings and actual scores, although these latter two measures correlated perfectly. These results suggest that correlation is not the proper statistical technique to use in self-estimate research.

Additional problems are involved in a determination of the adequacy of comparisons of measures of central tendency in self-estimate research. It will be recalled that in Johnson's study (3) tests of significance were made of the difference between the means of each rating and the available objective information. The authors would like to suggest that it may, under certain conditions, be profitable to carry the tests of significance an additional step since tests of significance between means might sometimes tend to obscure the real nature of the data. One rating might demonstrate estimates very

TABLE 1

Scores on X Test

$(n = 10)$

Pre-Counseling Self-Estimate A*	B*	Actual Score C*	D*	Post-Counseling Self-Estimate E*
24	+4	20	−9	11
23	+2	21	−9	12
22	0	22	−9	13
21	−2	23	−9	14
20	−4	24	−9	15
29	+4	25	−9	16
28	+2	26	−9	17
27	0	27	−9	18
26	−2	28	−9	19
25	−4	29	−9	20
	$r_{AC} = .52$		$r_{EC} = 1.00$	

* A = Distribution of pre-counseling self-estimates
  C = Actual scores
  E = Distribution of post-counseling self-estimates
  B = Discrepancy between A and C
  D = Discrepancy between E and C

close to the actual scores while the other rating might, on inspection, indicate estimates widely dispersed on both sides of the mean so that the discrepancies have a canceling effect. In this situation the means might be identical and only additional tests of significance of the differences in the standard deviations would make possible meaningful interpretation of the data.

If, when this is done, it is found that the variability of the discrepancies is significantly less on the post-counseling estimate than on the pre-counseling estimate, it seems reasonable to assume the lessened variability derives from the counseling process.

This test of the significance of the differences in the standard deviations would be particularly useful in those cases where the means of the discrepancies shifted across the zero point from the pre-counseling to the post-counseling measurement. An example would be a situation where the pre-counseling discrepancy mean was -2 and the post-counseling discrepancy mean was $+2$. In such a case, the means might be significantly different but interpretation of this finding would be impossible without the additional evidence offered by an examination of the standard deviation.

To illustrate these methodological considerations the present paper considers the application in self-estimate research of variability of the standard deviations as well as tests of significance between the means.

In the present study, the subjects were seniors at two Los Angeles high schools who received vocational advisement including testing and interviewing.

The students were twice asked to estimate their degree of interest in the six fields measured by the *Occupational Interest Inventory*. The first estimates were made after a discussion explaining the nature of the fields of interest and before any testing was done. The second estimates were made three months after counseling had been completed. The difference between the actual interest inventory score and the student's estimate of his interest was designated as his "discrepancy score." (Since the difference between the estimate and the actual score might be either positive or negative, depending on whether the interest was overestimated or underestimated, 30 points were added to each difference to make every discrepancy score positive and thus facilitate computations. Because of this weighting, it must be kept in mind throughout that a discrepancy score of 30 actually represents perfect agreement between estimate and actual score—in other words, no real discrepancy.)

Statistical checks were made to determine whether the discrepancy scores which were found before counseling differed to a significant degree from those found after counseling.

The null hypothesis is that counseling does not decrease the discrepancy between a student's self-estimate of his interest and his scores on an interest test. This hypothesis was tested by applying the *t* test to the means of the pre-counseling and post-counseling discrepancy scores and by testing the significance of the differences in the two standard deviations.

Table 2 (males) indicates that although there were no significant differences between the means of the two discrepancy scores, there

TABLE 2

($n = 72$ Los Angeles High School Senior Males)

Category	M 1 *	S.D. 1 *	M 2 *	S.D. 2 *	t M	t S.D.
Personal-Social	28.01	4.72	28.81	4.08	−1.10	1.78
Natural	27.94	6.40	28.58	6.00	−.62	.64
Mechanical	30.33	4.90	30.92	3.21	−.86	3.76 **
Business	27.61	6.87	28.53	6.04	−.84	1.19
Arts	27.63	5.98	28.67	5.45	−1.08	.96
Science	28.99	3.36	29.89	2.83	−1.70	1.51

* 1 = Before counseling

* 2 = Three months after counseling

** = 1% level of confidence

was a significantly smaller standard deviation in the distribution of the second estimate on mechanical interest as compared with the first estimate. This is a good illustration of the value of this statistic in research of this type. In the mechanical area the mean of the second estimate deviated slightly more from the actual score than did that of the first estimate. However, the difference between standard deviations indicates that there was significantly less variability on the post-counseling estimate. It can be seen that in the distribution of the pre-counseling discrepancy scores, a range of 25.43 to 35.23 is needed to take in the middle two-thirds of the group, whereas in the post-counseling discrepancy scores two-thirds of the group can be included in a range of 27.71 to 34.13. Thus it seems apparent that after counseling there was a greater concentration of scores around the point indicating no discrepancy between estimate and actual score, i.e., around the 0 (30) discrepancy point. It is also of note that in all cases the standard deviation of the second discrepancies was smaller than the first. This suggests that in every case there is a tendency for the variability between estimates of interest and test scores on interest measures to diminish as a result of counseling since the second mean was in all cases very near a 0 (30) discrepancy point.

Table 3 (females) shows that the means of the discrepancies for mechanical and science interest were significantly closer to 0 on the

TABLE 3
DISCREPANCY BETWEEN SELF-ESTIMATES AND MEASURED INTERESTS BEFORE AND AFTER COUNSELING
($n = 121$ LOS ANGELES HIGH SCHOOL SENIOR FEMALES)

Category	M 1*	S.D. 1*	M 2*	S.D. 2*	t M	t S.D.
Personal-Social	29.54	4.50	29.88	3.44	−.65	3.53**
Natural	26.99	6.23	28.00	5.64	−1.31	1.40
Mechanical	26.56	4.83	28.95	3.38	−4.43**	4.03**
Business	29.79	5.68	29.20	6.12	.78	−.90
Arts	31.19	5.98	30.14	6.44	1.31	−.94
Science	25.80	6.26	28.08	5.33	−3.04**	1.90

* 1 = Before counseling
* 2 = Three months after counseling
** = 1% level of confidence

post-counseling estimate. The standard deviation of the post-counseling discrepancy distribution was significantly smaller than that of the pre-counseling distribution in the case of the personal-social and mechanical fields.

SUMMARY

1. Previous studies using self-estimates as a measure of counseling success were reviewed and some questions raised regarding methodology.

2. In the present illustrative study, students' estimates of their in-

terest were taken before and three months after counseling and were compared with their scores on an interest test to arrive at their "discrepancy" score. Significant differences between the means, all in the direction indicating less discrepancy between actual scores and self-estimates after counseling when compared with before counseling, were found for boys in no field but for girls in the mechanical and science fields. Significant differences between the standard deviations, all in the direction indicating greater clustering of scores near the 0 discrepancy point after counseling when compared with before-counseling, were found for boys in the mechanical field and for girls in the personal-social and mechanical fields.

3. Tests of significance between standard deviations can provide helpful clues in interpreting pre-counseling and post-counseling estimates when the mean discrepancy scores are highly similar. Such tests of significance may reveal information which would not be apparent from tests of significance between means or from correlation coefficients.

Received July 15, 1954.

REFERENCES

1. Berdie, R. F. Changes in self-ratings as a method of evaluating counseling. *J. counsel. Psychol.,* 1954, **1**, 49-54.
2. Froehlich, C. P., & Moser, W. E. Do counselees remember test scores? *J. counsel. Psychol.,* 1954, **1**, 149-153.
3. Johnson, D. G. Effect of vocational counseling on self-knowledge. *Educ. psychol. Measmt.,* 1953, **13**, 330-338.
4. Russell, D. H. What does research say about self-evaluation? *J. educ. Res.,* 1953, **47**, 561-571.

39. EFFECTS OF COUNSELING

J. David O'Dea and Franklin R. Zeran

Professional counselors have had the benefit of relatively few studies to assist with *the problem of evaluating the effects of coun-*

Reprinted by permission of the authors and *Personnel and Guidance Journal,* XXXI, No. 4 (January, 1953), 241-44.

seling. Coe and Habbe (3:338) stated that counselors are generally ". . . so preoccupied with the day-to-day routine of counseling and office duty that they neglect matters of research and evaluation." As emphasized by Froehlich (6), O'Dea (8), Rogers (9), and by Williamson and Bordin (10), progress in counseling is dependent upon research.

Some researchers have accused counselors of applying new counseling methods and then, as Wrenn (12:409) stated, "trust in God that it will prove to be all we expect of it." Wischner and McKinney (11:180) suggested in a review of the status of counseling that ". . . since there has been an introduction of new methods without adequate evaluation of the old, it would seem desirable to take stock. . . ." In a critique of the guidance movement, Wrenn (12:409) wrote ". . . a constant check must be made upon what had been done so that procedures can be changed in the light of what is learned . . . no large claims as to the value of these new procedures should be made unless there is at least some objective proof."

Professional groups interested in improving the practices of counselors are keenly aware of the impelling need for coordinated research to bind together and give larger meaning to the continued efforts of the individual researcher. Hahn (7) pointed out that the need for evaluating the effects of counseling has been so severely felt that at present several divisions of the American Psychological Association are pushing over-all and team-research activities. The American College Personnel Association has been directing increasing attention to the evaluation of counseling. The National Vocational Guidance Association has interested itself in the assessment of total programs. Despite these past and current over-all efforts, counselors have been lacking in direction because of the need for more research on specific ways of evaluating the effects of counseling.

Summary of the Literature

The eighty references reviewed by the writers pertaining to an evaluation of the effects of counseling led to the following summary:

- There is a need for research to discover the relative efficacy of the known criteria for evaluation of counseling.

- There is a need for evaluative methods which meet acceptable research standards, but which are not beyond the reach of the practicing counselor.
- The lack of suitable criteria has been the greatest single difficulty of evaluation.
- To date, there is no clear-cut set of criteria that would be applicable in evaluating the effects of counseling in all situations.
- Every criterion that has been used in evaluating counseling has elements of error.
- In any experiment measuring the outcomes of counseling, a range of three or more criteria needs to be used not only to get at the many aspects of counseling outcomes but also to overcome the unreliability and the biasing effects of single criterion.
- It is extremely difficult to design studies to evaluate counseling and at the same time even partially eliminate extraneous factors in causing counselee gains.
- In order to have relatively complete evaluative methods, both immediate and delayed effects of counseling should be measured.
- There is wide disagreement among counseling specialists as to what criteria should be used to measure counseling outcomes.
- Different criteria measure different aspects of the effects of counseling.

The literature revealed that more than 16 different criteria have been used by investigators for purposes of evaluating the effects of counseling. Certain criteria were not considered in the study because they did not lend themselves to research facilities available at Oregon State College (4). Ten criteria, Table 1, were considered by the writers in evaluating the effects of counseling.

On the basis of a review of the research pertaining to the 10 criteria and the results of findings of an opinionnaire reported in Table 1, three criteria were selected by the writers for the purposes of the study. The criteria selected as being, in general, most acceptable for evaluating the effects of counseling were: (a) *counselee satisfaction,* (b) *counselee understanding of test data,* and (c) *before-and-after tests of personality and social adjustment.* The writers combined social adjustment and personality as one criterion.

RESULTS OF OPINIONNAIRE

The 10 criteria considered were listed on double postcards and mailed to those people who had recently published articles concerning the criteria being considered. In addition, cards were mailed to 71 of the members of the American Psychological Association who have a fellow rating in the Division of Counseling and Guidance Psychologists. These specialists were requested to select from the list the five criteria which they considered most useful and to indicate the order of their preferences. Forty-eight usable cards were returned.

Table 1 reports the preferences of the specialists. The votes were also given weighted scores in order that a combined rank preference of the 48 specialists could be recorded. Even though some of the criteria received a limited number of votes, it is evident that there are authorities who merit the same criterion as a first choice.

PROCEDURES OF THE STUDY

The writers attempted to evaluate the effects of the counseling with 36 counselees using the three criteria selected.

Step One: When a student came to the Counseling Bureau to make an appointment, the student or counselee was given an autobiographical form to fill in. In addition, a pamphlet explaining the services of the Counseling Bureau was given to each counselee along with a form letter explaining a desire to administer some inventories to him before his first appointment with a counselor.

Step Two: The counselee completed the autobiographical form and took the Minnesota Multiphasic Personality Inventory, the California Test of Personality, and a Test of Self-Understanding (5). The counselee then arranged for his sessions with the counselor.

Step Three: In the early stages of his counseling, the counselee completed a uniform battery of tests. In addition, the counselor may have assisted the counselee in the selection of additional tests which would apply to the particular counseling situation (1).

Step Four: One month after the termination of the counseling sessions, the counselee was asked to return to the Counseling Bureau.

At this time he was again given the Minnesota Multiphasic Personality Inventory and the Test of Self-Understanding. The counselee also indicated his satisfaction with the counseling services by use of an opinionnaire (5).

Step Five: Four to five months after the termination of the counseling sessions, the counselee was again asked to retake the California Test of Personality.

TABLE 1

RESULTS OF THE PREFERENCE OF FORTY-EIGHT SPECIALISTS FOR TEN
SELECTED CRITERIA USED TO EVALUATE THE EFFECTS OF COUNSELING

Criteria for Evaluation	Votes					Weighted Scores	Rank
	1	2	3	4	5		
1. Congruence of Objectives (Counselor and Counselee)	8	3	2	4	1	67	6
2. Counselee Satisfaction (Student Opinion)	9	8	9	7	4	122	1
3. Counselee understanding of opportunities, test data, "advice," at termination of sessions	9	6	10	5	2	111	2
4. Judgment of an "outside-expert" counselor (from case records)	5	9	5	1	6	84	4
5. Before-and-after tests of personality and changes of self-attitude	7	7	4	6	5	92	3
6. Grades: Academic achievement	4	3	3	5	5	56	7
7. Social adjustment	4	4	2	10	11	73	5
8. Continuance in College training	1	1	2	1	1	18	10
9. Observations of student training	0	3	7	6	3	48	8
10. Counselor's judgment of progress	0	3	4	3	6	36	9

Of the 36 counselees, six cases were written in complete detail for the purpose of demonstrating in full the methods used in this study. Additional information about this study may be obtained from J. David O'Dea at the University of Wisconsin at Milwaukee.

CONCLUSIONS

The following conclusions are based upon the information the writers have obtained from this study and from the literature reviewed.

• The use of pre-test personality inventories, preferably the Minnesota Multiphasic Personality Inventory, can function as a definite counseling and screening aid to the counselor.

• One element related to the criteria of personal adjustment is indicated by the MMPI profiles. An examination of the L, F, and K scores of the counselees pointed out and supported the claim that the criteria for the success of counseling should in part be concerned with the degree and the direction of change in the self-concept with its concomitant effects upon behavior.

• The results of the study seemed to indicate that a change does not occur in the basic personality structure of the counselee as a result of a limited number of two or three sessions. However, some of the cases experiencing five or more sessions did seem to demonstrate limited changes in personality structure.

• With the development of an increasing awareness on the part of the counseling profession of the significance of client attitudes the study supports the growing trend for counselor-trainees to be required to obtain a fundamental background in individual differences as well as in testing.

• Contrary to the opinion held by some counselors, the results of the study indicated that the administration of the tests did not hinder the counseling process in any way; rather, on occasion the tests seemed to facilitate the development of the counseling process (2).

• The results of the study do not appear to disagree, except on emphasis, with the findings of other studies related to the area of evaluation of the effects of counseling.

• Due to the acknowledged crudity of the Test of Self-Understanding, the writers temporarily exclude its use in evaluative studies until such time as the instrument has been refined and improved. Necessary revisions to this potential instrument are currently being made.

• In view of the findings of the literature reviewed and the results of the study, the writers encourage the use of the counselee opinionnaire (5) and the Minnesota Multiphasic Personality Inventory in future studies.

• Changes of self concept is considered to be one of the most important factors in evaluating the effects of counseling.

The conclusions from the study have been made with caution to prevent distortions in the interpretation of the results. The conclusions are limited because of the small numbers of counselees involved and because of the acknowledged crudity of some of the instruments used.

BIBLIOGRAPHY

1. Bixler, R. H., and Bordin E. S. "Test Selection: A Process of Counseling," *Educational and Psychological Measurement*, XI (Fall, 1946), 361-373.

2. Carr, A. C. "An Evaluation of Nine Non-Directive Psychotherapy Cases by Means of the Rorschach," *Journal of Counsulting Psychology*, XIII (June, 1949), 196-205.

3. Coe, B. A., and Habbe, S. N. "Adult Guidance Services in New Haven: An Evaluation Study," *Occupations*, XVIII (February, 1940), 338-342.

4. Darley, J. C., and Anderson, G. V. "The Function of Measurement in Counseling," *Educational Measurement*, ed. E. F. Lindquist. Washington: American Council on Education, 1951.

5. Dressel, P. L., and Matteson, R. W. "The Effects of Client Participation in Test Interpretation," *Educational and Psychological Measurement*, X (Winter, 1950), 139-149.

6. Froehlich, C. P. *Evaluating Guidance Procedures: Review of the Literature*, Washington: Federal Security Agency, Office of Education, Miscellaneous Publication, 1949.

7. Hahn, M. E., and MacLean, M. S. *General Clinical Counseling*. New York: McGraw-Hill, 1946.

8. O'Dea, J. D. "A Study of Teaching Potentialities," *The Journal of Educational Psychology*, XLI (December, 1950), 473-479.

9. Rogers, C. R. *Client Centered Therapy*. Boston: Houghton-Mifflin, 1951.

10. Williamson, E. G., and Bordin, E. S. "The Evaluation of Vocational and Educational Counseling: A Critique of the Methodology of Experiment," *Educational and Psychological Measurement*, I (Spring, 1941), 5-24.

11. Wischner, G. A., and McKinney, F. "Counseling," *Review of Educational Research*, XVIII (April, 1948), 175-183.

12. Wrenn, C. G. "The Evaluation of Student Personnel Work: A Critique of the Guidance Movement," *School and Society*, LII (November, 1940), 409-414.

40. EVALUATING THE EFFECTS OF COUNSELING—EIGHT YEARS AFTER

Peter F. Merenda[1] and John W. M. Rothney

The great need for basic research in the evaluation of the counseling process has been cited by many (1, 2, 3, 7, 8) but principally by Froehlich (5). As late as 1949, he could find in a comprehensive review of the literature only 177 published studies relating to the evaluation of guidance practices. Of these only 24 reported findings based on the results obtained by employment of experimental and control groups. Each of these was concerned primarily with such single aspects of the counseling process as occupational and educational placement, academic achievement, occupational information and orientation, and personality development and change. The findings of most of these studies were based on relatively small samples. In some cases they were based on only the small portions of these samples who responded to follow-up questionnaires.

Recently, however, several attempts have been made to conduct comprehensive research in the evaluation of counseling through longitudinal studies attempting to cut across the whole counseling process. Among these are the works of Rothney and Roens (10), Super (12), Tiedeman (13), and Rothney (9). The study reported here is part of the latter investigation.

METHOD

In 1948, all 870 sophomores in four Wisconsin High Schools were selected for study. These 870 students were alternately assigned to two distinct groups: experimental and control. During the three remaining years of high school the members of the experimental group

Reprinted by permission of the authors and *Journal of Counseling Psychology*, V, No. 3 (Fall, 1958), 163-68.

[1] This paper is based upon a portion of a Ph.D. thesis submitted to the graduate faculty of the University of Wisconsin by the senior author. He wishes to acknowledge the guidance of his advisors, John W. M. Rothney, Chester W. Harris, Julian C. Stanley, and A. Harold Edgerton.

received intensive counseling from qualified counselors who were members of the University of Wisconsin staff. The members of the control group received no such counseling. No intensive formal counseling was available to the students from the regular school staff.

Six months after high school graduation all 690 subjects who remained in school to complete their educational programs were contacted by a post card questionnaire inquiring about their present individual status and degree of satisfaction with this status. One hundred per cent return of questionnaires was achieved in this follow-up study.

In 1953, two and one half years after high school graduation, a much more comprehensive questionnaire was sent to the 688 graduates who were still alive at that time. The questionnaire was designed to elicit responses from the subjects which would yield both descriptive data concerning their current educational, vocational and marital status, and other personal history information since graduation. It was also expected to yield responses from which inferences could be made regarding their post-high school educational, vocational, social, and personal adjustments, attitudes, reflections, and outlooks. Again one hundred per cent return was achieved in this follow-up.

The follow-up research from which the data were largely gathered for this study was conducted in 1956-57, after the subjects had been out of high school for a period of five years. A comprehensive three-page questionnaire was sent to the 685 subjects remaining in the study in the fall of 1956. One hundred per cent return was achieved also in this follow-up research.

In addition to the purely descriptive data regarding the present status of subjects, their whereabouts, armed forces experiences and activities, an attempt was made to elicit responses which would yield data for criteria in the evaluation of the effectiveness of counseling. These evaluative criteria can be classified principally into four major categories: (a) Measures of satisfaction with, and adjustment to, post high school status; (b) Measures of optimism in outlook toward the future; (c) Measures of reflection on high school training received—how it helped and failed; and (d) Measures of persistency in post-high school endeavors.

Evaluative Criteria

Four scales were developed for evaluating the effectiveness of counseling in terms of the above criteria. The Satisfaction-Adjustment scale was a 26-unit composite. A 21-unit scale was developed for measuring the Optimism criterion, and an 11-unit scale measured the students' attitudes concerning how they felt that high school either helped or failed to prepare them for life beyond graduation.

Examples of items for each of these three scales follow: Item 1 in the *Satisfaction-Adjustment Scale* was the question: "Regardless of what you are doing show how you like it by checking below." The following numerical values were assigned: 4—"I really like it"; 3—"My likes just balance my dislikes"; 2—"I don't like it, but have to put up with it"; 1—"I hate it."

Item 3 in the *Optimism Scale* was the question, "Looking forward to the future do you think things are going to work out well for you?" The following scale values were assigned to the responses: 6—"enthusiastically yes"; 5—"yes"; 4—"yes and no"; 3—"undecided"; 2—"probably not"; 1—"definitely not."

Reflection on high school training was scaled in the following manner from the responses given to the question, "Looking back at your high school training, tell us how it helped you—how it failed you." 11—very enthusiastic about high school experiences, no unfavorable comments; 10—several comments, all favorable or "did not fail" with no unfavorable comments; 9—only one comment, but favorable; 8—helped more than failed; 7—helped as much as failed; 6—neither helped nor failed; 5—"don't know" or no expression favorable or unfavorable; 4—failed more than helped; 3—only one comment, but unfavorable; 2—several comments, all unfavorable or "did not help"; 1—strongly, adversely critical of high school training received.

A direct measure of persistency in post-high school endeavors and relation to educational and vocational choice of individual subjects of this study was obtained by investigating the status at six-month intervals and recording the number of significant changes made during the eight-year period covering the study.

Reliabilities of these criterion measures were estimated in several

TABLE 1

COEFFICIENT OF EQUIVALENCE FOR SATISFACTION-
ADJUSTMENT AND OPTIMISM SCALES

Scale	No. of Items	Coefficient of Equivalence
Satisfaction-Adjustment	5	.42
Optimism	4	.62

ways. A measure of "inter-rater" reliability was established by drawing a random sample of 100 subjects and comparing the original rater's scores with those given by an independent rater. These coefficients of agreement were as follows: *Satisfaction-Adjustment* (.95), *Optimism* (.93) and *Reflection on High School Training* (.92). Since the *Persistency* scale merely represented the number of changes in status, no attempt was made to establish an "inter-rater" reliability coefficient for this measure.

An internal consistency coefficient for each of the two scales in which sub-scores were present was obtained by using a procedure developed by Stanley (11). The same random sample of 100 subjects as was drawn for establishing the "inter-rater" reliabilities was used. These coefficients of equivalence are given in Table 1.

Item intercorrelations and item vs. total score correlations were also computed for these two scales. These matrices are presented in Tables 2 and 3. These coefficients are indicative of a relatively high

TABLE 2

ITEM INTERCORRELATIONS AND ITEM VS. TOTAL SCORE
CORRELATIONS FOR SATISFACTION-ADJUSTMENT SCALE

	Item					Total Score
	1	2	3	4	5	
1		.13	.41	.08	.06	.45
2			.03	.21	.21	.62
3				.16	.04	.55
4					.07	.70
5						.37

TABLE 3

Item Intercorrelations and Item vs. Total Score Correlations for Optimism Scale

	Item				Total Score
	1	2	3	4	
1		.50	.23	.40	.72
2			.14	.29	.85
3				.33	.50
4					.61

degree of homogeneity among the items in these scales and suggest that the evaluative criteria used in this study are sufficiently reliable for group comparisons.

Distribution of Sub-Samples

Upon graduation from high school, students generally tend to follow one of three directions: (a) toward further education; (b) toward employment; and (c) toward marriage. Since one of the major functions of the counseling process is to help students with their problems and plans concerning the future, it becomes apparent that early attempts are made by the counselor to assist the student in formulating post-high school plans and carrying them through to realization. The result may well be that the nature and degree of the counseling for each student is affected by these conditions. For the purpose of evaluating the effectiveness of counseling, therefore, it was deemed necessary to take these factors into consideration. Furthermore, the actual post-high school individual status of the graduates and their individual experiences would tend to result in systematic differences among the different subsamples. Finally, the phenomenon of sex differences as it affects a number of personal characteristics and attributes which had already been shown by Kaczkowski (6) to exist for the same population of this study was taken into consideration. Accordingly, this population of high school graduates was divided into the following five categories:

1. Male subjects who had attended for at least one full year, a postsecondary level school of higher education or training and/or were in fulltime residence in such an institution five years after high school graduation.

2. Unmarried females in the above status.

3. Male subjects whose most significant post-high school experiences were in the field of employment and/or whose post-secondary training, if any, was limited to less than one year. All apprenticeships were classified in this category.

4. Unmarried female subjects in the above status.

5. All females who were married within the first five years after high school graduation and who were still married at the time of the study.

Statistical Treatment and Results

Raw scores on the criterion scales were transformed to normalized stanine scores (Mean = 5.00; Sigma = 1.96). The Fisher (4) two-group method of discriminant analysis was applied to the data, and the resulting discriminant functions were tested for significance. The results reported in Tables 4 and 5 show the effectiveness of the counseling given to the experimental subjects. The mean criterion values are in favor of the experimental subjects. With one exception, the discriminant function extracted for each category of subjects indicated statistical significance at least at the .07 level of confidence. These results are an indication that counseling appeared to produce, for the population studied, desirable outcomes in terms of educational, vocational, and personal satisfaction and adjustment; degree of optimism in outlook toward the future; reflection on value of high school training received; and persistency in post-high school endeavors when measured five years after high school graduation. Except in the case of the unmarried nonschool females, the probabilities are at least 93 in 100 that the differences in profiles on the criterion are not due to sampling fluctuation or other chance occurrences.

The criterion which appeared to be the best over-all single discriminator between the counseled and uncounseled subjects is the self-report measure of *Satisfaction-Adjustment*. The Reflection on High School Training variable assumed the second greatest over-all

TABLE 4

Sample	Evaluation Criterion	Counseled		Uncounseled	
		$\overline{X}$	σ	$\overline{X}$	σ
School Males	1. Satisfaction-Adjustment	5.33	1.77	4.29	1.82
	2. Optimism	5.14	1.84	4.91	1.58
	3. Reflection on H. S. Training	5.25	2.04	4.98	1.68
	4. Persistency	5.05	1.46	4.70	1.44
School Females (unmarried)	1. Satisfaction-Adjustment	5.65	2.06	4.58	1.73
	2. Optimism	4.57	1.69	5.16	1.33
	3. Reflection on H. S. Training	5.09	1.67	4.58	1.63
	4. Persistency	5.17	0.82	4.21	1.51
Non-School Males	1. Satisfaction-Adjustment	5.21	2.12	4.53	1.78
	2. Optimism	5.14	1.94	4.63	1.94
	3. Reflection on H. S. Training	4.92	1.89	4.27	1.75
	4. Persistency	5.32	1.72	5.28	1.65
Non-School Females (unmarried)	1. Satisfaction-Adjustment	5.07	1.87	5.47	1.35
	2. Optimism	4.64	1.80	4.37	1.78
	3. Reflection on H. S. Training	4.93	1.53	5.21	1.67
	4. Persistency	5.28	1.22	4.68	1.78
Married Females	1. Satisfaction-Adjustment	5.47	1.81	4.79	1.73
	2. Optimism	4.98	1.56	4.45	1.53
	3. Reflection on H. S. Training	5.07	1.64	4.57	1.76
	4. Persistency	4.69	1.34	4.71	1.51

weight in providing maximum separation between the groups in the four categories in which the discrimination proved to exceed or at least approach statistical significance. The other self-report criterion (optimism) proved to be the least effective discriminatory measure. This was particularly true in the case of those students who went on with their training beyond high school.

The sole criterion which was not a self-report measure (persistency) assumed relatively high weight for students in this category and relatively low weight for students with no significant education beyond high school. The reversal of the relative influence of these two evaluative criteria in assessing the effectiveness of counseling can possibly be explained by the following facts. Students with signifi-

TABLE 5

ANALYSIS OF MAXIMUM SEPARATION BETWEEN
COUNSELED AND UNCOUNSELED SUBJECTS

Sample	N	Difference in Means (Exp.-Con.)	Discriminant Weights	F	P
School Males	$N_E = 63$	$d_1 = 1.0355$	$V_1 = 0.00278$		
	$N_C = 47$	$d_2 = 0.2280$	$V_2 = -0.00012$	2.24	.07
	$N = 110$	$d_3 = 0.2753$	$V_3 = 0.00018$		
		$d_4 = 0.3455$	$V_4 = 0.00077$		
School Females (unmarried)	$N_E = 23$	$d_1 = 1.0732$	$V_1 = 0.00322$		
	$N_C = 19$	$d_2 = -0.5927$	$V_2 = -0.00617$	2.36	.07
	$N = 42$	$d_3 = 0.5107$	$V_3 = 0.00529$		
		$d_4 = 0.9634$	$V_4 = 0.01527$		
Non-School Males	$N_E = 97$	$d_1 = 0.6741$	$V_1 = 0.00067$		
	$N_C = 109$	$d_2 = 0.5113$	$V_2 = 0.00046$		
	$N = 206$	$d_3 = 0.6515$	$V_3 = 0.00069$	2.91	<.05
		$d_1 = 0.0444$	$V_4 = -0.00020$		
Non-School Females (unmarried)	$N_E = 14$	$d_1 = -0.4023$	$V_1 = -0.00400$		
	$N_C = 19$	$d_2 = 0.2744$	$V_2 = 0.00046$		
	$N = 33$	$d_3 = -0.2820$	$V_3 = -0.00439$	0.49	
		$d_4 = -0.6025$	$V_4 = -0.00937$		
Married Females	$N_E = 144$	$d_1 = 0.6850$	$V_1 = 0.00067$		
	$N_C = 141$	$d_2 = 0.5322$	$V_2 = 0.00056$		
	$N = 285$	$d_3 = 0.4950$	$V_3 = 0.00048$	4.99	<.01
		$d_4 = -0.0217$	$V_4 = -0.00028$		

Criterion 1 = Satisfaction-Adjustment
Criterion 2 = Optimism
Criterion 3 = Reflection on High School Training
Criterion 4 = Persistency

cant postgraduate training generally expressed an exceptionally high degree of optimism in their outlook toward the future. This result presumably reflected increased levels of aspiration resulting from expectations of rewarding vocational and personal experiences. Students in the other categories were more variable with respect to this criterion. On the other hand, the counseled students in this category tended to begin their further education and training directly upon high school graduation and follow their educational plans to completion, whereas a sizable portion of the noncounseled students tended either to postpone their future schooling or fail to carry through with their educational plans. In this light the counseled students showed an exceptionally high degree of persistency. For the nonschool students and married females, the greater opportunities for varied and exploratory experiences apparently caused both counseled and uncounseled students to show relatively low persistency in post-high school endeavors.

CONCLUSIONS

The data of this study suggest that desirable outcomes may be enhanced by providing intensive counseling services to high school students. The fact that the counseled subjects tended to show a pattern of more favorable adult behaviors and attitudes is an indication that intensive counseling does produce certain significant and desirable results which are achieved to a lesser degree by the usual informal type of counseling that is typically offered in the majority of our high schools today.

The differences were not large between counseled and uncounseled students on the criterion variables of this study for measures obtained five years after high school graduation. This may be due, in part, to the fact that the more subtle and lasting effects of counseling require a longer period of time to elapse in order to become more clearly apparent. Five years may be too short a period of time to allow these effects, if they truly exist, to appear. This likelihood is suggested by the fact that the early years after high school graduation largely constitute an exploratory and continuing training period for many young people planning life careers. Probably in another five years the differences in this study will be widened. The generally consistent trend of the criterion differences in favor of the counseled subjects is nearly conclusive evidence that they are not due merely to random variation.

Received December 3, 1957.

REFERENCES

1. Baier, D. E. The role of research in improving standards for counseling and guidance services. *Educ. psychol. Measmt.,* 1949, **9,** 313-319.
2. Bixler, H. H. Conditions affecting personnel work. *Rev. ed. Res.,* 1945, 25, 121-122.
3. Dressel, P. L. Research in counseling; some approaches to evaluation. *Personnel & guid. J.,* 1953, **31,** 284-287.
4. Fisher, R. A. The use of multiple measurements in taxonomic problems. *Ann. Eugenics,* 1936, **6,** 376-386.
5. Froehlich, C. P. Evaluating guidance practices. Washington, D. C.: U. S. Office of Education, 1949.
6. Kaczkowski, H. R. Discrimination among eight groups of high school students. Unpublished doctoral dissertation, Univer. of Wisconsin, 1954.
7. Kirk, B. A. How counseling affects vocational goals. *Educ. psychol. Measmt.,* 1952, **12,** 692-698.
8. O'Dea, J. D. & Zeran, F. R. Evaluating effects of counseling. *Personnel & guid. J.,* 1953, **31,** 241-244.
9. Rothney, J. W. M. Guidance practices and results. New York: Harper & Bros., 1957 (In press).
10. Rothney, J. W. M. & Roens, B. A. Guidance of American youth. Cambridge: Harvard Univer. Press, 1950.
11. Stanley, J. C. K-R 20 as a stepped-up mean r among items. Paper read at NCMUE, Atlantic City, April, 1957.
12. Super, D. E. Career development programs. *Amer. Psychologist,* 1953, 8, 185-190.
13. Tiedeman, D. V. The Harvard studies in career development, *J. counsel Psychol.,* 1956, 3, 67-68.

41. THE COUNSELING FUNCTION

Herman J. Peters and William J. Mueller

Definition of the field of counseling, as distinguished from guidance and psychotherapy, continued during the period covered by this review (4, 46, 54, 56, 59). Two related approaches to definition were observed. One effort to fix boundaries of the counseling field

Reprinted by permission of the authors and *Review of Educational Research,* XXX, No. 2 (April, 1960), 131-39.

placed it on a continuum according to the degree of affective involvement. In this lies danger that theory becomes the province of the psychotherapist and only surface applications are made by the counselor. A second approach was made in terms of where the interview takes place: in a school, it is guidance; in a counseling center, counseling; in a clinic, psychotherapy. Despite attempts to define counseling as leading to acceptance of one's personality attributes and the best use of them, and to define psychotherapy as efforts toward basic personality change, counselors of all persuasions have not effected a commonality for the meaning of counseling.

The counseling function needs definition for many reasons. Recent attempts in California and in Ohio to enact legislation call for a definition. The impact of counseling and guidance institutes under the National Defense Education Act necessitated some working definitions. Hydra-headed approaches to the problem may result in lessened public approval of the role of counseling in assisting students and youth. English and English (14) observed that "goodness of terminology is not merely statistical; it is psychological and social. Our goals are clarity of thinking and effectiveness of communications. Misleading terminology does not become better by being widely diffused; it merely does greater damage."

The persistent dilemma with regard to terminology is well stated by Peltz (43): "Guidance work may be conducted by homeroom teachers, advisors, or trained counselors, and may involve working with parents as well as with students. The difference between guidance or counseling on the one hand and psychotherapy on the other is a hard one to define precisely. In general, however, it can be said that the former is more apt to be concerned with external situations or factors dealing primarily with conscious material and usually lasting a short time whereas psychotherapy deals with internal conflicts as well as conflicts with the external world, handles unconscious factors as well as conscious material, and is frequently of fairly long duration."

THEORETICAL CONSIDERATIONS

No new formulations were found, nor were there any major polemics about directive versus nondirective counseling. Yet, theoretical considerations received their fair share of attention and focused on the total concept of guidance, personality, the counseling process, and counseling in relation to particular psychological and sociological problems.

Beechy (3) developed a theoretical framework of guidance through an analysis of adjustment, individualization, socialization, vocation, and love. His conceptual framework offers a broad sociopsychological screen against which the counselor may project his counseling functions. Looking at the problem somewhat differently, Masserman (34) pointed out the essentials in a large, encompassing, and responsible base for the counseling function in analyzing (a) the maintenance of the scientific prestige, (b) ethical integrity, and (c) social influence of allied professions.

Thorne (55) pointed out the importance of periodic examinations of various theoretical foundations of counseling and discussed psychoanalytically oriented therapies, client-centered counseling, disciplinary counseling, and the semantic impact on counseling. This article is recommended as a provocative stimulus for students and scholars to analyze the similarities of, and differences between, various theoretical bases for counseling. Thorne's view was also expressed by Lewis (30).

Fundamental principles of counseling theory were considered in terms of man's integrating relationship between mind and body (35), clarifying dogma or a set of principles involved in having a theory (4, 5), thinking through one's theory of counseling (60), and counselors' values operative in the helping relationships (19). Patterson (39) argued for a systematic view of counseling theory rather than an eclectic perspective. Various writers emphasized a particular bent in looking at the counseling function, such as the place of limits (18), the therapeutic effort (67), the impact of culture (51), counseling for personal adjustment (33), the vocationally handicapped (32), the emotionally disturbed (40), the interview with emphasis on communication (25), and multiple counseling (12).

Prompted by analysis of the writings on counseling and adolescent development, Peters and Farwell (45) urged a study of principles and procedures in the secondary- and elementary-school settings. They remarked that the following factors may necessitate modification of current counseling theory and procedures when applied to the pupil in the school setting: (a) differential factors of maturation level of pupils, (b) school organization, (c) concept of authority in the school setting, (d) involuntary nature of the counseling process, (e) the kind of limits which may be set on counseling, and (f) the professional education of the counselor. Books on guidance at the elementary-school level gave considerable space to counseling (28, 29), but their material was vague and unsubstantiated by research or theoretical models applicable to the child.

THE DETERMINANTS OF THE COUNSELING PROCESS

The studies in this section are classified according to the variables which the researcher was interested in isolating. Articles that were not strictly experimental in the sense that they relied heavily on the author's intuition are included, since they differed from others only in the degree to which the author was able to specify and subject his clinical observations to rigid tests of his hypothesis. Studies clustered around (a) the person of the counselee, (b) that of the counselor, and (c) the interaction between counselee and counselor.

THE COUNSELEE

Subsumed under the first heading is a group of studies about counselees' expectations of counseling and satisfaction with counseling. Solely on intuitive grounds, one would expect a strong positive relationship between congruence of counselee-counselor concepts of what counseling ought to be (expectations) and counselee satisfaction. The conflict evident in the studies reported below supports Rogers' statement (50) that the area of client expectations is one of the least understood in the counseling process.

Operating solely within the framework of the counselee, Grigg and Goodstein (21) attempted to evaluate the outcomes of counseling in terms of such evaluations by the counselee of the counseling process itself as his feelings of comfort and his appraisal of the counselor's activity and participation. As defined by response of

counselees to two questions about the number of opinions, suggestions, and interpretations that were given by the counselors, counselees seemed to prefer a counselor who was more directive.

Utilizing a sample of high-school seniors, Sonne and Goldman
(52) sought to determine whether clients with authoritarian or
equalitarian personality structures differed in their responses to
client-centered or eclectic counseling. The "unpredicted preference
of . . . three groups for the eclectic over the client-centered interview" seemed to be one source of stimulation for a series of critical
comments and replies regarding the use of the client's satisfaction
as a criterion in evaluating the outcomes of counseling.

Patterson (37), arguing that the counselee's expectations were a
function of his social conditioning, questioned the advisability of
the counselor's acquiescing to the student's dependency need rather
than continuing to work with the counselee toward such an ultimate
goal as the counselee's acceptance of responsibility. This same issue
recurred in Patterson's recent text (39), and it is clear from the
way in which the problem was handled that the author recognized
the strength of the cultural learning question involved. Responding
to Patterson's study, Goodstein and Grigg (20) contended that, although multiple-criterion measures are necessary, client satisfaction
is a valid criterion for evaluating counseling success.

A different point of view, but one affected by the same issue, was
presented by Froehlich (17) in a recent summary of studies, principally multiple-counseling research. The general counseling objectives advocated by Froehlich, as revealed by these studies, were to
provide relationships which maximized counselee participation and
minimized counselor-centered activities.

Nelson (36) attempted to refine the use of client satisfaction as a
variable by examining its relationship to vocational maturity. Results of aptitude tests and inventoried interests constituted the
experimental variables with which the criterion variable was correlated, and vocational maturity as defined above was found to be
related to reported satisfaction with counseling.

Other studies attempted to relate outcomes of counseling to the
personality structure of the counselee. Cartwright (10) applied the
Rorschach Prognostic Rating Scale to the 13 clients' pretherapy
Rorschachs and, with reasonable success, predicted the successful
client from response patterns. Utilizing rating scales derived from a

pretherapy *Thematic Apperception Test* and a first interview, Kirtner and Cartwright (27) extended this kind of research into a second dimension and found a relationship between the client's personality structure and the length by outcome of the interview. Wrenn (66) reviewed the growing body of research on self-perceptions and interpersonal perceptions, especially as these studies relate to growth through counseling. Cartwright (8) presented an excellent current accounting of research, methodology, and theory construction in client-centered therapy.

Cartwright (9) hypothesized that counseling increases the consistency of the self-concept which one brings to varied situations involving interaction with other persons, that is, the person's "self" would have been enlarged. A Q-sort technique revealed less item variance after therapy. Of special interest are the implications of the finding that for the successfully counseled persons, the increase in consistency came from pretherapy low-relevance items that had changed to high-relevance post-therapy.

Using as a counseling criterion the shift in the discrepancy scores between counselees' self-ratings and such external measures as test and inventory scores, Froehlich (16) found a significant shift in the direction of increased self-knowledge in a counseled group with whom the counselor interpreted test data.

The Counselor

Other studies were directly concerned with the effects of the counselor's personality, behavior, or training on the outcomes of counseling. Weitz (63) set down security, sensitivity, and objectivity as three personality characteristics that a counselor ought to possess.

According to Weitz, the secure counselor accepts himself and others. His acceptance of others flows from his self-acceptance, and it is the basic stuff on which sensitivity thrives. Lastly, the objective counselor is aware of such distinctions in counseling as those between the person and the norm, the label and the behavior, the symbol and the object. Similar characteristics were cited by Rogers (49) as the guidelines of a helping relationship.

Operating within the framework of the discussion unit proposed by Robinson (48), Weeks (62) attempted to circumvent the diffi-

culties experienced by Dipboye (11) in classifying counselor style
according to the dimensions of previously proposed schemata. In
Week's system, the style of counselor is plotted against an analysis
of the content of the discussion unit in terms of the level of affect
involved. A significant finding of the study was that the counselor's
style differed between high-affect and moderate- or low-affect discussion units; a wider range of responses was evinced by the counselor
at the level of high affective involvement.

Poole (47) compared judgments by counselors and by typescript-
readers of the counselor's objectives in counseling and the achievement of these objectives. Apparently the readers and counselors
judged consistently in terms of their own interpretations of the goals
of the counselor and the achievement of these goals by counselees,
but the interesting phenomenon was that these systems were independent. Poole contended that, had she utilized a research design
in which evaluation of outcomes had been made solely in terms of
readers' judgments of the achievement of counseling goals, she
might have concluded that counseling was successful.

Whereas the research has often been directed at the expectations
of clients, Truax (57) investigated the expectations that administrators, teachers, counselor trainers, counselors, supervisors, and state
directors of guidance have of small-school counselors. Although
Truax's completed job analysis revealed a strong emphasis on the
counselor's duty to individual students, the study indicated that the
counselor is also perceived as a resource person with major school
and community responsibilities. King (26) confirmed this concept of
the counselor in a study of behaviors used by teachers to differentiate
between effective and ineffective counselors. It is worthy of note
that the critical-incident technique proposed by Flanagan (15) has
been applied in both these studies. In still another instance, this
same technique was used by Eilbert (13) as a semantic tool to re-
classify the meaning of emotional immaturity.

Brams (7) compared the scores made by a group of counselor-
trainees on a *Communication Rating Scale* with their scores on a
series of personality and interest inventories. A positive relationship
was found only between the trainees' tolerance for ambiguity (Berkeley Questionnaire) and their effectiveness in communication.

Arbuckle and Wicas (2) attempted to develop a free-response appraisal instrument to measure the agreement between the counseling

orientations of counselor-trainees and expert counselors. Because all but one of the items measure accurate clarification of feeling, other aspects of the counseling relationship are ignored and the instrument's usefulness is limited.

In a stimulating presentation, Horst (23) differentiated between the actuarial and other nonintuitive views in counseling evaluation as one of degree, not kind. The essential evaluative problem centers around the counselor's willingness to "specify the factors which he takes into consideration in making a prediction."

Editors allotted considerable space to philosophical issues, especially to questions of value orientation in counseling. Perhaps, as Walters (61) has suggested, psychology's scientific antithesis has been fulfilled, and a synthesis of philosophical issues is in order. Regardless of their orientation, counselors seem agreed that the value structures of the counselor, *ipso facto,* become a part of the counseling process (1, 39, 42, 64, 65). This seems to be a departure from popular misconceptions of theorists' positions, rather than from the positions themselves. At any rate, the articles reflect a need for clarification of some philosophical bases of counseling. The issues generally center around (a) what the counselor's values ought to be and (b) whether these values ought to be consciously imposed. The second issue quickly dissolves, however, when the discussants come to terms on what the value orientation of the counselor ought to be, since the nature of the acceptable counselor-held values is incompatible with the imposition of lesser values.

THE INTERACTION BETWEEN COUNSELEE AND COUNSELOR

A growing concern was shown (6, 22) for a need to study the interaction between counselor and counselee in the counseling relationship, despite the required complexity of research design and multivariate analysis. Gustad (22) has nicely stated the problems involved in this kind of research, and his own work (58) reflects an attempt to meet the need for research in counselor-counselee interaction. Tuma and Gustad (58) studied the effects of difference of personality characteristics of client and counselor on self-learning. They found that the amount of client self-learning was related to the existence of an original similarity in the personalities of counselor and counselee on three of the selected personality traits. As interesting as the article itself was the critique of the research design by Pepinsky (44), who commented that the methodological question was logically prior to the substantive one in the interpretation of research studies.

In an over-all summary of findings of a 15-year, three-phase integrated program of interview research, Berdie (6) emphasized the need for a research design that allows for an analysis of counselor-counselee interaction at many levels.

The fuller analysis by Patterson (41) of methodology in research on counseling ought to be studied carefully for its implications for determining whether the results of counseling research can be trusted and its findings put to use. The same research-design theme is repeated in another article by Patterson (38) in a consideration of his own research on counseling.

Lifton (31), in an intriguing study, reported on the relationship of empathy to aesthetic sensitivity. Despite the many problems encountered, this attempt to establish the validity of the criterion variable of empathic ability in some way other than through such an external agent as the consensus of judges deserves recognition. Lifton correctly recognized empathy as a *relationship,* thereby calling into question the usual self-description-prediction methodology as a means of measuring empathic ability.

Utilizing interview data from the Career Pattern Study (53) and operating within a definition of the appraisal interview as one whose purpose is to learn about the counselee, Hummel (24) attempted a content-analysis of the data. He found that the utterance category in which the content of the previous communication was reflected received highest rank among the prediction weights for responsiveness.

SUMMARY

There is increased awareness of the need for adequate research design on interaction between counselor and counselee. Significance of contributions to counseling research may be a function of the number of variables that can be handled by the investigator in an unstructured counseling contact.

High-school populations furnished an increasing number of subjects for counseling studies. Perhaps this is the most important development reported here. It will be interesting to note whether modifications of counseling theory may result from increased controlled observation at the school-counseling level.

Finally, philosophical issues in counseling received considerable attention. Generally, discussion of the question of "neutrality" in counseling has been replaced by an examination of the nature and strength of the impact of the person of the counselor on the counseling relationship.

BIBLIOGRAPHY

1. Arbuckle, Dugald S. "Five Philosophical Issues in Counseling." *Journal of Counseling Psychology* 5: 211-15; Fall 1958.
2. Arbuckle, Dugald S., and Wicas, Edward A. "The Development of an Instrument for the Measurement of Counseling Perceptions." *Journal of Counseling Psychology* 4: 304-10; Winter 1957.
3. Beechy, Atlee. *A Conceptual Framework for Guidance.* Doctor's thesis. Columbus: The Ohio State University, 1958. 456 p. Abstract: *Dissertation Abstracts* 19: 2281-82; No. 9, 1959.
4. Berdie, Ralph F. "Counseling." *Annual Review of Psychology.* (Edited by Paul R. Farnsworth.) Palo Alto, Calif.: Annual Reviews, 1959. Vol. 10, p. 345-70.
5. Berdie, Ralph F. "Counseling Principles and Presumptions." *Journal of Counseling Psychology* 6: 175-87; Fall 1959.
6. Berdie, Ralph F. "A Program of Counseling Interview Research." *Educational and Psychological Measurement* 18: 255-74; Summer 1958.
7. Brams, Jerome M. *The Relationship Between Personal Characteristics of Counseling Trainees and Effective Communication in Counseling.* Doctor's thesis. Columbia: University of Missouri, 1957. 122 p. Abstract: *Dissertation Abstracts* 17: 1510-11; No. 7, 1957.
8. Cartwright, Desmond S. "Annotated Bibliography of Research and Theory Construction in Client-Centered Therapy." *Journal of Counseling Psychology* 4: 82-100; Spring 1957.
9. Cartwright, Rosalind Dymond. "Effects of Psychotherapy on Self-Consistency." *Journal of Counseling Psychology* 4: 15-22; Spring 1957.
10. Cartwright, Rosalind Dymond. "Predicting Response to Client-Centered Therapy with the Rorschach PR Scale." *Journal of Counseling Psychology* 5: 11-17; Spring 1958.
11. Dipboye, Wilbert J. "Analysis of Counselor Style by Discussion Units." *Journal of Counseling Psychology* 1: 21-26; February 1954.

12. Driver, Helen I., and Others. *Counseling and Learning Through Small-Group Discussion*. Madison, Wis.: Monona Publications (803 Moygara Road), 1958. 464 p.

13. Eilbert, Leo R. "A Tentative Definition of Emotional Immaturity Utilizing the Critical Incident Technique." *Personnel and Guidance Journal* 35: 554-63; May 1957.

14. English, Horace B., and English, Ava C. *A Comprehensive Dictionary of Psychological and Psychoanalytical Terms: A Guide to Usage*. New York: Longmans, Green and Co., 1958. 594 p.

15. Flanagan, John C. "The Critical Incident Technique." *Psychological Bulletin* 1: 327-58; 1954.

16. Froehlich, Clifford P. *A Criterion for Counseling*. Psychological Monographs: General and Applied, Vol. 71, No. 15 (Whole Number 444). Washington, D. C.: American Psychological Association, 1957. 12 p.

17. Froehlich, Clifford P. "Stars, Parsons and Clients." *Personnel and Guidance Journal* 36: 10-16; September 1957.

18. Ginott, Haim G. "The Theory and Practice of Therapeutic Intervention in Child Treatment." *Journal of Consulting Psychology* 23: 160-66; April 1959.

19. Glad, Donald D.; Glad, Virginia M.; and Barnes, Robert H. *Operational Values in Psychotherapy: A Conceptual Framework of Interpersonality*. New York: Oxford University Press, 1959. 326 p.

20. Goodstein, Leonard D., and Grigg, Austin E. "Client Satisfaction, Counselors, and the Counseling Process." *Personnel and Guidance Journal* 38: 19-24; September 1959.

21. Grigg, Austin E., and Goodstein, Leonard D. "The Use of Clients as Judges of the Counselor's Performance." *Journal of Counseling Psychology* 4: 31-36; Spring 1957.

22. Gustad, John W. "The Evaluation Interview in Vocational Counseling." *Personnel and Guidance Journal* 36: 242-50; December 1957.

23. Horst, Paul. "Educational and Vocational Counseling from the Actuarial Point of View." *Personnel and Guidance Journal* 35: 164-70; November 1956.

24. Hummel, Raymond C. *Interviewee Responsiveness as a Function of Interviewer Method*. Doctor's thesis. New York: Columbia University, 1958. 130 p. Abstract: *Dissertation Abstracts* 19: 1846; No. 7, 1959.

25. Kahn, Robert L., and Cannell, Charles F. *The Dynamics of Interviewing: Theory, Techniques, and Cases*. New York: John Wiley & Sons, 1957. 368 p.

26. King, William B. *Certain Critical Requirements for the Secondary School Counselor Determined from an Analysis of Critical Incidents Reported by Teachers*. Doctor's thesis. New York: New York Univer-

sity, 1956. 134 p. Abstract: *Dissertation Abstracts* 17: 575-76; No. 3, 1957.

27. Kirtner, William L., and Cartwright, Desmond S. "Success and Failure in Client-Centered Therapy as a Function of Client Personality Variables." *Journal of Consulting Psychology* 22: 259-64; August 1958.

28. Knapp, Robert H. *Guidance in the Elementary School.* Englewood Cliffs, N. J.: Allyn and Bacon, 1959. 394 p.

29. Kowitz, Gerald T., and Kowitz, Norma G. *Guidance in the Elementary Classroom.* New York: McGraw-Hill Book Co., 1959. 314 p.

30. Lewis, Nolan D. C. "Historical Roots of Psychotherapy." *American Journal of Psychiatry* 114: 795-99; March 1958.

31. Lifton, Walter M. "The Role of Empathy and Aesthetic Sensitivity in Counseling." *Journal of Counseling Psychology* 5: 267-74; Winter 1958.

32. Lofquist, Lloyd H. *Vocational Counseling with the Physically Handicapped.* New York: Appleton-Century-Crofts, 1957. 384 p.

33. McKinney, Fred. *Counseling for Personal Adjustment; in Schools and Colleges.* Boston: Houghton Mifflin Co., 1958. 584 p.

34. Masserman, Jules H. "Evaluation vs. 'Revolution' in Psychotherapy: A Biodynamic Integration." *Behavioral Science* 2: 89-100; April 1957.

35. Mowrer, O. Hobart. "Some Philosophical Problems in Psychological Counseling." *Journal of Counseling Psychology* 4: 103-11; Summer 1957.

36. Nelson, A. Gordon. "Vocational Maturity and Client Satisfaction." *Journal of Counseling Psychology* 3: 254-56; Winter 1956.

37. Patterson, Cecil H. "Client Expectations and Social Conditioning." *Personnel and Guidance Journal* 37: 136-38; October 1958.

38. Patterson, Cecil H. "A Comparison of Counseled and Non-Counseled Industrial School Students." *Journal of Applied Psychology* 41: 240-42; August 1957.

39. Patterson, Cecil H. *Counseling and Psychotherapy: Theory and Practice.* New York: Harper & Brothers, 1959. 322 p.

40. Patterson, Cecil H. *Counseling the Emotionally Disturbed.* New York: Harper & Brothers, 1958. 458 p.

41. Patterson, Cecil H. "Matching Versus Randomization in Studies of Counseling." *Journal of Counseling Psychology* 3: 262-71; Winter 1956.

42. Patterson, Cecil H. "The Place of Values in Counseling and Psychotherapy." *Journal of Counseling Psychology* 5: 216-23; Fall 1958.

43. Peltz, William L. "Psychotherapy of Adolescents at Private Practice Plus School Practice Level." *Psychotherapy of the Adolescent.* (Edited by Benjamin H. Balser.) New York: International Universities Press, 1957. p. 40-41.

44. Pepinsky, Harold B. "Comment." [On article by Tuma and Gustad (58)]. *Journal of Counseling Psychology* 4: 142-43; Summer 1957.

45. Peters, Herman J., and Farwell, Gail F. "What Is Different About High School Counseling?" *School Counselor* 5: 67-70; May 1958.
46. Philips, Ewing Lakin. *Psychotherapy: A Modern Theory and Practice.* Englewood Cliffs, N. J.: Prentice-Hall, 1956. 334 p.
47. Poole, Aileen. "Counselor Judgment and Counseling Evaluation." *Journal of Counseling Psychology* 4: 37-40; Spring 1957.
48. Robinson, Francis P. "The Unit in Interview Analysis." *Educational and Psychological Measurement* 9: 709-16; Winter 1949.
49. Rogers, Carl R. "The Characteristics of a Helping Relationship." *Personnel and Guidance Journal* 37: 6-16; September 1958.
50. Rogers, Carl R. "Counseling Points of View." *Proceedings of the Minnesota Counselors Association Midwinter Conference, 1958.* (Edited by Willis E. Dugan.) Minneapolis: University of Minnesota Press, 1958. p. 14-26.
51. Seward, Gorgene. *Psychotherapy and Culture Conflict: With Case Studies by Judd Marmor.* New York: Ronald Press Co., 1956. 299 p.
52. Sonne, Thomas R., and Goldman, Leo. "Preferences of Authoritarian and Equalitarian Personalities for Client-Centered and Eclectic Counseling." *Journal of Counseling Psychology* 4: 129-35; Summer 1957.
53. Super, Donald E., and Others. *Vocational Development: A Framework for Research.* Career Pattern Study Monographs, No. 1. New York: Teachers College, Columbia University, Bureau of Publications, 1957. 142 p.
54. Symonds, Percival M. *Dynamics of Psychotherapy: The Psychology of Personality Change.* New York: Grune and Stratton, 1956. Vol. 1, 210 p.
55. Thorne, Frederick C. "Critique of Recent Developments in Personality Counseling Theory." *Journal of Clinical Psychology* 13: 234-44; July 1957.
56. Tolbert, Elias Lake. *Introduction to Counseling.* New York: McGraw-Hill Book Co., 1959. 322 p.
57. Truax, William E., Jr. "Critical Requirements of Small School Counselors." *Personnel and Guidance Journal* 35: 103-106; October 1956.
58. Tuma, Abdul H., and Gustad, John W. "The Effects of Client and Counselor Personality Characteristics on Client Learning in Counseling." *Journal of Counseling Psychology* 4: 136-41; Summer 1957.
59. Tyler, Leona E. "Counseling." *Annual Review of Psychology.* (Edited by Paul R. Farnsworth.) Palo Alto, Calif.: Annual Reviews, 1958. Vol. 9, 375-90.
60. Tyler, Leona E. "Theoretical Principles Underlying the Counseling Process." *Journal of Counseling Psychology* 5: 3-8; Spring 1958.
61. Walters, Orville S. "Metaphysics, Religion, and Psychotherapy." *Journal of Counseling Psychology* 5: 243-52; Winter 1958.

62. Weeks, James S. "Level of Affect in the Counseling Responses of High School Senior Boys." *Journal of Counseling Psychology* 4: 297-303; Winter 1957.

63. Weitz, Henry. "Counseling as a Function of the Counselor's Personality." *Personnel and Guidance Journal* 35: 276-80; January 1957.

64. Williamson, Edmund G. "The Meaning of Communication in Counseling." *Personnel and Guidance Journal* 38: 6-14; September 1959.

65. Williamson, Edmund G. "Value Orientation in Counseling." *Personnel and Guidance Journal* 36: 520-28; April 1958.

66. Wrenn, Charles Gilbert. "The Self Concept in Counseling." *Journal of Counseling Psychology* 5: 104-10; Summer 1958.

67. Wyatt, Frederick. "Therapeutic Effort and Therapeutic Situation." *American Journal of Orthopsychiatry* 27: 616-20; July 1957.

INDEXES

INDEX OF NAMES

SUBJECT INDEX

Acceptance, 43, 212
Achievement, 60-61
Adolescence, 55
Adolescent, 68-76
Aesthetic sensitivity, definition, 194-
195

Behavior, 125-127
  development of, 128-131

Communication
  effect of culture, 281-283
  dynamics of, 206-217
  in counseling process, 184-185,
    206-217
  value of non-verbal, 217-227
Counselee (see also Student)
  acceptance of counseling, 85-95
  attitudes toward therapist, 277-279
  characteristics, 441-445
  dimensions of, 208-210
  evaluation of counseling, 312-321
  preferences for counseling, 56
  understanding, 43
Counseling
  authoritarianism, 249-263
  characteristics, 101
  clinical, 9
  confidentiality, 41, 187, 289-298
  counselor initiated, 78-81
  culture, 186-187, 276-289
  defined, 3, 40-41
  diagnosis, 101
  difference between clinical and
    high school, 165-169

different from guidance, 29
differential factors, 101
directive, 111-123
disciplinary, 408-412
dogmatism, 186, 263-266
doubts about, 347-348
eclectic, 9-10, 101, 404-408
effects of, 422-428
empathy, 192-206
  criteria for, 200-202
  defined, 193
experiencing, 235-249
function, 439-451
influence of philosophy, 363-366
in secondary schools, 3
life experience, 40
methodology, 100, 104-107, 116-
  117, 131-135
national emergency, 379-380
need for, 163-164
non-directive, 8-9, 136-154, 399-404
non-verbal, 217-227
outcomes, 213-214
preparation for, 187
pupil initiated, 76-78
rapport, 82-84, 188-192
rationale, 117-121
referral, 81-82
silence, 227-235
value system, 375-377
vocational development, 379
volition, 266-276
Counseling process
  authoritarianism, 261
  communication in, 184-185
  degree of lead, 213
  dependency, 271-272

461